Readings in Law and Popula Culture

Readings in Law and Popular Culture is a key text in the burgeoning field of law and popular culture. It is the first book to bring together high quality, state of the art, research from recognized scholars working at the cutting edge of law and popular culture.

The volume crosses many boundaries, dealing with areas as diverse as computer games; TV programmes such as *Buffy the Vampire Slayer*; the contentious practice of digital sampling in the music industry; and an analysis of the legal films of Sidney Lumet. These topics, and others, are linked together through the key thread of the role of, or absence of, the law. The book includes important theoretical and truly innovative and relevant material that will enliven and inform a legal audience, and will be of interest to a far wider readership.

Steve Greenfield and **Guy Osborn** are academics in the law school at the University of Westminster, UK. They are the editors of the series Routledge Studies in Law, Society and Popular Culture.

Routledge studies in law, society and popular culture

Series Editors: Steve Greenfield and Guy Osborn, School of Law, University of Westminster, UK.

Routledge studies in law, society and popular culture is an inter-disciplinary series that examines the relationship between the law and all areas of popular culture. Particular foci include the regulation of spheres of popular culture and representations of law within popular culture. 'Popular Culture' is a broad and inclusive church that includes all aspects of leisure and culture, including but not confined to music, sport, film, media, the night-time economy, art, literature, the Internet, and so on. Whilst law may well provide a useful vehicle for an analysis of cultural activities within society the absence of law in the field may be just as important and worthy of consideration.

The Editors are interested in receiving proposals and manuscripts for this series: please contact Dr Guy Osborn or Steve Greenfield at the University of Westminster (G.Osborn@wmin.ac.uk or S.Greenfield@wmin.ac.uk).

Previous books published in this series:

1 **Cricket and the Law**
   The man in white is always right
   David Fraser

2 **Gigs**
   Jazz and the cabaret laws in New York City, second edition
   Paul Chevigny

3 **Readings in Law and Popular Culture**
   Edited by Steve Greenfield and Guy Osborn

Readings in Law and Popular Culture

Edited by Steve Greenfield and
Guy Osborn

Routledge
Taylor & Francis Group

LONDON AND NEW YORK

First published 2006
by Routledge
2 Park Square, Milton Park, Abingdon, Oxon OX14 4RN

Simultaneously published in the USA and Canada
by Routledge
711 Third Ave, New York, NY 10017

First issued in paperback 2012

Routledge is an imprint of the Taylor & Francis Group

© 2006 selection and editorial matter Steve Greenfield and Guy
Osborn; individual chapters, the contributors

Typeset in Garamond by Wearset Ltd, Boldon, Tyne and Wear

British Library Cataloguing in Publication Data
A catalogue record for this book is available from the British Library

Library of Congress Cataloging in Publication Data
A catalog record for this book has been requested

ISBN: 978-0-4156–5134–9

Contents

Contributors

Professor Andrew Blake, Faculty of Arts, University of Winchester.

Professor Anthony Bradney, School of Law, University of Sheffield.

Professor Richard Collier, Newcastle Law School, University of Newcastle upon Tyne.

Penny English, Centre for Legal Research, Middlesex University.

Ken Foster.

Dr Lieve Gies, Department of Law, Keele University.

Steve Greenfield, School of Law, University of Westminster.

Kwela Hermanns, School of Media Language and Music, Ayr University.

Dr Mark James, School of Law, Manchester Metropolitan University.

Yvonne Sarah Morris LLB LLM.

Dr Guy Osborn, School of Law, University of Westminster.

Dr Geoff Pearson, Management School (Football Industry Group), University of Liverpool.

Professor Peter Robson, School of Law, University of Strathclyde.

Dr Peter Sanderson, School of Education and Professional Development, University of Huddersfield.

Professor Hilary Sommerlad, School of Law, Leeds Metropolitan University.

1 Law, legal education and popular culture*

Steve Greenfield and Guy Osborn

> Given the likely value of popular culture to the law school and given the fact that the existence of academic freedom in both research and teaching is one of the defining features of a university law school, how law schools meet the challenges set by the study of law and popular culture is indicative of the intellectual and professional state of health of those law schools.[1]

In terms of the undergraduate programme, the law school curriculum is in many ways a narrow one. This is partly due to the professional requirements of legal study, and the concomitant requirement of the core subjects demanded in order for a degree to be a qualifying one, and partly because of a broader adherence to the black-letter tradition.[2] This is not meant to be a dogmatic statement. It is of course apparent that there are some attempts to go beyond a black-letter approach to legal study, both outside and within the core elements of study.[3] The professional requirements dictate the pre-scriptive nature to a degree, but legal education has changed – in fact, the skills agenda which came to prominence in the 1980s[4] was driven by the professions and their desire for a more skills-based curriculum. On a related issue it is important to make clear that a subject is not necessarily outside of the black-letter tradition just because it is a novel or different area, it is a question of approach.[5]

In terms of academic research this black-letter hegemony has manifested itself historically with a conservative approach both to 'acceptable' subject matter and the ways in which the subjects were treated.[6] Of course, not all law schools are the same and a number of approaches persist. Often conflicting approaches may reside in the same school, and while the black-letter tradition is not all pervasive it still exerts a powerful influence.[7] In addition to this, legal academics may themselves have difficulties when attempting to locate the law within wider social structures and contexts, as Macaulay puts it; '. . . many law professors experience vertigo when they open the doors and look outside appellate courtrooms'.[8] Taking a wider vista, Sugarman notes the position of the law in relation to other academic disciplines, and in particular law's isolation from these disciplines and its reluctance to embrace change.[9] That said, the law curriculum has evolved, partly as a response to external pressure[10] partly because of dynamism on the part of the law itself and shifts within approaches within individual law schools:

> University law schools are not, of course, fixed entities, wholly unable to escape their past. A number of writers have argued that the research paradigm in university law schools is changing and that theoretical work or socio-legal studies rather than doctrinal law now represents the dominant mode.[11]

The point is further made by Cownie and Bradney that teaching developments tend to lag behind research ones, so the impact of the research paradigm upon the student experience may well be minimized, at least initially. The developments that have occurred illustrate that whilst internally there may have been a reticence to embrace change for all sorts of reasons, not least perhaps this endemic inertia of substance and delivery, governmental bodies such as that overseen by Ormrod in the form of the *Report of the Committee of Legal Education*.[12] have pointed out that academic legal education should be seen within a broader social and economic context. That there have been attempts to embrace this has been vividly illustrated by the growth in a series of welfarist-focused courses within the UK. Those fairly recent law subjects that have attempted to stress their relevance and position to society. These could include Labour Law, Family Law, Social Security Law and perhaps today, Human Rights and the Law. Again the point needs to be made that these subjects could just as easily be taught within a black-letter framework, it is a question of approach and context.

In addition to this, developments such as that of the Critical Legal Studies Movement further attempted to map the 'politics of law' by offering different readings of legal texts, and to encourage the use of other interpretative techniques to analyse the law; witness for example the various approaches in Kairys' collection.[13] On a similar basis, the Socio-Legal Studies Association in the UK posited a view of law that embraced other disciplines and approaches and was concerned with '. . . the study of legal phenomena which is multi- or inter-disciplinary in its approach. Our theoretical perspectives and methodologies are informed by research undertaken in many other disciplines'.[14] This undoubtedly had some influence, and these approaches will have impacted upon syllabi and research of adherents to this socio-legal philosophy. That said, the black-letter tradition has persisted. As Redhead notes:

> Whether the depth of this challenge of a new legal conceptualism was actually maintained in the 1980s and even into the 1990s, either in the United States or elsewhere, is a moot point . . . suffice it to say that by the end of the 1980s a positivist-dominated law curriculum was still the norm in most British law schools.[15]

However, in terms of popular culture, a further problem can be identified. Not only was there a hurdle of establishing a 'law and...' element within the context of a predominantly black-letter tradition within the law school, but also the difficulty of confronting debates in some quarters (both inside and outside the legal academy) as to the relevance of popular culture.

This rejection, or marginalization, of popular culture, is charted by Turner in his exemplary history of British Cultural Studies.[16] As Newman notes, echoing Redhead's point about 1980s dominant traditions:

> [p]opular culture theorists have claimed that their field has been ignored by elitist scholars, who view popular culture as not worthy of serious study, because it is popular ... This attitude toward popular culture has prevailed since Matthew Arnold's *Culture and Anarchy* (1869). Popular culture began to receive scholarly attention in the 1960s and 1970s, but the 1980s saw a resurgence of the 'back to basics' movement in education exemplified by the Harvard Core Curriculum'.[17]

So, 'law and popular culture' is afflicted by a double jeopardy – a narrow approach to the law curriculum, and a cautious attitude to popular culture. Yet here lies the conundrum – the area attracts interest by virtue of the fact that it is popular and relevant, yet there may be a reluctance to accept it because of its popular status. However, this accessibility and contemporaneity has nurtured developments throughout the 1990s in terms of research initiatives within the field of law and popular culture. This has been in terms of research centres focusing upon the law/popular culture interface more generally (such as the Centre for the Study of Law, Society and Popular Culture at the University of Westminster and the Unit for Law and Popular Culture at Manchester Metropolitan University) as well as more specific areas e.g. sport and law (such as the Sports Law Centre at Anglia Polytechnic University).

So law and popular culture faces two initial problems. The first an internal legal one where the academic hegemony determines that law is a text in need of interpretation, rather than a system of social relations.[18] Second, a persistent (elitist) perception in some quarters of popular culture as 'cheap', 'trashy' and lacking in value. However, running counter to these two positions is a strong movement which suggests that in fact much may be learned about the law, and legal processes from an interrogation and understanding of this very relationship.[19] Indeed, this book hopefully adds further weight to that argument, or at least goes further to support the acceptance of the fact that a contextual inquiry of the law, and an understanding of how the law interacts with the everyday, has a useful and valid purpose.

Law's engagement with popular culture

Before looking at the ways in which the law has engaged with, and often colonized, popular culture, it is useful to briefly illustrate how popular culture has engaged with the law. At this juncture it is also helpful to consider what is meant by popular culture itself. It is in fact very difficult to frame a definition as all cultures, groups and historical periods can have their own notions of popular culture[20] and part of the joy of the area is its inclusivity. That said, the definition provided by Dick Hebdidge, that popular culture is '. . . a set of generally available artefacts: films, records, clothes, TV programmes, modes of transport, etc.'[21] is a useful marker for these purposes.

Popular culture in this sense has engaged with the law in a number of ways. In an age dominated by the visual image, the most overt manifestation of this is undoubtedly through television and film.[22] Much in the same way that the film industry has a fascination for the law, 'the law', in all its forms has had a strong presence within the medium of television. This has ranged from fictional police dramas, detective series, law-firm centred dramas etc., to fact-based documentaries, usually focusing on criminal issues.[23] Certainly the law has been often represented within film; from *Young Mr Lincoln* (1939) to *Legally Blonde* (2001) the law has provided a popular focal point for cinematic treatment.[24] Similarly, although this is not so marked, the popular song has also utilized the law as a focus. Often these instances have focused on critiques of the law as it applies particularly to the music industry and an artist's own particular situation; examples of this include the work of The Clash and The Sex Pistols. Similarly, an approach might focus more broadly on the legal machinations of the music industry from a more objective, less artist-centred stance, such as a critique of copyright law (as with Pop Will Eat Itself's exhortation to *Sample it, Loop it, Fuck it and Eat it*) or record-industry practice (as in The Smiths' *Paint a Vulgar Picture*).[25]

However, aside from representations of the law in popular culture, another aspect of this has been the use of popular culture as a tool in the delivery of legal teaching. This basically covers the use of instances of popular culture as vehicles to illustrate legal issues or practice.[26] The legal academy has become less resistant to the use of popular culture in this way, partly because it allows a black-letter focus to have a veneer of hipness (the use of a film clip to illustrate a point of evidence perhaps), but also because it allows a contextualization or an appreciation of the law's operation in practice. Johnson makes the point that aids of a basic kind are commonplace and that developments can be used to enhance teaching on a number of levels; 'the idea that audiovisual devices can be used to enhance law teaching is certainly accepted to some degree for even the most hardened skeptic would find it difficult to picture a professor – even a law professor – without a blackboard and chalk close at hand',[27] and the rise of multi-media has seen an acceleration of the use of sources such as this within law teaching, partly as a way of 'livening up' teaching. Studies such as that of Hausermann also

illustrate that such approaches can promote student attendance and participation.[28] So, the law is used as a focus of popular culture for a number of
reasons. This is partly because of the visual and literary images it conjures,
partly because of the subject matter itself (and the binary themes of
right/wrong, black/white, good/bad etc.) and partly because in a media-
saturated age it provides a useful way into discussing other issues on an
educative level.

Whilst areas of popular culture have become sites for representation of
the law, and as noted above it may be used as a vehicle for teaching areas of
law, the flipside of this is its inversion – the way in which the law has
engaged with areas of popular culture. There are myriad examples of the
ways and methods by which areas of popular culture have been policed. The
chapters in the book further interrogate such 'ways and methods', but it is
useful in this introduction to briefly illustrate some of the arenas of popular
culture that have been policed by way of context.

One area of popular culture that has been heavily policed is that of
popular music. Examples of the ways in which this has been policed include
the regulation of dissemination on grounds of censorship;[29] intellectual
property disputes that may also have the effect of preventing production and
dissemination of material[30] and contractual disputes.[31] All of these areas of
intervention have potential implications in terms of the ability of artists to
fully voice their creativity, in addition to wider issues about the commodification of a cultural entity. Fraser and Black cite these tensions within the
context of the legal contradictions that surround(ed) the band the Grateful
Dead. These are neatly exemplified by juxtaposing the image of 'the outlaw
band', whose concerts are viewed as a site to escape the mundane and whose
fans see in the Grateful Dead a potential to exist outside everyday legality,
with a broader picture of their position within the rock 'n' roll industry;

> Here we come to what we see as the central contradiction between the
> myth and reality of the Grateful Dead and the law, or perhaps more
> accurately, two competing realities of the Grateful Dead and the law.
> On the one hand, we find LSD, 'Me and My Uncle', taper's sections, and
> the experiential reality of a Dead show as a place and time where things
> are in fact different. On the other hand we have the Grateful Dead
> incorporating in 1971 and vigorously pursuing copyright infringement
> actions against bootleggers; BMWs; and millions of dollars in annual
> revenues from shows, CDs, and licensed T-shirts.[32]

Here we see a dialectic between, for example, allowing 'Deadheads' to tape
shows and create their own bootlegs on the one hand, and the legal protection of the name and output on the other. Here the tension is an internal one
– a question for the Grateful Dead as to whether they exist as a cultural or
commercial enterprise, a debate that has caused innumerable problems for
popular cultural artists from Bette Davis to George Michael,[33] and indeed

provides for wider fissures within approaches to legal areas. These tensions have become more pronounced, and more in need of resolution, as the global economy develops. Witness the difficulties of enacting sufficient moral rights protection in a number of common law jurisdictions and the contrasting approaches in civil law traditions that often privilege the artistic over the economic[34] or the set of jurisdictional and regulatory problems created by the Internet.[35] The music industry does in fact provide a number of examples of legal regulation, largely through its twin focal points of control; contract and copyright.

Within popular music, the different levels of regulation can be fairly easily identified; one way of classifying this is to distinguish how the law regulates the consumption of music (censorship, copyright issues, criminal regulation) on the one hand and the creation of, or participation in, music (censorship or copyright issues preventing artistic endeavours, contractual issues) on the other. The distinction between these two concepts is important in terms of approaches to legal regulation of popular culture, but it is also important to appreciate that there is a considerable blurring taking place. In terms of popular music, one way that this manifests itself is in terms of technology allowing a democratization in terms of music production and dissemination – the line between being a consumer and a creative artist is a fine one in an age when it is relatively easy to produce material cheaply and easily on a home computer for example.[36] In terms of football, this blurring is seen in terms of developments such as 'Supporters Direct', a movement allowing supporters to take a more direct, or participative role within the game, thus blurring the consumer/participator divide. Within sport there are a number of approaches that could be taken in order to illustrate the shifts that have occurred within its regulatory frameworks. There certainly appears to be a shift from a primarily criminal framework (public order), via a narrower private law approach (footballer's contracts, injuries etc.) towards broader regulatory issues that impact upon commercial aspects (the relevance of company law for example) within the regulation of football generally;

> Sporting legal disputes take many forms and tend to fall into two categories: participatory and consumptive. Participatory disputes tend to concern contractual and licensing disputes between players and clubs or governing bodies, contested disciplinary procedures and criminal and civil claims made between sporting participants. Consumptive disputes relate to the regulatory powers that might affect how sports can be consumed – these range from laws dealing with safety and public order when travelling to and attending sporting events, to the increasingly important areas of television rights, ownership and merchandising.[37]

In terms of consumption, the policing of rave culture in the 1980s and 1990s provides a neat example of regulatory pressure being placed upon a cultural phenomenon. While Thornton[38] has charted the social significance and cultural impact of this movement, others have charted the attempts made to police it.[39] Redhead has further argued that legislative provisions such as the *Entertainment (Increased Penalties) Act 1990* and *Criminal Justice and Public Order Act 1994* (and he would undoubtedly include the later *Public Entertainment (Misuse of Drugs) Act 1997*) have all been prompted by a moral panic, and the resultant legal manifestation of this he has termed 'panic law'.[40] Redhead's model of panic law can equally be applied to other areas of popular culture,[41] and as regards football this can arguably be used as a tool for analysing the responses to football hooliganism of the last two decades of the twentieth century, and perhaps even earlier antecedents of disorder reactive legislation. Indeed, this panic law approach can be seen as a motif to much of the legislative reactions charted within football,[42] and illustrates one way in which the consumption of popular culture might be regulated.

So, the law interacts with popular culture in a number of ways. In particular, there is a long history of regulating popular culture and selected examples of how popular culture has been (and is) regulated are illustrated within this book. On one level, this book is solely a collection of articles based upon papers presented for the Law and Popular Culture stream of the Socio Legal Studies Association over the past few years.[43] In a broader sense, however, this book marks a key point in the emergence of the field of law and popular culture – a clarion call to friend and foe that law and popular culture has truly arrived. Bradney, in his chapter places the difficulty of the acceptance of new areas within the context of the policy of the law school, and argues, amongst other things that a failure to accord popular culture a place within the legal academy does law schools and legal academia a disservice – such a 'monolithic approach' has a negative effect not only on law and popular culture but on all new areas of scholarship. All of the chapters here provide evidence of the health of the area and hopefully illustrate that notwithstanding myopic academic agenda, the area is thriving.

The chapters in this book are divided into three parts. Part One deals with Theory and Academia; all these chapters provide a fascinating underpinning to the area – a theoretical understanding is one element that has perhaps been under-represented in law and popular culture historically and this section helps with the 'authentication' of the area.

The other parts are loosely constructed around the areas of 'sport' and 'film, literature and music'. Whilst we have chosen to categorize in this way for the purposes of this book, we are keen to stress that there is a crossover in many of these approaches and that in some ways such categorization is artificial. In addition, we do not mean this to be construed as a definitive list of areas of popular culture, one of the joys of the area is its elastic parameters and potential for trawling new areas – inclusivity is all.

Underpinning all of this is a feeling that, today, law attempts to colonize everything in its path, partly because of commercial lure, partly because of a desire to regulate, to systemize. This can certainly be witnessed in terms of the increased legalization of sport; on a micro level even the increasing juridical nature of the rules of the sports themselves support this onward march of legalization. Perhaps most tellingly, the rules of some sports are actually called 'Laws' as if to reiterate this point. Indeed, increasingly everything is becoming legal; 'Now law comes to us, whether we want it or not. Legal modes of vocabulary and behaviour pervade even the most quotidian social interactions; the workplace, the school and even the home mimic the language of the law, and as a consequence replicate its conceptual schemes'.[44] So, internal regulations of sports mimic the law more and more, and the relationships with which we define ourselves become ever more legal. At the same time, the law and popular culture interface can be seen as a two-way street. Even beyond increasing legalization of these relationships, the area of popular culture still has a valid and important role in terms of legal education more generally, and hopefully both the chapters in this book and the work relied upon and referred to within, support the view that the relationship between law and popular culture is a valuable one, worthy of charting;

> My view is that once sufficient time and care have been devoted to analysing the emerging set of problems and materials which connect the world of popular art and everyday experience to that of legal institutions and practices, it will become apparent that useful contributions have been made to the sociology of culture, including legal culture. Understanding popular legal culture might even make possible more rigorous thinking about the relation between law, politics and social change . . .[45]

Notes

* This chapter is partly based upon a chapter of G. Osborn (2002) 'Folklore, Folkdevil, Folklaw? Football and the Regulation of its Consumption' Unpublished PhD thesis, Manchester Metropolitan University.
1 Bradney, A. (2006) 'The case of Buffy the Vampire Slayer and the Politics of Legal Education', in chapter 2 at p 15.
2 Stanley, C. (1988) 'Training for the hierarchy? Reflections on the British Experience of Legal Education' *The Law Teacher* 78.
3 Cownie, F. and Bradney, A. (2000) *English Legal System in Context* Butterworths: London.
4 Twining, W. (1989) 'Taking skills seriously' in Gold, N., Mackie, K. and Twining, W. (1989) *Learning Lawyers Skills* Butterworths: London.
5 Osborn, G. (2001) 'Borders and Boundaries. Locating the Law in Film' *Journal of Law and Society* Volume 28, Number 1, 164; Redhead, S. (1995) *Unpopular Cultures: The Birth of Law and Popular Culture* Manchester University Press: Manchester.
6 See here generally Bradney, 'The Case of Buffy the Vampire Slayer'.
7 Cownie and Bradney (2000).
8 Macaulay, S. (1989) 'Popular Legal Culture: An Introduction', *Yale Law Journal* 1548–1549.

9 Sugarman, D. (1991) '"A Hatred of Disorder": Legal Science, Liberalism and Imperialism' in Fitzpatrick, P. (ed.) (1991) *Dangerous Supplements. Resistance and renewal in jurisprudence*, Pluto Press, London. On a very personal level, our own early teaching was based in a building (the law school) in which no other member of the University or even Faculty resided and which was some distance from the other parts of the University. This effect of this dislocation was easy to see, both in terms of a certain privileging of the law school itself by certain staff, and a view of suspicion being exhibited by 'outsiders'. See Chris Stanley, 'Training for the Hierarchy?' (ibid.) for an analysis of the position of the law school in relation to the University as a whole.

10 See generally here Osborn, (2001), 'Borders and Boundaries'.

11 Cownie, F. and Bradney, A. (2000) *English Legal System in Context* Butterworths: London 133–134.

12 *Report of the Committee of Legal Education* 1971 (Ormrod) Cmnd 4595.

13 Kairys, D. (ed.) (1982) *The Politics of Law: A progressive critique* Pantheon Books: New York.

14 SLSA, 2002, xii. Available online: http://www.kent.ac.uk/slsa/home_links/aboutslsa.htm (date accessed 5 October 2005).

15 Redhead, S. (1995), *Unpopular Cultures*, 19.

16 Turner, G. (1996) *British Cultural Studies. An Introduction* Routledge: London.

17 Newman, G. (1990) 'Popular Culture and Criminal Justice: A Preliminary Analysis' *Journal of Criminal Justice* Volume 18, 261, 270.

18 Chase, A. (1988) 'An Obscure Scandal of Consciousness' *Yale Journal of Law and the Humanities* 105.

19 Friedman, L. (1989) 'Law, lawyers and popular culture' *Yale Law Journal* Vol. 98 1579; Chase, A. (1986a) 'Toward a legal theory of popular culture' *Wisconsin Law Review* 527; Chase, A. (1986b) 'Lawyers and Popular Culture: A Review of Mass Media Portrayals of American Attorneys' *American Bar Foundation Research Journal* 281; Chase (1988) 'An Obscure Scandal of Consciousness'; Hunt, A. (1995) 'The Role of Law in the Civilizing Process and the Reform of Popular Culture' *Canadian Journal of Law and Society* Volume 10, Number 2, 5, Macaulay (1989) 'Symposium: Popular Legal Culture'; Redhead, S. (1995) *Unpopular Cultures*.

20 Strinati, D. (1995) *An Introduction to Theories of Popular Culture* Routledge: London.

21 Hebdidge, D. (1988) *Hiding in the Light: On Images and Things* Routledge: London 47.

22 Of course, literature has a far longer historical and cultural lineage, and there is no shortage of literary material that utilizes the law – Ward, I. (1993) 'The educative ambition of Law and Literature' *Legal Studies 323* illustrates how this might be used within a legal teaching context. However, the film industry has a pre-eminence in terms of its accessibility and connection with society. Certainly most law students have their first view of law from the TV or cinema rather than the written word. See Greenfield, S., Osborn, G. and Robson, P. (2001) *Film and the Law* Cavendish Publishing: London.

23 Greenfield, S., Osborn, G. and Robson, P. (2001), *Film and the Law* Cavendish Publishing: London.

24 Denvir, J. (ed.) *Legal Reelism. Movies as Legal Texts* University of Illinois Press: Urbana and Chicago; Bergman, P. and Asimow, M. (1996) *Reel Justice – the Courtroom goes to the movies* Andrews and McMeel, Kansas City; Greenfield *et al.*, (2001), *Film and the Law*.

25 The Sex Pistols for example included a song entitled 'E.M.I' on their *Never mind the Bollocks . . . here's the Sex Pistols* LP (Virgin Records, 1978) which outlined

their views on one of their record companies during a period when they seemed unable to remain with any company for more than a few days. This theme was returned to on the title track of the *The Great Rock 'n' Roll Swindle* LP (Virgin Records, 1979). A verse of The Clash's *Complete Control* was used to conclude the final chapter of Greenfield and Osborn (1998) *Contract and Control in the Entertainment Industry. Dancing on the Edge of Heaven*, Dartmouth: Aldershot as it encapsulated a typical record industry view of artists.

Pop Will Eat Itself are a good example of a UK band who 'sampled' other people's work to create their own sound. Sound sampling is a form of musical collage that utilizes, literally samples or excerpts of the sound recordings of others. The quote in the text illustrates their approach and attitude to others' work. The Smiths' reference is to a Morrissey lyric as the Smiths were coming to an end, on the final album (*Strangeways Here We Come*, Rough Trade, 1987) where he posited the music industry attitude to their artists thus:

> At the record company meeting
> On their hands – a dead star
> and ooh, the plans that they weave
> and ooh, the sickening greed
> At the record company party
> on their hands – a dead star
> The sycophantic slags all say:
> 'I knew him first, and I knew him well!'
> Re-issue! Re-package! Re-package!
> Re-evaluate the songs
> double-pack with a photograph
> Extra track (and a tacky badge)…
> (Morrissey and Marr, 1987,
> Warner Brothers Music Ltd)

26 See Osborn (2001) 'Borders and Boundaries', Greenfield *et al.* (2001), *Film and the Law*.

27 Johnson, V. (1987) 'Audiovisual enhancement of classroom teaching: a primer for law professors' *Journal of Legal Education* 97.

28 Hausermann (1995) 'Learning can be fun: high tech meets undergrad law' *ABA Focus on Law Studies*.

29 Cloonan, M. (1996) *Banned! Censorship of Popular Music in Britain: 1967–92* Arena: Aldershot; Cloonan, M. and Garafolo, R. (2002) *Policing Pop* Temple University Press.

30 Bentley, L. (1989) 'Sampling and Copyright: is the Law on the Right Track?' *Journal of Business Law* 113; Frith, S. (1993) 'Music and Morality' in Frith, S. (ed.) (1993) *Music and Copyright* Edinburgh University Press: Edinburgh.

31 Greenfield, S. and Osborn, G. (1992) 'Unchained Melody. Restraint of Trade and Music contracts' *Business Law Review*; Greenfield, S. and Osborn, G. (1992). 'Unconscionability and Contract. The creeping shoots of Bundy' *Denning Law Journal* 65; Greenfield, S. and Osborn, G. (1994) 'Sympathy for the Devil? Contractual restraint and artistic autonomy in the entertainment industry' *Journal of Media Law* 117; Greenfield, S. and Osborn, G. (1998); Coulthard, A. (1995) 'George Michael v. Sony Music – a challenge to artistic freedom?' *Modern Law Review* 58, 731.

32 Fraser, D. and Black, V. (1999) 'Legally Dead: The Grateful Dead and American Legal Culture' in Weiner, R. (ed.) (1999) *Perspectives on the Grateful Dead. Critical Writings* Greenwood Press: Westport Connecticut, 21.

33 Both of these contract cases are covered in depth in Greenfield and Osborn,

(1998). It is of course undoubtedly possible to exist contemporaneously as a commercial and cultural being, but the competing interests will inevitably create tensions managing the two.

34 See for example Frith, (1993), *Music and Copyright*.

35 Akdeniz, Y., Walker, C. and Wall, D. (2000) *The Internet, Law and Society* Longman: Harlow.

36 There is an interesting shift that has taken place in terms of who is deemed a musician, and in particular whether a DJ could become a member of the Musicians' Union (MU). Whilst historically a DJ might not have been deemed to merit recognition as a musician because of a perceived low level of creativity, the MU now deems DJs to be a creative artist and therefore qualifies as a musician. See chapter 14 of the current text.

37 Greenfield and Osborn (1999) 'The legal colonisation of cricket' *Soundings* Issue 13.

38 Thornton, S. (1995) *Club Cultures. Music, Media and Subcultural Capital* Polity Press: Cambridge.

39 Collin, M. (1997) *Altered States* Serpents Tail: London.

40 Steve Redhead (1995) *Unpopular Cultures*, 112 defines panic law as '. . . the frenzied-but-simulated state of the law and justice at the end of the century, as in Jean Baudrillard's use of "panic crash" to describe global economic stock exchange breakdowns'. Panic law is predicated upon notions of moral panic as outlined by Stanley Cohen (2002) *Folk Devils and Moral Panics*, Routledge: London.

41 See for example Greenfield, S. and Osborn, G. (1998) 'When the writ hits the fan; panic law and football fandom' in Brown, A. (ed.) (1998) *Fanatics! Power, identity and fandom in football*, Routledge: London.

42 See Greenfield, S. and Osborn, G. (2001) *Regulatory Football*, Pluto Press: London.

43 The Law and Popular Culture stream has successfully run at the SLSA at Bristol (2001), Aberystwyth (2002), Nottingham (2003) and Glasgow (2004). We have seen over 30 papers presented here across over a dozen sessions, thanks to all the participants in these, not just those that have been selected for publication here.

44 Campos, P. (1998) *Jurismania. The Madness of American Law* Oxford University Press: New York, 5.

45 Chase (1988) 'An Obscure Scandal of Consciousness' Yale *Journal of Law and the Humanities* pp. 105–106.

Part I

Theory and academia

2 The case of Buffy the Vampire Slayer and the politics of legal education

Anthony Bradney

Introduction

This chapter will argue that the approach taken by law schools to scholarship that treats law and popular culture as its focus is a good indicator of whether or not the intellectual vibrancy that currently characterizes both research and teaching in United Kingdom university law schools will continue. Using the example of the television series Buffy the Vampire Slayer (hereinafter BtVS), this chapter illustrates some of the ways in which popular culture can be both a stimulating site for research and, at the same time, provide a fruitful resource for learning and teaching in the law school. Despite this potentiality inherent in the study of popular culture, the chapter suggests that some of the dynamics within the politics of university legal education may inhibit the development of work on law and popular culture, resulting in the area receiving less attention than it deserves. This chapter contends that such an outcome would not only impoverish law schools but also constitute an infringement on academic freedom since it would result from an attempt to circumscribe the research paths, teaching objectives or methods that have been chosen by individual academics. Given the likely value of popular culture to the law school and given the fact that the existence of academic freedom in both research and teaching is one of the defining features of a university law school, how law schools meet the challenges set by the study of law and popular culture is indicative of the intellectual and professional state of health of those law schools.

BtVS

The basic setting for BtVS is straightforward.[1] Human beings share the world with vampires, demons and other supernatural creatures that are usually hostile to humanity.

> Into every generation, a Slayer is born. One girl, in all the world, a Chosen One. One born with the strength and skill to hunt the vampires...[2]

The Slayer is human but possesses greater '[a]gility, clarity, stamina and strength' than normal people.[3] Slayers also heal much faster than other human beings.[4] The Slayer's main purpose is to kill vampires and demons. She works for a Watcher who is, at least in principle, her 'commander' and who trains her.[5] The Watcher, again in principle, is, 'in matters of tradition and protocol', responsible to the Watcher's Council who base their decisions about what the Slayer should do on 'laws that have existed longer than civilization'.[6] The programme is set in contemporary southern California. Buffy, who is 16-years-old when the series first starts and a 24-year-old when it ends, is supported through the seven series by a changing group of characters, first referred to as the Slayerettes and later as the Scooby Gang, who also fight vampires and demons and seek to avert the apocalypse that is threatened in each series.[7]

Two things about BtVS are of consequence for the purposes of this chapter; its worldwide popularity and the academic attention that has been paid to the programme. The fact of BtVS' popularity is not open to dispute, given both the viewing figures that it received and the ever-increasing number of websites (located in countries from Argentina to the Ukraine) devoted to it.[8] Evidence of the academic attention paid to the programme comes from a number of different sources. To date, three volumes of essays on the programme have been published and one more is in press. Two monographs have also been published.[9] BtVS has been the focus of analysis both in academic journals concerned with television studies or cultural studies and, more tellingly, in a wide range of other places as diverse as the journal of the American Library Association, 'American Libraries', and the United States Center for Strategic and International Studies.[10] The academic journal, S*layage: the Online International Journal of Buffy Studies*, now in its fifteenth issue, is entirely devoted to the programme.[11] The University of East Anglia, the University of Melbourne and the Middle Tennessee State University have all hosted major conferences on the programme, with the University of Melbourne's conference leading to a special issue of the cultural studies journal, *Refractory*.[12] Such examples could be expanded on almost endlessly.

The popularity of the BtVS with the general public justifies the law school turning its attention to the series because its students are a segment of that population and, as will be shown below, BtVS can be used to improve learning and teaching for those students. The programme's fascination for academics indicates that the law school should examine the series because, if the programme has been seen as having so much significance by others in the academy, the question of whether it might be of any interest to academics in the law school is raised.

BtVS and the law school's research agenda

Analysis of BtVS in the law school can broadly take one of two directions; consideration of how viewers respond to the ideas about law and justice that arise in BtVS or critical analysis of those themes.[13]

Reception studies in relation to television, the question of how and why audiences react to particular programmes in the way that they do, is an area of academic enquiry that has now been established for some decades.[14] Its importance to the law school lies in the fact that people's ideas about law are, in terms of social effect, just as important as the law itself. What people think about law and what people think about the content of legal rules helps to determine their behaviour. If people think law is fair and just they are more likely to both respect and use it than if they do not. Equally, if people are aware that a legal rule has been framed so as to give them legal protection in a particular situation they may use it whilst, if they are unaware of the rule, or misunderstand its content, they may not.[15] Popular culture provides one important source of knowledge about law; and television is now the 'main, mass medium'.[16] Thus the question, how do audiences react to images of law on television in general and BtVS in particular, becomes pertinent to the law school.

Reception studies in relation to BtVS are still in their nascence.[17] Two issues about the audience reception of BtVS are, however, already clear. First, whilst Levine and Schneider *might* be right, in general, in arguing that BtVS' high audience figures do not result from 'anything remarkable (much less unique) about the series, its scripts, acting, language, or message' and that to focus on the themes frequently discussed in much of the academic literature on BtVS 'misplaces the show's value and appeal', for at least some of the people who view BtVS, the themes relating to law and authority that permeate the programme are a matter of engrossing concern and a reason for their watching the programme.[18] Illustrative of this proposition is the fact that discussion on at least one well-established website, 'Above the Law', focuses solely on these issues whilst another equally well-known website, 'All Things Philosophical on Buffy the Vampire Slayer and Angel the Series', also has commentary on some of these matters.[19] The way in which law is portrayed on BtVS is a matter of interest to some viewers. How widespread or deep this interest is amongst those who view BtVS is, of course, another matter.[20] Equally, viewers of BtVS who manifest no interest in the programme's portrayal of law and justice may still have their ideas about these matters subliminally affected by the series. However, in both cases, the effect of BtVS on the viewer is a complex matter. The fact that a viewer reacts to ideas in BtVS, whether consciously or unconsciously, does not necessarily mean that he or she takes on the ideas passively; reacting to ideas and accepting ideas are different matters and the degree to which audiences are active or passive in their viewing has been a matter of much debate within reception studies.[21] Second, as regards audience reception of BtVS, it seems plain that the BtVS audience should in fact be conceived of as the BtVS audiences. 'The actual television viewer is a primarily social subject.'[22] Thus class, gender, age, religion and so forth alter how the viewer perceives BtVS and divide the audience into 'audiences'. Equally the distinction drawn between fans and viewers in studies of some other television programmes such as *Star Trek* is pertinent to BtVS.[23] Fans are the paradigmatic example of active viewers in that they produce a '*material* culture of their own' in the form of stories, videos and other matter based on the subject of their fandom. Moreover, classically, they form their own communities, either by attendance at conventions, or in a virtual form via the web.[24] How fans as an audience react to BtVS and questions of law in BtVS may be very different from how non-fan audiences react.

Amongst the wealth of literature on BtVS, comparatively little has been published that focuses its analysis on the themes of law and justice in BtVS.[25] This is not because these matters are not touched on in BtVS but, rather, because other things in the programme are of greater weight and have thus more quickly attracted commentary, and also because the law school has shown its customary tardiness in considering new areas for analysis and therefore has tended to ignore BtVS. Nevertheless, just as a range of literary works from the obvious King Lear to the less well-known Super-Cannes provide a starting point for the analysis of law, so BtVS can stimulate reflection on legal issues.[26]

Law does not, at first sight, appear to be central to BtVS. BtVS is about vampire slaying, but it is also about the 'problems of middle-class, Anglo, heteronormative, North American teenage socialization'.[27] Early's description of BtVS as being 'preeminently a narrative of the disorderly rebellious female' is a good general description of the series.[28] Law, if not irrelevant to the programme, seems peripheral to it. In terms of plot, only two out of the 144 episodes concentrate on the difficulties of a legal decision that has to be made, 'Pangs' (4008) which centres on the question of whether the rule 'kill vampires and demons' applies to Hus, a vengeance spirit and 'Selfless' (7005) where the same question is asked in relation to Anya, one of the Scooby Gang, who has returned to being a vengeance demon. Nevertheless, notwithstanding the paucity of overt references to law, there is much for the law school in the programme.

The basic structure in which Buffy operates for much of the first three series of BtVS, working for the Watcher's Council with its laws that are older than civilization and being directly responsible to a Watcher, means that Buffy works within the context of 'an alternate system of power and control'; to the legal theorist's eyes a pluralistic legal system, that ignores or contradicts the state legal system.[29] Her role, I have argued elsewhere, is that of a police officer and, at this juncture, the series can be seen as being an unusual variant of that genre.[30] Superficially challenging to the notion of the value of law because of Buffy and the Scobby Gang's apparent disregard of the state legal system, the programme in fact largely follows the conservative traditions of the police series genre by portraying a police officer and a policing system that can defeat or at least suppress the criminality that is represented by vampires and demons.[31] Buffy's resignation from the Watcher's Council in the penultimate programme of the third series, *Graduation: Part I* (3021), a resignation resulting from the fact that she has decided that she rejects the law of the Watcher's Council, changes the nature of BtVS. Given her refusal to accept the idea that Slayers are above the law, and in the absence of established legal systems that she can accept, Buffy must for the next four series, in cooperation with her surrogate family the Scooby Gang, make up her own law.[32]

Because the first three series of BtVS are, in part, police series, because of the problematic relationship that the central characters have with state law during these series and because Buffy has doubts about the law of the Watcher's Council from the moment, in series one, when she realizes her developing friendship with Angel, a vampire, brings her into conflict with a law that tells her to kill all vampires, the first three series of BtVS are of interest to the law school.[33] Questions about the nature of law and about the extent of one's duty to obey the law are implicitly, and sometimes explicitly, raised in these series. However, the final four series of BtVS offer even more to the law school as they deal with the questions of how the characters are to arrive at rules that will serve them as law, how they will interact with state law, how they will relate to the Watcher's Council and its law and how far, if at all, Buffy's role as a Slayer gives her a special status in these decisions. It is significant that the two episodes, 'Pangs' and 'Selfless', which explicitly address the question of the interpretation of a legal rule are to be found in these final four series. Moreover, for the law school it is important that BtVS, a programme that 'refuses the black-and-white moral distinctions of a more self-evident and sanctimonious style of politics', acknowledging the complexity of the world, avoids quick and over-easy answers to these questions about law.[34] In drawing a contrast between systems of rules such as state law and the law of the Watcher's Council which are legitimated externally and a system of law which is arrived at by personal reflection and in finally suggesting that the latter is to be preferred, even though the former systems still need to be heeded on occasion, BtVS offers a complex and unusual text for the law school to reflect on.[35]

Pedagogy in the law school and BtVS

Ausubel, in his book on educational psychology, remarks on the importance of starting with the experience of the student and building on that if the student's learning is to reach its full potential.[36] Given the very limited experience that each student possesses, this contention has to be treated with some caution in the context of university education, where the purpose of the education is to challenge, contradict, go beyond and in some instances simply disregard what the student has previously believed to be either valuable or valid.[37] However, the more conservative proposition that it is sometimes useful to start with the actual experience of students when exploring complicated concepts seems relatively uncontroversial. It is in this context that BtVS becomes of importance for pedagogy in the law school.

Given the demographics of the viewing figures for the BtVS it is likely that a significant proportion of the students in any law school will be familiar with the programme.[38] This is so despite the fact that the social milieu of the programme, white, middle-class, suburban, southern California, is different from and in some instances far-removed from the cultural circumstances of students in a United Kingdom law school. The programme has resonances for those with backgrounds that are, at least superficially, very different from the backgrounds of the characters in the series. The complexity of the programme noted above is in part responsible for this. Chin asks of herself, '[h]ow can a woman of color be a fan of the blond and very white Buffy the vampire slayer?'.[39] Her answer is to point to the essential ambiguity in Buffy as a character. Buffy is neither simply a superhero, nor is she simply a woman with the normal experiences of adolescence and post-adolescence, she is not always good; she is not always right; she is not always reliable; she is not always just; she is not always tough (though she is also all of these things) and so on, and so forth.[40] Chin comments, 'Buffy's ambiguity provides some space to grant her the benefit of the doubt' and, quoting Inness, goes onto remark 'she is a multivalent representation that can be read in numerous and even paradoxical ways'.[41] For this reason, it is not surprising that Bloustein notes that her Australian Screen Studies students like BtVS because it 'is so real' and then observes that

> speculative fictions such as *Buffy* can resonate with the adolescent experience – albeit nuanced by gender, ethnicity, race and class – even in social experiences far from their geographic origin.[42]

However, even if it is safe to assume that BtVS is something that most law students, no matter what their background, are to some extent familiar with and responsive to, how can it help teaching and learning in the law school?

As I have shown above, notions of law and justice permeate BtVS and thus give rise to opportunities to pose questions about the nature of law, the way in which it should be applied and the purposes that it should have.[43] South's edited collection *Buffy the Vampire Slayer and Philosophy* shows how, in the context of the study of philosophy, the series can be used in learning and teaching. Authors in the collection rehearse themes as diverse as Kantian morality, Aristotle's analysis of love and feminist ethics, using BtVS as the starting point for their discussion.[44] The central concern in these essays is not, as is the case with most other academic writing about BtVS, to say something new but, rather, to use BtVS as a vehicle for providing an accessible explanation of existing debates within philosophy.[45] Law as much as philosophy can employ BtVS in this way. Here the pedagogic advantage offered by BtVS is not that it necessarily says anything novel about issues relating to law or justice (although sometimes it does) but that it allows students to begin an examination of such issues on ground that is familiar to them.[46]

BtVS can also be used in the curriculum in the law school in a completely separate, second way. Law has reality only in a social context and most legal academics working in United Kingdom law schools would now accept that that social context must inform the way in which we study law.[47] BtVS provides an example of a social context in which to discuss law that is both known to the students but, because it is not personal to any of them, does not give any individual a privileged position in discussion. Used in this way, BtVS' treatment of issues directly pertaining to law or justice is irrelevant. Rather it is the fact that, when it is thought necessary to give students a 'real life' example of something, BtVS may be more meaningful to students than other sources.

In a course I once taught I tried to show students that a knowledge of non-legal theory is necessary if one is to understand what some legal rules mean. Taking the example of duress in marriage I asked, what do judges mean when they talk about the idea of the overborne will?[48] Existentialist philosophy, with its emphasis on the idea that choice is part of the signature of the human condition, offers an obvious theoretical context for an examination of the idea of wills being overborne. Sartre's book *Being and Nothingness* is the most complete statement of the existential position whilst his *Roads to Freedom* trilogy gives a literary 'real life' view of his theoretical stance.[49] However, more immediately relevant than Sartre to students, in understanding the thesis that human beings always have a choice and thus that minds cannot be overborne, is the episode of BtVS *Lie to Me* (2007). In *Lie to Me* Buffy is joined at her school by Billy Fordham, a friend from a previous school. Fordham wishes to become a vampire and intends to offer both Buffy and a group of people, who also want to become vampires, as a sacrifice to the vampire Spike who Fordham hopes will then facilitate his desire. He justifies his actions to Buffy by explaining that he has a brain tumour that will soon kill him in a very painful manner; being a vampire will give him eternal life free of pain. The following exchange exemplifies the existentialist argument.

> Fordham: . . . you try vomiting for twenty four hours straight because the pain in your head is so intense and then we'll discuss the concept of right and wrong . . . I don't have a choice.
> Buffy: You have a choice. You don't have a **good** choice: what's behind door number three is pretty much a dead fish but you have a choice.

The point is not that this exchange in *Lie to Me* contains a better explanation of the existentialist position than that found in Sartre. On the contrary, it is obvious that even Sartre's exposition of existentialism in his novels is more subtle and sophisticated than the brief examination of the nature of choice in *Lie to Me*. However, because of their familiarity with the programme, BtVS is a good starting point for a student's exploration of existentialist ideas that may then lead them on to Sartre.[50] Discussing whether or not Fordham has a choice leads to discussing what we individually mean when we say we did something because we did not have a choice which in turn leads to discussing what a judge means when they say a person who had repeated the marriage vows and signed the marriage register had their mind overborne so that they did those things. Fiction offers a more accessible route to reality than reality itself and a fiction that is familiar to students offers the most accessible route of all.

The pedagogic advantage offered by BtVS when used as a proxy for 'real life' is small but the fact that it is small does not mean that it should be dismissed. The series can be used in many different contexts. Thus, for example, the potentially destructive nature of families is central to any course on family law. In BtVS traditional biological families are invariably dysfunctional in some way. BtVS therefore offers opportunities for academics to raise questions which are central to a family law course in a way that is both familiar to students, whilst at the same time it is less threatening than trying to raise such issues in the context of the cultures that the students come from.[51] Many other similar examples could be given.

It is clear from the above that using BtVS in the law school curriculum has the potentiality to enhance learning and teaching in a number of different ways. The question is, will this potential in either BtVS or other examples of popular culture be realized?

BtVS and academic freedom

In the sections above I have sought to show that BtVS (and thus by extension popular culture) provides something that should be of interest to the law school. In doing this I do not suggest that popular culture in general or BtVS in particular should be of more interest than other things that the law school has hitherto focused on. Instead, I merely wish to argue that popular culture should be added to the list of things that the law school attends to and that, if it does not do so, there will be a consequent loss to both its research activities and its pedagogy. If individual academics wish to pursue this work, law schools as a whole will receive a collective benefit. How big the collective benefit is a matter for debate and speculation. Even if the gain offered by looking at law and popular culture is small, the gain is unarguably still there to be made. Yet there is good reason to suppose that academics who do wish to pursue such work are likely to face far greater difficulties than those who work in more traditional areas.

The threat to work on law and popular culture comes from two main sources. The first source is the Research Assessment Exercise (RAE), or, to be more precise, perceptions about the RAE, whilst the second source is those people who have a monolithic view of the research agenda that university law schools should have.

It is clear that many academics in both the university at large and in the law school believe that the RAE has affected the focus of research in universities.[52] Some writing, it is argued, is acceptable for the RAE and some is not, and if a form of writing is not acceptable for the RAE then it is no longer acceptable as research in the university. In the case of the law RAE panels there is plainly some justice in at least the first part of this suggestion. Successive panels have, for example, made it plain that new editions of student textbooks are unlikely to receive a high research ranking.[53] Equally, writing which is simply of an explanatory form directed towards practitioners is not likely to be well regarded by the panel. Such judgements are almost wholly uncontroversial since both these kinds of work, however well they perform their intended task, cannot be regarded as being high-level research because they bring no significant contribution to the expansion of knowledge.[54] Instead, such writing should properly be regarded as being part of the teaching mission of the law school. What is problematic for the law school and for the development of work on popular culture in the law school, however, is the view that, in order to receive a high ranking in the RAE, work must be published in certain supposedly prestigious journals or, in the case of monographs, be published by one of a select group of publishers.

None of the reports and presentations of successive law RAE panels sustain an argument that the choice of where to publish has to be restricted in any way. Indeed, in the light of the behaviour of past RAE panels, it is difficult to see how anyone could rationally support the thesis that place of publication matters. A vast range of work within law school has, by virtue of the fact that very different kinds of law schools have received high research rankings, implicitly received the approval of RAE panels. Even a casual reading of RAE returns demonstrates the very wide range of places that individuals in top-ranking law schools are choosing to publish in.[55] Nevertheless, it is plain that some academics do hold the view that publication must be in one of a small number of journals or with one of a small group of publishers.[56] As a result it would appear that some people go through a process of self-policing, entering onto research projects only if they believe they will lead to publication in what they think, or what they think other academics think, are suitable places, whilst other academics take it upon themselves to indicate to their colleagues where they should be publishing their research in order, supposedly, to enhance the RAE rating for their department.[57] Both forms of behaviour are likely to inhibit the development of research into law and popular culture.

If the publication of research has to be in a limited number of established and acceptable places the development of new research areas such as law and popular culture is inhibited in two ways.[58] First, new areas of research will not, by definition, have established specialist journals. Thus, whilst those who are pursuing research in more traditional areas have a home for publication in journals particular to their field, those working in new areas can only publish in such specialist journals if their work happens to overlap with the areas that those journals already cover. This is not impossible. Work in law and popular culture might at the same time be, for example, work in the field of criminal law. However, it is clear that occasional instances of fortu-itous overlap do not alter the fact that scholars in a new research field such as law and popular culture are disadvantaged if they are forced to publish their work in a select group of established journals. Second, a scholar in the field of law and popular culture suffers even when it comes to placing an article in a general journal. A general journal may be willing to take one article on law and popular culture but it is unlikely to take two within a very short period of time and still less likely to take three. If a general journal is to remain general it must demonstrate that it carries articles across a range of fields and cannot be seen to favour just one or two.[59] Moreover, it might well take the view that established areas of research are so sub-divided into various categories that it is justified in taking articles in all or some of those categories in a short period of time, whilst at the same time viewing some-thing like law and popular culture as one undivided area of research. Similar arguments to those given above for journals could be applied to publishers of monographs who have both general and specialist lists. Restricting publi-cation to approved sites makes it more difficult for those interested in law and popular culture to follow their chosen research agenda than it does for those who follow traditional research areas and thus, for some, makes it less likely that they will continue with such an agenda.[60]

Monolithic views of the law school's research agenda have a deleterious effect on the development of new areas of scholarship that is similar to the effect of the perceptions about the RAE noted above. Fiss, in the response to a suggestion that those academics who held nihilistic views about law should withdraw from law schools observed that the academic's job in a uni-versity law school is simply 'to study law and to teach their students what they happen to discover'.[61] An agenda-less agenda of this kind protects the freedom of scholars to pursue their individual interests. Once one abandons this position and begins to think of missions for the law school the margin-alization of some forms of scholarship becomes an inevitable, if sometimes unexpected and undesired, consequence. New, less well-known scholarship, such as that on law and popular culture, is almost certain to be a part of the marginalized group. This is so, no matter whether the mission of the law school is seen as being, to take two very different examples of such a mission, to train lawyers or to ameliorate the conditions of the poorest members of society.[62] Law schools exist for the purpose of studying law.[63] Leaving individual members of those law schools to decide for themselves what that study should entail creates the most propitious conditions for new forms of scholarship such as the study of law and popular culture.

The future of law and popular culture in the law school

A number of things, including panel sessions at recent Socio-Legal Studies Association and Society of Legal Scholars conferences, the special issue of the *British Journal of Law and Society* devoted to film, the 2003 Current Legal

Problems conference on law and popular culture and publication of this collection of essays, suggest that the study of law and popular culture is becoming both more common and more acceptable within the law school.[64] The arguments in this chapter indicate both some of the reasons why this is desirable and some of the tensions that may delay this development. The study of law and popular culture deserves a future in the law school. However, new areas of research and scholarship are fragile flowers that need to be nurtured and cosseted in a way that is not true for more established areas. In the light of the arguments above, one cannot be complacent that this will be done and the study of law and popular culture may thus not achieve the success that it merits. If this is so, the loss is to all legal academics, whatever their interests, both because of the consequent loss to scholarship that would be entailed, but also, more importantly, because of what it would say about the atmosphere that prevails in university law schools.

Notes

1 In addition to the television series BtVS takes a large number of other forms including a film and a series of books. (For a full analysis of the different forms see A. Bradney 'Choosing Laws, Choosing Families: Images of Law, Love and Authority' in *Buffy the Vampire Slayer* (2003a) 2 Web Journal of Current Legal Issues (http://webjcli.ncl.ac.uk/).) This chapter looks only at the television series and the scripts for that series. The first episode of BtVS, *Welcome to the Hellmouth*, was first broadcast in the USA on 10 March 1997. The final, one hundred and forty-fourth episode, *Chosen*, was broadcast in the USA on 20 May 2003. All seven series are currently available in video format. Scripts for all the episodes of the first two series and the first six programmes of the third series have been published by Pocket Books. The scripts for all 144 episodes are available on a variety of websites such as 'The Buffyverse Dialogue Database' (http://vyra.net/bdb/index.php) and 'Buffworld.com' (http://www.buffyworld. com/). The analysis in this chapter would not have been possible without these scripts.
2 *Welcome to the Hellmouth*, 1001. The first figure refers to the number of the series, the last figure(s) refer to the number of the episode in the series. Thus, the final, twenty-second programme in the seventh series, *Chosen*, is denoted as 7022.
3 *Checkpoint*, 5012.
4 *End of Days*, 7021.
5 *Consequences*, 3015; *Welcome to the Hellmouth*, 1001.
6 *Helpless*, 3012; *Graduation: Part One*, 3021.
7 *The Witch*, 1003; *What's My Line – Part One*, 2010. For detailed descriptions of each episode in the first six series of BtVS see K. Topping *Slayer: An Expanded and Updated Unofficial and Unauthorised Guide to Buffy the Vampire Slayer* (2002) Virgin Books, London, and K. Topping *Slayer: The Next Generation* (2003) Virgin Books, London. For an introduction to themes in BtVS see R. Kaveney 'She saved the world. A lot': An introduction to the themes and structures of *Buffy* and *Angel* in R. Kaveney (ed.) *Reading the Vampire Slayer* (2004) (2nd edn) Tauris Parke Paperbacks.
8 For audience ratings in the USA see 'Nielsen Ratings for Buffy the Vampire Slayer, Angel, and Firefly' (http://home.insightbb.com/~wahoskem). See also M. Adams *Slayer Slang: A Buffy the Vampire Slayer Lexicon* (2003) Oxford University

Press, Oxford, p. 4. The number of websites devoted to the series runs into the thousands, with it being impossible to give a precise figure since sites both start and close on a daily basis. 'Sonya Marie's Buffy' (http://wwww.bitterwisodom. com/btvsurls/) and 'Buffy-Slayer.org' (http://buffy.cs.caltecg.edu/www/) both provide a list of such sites though neither list can be regarded as being definitive.

9 The volumes of essays already published by December 2004 are Kaveney (ed.) *Reading the Vampire Slayer* (new essays have been added to the second edition and some of the original essays in the first, 2002, edition left out), R. Wilcox and D. Lavery (eds) *Fighting the Forces: What's at Stake in Buffy the Vampire Slayer* (2002) Rowman and Littlefield Publishers, New York and J. South (ed.) *Buffy the Vampire Slayer and Philosophy: Fear and Trembling in Sunnydale* (2003) Open Court, Chicago. L. Parks (ed.) *Red Noise: Television Studies and Buffy the Vampire Slayer* (Duke University Press) is currently listed as to be published in 2005. The monographs are by Adams (*Slayer Slang*) and G. Stevenson *Televised Morality: The case of Buffy the Vampire Slayer* (2003) Hamilton Books, Lanham, Maryland. In addition to this a volume of essays on the programme by other writers has been published (G. Yeffeth (ed.) *Seven Seasons of Buffy: Science Fiction and Fantasy Writers Discuss Their Favorite Television Show* (2003) Benbella Books, Dallas, Texas) and Reiss has written a book on the spiritual aspects of BtVS (J. Reiss *What Would Buffy Do Next? The Vampire Slayer as Spiritual Guide* (2004) Jossey-Bass, San Francisco). A number of other volumes are planned.

10 See, for example, K. Harte Deconstructing Buffy: *Buffy the Vampire's Contribution to the Discourse on Gender Construction* (2001) 12 *Popular Culture Review* 79, G. DeCandido Bibliographic Good vs. Evil September *1999 American Libraries* 44 and A. Cordesman *Biological Warfare and the 'Buffy Paradigm'* (2001) http://csis.org/burke/hel/reports/Buffy012902.pdf.

11 http://www.slayage.tv/. McKee has argued that Slayage is 'both fan work and academic work' (A McKee Fandom in T. Miller (ed.) *Television Studies* (2002) British Film Institute, London at p. 69. Whilst it is true that a very small minority of authors writing in Slayage are not working in academic institutions this does not seem to justify his description of the journal. A very small number of authors of articles in the *Criminal Law Review* are practising lawyers rather than academics. This does not, of itself, mean that the *Criminal Law Review* is not an academic journal. What makes a journal academic is the nature of the concerns addressed by articles in the journal not the provenance of its authors.

12 (2003) 2 *Refractory: a Journal of Entertainment Media* http://www.sca.unimelb. edu.au/refractory/journalissues/vol2/.

13 This, of course, is not to say that this is all that can be done when looking at the intersection of law and popular culture. For very different kind of work see, for example, R. Sherwin *When Law Goes Pop: The Vanishing Line Between Law and Popular Culture* (2000) University of Chicago Press, Chicago.

14 See J. Fiske *Television Culture* (1987) Routledge, London, ch 5.

15 H. Genn *Paths to Justice: What People Do and Think About Going to Law* (1999) Hart Publishing, Oxford; A. Bradney 'Making Cowards' (1990*) Juridical Review* 129 at pp. 145–147.

16 D. Strinati *An Introduction to Studying Popular Culture* (2000) Routledge, London, p. 174.

17 Early studies include L. Parpart 'Action, Chicks, Everything': On-Line Interviews with Male Fans of *Buffy the Vampire Slayer* in F. Early and K. Kennedy (eds) *Athena's Daughters: Televisions New Women Warriors* (2003) Syracuse University Press, Syracuse, L. Roseneld and S. Wynns 'Perceived Values and Social Support' in *Buffy the Vampire Slayer* (2003) 10 *Slayage: The On-Line International*

Journal of Buffy Studies and 'Discovering *Buffy*', a page on the website of Slayage: The International Journal of Buffy Studies, which contains short autobiographical descriptions of how viewers came to be interested in BtVS (http://www. slayage.tv/discovering buffy/). Studies of fan fiction, stories written by fans that take the characters and storyline of BtVS but develop in ways personal to the author, offer an insight into how those fans understand BtVS. For two such studies see E. Saxey 'Staking a claim: The series and its fan fiction in Kaveney (ed.) *Reading the Vampire Slayer* and K. Busse Crossing the Final Taboo: Family, Sexuality, and Incest in Buffyverse Fan Fiction in Wilcox and Lavery (eds) *Fighting the Forces*.

18 M. Levine and S. Schneider Feeling for Buffy: The Girl Next Door in *South Buffy the Vampire Slayer and Philosophy* at p. 296 and p. 299. I stress the word 'might'. In the absence of developed reception studies we cannot know what the reason is for the programme's success with its audiences.

19 http://www.geocities.com/voxsententia/abovethelaw/; http://www.atpobtvs.com/index.html.

20 One fruitful site for enquiry into these questions would be the many websites that publish fan fiction about BtVS.

21 See further J. Tulloch *Television Drama: Agency, Audience and Myth* (1990) Routledge, London Part Three.

22 Fiske *Television Culture* p. 62.

23 On fans and *Star Trek* see J. Tulloch and H. Jenkins *Science Fiction Audiences: Watching Doctor Who and Star Trek* (1995) Routledge, London, ch 1.

24 McKee *Television Studies* at pp. 67–68.

25 The only example of published work to date is Bradney (2003a) *Choosing Families*, A. Bradney 'I Made a Promise to a Lady': Law and Love in BtVS (2003b) 10 *Slayage: The On-line International Journal of Buffy Studies* and W. McNeil 'You slay me!: Buffy as Jurisprude of Desire' (2003) 24 Cardozo Law Review 2421. Other essays which have dealt with the wider question of the treatment of authority in BtVS contain references to notions of law and justice. See, for example, B. McClelland 'By Whose Authority? The Magical Tradition, Violence, and the Legitimation of the Vampire Slayer' (2001) 1 *Slayage: The On-Line International Journal of Buffy Studies* http://www.slayage.tv/ and D. Clark and P. Miller 'Buffy, the Scooby Gang, and Monstrous Authority: *BtVS* and the Subversion of Authority' (2001) 3 *Slayage: The On-Line International Journal of Buffy Studies* http://www.slayage.tv/.

26 P. Kahn *Law and Love: The Trials of King Lear* (2000) Yale University Press, New Haven; M. Williams *Empty Justice: One Hundred Years of Law, Literature and Philosophy* (2002) Cavendish publishing, London.

27 A. Susan Owen 'Vampires, Postmodernity and Feminism' (1997) No. 2 *Journal of Popular Film and Television* 24 at p. 27.

28 F. Early 'Staking Her Claim: Buffy the Vampire Slayer as Transgressive Woman Warrior' (2002) 6 *Slayage: The On-Line International Journal of Buffy Studies* http://www.slayage.tv/.

29 M. Buinicki and A. Enns 'Buffy the Vampire Disciplinarian: Institutional Excess and the New Economy of Power' (2001) 4 *Slayage: The On-Line International Journal of Buffy Studies* http://www.slayage.tv/.

30 See further Bradney (2003a) *Choosing Families*. BtVS is an unusual variant in both the sense of, for example, things such as the age of the police officer and in the much more important sense of the emotional connections that she makes from a very early stage with Giles, her Watcher and thus superior officer (*Never Kill a Boy on the First Date*, 1005) which contradict the basic conventions of the genre. For a preliminary assessment of these conventions see C. Bazalgette

Regan and Carter, Kojak and Croker, Batman and Robin (1976) 20 *Screen Education* 54.

31 Malach writes of police officers in police series, 'he or she represents cultural categories of correctness, acting out what it means to be normal, mainstream, not-marginalized...' (M. Malach 'I Want to Believe ... in the FBI': The Special Agent and *The X-Files* in D. Lavery, A. Hague and M. Cartwright (eds) *'Deny All Knowledge: Reading the X Files* (1996) Syracuse University Press, Syracuse p. 64).

32 *Consequences*, 3015.

33 *Angel*, 1007.

34 P. Pender 'I'm Buffy and You're ... History': *The Postmodern Politics of Buffy* in Lavery and Wilcox (eds) *Fighting the Forces* at p. 43.

35 *Chosen*, 7022; *Villains*, 6020.

36 P. Ausubel *Educational Psychology: A Cognitive View* (1968) Holt Rinehart and Winston, New York pp. 37–38. On the application of Ausubel's thesis to the law school see D. Tribe 'How Students Learn' in J. Webb and C. Maughan (eds) *Teaching Lawyers' Skills* (1996) Butterworths, London at pp. 7–10.

37 See further A. Bradney *Conversations, Chances and Choices: The Liberal Law School in the Twenty-First Century* (2003c) Hart Publishing, Oxford, ch 4. Ausubel himself notes the danger of taking his proposition too far and writes of 'the seemingly indestructible myth that, under any and all circumstances, abstractions cannot be meaningful unless preceeded by direct empirical experience' (Auausbel *Educational Psychology* p. 87).

38 The audience is composed 'primarily of teens and twenty-somethings' (Adams *Slayer Slang* p. 4).

39 V. Chin 'Buffy? She's Like Me, She's Not Like Me – She's *Rad*' in Early and Kennedy *Athena's Daughters* at p. 92.

40 This is also true for the other main characters in the show. See, for example, M. Money 'The Undemonization of Supporting Characters in Buffy' in Wilcox and Lavery *Fighting the Forces* and J. Battis 'She's Not All Grown Yet': Willow as Hybrid/Hero in *Buffy the Vampire Slayer* (2003) 8 *Slayage: The On-Line International Journal of Buffy Studies* http://www.slayage.tv/.

41 Chin *Athena's Daughter* p. 101. It should, however, be noted that some commentators have suggested that the series is nothing more than a celebration of the supremacy of the values of white, middle-class America (see, for example, K. Ono 'To Be a Vampire on *Buffy the Vampire Slayer*: Race and ("Other") Socially Marginalizing Positions on Horror TV' in E. Helford (ed.) *Fantasy Girls: Gender and the New Universe of Science Fiction and Fantasy Television* (2000) Rowman and Littlefield, New York) whilst others sought to 'expose the Buffy-verse as the product of a very traditional patriarchal world view which pays lip service to a superficial feminist fashioning' (G. Bodger 'Buffy the Feminist Slayer? Constructions of Femininity in *Buffy the Vampire Slayer*' (2003) 2 *Refractory: a Journal of Entertainment Media* http://www.sca.unimelb.edu.au/reractory/journalissues/vol2).

42 G. Bloustein 'Fans with a lot at stake: *Serious play and mimetic excess in* Buffy the Vampire Slayer' (2002) 5 *European Journal of Cultural Studies* 427 at p. 428.

43 See further Bradney (2003a) *Choosing Families*.

44 South *Buffy the Vampire Slayer and Philosophy*.

45 In a similar vein see Schlozman's argument that BtVS provides valuable educational examples of important psychological constructs (S. Schlozman 'Vampires and Those Who Slay Them: Using the Television Program *Buffy the Vampire Slayer* in Adolescent Therapy and Psychodynamic Education' (2000) 24 *American Psychiatry* 49 at p. 54).

46 Burr writes that BtVS provides a potential 'opportunity to engage in a dialogue with ourselves about what we think is right and wrong, acceptable and unacceptable. It is part of our moral education. TV is as important as real experience in this respect; perhaps more so since many of us will never experience at first hand some of the life events that raise ethical and moral issues upon which a person should take a view.' V. Burr 'Buffy vs. the BBC: Moral Questions and How to Avoid Them' (2003) 8 *Slayage: The On-Line International Journal of Buffy Studies* http://www.slayage.tv/ 12.

47 Only a very small number of academics now give allegiance to doctrinal law in its purest form where the study is just of the rules and principles from a perspective internal to the law itself. In the modern law school even those academics who call themselves black-letter lawyers usually accept the need to put their analysis of legal rules and principles into some kind of social and philosophical context. On this see further F. Cownie *Legal Academics: Culture and Identities* (Forthcoming) Hart Publishing, Oxford.

48 See, for example, *Singh* v. *Singh* [1971] P 226.

49 J. Sartre *Being and Nothingness* Philosophical Library, New York; J. Sartre *The Age of Reason* (1947) Hamish Hamilton, London; J. Sartre *The Reprieve* (1947) Hamish Hamilton, London and J. Sartre *Iron in the Soul* (1950) Hamish Hamilton, London.

50 In the spin-off series from BtVS Angel, Angel refuses to accept Lindsay's argument that he has no choice but to work as a lawyer for the evil law firm Wolfram and Hart because of his desire to escape his poor background, saying 'You always have a choice. I mean, you sold your soul for a fifth-floor office and a company car' (*Blind Date*, 1021). This may seem even more pertinent to their concerns for law students than *Lie to Me*. However, the nature of choice is less central to *Blind Date* than it is to *Lie to Me*.

51 On the notion of parenting in BtVS see C. Bowers 'Generation Lapse: The Problematic Parenting of Joyce Summers and Rupert Giles' (2001) 2 *Slayage: The On-Line International Journal of Buffy Studies* http://www.slayage.tv/.

52 See, for example, D. Vick, A. Murray, G. Little and K. Campbell 'The Perceptions of Academic Lawyers Concerning the Effects of the United Kingdom Research Assessment Exercise' (1998) *Journal of Law and Society* 536.

53 See, for example, 'RAE 2001: Law Panel: General Overview' Spring 2002 *The Reporter* 6 at p. 6.

54 For a contrary view see A. Hicks 'Legal Practice is an Academic Matter' Spring 1995 *SPTL Reporter* 6. On the role of the university law school in furthering knowledge see Bradney (2003c) *Conversations, Chances and Choices*, ch 5.

55 Moreover, law RAE panels have been explicit in saying 'that it would not be safe to determine the quality of research outputs on the basis of the place in which they have been published' ('RAE 2001: Law Panel: General Overview' op. cit. n 53).

56 Vick *et al.*, 'The Perceptions of Academic Lawyers' pp. 556–557.

57 Irrespective of its effect on the development of the discipline, it is, of course, a matter of supreme impertinence for any academic to tell a colleague what they may or may not research into or where they may or may not publish. Cloaking such instructions under the guise of advice merely adds the cowardliness of being unwilling to take responsibility for one's actions to the impertinence.

58 The arguments that follow could be equally well-made for any new area of study within the law school or, probably, for any well-established area that remains the interest of a small minority of legal scholars.

59 This is not the case, of course, with special issues. However, special issues are precisely special and therefore infrequent. Law and popular culture might be the

subject of one special issue in a general journal; it is not likely to be the subject of two.

60 There is equal fault in those who contrive to bring about such pressures and those who succumb to them. Academic freedom is a right that should be respected by everyone in the academy. Equally it is the duty of all academics, in both their research and their teaching, to say the things they believe to be true not the things that they believe to be popular (see further D. Kennedy *Academic Duty* (1997) Harvard University Press, Cambridge ch 8).

61 O. Fiss 'Of Law and the River' and Nihilism and Academic Freedom (1985) 35 *Journal of Legal Education* 26 at p. 26.

62 P. Carrington 'Of Law and the River' (1984) 34 *Journal of Legal Education* 222; P. Hillyard 'Invoking Indignation: Reflections on Future Directions of Socio-Legal Studies' (2002) 29 *Journal of Law and Society* 645 at p. 656.

63 See further Bradney (2003b) 'I Made a Promise to a Lady' ch 4 and ch 5.

64 S. Machura and P. Robson (eds) Law and Film (2001) 28(1) *Journal of Law and Society*.

3 Peter's choice

Issues of identity, lifestyle and consumption in changing representations of corporate lawyers and legal academics

Richard Collier

Introduction

> Somebody told *you*, and you hold it as an article of faith, that higher education is an unassailable good. This notion is so dear to you that when I question it you become angry. Good. Good, I say. Are those not the very things which we should question? I say college education, since the war, has become so a matter of course, and such a fashionable necessity, for those either of or aspiring *to* the new vast middle class, that we *espouse* it, as a matter of right, and have ceased to ask, 'What is it good for?'[1]

A number of years ago the following exchange took place between myself and a third-year undergraduate law student in the UK university law school in which I work (who I will, in the course of this paper, refer to simply as Peter).[2] Presented from memory, and if not the exact words as stated, what follows nonetheless conveys what I believe to be an accurate reflection of the conversation which occurred. 'Why', I was asked, 'did I choose to teach law when I could earn so much more money as a practising lawyer?' Why did I and my colleagues work to 'facilitate the careers of others' when, it seemed to this student, given that universities were so clearly under-funded and, increasingly, resembling private sector organizations in terms of their working practices and dominant cultures – as well as, in his view, being beset by low morale – a far more rewarding and financially advantageous career could be found elsewhere? By way of illustrating what he saw as the limited material ambition of the legal academic, the student pointed out that he had noted the fact that the car he was already driving[3] as an undergraduate was markedly better than that any lecturer in an English provincial 'red-brick' university could afford[4] – at least judging from what he had observed in the small car park located at the rear of the law school building. In summary, 'why', he asked, would one of the 'brightest students', an individual with a projected (at least) very good upper second class degree (such as himself) 'in their right mind' choose to enter academia at the present moment? Especially if they had, as this student did, the alternative prospect of securing potentially lucrative employment with a large corporate law firm?

It is, of course, all too easy to answer such comments and to counter – if not, I want to suggest in this paper, to dismiss the social significance of – these views; as being, for example, the misguided and unrepresentative opinion of just one individual (and, as such, not to be taken seriously); as encapsulating aspects of the familiar idea that 'those who can, do: those who can't, teach'; or as signalling a certain immaturity and, without doubt, a profoundly anti-intellectual world-view – there is, of course, more to life than money (after all, 'whoever dies with the most toys' still dies).[5] The exchange also betrays on the part of the student, I would once have argued, a profound misunderstanding of the nature of higher education and the place and purpose of universities and of academics in society;[6] as well as an inability to empathize with and appreciate, even if this particular individual did not share, any notion that there might be an academic 'vocation'.[7]

Notwithstanding the force of such responses, however, this is an exchange which has remained with me over subsequent years. Perhaps it taps into a personal sense of, if not regret, then of 'what might have been' for an individual who has never been in legal practice but one who has, certainly, witnessed on the part of friends and acquaintances something of the clear material rewards which can, for some at least, follow from developing a successful career in the legal profession, particularly in the large commercial firms. As academic life continues to change at a rapid rate, and as a considerable number of those presently working in universities express doubts about the present direction of many policies relating to higher education,[8] this paper presents an attempt to socially contextualize the above conversation; to explore the views expressed by this student and ask why they might have come to have (as I believe they do) a resonance for many of today's law students in UK universities.

In approaching this question this chapter seeks to develop a greater understanding of the social context in relation to which, I shall argue, the relationship between law lecturers and their students, and legal academics and the universities in which they work, has changed considerably. This is, of course, a vast topic, encompassing issues far beyond the reach of a paper such as this. The scope of this chapter is modest. In what follows I want to focus on a number of interrelated areas, each of which, I shall suggest, have been neglected in much of the relevant literature on the law school, legal education and the legal profession to date; but which remain areas an exploration of which can usefully, I shall suggest, shed light on understanding the social context in which Peter, above, is making his comments about what he sees as the respective appeal of legal practice and the (relative) lack of 'career opportunity',[9] for him at least, within the legal academy; questions about changing youth cultures and identity, of the changing city, lifestyles and economic opportunity; and, relating to each of the above, of a fragmentation which has taken place within (middle) class formations and consumption practices. It is around an engagement with each of these issues that I wish to structure the following argument.

This chapter presents, in short, an attempt to understand *why* it should be that for Peter – and, I will suggest, many others like him – securing a training contract with the large commercial law firms, based in the City of London and other regional financial centres in the UK, should continue to have such an allure.[10] My argument draws, in part, on research discussed in detail elsewhere deriving from a qualitative study of changes in the visual images and text contained within a range of materials depicting the nature of corporate legal employment and aimed at 'selling' a career in law to prospective trainee solicitors within the large corporate law firms.[11] In this chapter I wish to turn, by way of contributing to a developing scholarship in the broad field of law and popular culture,[12] to three fields of literature, mapping to each of the research questions above, often considered 'outwith' the sociology of the legal profession;[13] that is, to an engagement with changing ideas of youth cultures and lifestyle; to urban geography (notably in relation to what has been termed the 'new urbanism'); and, in particular, to what I shall suggest are the distinctive dynamics of consumption, social capital and identity formation increasingly at play, for students like Peter,[14] within both university law schools and the large commercial or 'big City' law firm to which he had successfully applied.

It is necessary, at the outset, to sound a note of caution. I do not wish to claim that law teaching and legal research has ever been a 'first choice' destination, as it were, for law graduates. An argument can be made that the 'brightest'[15] law students (whatever 'brightest' means in this context), particularly those from the most 'prestigious' institutions,[16] have long gravitated to certain areas of professional practice and to business, and not to the universities. I am not concerned, directly at least, with the career trajectories of law students in any general sense post-graduation;[17] nor with the diversity of professional practice[18] or the historical, political and philosophical dimensions of a 'liberal' legal education – the question of what a (legal) university education is (or should be) 'for'. Each of these are issues discussed in depth elsewhere.[19] I am concerned, rather, with surfacing aspects of the aforementioned changing socio-cultural context which has, I shall to argue, served to shift in some far-reaching ways ideas about the purported utility of legal education.

Approaching Peter's choice:[20] the law school and the large commercial law firms – why are they important?

> Be Smart . . . what sort of person thrives in a premier international law firm?
> Be Successful . . . [we offer] the ideal environment for realising your ambitions.
> Be Yourself . . . we believe that people perform better *when being themselves*.[21]

It is necessary, to begin, to understand something of the allure of the profession for many law students and, in particular, the appeal of securing employment in the large commercial firms. The 'prestige and power' of these firms has long, it has been suggested, been 'out of all proportion to their number'.[22] If the training contract itself remains a relatively under-explored stage of socialization into the legal profession,[23] research suggests Peter is by no means alone amongst undergraduate law students in seeing considerable appeal in securing employment with a large commercial law firm, whether they be based in the City of London or any of the regional financial centres in the UK.[24] These firms are widely perceived to offer, and explicitly present themselves within their recruitment material as offering,[25] a challenging, rewarding and undoubtedly potentially lucrative career for the students they accept as trainees.[26] Their further attraction in terms of the significant economic imperatives of securing funding for further training and paying off, often considerable, undergraduate debts has been well-documented.[27] In recognizing at the outset the diversity of the term 'university law school'[28] – and of the law students who study in them,[29] as well as the open-ended and contested nature of legal education – application rates suggest that a significant percentage of those students who do contemplate entering the profession end up applying to such firms.[30] This is notwithstanding what is known (or can easily be discovered) about the realities of attrition rates in this area of the profession and the possible potential difficulties, for some, around access and recruitment; issues of diversity,[31] equity and discrimination;[32] the well-documented concerns about quality of life and working-hours in these firms,[33] future security of employment and the contingencies around promotion to partnership in this field.[34] As Lee observes in relation to the largest law firms generally:

> Disaffection with professional life [is leading] to the departure of talented and trained personnel, leaving shortages of experienced and qualified lawyers. In a situation of short supply, the wage rates for solicitors in these firms are rising rapidly. But this is being paid for by ever-increasing billable hours, leading to yet more disaffection. In short, and in both senses of the word, the result is a vortex.[35]

Notwithstanding any such 'vortex' – and in noting the clear gendered dynamics of such a retention drift from the profession[36] – the corporate law firm would appear to exert a considerable (and, it has been suggested, increasing)[37] cultural, political and economic hold not only over university *students* but also, importantly, on the practices and cultures of law *schools* themselves. The direct influence of the large law firms on curricula content in law schools remains, at the time of writing, contested, the subject of an ongoing debate.[38] Evidence does suggest, nonetheless, that the perceived broader recruitment demands of the corporate law firms, as well as the more general ethic of 'commercial endeavour' they embody, now frames many aspects of legal education provision in the UK; and that this is an influence which is pervasive in the sector, regardless of the question of any individual and/or organizational/institutional orientation towards commercial law in any broader sense. Importantly, what is at issue here is not simply the way in which many law schools seek, with ever greater enthusiasm, to secure the 'grace and favour' of the large firms in the form of alumni donations, the sponsorship of (at least certain commercial-oriented) academic posts, student competitions, estates developments and so forth (each of the above, it is important to remember, increasingly significant activities for cash-strapped Higher Education institutions in search of 'third strand' income).[39] Nor is this influence confined to the way in which – for contemporary UK law schools, like the law firms themselves, increasingly ranked in terms of their brand name, size and wealth – the securing of student employment with the large transnational firm has become a significant marker of success within a competitive legal labour market.

The question of the influence of the large firms cannot, in short, be confined to the way in which many law school cultures and practices have historically facilitated (whether they were explicitly designed to or not) the gravitation of considerable numbers of students to the commercial/business oriented subjects as the embodiment of 'real' and, in career terms, 'useful' law. A growing body of research suggests, rather, that something else may now be happening; specifically, that the twin pincers of (a) the development of the new (global) knowledge economy and (b) the contemporary 'massification' of Higher Education have each, taken together, served to heighten the appeal and influence of the corporate law firms and of commercial cultures and markets within legal education in a number of ways.[40] And one result of this two-fold process, it has been suggested, is the more general move now underway in legal education internationally towards the inclusion of what has been termed an increasingly 'corporatized market-oriented curriculum' within law schools;[41] a process which, in the UK, is taking place within the context of a number of 'entrepreneurially-driven'[42] institutional reforms and organizational restructurings explicitly geared towards shifting '. . . the orientation and purpose of universities generally [away] from intellectual inquiry [and] to instrumentalism and vocationalism'.[43]

It is not difficult in such a context to link the wider economic and political imperatives associated with the 'new knowledge economy' to the cultural and economic turn towards commercial-law-related subjects in law schools; and to what would appear to be, as above, the heightened appeal of this area for many law students in considering future employment opportunities. As universities struggle to cater for large numbers of school-leavers (to satisfy the demands of the new economy) one consequence, Thornton suggests, is that 'even though massification . . . has meant that the vastly increased number of law graduates are not all able to obtain positions as practising lawyers, *the institutional aspiration that they will do so*' remains a powerful influence on universities and their law schools.[44] In the context of this institutional aspiration – and within an increasingly marketized Higher Education sector, as outlined above – Peter's observation that universities themselves are increasingly resembling private sector organizations in terms of their working practices and dominant culture betrays a certain acuity (he has, as it were, done the research). For, in the context of what Slaughter and Leslie have termed the rise of 'academic capitalism',[45] a growing international literature is suggesting that, across jurisdictions, the aspirations and values of both students *and* (legal) academics have been (and are being) reconstituted in some far-reaching ways;[46] and that, in particular, as the parameters of university research and education are reframed along the lines of a utility model of knowledge production – the parameters of which, it is important to remember, explicitly frame many aspects of present government policy in the UK[47] – both academics and students are being exhorted to 'attend to the market' and to structure their career choices accordingly; according, that is, to the dictates of an economically driven, business-focused notion of use value.

One result of this turn towards a model of universities as, essentially, 'knowledge factories', it has been suggested, is the further marginalization of critical approaches across disciplines,[48] alongside a growing technocratic conformity on the part of students and staff to the dictates of the market. This is a development which has been identified as gathering pace across the boundaries of specific subject disciplines (including law) and as having informed what is now widely seen as the profound shift which has taken place in understandings of 'acceptable' workplace performances within universities; in relation to such issues, for example, as the determination of what grants to apply for,[49] how to manage a career and, indeed, how to dress and present oneself.[50] It is in a context such as this that, in looking to the trade off once, it is suggested, assumed to exist between relative financial reward and autonomy/'quality of life' issue in informing recruitment and retention in academia,[51] the contemporary law school has itself moved, like the universities of which it is part, 'to market'.

Yet whatever the changes which have taken place in higher education, and regardless of the undoubted continued allure of this part of the profession for many students, as outlined above, such a picture of a changing university sector can only tell us so much. Let us assume that Peter was himself of 'academic disposition', as it were. For the ambitious and able individual one could argue that, in the future, an increasingly marketized higher education sector might well come to offer, arguably, potentially greater rewards – that it might, for example, become more, not less, attractive as a career choice for personal advancement as pay scales fracture and as salaries, at least in some elite institutions, rise to attract the 'star' players. In developing this discussion of 'Peter's choice' I wish to turn at this moment to three rather different areas, a consideration of each of which can, I now want to suggest, shed a rather different light on any such vision of the future. I shall consider, in turn, issues around changing ideas of lifestyle and consumption; of urban change, economic opportunity and 'success'; and, finally, of class and culture in relation to both the legal academy and the legal profession. I shall conclude by drawing together the arguments of the chapter thus far and consider again the conversation which took place between myself and Peter.

Buying (into) the 'complete lifestyle': work, pleasure and consumption

> Herbert Smith London is based in stunning offices above Liverpool Street Station, in the heart of the Broadgate complex. Surrounded by City banks and other institutions, this area was built in the 1980s to cater for *the City worker's lifestyle*.[52]

If Peter was not attracted by what he saw as the 'lifestyle' of the contemporary legal academic, what exactly did he mean by that? Within the modern era the idea of developing a distinctive lifestyle has been widely understood to be a project invested with both an ethical and aesthetic significance; as a way of denoting the 'creative use of consumer facilities'[53] and, importantly, as a key element within the formation of both individual and collective social identities – part of how we identify ourselves as similar *to* and, simultaneously, as different *from*, others. Lifestyles are '. . . patterns of action that differentiate people. In everyday interaction we . . . employ a notion of lifestyle without needing to explain what we mean':[54]

> Social worlds are organised, structured and imbued with meaning by reference to *what sort of people the protagonists are*, that is their sense of their own social identity . . . lifestyles are reflexive projects: we (and relevant others) can see (however dimly) who we want to be seen to be through *how we use the resources of who we are*'.[55]

The idea of developing a distinctive lifestyle has been a central feature of how the career progression of the successful commercial solicitor is presented to would-be trainees such as Peter in the advertising and publicity material produced by law firms.[56] Quite explicitly, what is employed is an appeal to a lifestyle in which certain ideas of what constitutes 'lawyer's work' are mobilized in both ethical and aesthetic terms; in such a way, importantly, as to position the lawyer via reference to a range of ideas which tend to focus, I have argued elsewhere,[57] around two key or recurring concerns; first, via reference to certain ideas about practices of *consumption*; and, second, around ideas of *urbanism* and, more specifically, to a particular understanding of the shifting spatiality of corporate legal work.

   To clarify. There is one recurring theme in representations of the articled clerk/trainee solicitor drawn from recruitment materials produced by law firms during the 1980s and early 1990s. It is of the young solicitor – male or female – facing direct to camera, looking (usually) thoughtful or smiling and, time and again, holding an open book. Against the backdrop of the bookshelves of a library these figures depict a thoughtfulness and studiousness more commonly associated with university study (the 'bookish' academic lawyer perhaps). The past ten years or so, however, have witnessed a shift away from this once ubiquitous image of a lawyer 'holding the book', as it were, and towards a more complex, sophisticated and multi-layered representation of the legal practice: one which has focused, in particular, around the notion of how the novice trainee will, in the course of their career, buy into the 'Complete lifestyle' of the lawyer.[58] This is not simply a matter of depicting the now familiar 'one shop' package of employment and leisure activities, a theme noted elsewhere in literature on the corporate employer as 'total institution' within the global economy.[59] On closer examination, a range of ideas about youth cultures and consumption practices have emerged as central to the representation of how the would-be-lawyer will, if successful in their application (as Peter himself was), 'buy into' the 'Complete Lifestyle' of the modern lawyer.

In effect, there is, I would suggest, a distinctive lifestyle being presented here. Traditionally, the imaging of the leisure pursuits associated with corporate legal employment tended to be presented by the firms in their recruitment material via the depiction of a number of organized – and, for some recruits at least, culturally familiar[60] – array of social and sporting events:

> Working in a city law firm is often hard, but its not all long hours. The quality and frequency of Ashurst's sporting and social events are well known. Apart from the annual party for the whole firm and a variety of departmental functions, there are also periodic quiz evenings, wine tastings and many other one-off events . . . Roger Finnow . . . hosts a garden party each summer for all trainees, and all members of the firm are invited to attend the annual tennis evening, and barbecue and cricket event. We also have groups of musicians who play at suitable firm occasions . . .[61]

It is in contrast to the above, however, that representations produced during the past ten years or so have tended to be increasingly marked by something else; not just a heightened emphasis on the 'total package' of body care now being offered by firms, as noted above, but also what has become a far more vigorous, knowing and sophisticated attempt to connect aspects of the trainee experience to some wider trends around youth consumption and popular culture. The general legal press aimed at undergraduate student market[62] has itself, for some time, engaged in an appropriation of the visual styles, images and products associated with youth in the presentation of articles on different aspects of law, legal education and legal careers.[63] What is notable in recent years, however, and what I shall proceed to suggest is particularly significant, is how the law firms themselves are now connecting the trainee experience and the idea of a distinctive 'lawyer's lifestyle' to a range of cultural reference points each of which, it is assumed, will have a resonance for the readers of their recruitment and publicity material; that is, alongside the general legal press aimed at undergraduate market, the law firms themselves are now appropriating the visual styles, images and products associated with youth in the presentation of diverse aspects of the development of a career in law.

This can be seen in terms of both content and style in the presentation[64] of 'core' information;[65] and it has involved, in particular, the use of a range of popular cultural reference points relating to themes such as contemporary television and film,[66] popular music,[67] trends in art[68] and, perhaps most visibly (a theme it is difficult to underestimate the general pervasiveness of in the literature) the place of alcohol consumption within bars and clubs as part of the 'everyday life' of the firm.[69] These kinds of representations are themselves just part of what is the far broader appeal taking place here to the idea of (conspicuous) consumption and to 'having fun',[70] a theme which maps onto what research within the fields of the sociology of youth and cultural studies would suggest has been a broader shift around the place of leisure and consumption within the formation of identities.[71] That is, as traditional social relations and sites of identity for young adults have weakened within late-modern societies the focal concerns of consumption, leisure and popular culture – especially in urban centres – have each become central elements in the formation and experience of a range of distinctive youth identities.[72] And this is a cultural and political economy around youth which has itself, Chatterton and Hollands have argued, been increasingly characterized over the past decade in the UK by a threefold process which has involved: (a) the increasing 'mainstream' *production* of youth leisure, notably through the corporatization and branding of the ownership of the spaces in which young people tend to socialize (clubs, bars, pubs, venues and so forth); (b) the heightened *regulation* of the emerging 'urban playscapes'[73] of major UK cities (a process which has resulted, Chatterton and Hollands suggest, in the marginalization of radical/non-conformist youth cultures, an issue outside the scope of this paper); and (c) a shift in the location and patterns of youth *consumption* practices – more specifically, '...through new forms of segmented nightlife activity based around more 'exclusive' and 'up-market' identities amongst young adults'.[74]

In considering how the appeal being made to a distinctive 'lawyer's lifestyle' is constructed here these insights are useful, for what is both intriguing and revealing is the extent to which each of these themes of production, regulation and consumption can be seen to pervade the imaging of the trainee commercial lawyer within the recruitment materials being produced by the firms – as well as, and more generally, the student cultures which themselves surround many university law undergraduates.

Understanding consumption as a '...symbolically meaningful and active relationship', one which 'produc[es] experiences and identities',[75] it is, by itself, perhaps unsurprising that in these attempts to 'sell' the corporate law firms young adults should be viewed both as the recipients of economically produced and regulated activities (of, let us say, drinking in particular 'branded' themed bars such as *All Bar One*);[76] and, simultaneously, as active participants in a cultural realm as the purchasers/consumers of a distinctive image and lifestyle, of the positional goods being associated with the 'successful' commercial lawyer:[77]

> 'Spend, spend spend . . . It's a Lifestyle Thing!' 'What to spend the "first glorious pay check" on? What do partners of the future dream of?'. The answer; 'Rent an Aston Martin for the weekend; a visit to a country club; bachlorette pad in Regents Park; a surround sound stereo system; pool table; pale blue BMW 73 . . . my own beautiful boat . . . pay off the Peugeot 206 coupe.'[78]

> 'Every girl's crazy 'bout a sharp dressed man': 'I'm gonna get dressed for success': 'All your suits are custom-made in London'. Matt, Lisa and Sarah advise on 'office essentials' and, most importantly, how not to get caught out. (On the 'Magic Wardrobe' for the 'Ambitious Trainee').[79]

The idea that the trainee solicitor will be both the recipient of commercially produced activities and participant in a (corporate) cultural realm has become something of a key leitmotif in how the legal career is being represented in this context. Peter himself would undoubtedly have been (as, indeed, I know he was) familiar with these kinds of texts, this kind of depiction of legal practice. And what is being presented here is, in effect, an overarching and dominant discourse of 'work hard, play hard' – framed by what might be termed an ethic of 'playful responsibility' – a dedication to pleasure which itself corresponds broadly with what is known about changing identifications amongst young adults in the UK.[80] However, if it is the case that these ideas of (mainstream, conformist) production and regulation frame the imaging of the lifestyle of the young commercial solicitor in these firms in this way, this process has itself been, I now wish to argue, premised on the making of certain other assumptions about patterns of consumption based on 'exclusive' and 'up-market' identities. And it is around this issue – of distinction,[81] success and economic advancement in the urban context – that the contrast becomes particularly revealing in seeking to understand, not only how an imaging of the trainee lawyer has shifted in recent years, but also how all this might relate to shifting perceptions of the legal academy in the context of the increasingly marketized university sector, as outlined above. To understand this relation, however, it is necessary to consider further how this lifestyle, and these issues of consumption, relate to some broader infrastructural changes which have taken place within the UK economy.

Relocating 'success': urbanism and the spatiality of (corporate) work and pleasure

Over the past two decades city centres in the UK, as well as internationally, have been remodelled as part of wider socio-economic processes of restructuring '...as places in which to live, work and be entertained'.[82] Contemporary urban sociology has charted[83] the erosion of the idea of the city strongly connected to a manufacturing and industrial past, and a move to an idea of city space as increasingly constituted and understood primarily as a locus for:

> ...private/corporate capital, knowledge-based activities, middle-class consumption and an entrepreneurial turn in urban governance *aimed at attracting and satisfying the demands of highly mobile global capital.*[84]

This process – one which continues apace across the UK[85] – has been marked by a '...renewed emphasis on business service employment', a '...dematerialized and knowledge-based economy' and by a greater economic role for '...corporately organized leisure, retail and consumption-based rather than production-based activities'.[86]

This urban shift constitutes, I would suggest, an important context in relation to which the kinds of consumption practices discussed above should now be understood. For, in considering how the large law firms are presenting the wider urban context in relation to which a legal career in their firm will be developed – let us say, developing the distinctive 'City Life' in relation to which the training contract will be lived and experienced – this structural shift around what has been termed the 'new urbanism' provides an important grounded context against which the changing imagery of corporate legal employment and of youth cultures can now be understood. Indeed, what is so striking about these representations is the extent to which the lifestyle of the City lawyer on display here exemplifies many aspects of the way in which certain consumption practices have become entwined with the economic logic and ethical and aesthetic codes associated with entrepreneurial, private/corporate capital within this new urban context; in the form, for example, of a commodification of the workplace cultures and practices associated with a rapidly expanding urban service class, not least in relation to ideas about body culture and the acquisition of a range of positional goods.[87]

Corporate lawyers within the largest firms are, I realize, just one employment grouping within the broader field of business service employment. However, the imaging of the profession more generally on display here engages in a particularly direct way with wider metaphors of consumption, work and order which have come to pervade the imaging of the cityspace associated with the new urbanism in a far more general sense. As a (relatively) 'cash-rich' group, the lifestyles of young City lawyers are, for example, explicitly now understood within both the brochures produced by the law firms, the related advertising materials and the student legal press as developing as much around the consumption of commodities and the acquisition of cultural experiences as they are through engaging in economic production (and, certainly, from engaging in any sense of public service, notwithstanding the occasional reference to pro bono work).[88] It is, in short, in the context of a wider urban change '. . . directed towards mobile, non-local and corporate capital, property developers and high income urban-livers. . .'[89] that those employed in corporate legal employment are, in effect, being presented as a social group especially well placed to *benefit* from the spoils of this wider socio-economic restructuring over the past two decades. These are individuals who, for example, can afford – or who will soon, in time, come to be able to afford, given the trajectory of salary advancement post-qualification – the 'redesigned' living spaces of contemporary 'lifestyle' urban dwelling; the individuals who can partake fully, or as fully as work demands allow, in the associated cultural provision of the newly corporatized leisure spaces; and, unlike so many of their public sector contemporaries – widely understood as now being priced out of urban centres – the individuals who themselves become '. . . implicated in a virtuous cycle of growth', positioned as the 'denizens of the reimagined urban landscape':[90]

> The Broadgate complex [the location of the offices of Herbert Smith] was built in the 1980s to cater for *the City worker's lifestyle*. It contains a number of smart bars and restaurants, summer seating areas, a croquet lawn, an ice rink, numerous cafe's and access to shops, banks and boutiques. However, being right on the edge of the City of London, it is also within a very easy stroll of the trendy Shoreditch area, historic Spitalfields Market and Brick Lane, renowned for the best and the cheapest curries in London . . . Five minutes walk from the office, it [the subsidised leisure club] has a swimming pool, Jacuzzi, steam rooms and sauna, as well as free classes and large multi – gym facilities.[91]

The lifestyle associated here with the new urbanism, intriguingly, plays out in different ways within, respectively, the national, global and regional contexts.[92] Yet in relation to each, it is a repeated theme in the depiction of the lifestyle of the commercial lawyer that ideas of space, place and status will be focused upon the idea of consumption and the acquisition of positional goods.[93] Within the global market in which many of the firms now operate, for example, the urban landscape presented is commonly that of the city at night; an association is made between the overseas office location and the night-time economy which itself speaks to the city as 'pleasure space', the city as site of play and entertainment, a space '. . . saturated with signs and images to the extent that anything can be represented, thematized and made an object of interest'.[94] At the national level, in contrast, and alongside the increasingly common play on the 'rebranded' urban in such a way as to denote certain (attractive) firm qualities,[95] reference continues to made to the ideas of lifestyle, consumption and an ethic of 'working hard, playing hard' in terms of the dominant framing of what 'being a lawyer' will now involve.

What we are dealing with here are, I would suggest, powerful, seductive images; images which, importantly, have a grounding in some real and profound social, economic and cultural changes – changes which, research suggests, have themselves impacted on the nature of youth identifications and cultures in a more general sense. When we turn to the legal academy, however, I now wish to suggest, the impact of these changes can be seen to have played out in some rather different ways.

'To be honest, I couldn't see myself living on your salary':[96] Dislocating Class

Social class is a notoriously fluid and contested concept and it is useful in this context, and drawing on recent sociological work, to see the lifestyle of the corporate lawyer discussed above as embodying aspects of what Savage *et al.* have referred to as a distinctively 'postmodern' kind of middle-class lifestyle; one, that is, which can be contrasted with it's 'ascetic' and 'undistinctive' middle-class variant.[97] 'If the public sector intellectuals of emergent modernity', in Chaney's observation:

> . . . have in the past acted as a vanguard in pioneering the use of cultural resources to mark out a distinctive social position, it seems that their distinctiveness is now being overtaken. Many elements in the stylistic baggage of those who claimed to be the agents of modernity *have been appropriated by later generations* and used indiscriminately in ways that subvert (and possibly transcend) the cultural codes of modernity.[98]

The imaging of the lifestyle of the corporate lawyer being deployed by the firms, as outlined above, exemplifies many aspects of this process of 'subversion' and 'appropriation'. And as, arguably, ideal typical 'public sector intellectuals of emergent modernity' *par excellence*,[99] this is something which has had particular implications for understanding the changing position of those who work in universities; and, perhaps especially, for those who work in disciplines closely associated with professional practice and the traditionally private sector – for a discipline, let us say, such as law. Interweaving with the specificities of gender, age, race, educational attainment and location,[100] the 'post-modern' middle-class lifestyle identified by Savage *et al.* points to a blurring of conventional stylistic distinctions which undercut many aspects of the cultural codes of modernity; something which is, interestingly, clearly evident in many features of the play of cultural artefacts within the representation of corporate (legal) youth discussed above, notably around the blurring of ideas of traditional 'high' and 'low' culture. For what is presented here is a world where an appeal to partaking in 'sexy' deals[101] and 'alcohol fuelled bonding' co-exists, all too easily, with the garden party, the opera and the wine-tasting evening;[102] a world where an appreciation of 'high' cultural forms of art (opera, classical music) rests cheek by jowl with a 'party hard' employee lifestyle which itself verges on the carnivalesque in the way in which it is characterized by appeals to hedonism, excess and this overarching appeal to 'having fun'.[103] This is a lifestyle, moreover, marked by a 'register of objectification' which serves to rupture some traditional ideas of masculinity and femininity in curious ways;[104] thus, for example, we see an increasingly explicit eroticism and turn to sexual imagery,[105] an appeal to playfulness and irony around gender which can be seen as the corollary of the symbolic restructuring which has accompanied the economic restructuring and the entry of women, in ever greater numbers, into the workforce. These images and texts are, above all, *knowing*; they play with, and subvert, many traditional ideas around gender, class, respectability – but they do so, crucially, in such a way as to consistently mark out the young lawyer as having, or as making a claim to, 'a distinctive social position' in a 'use of cultural resources'.

As an illustration of this kind of blurring of conventional stylistic distinction the 'pastiched and eclectic lifestyle' being presented here serves as a powerful illustration of '...how ... cultural practices [can] be sampled and juxtaposed in novel and heterodox patterns'[106] (resulting in what has been described by some as a '...demise of certain traditions of taste'). And yet it is precisely in keeping with this 'mix and mesh' approach to cultural styles that the themes of lifestyle, consumption and the new urbanism, discussed above, can be seen to work together in this context to evocatively position the lawyer as a member of a distinctive socio-spatial consumption group; one who is, I have suggested above, particularly well-placed to benefit from wider processes of economic restructuring and cultural change.[107]

The more I think of Peter's comments the more I see this as the context which surrounded him. And it is in this regard that the contrast with the vast majority, if certainly by no means all,[108] university law lecturers can be seen to be particularly – if not increasingly – marked. If the successful applicant to the larger law firms, such as Peter, has the potential to obtain salaries far in advance of both their contemporaries and those who taught them at university, for the latter group these are social shifts which have in so many ways undercut the cultural and economic social status of 'public sector intellectuals'.[109] For all the undoubted outward success of university law schools and the discipline of law in recent years, at least according to a range of performative criteria (not least the Research Assessment Exercise),[110] I wish to conclude this paper by considering further just why, from the position of Peter, there would appear to have been, for him at least, little career 'choice', ultimately, given what he saw around him as being the relative financial and personal rewards to be offered by the legal academy and legal practice.

Concluding remarks: on being (un)successful[111]

> I seldom know, in any detail, what it is that my friends really do in
> their work, because when we meet we talk of other things. Ironically, I
> think, I like them better when they are not succeeding, and they like
> me likewise, because there is more space and time for friends and fun.
> To put it crudely, they, and I, are less boring when less successful.[112]

Peter may well go on to be 'successful' in his legal career. He may not; he
may, like many others, leave the profession.[113] It is possible he might,
exhausted by long hours and often intellectually undemanding work, turn to
law teaching and, at some point in the future, enter academic life.[114] He may
experience the joys of teaching, of research, of administration and collegiality.
This paper has simply presented an attempt to understand how, from a
reading of a particular set of texts and images, ideas about what it means to
achieve professional success as a lawyer are currently being presented to students such as Peter; and how they can work in such a way as to produce what
is, I have suggested, a certain kind of social identity – one which positions an
individual as a member of a distinctive, segmented socio-spatial consumption
group,[115] one associated with '...private/corporate capital, knowledge-based
activities, middle-class consumption'[116] – and a spirit of entrepreneurialism
and material advancement which, there is reason to believe, continues to
make law students in general, and in particular amongst certain 'elite' institutions', well-attuned to any such representation of career success.[117]

I have suggested that the trainee commercial solicitor being presented
here embodies many aspects of what has become a now '...dominant mode
of young-adult consumption of urban ... culture'.[118] Indeed, these
representations of (corporate) legal youth can be seen themselves to exemplify some broader shifts which have taken place, as discussed above, around
the commodification of desire and pleasure within the social conditions of
late modernity.[119] The specific focal concerns of this group are, in keeping
with these wider processes of commodification, '...characterized by smart
attire ... pleasure seeking and hedonistic behaviour' and are routinely
framed within a largely corporately owned leisure context.[120] Profoundly
individualistic in nature,[121] they appear resolutely conformist and circumscribed by the 'bottom-line' imperatives of profit-making and maintaining
(individual, class) social/commercial status. At the same time, somewhat
ironically perhaps given this overarching individualism, their concerns are
nonetheless alluded to as involving a wider sense of civic identity, '...
of belonging or community'.[122] It is indicative of the cultural and
symbolic power of knowledge professionals and cultural intermediaries in a
broader sense that they are often presented as the saviours of the contemporary city's cultural economy *through* the consumption practices (the high cost,
status and profile) they are seen to bring with them to these renewed urban
spaces.

I have in this chapter, in short, charted something of the wider socio-cultural significance for the law school and legal practice of what I have suggested are these wider shifts taking place around ideas of lifestyle and consumption, the new 'urban playscapes' and dynamics of (middle) class fragmentation – each of which, it has been suggested, have served to position legal academics and law students who enter practice in some rather different ways as the beneficiaries or losers of social change.

I do *not* wish to present a picture – as simplistic as it would be misleading – of, on the one hand, a university system 'in crisis'; and, on the other, of a flourishing legal profession, somehow untouched by wider cultural and economic forces and pressures,[123] a profession immune to anxiety, low morale, dissatisfaction and disillusion; of a uniformly beleaguered and demoralized academy[124] and, in the case of law, a discipline beset with increasingly pressing problems around issues of the recruitment and retention in many institutions.[125] It is all too easy to make the point that the lifestyle of the contemporary university law teacher, prescribed by (relatively) poor public sector salaries, has become increasingly far removed – not just for early career scholars but for the majority of academics at all levels – from the material and symbolic images of social success now being presented to many law students across a range of cultural artefacts (regardless of whether or not they are associated with legal practice).[126]

Equally, and in the context of a mass higher education system, it is important to remember that not all can be 'winners', at least in the sense that Peter (one might assume) would understand it; that is, in terms of 'the lucky ones' who secure employment with the large commercial firms. Regardless of the vagaries of market demand, for a significant number of law students entering the profession is itself a matter of little consequence. The picture in relation to both law schools and professional practice is, of course, far more complex than any such simplistic picture would allow; although, undoubtedly, a now voluminous body of research does support the argument that there are many aspects of the 'decline of donnish dominion' and academic deprofessionalization which are only beginning to be addressed within the UK context.[127]

Notwithstanding the above, this paper has presented a reading of a number of social, economic and cultural changes which together, it has been suggested, can usefully be seen as *part* of the story – *part* of understanding, of seeking to explain – why it should be the case that for many law students, such as Peter, the legal academy should be seen as a primarily instrumental social good; and, certainly, not as something any ambitious individual should consider entering. Maybe, perhaps, it was ever so.[128] Within the political and social context of a neo-liberal hegemony the grounded context, as it were, of any such career choice has shifted considerably. At the present moment it is unsurprising that a social group which seeks – as its very *raison d'être* – to accumulate economic capital should also seek symbolic capital and status through engaging in certain kinds of 'up market' consumption practices. What we have here is, at its upper echelons, a social group both meritocratic yet exclusive, very highly paid yet powerfully convinced of the justice of their rewards and, increasingly, divorced from the rest of society by wealth, education, residence and lifestyle.[129] Peter's observation, with which I began, concerning the inferior quality of the cars being driven by his law lecturers is, in such a context, unsurprising. He is right. For what is explicitly being held out to prospective trainee solicitors in these firms is an individual and collective identity which *facilitates a differentiation of the self* from others – from those who will not 'make the grade', do not 'have what it takes' to succeed in this, most competitive, area of legal work.[130] These images and texts address cultural investments in what is, ultimately, an individual and collective sense of superiority and distinction; they provide the reader with a distinctive knowledge base about the sort of people these protagonists are, the social resources they have (or will soon obtain) and, crucially, of the social identity they will need to assume to succeed.

In the social context outlined in this paper it is not surprising that so many law students should, like Peter, see their lecturers as, in effect, if not 'failed lawyers' then as, ultimately, little more than the functionaries and facilitators of the professional success of their new demanding 'clients' – the paying customers of the new university as information factory.

Notes

1 D. Mamet, *Oleanna* (London: Methuen Royal Court Writers Series, 1993) p. 33.
2 Not his real name. I am focusing this discussion on one particular conversation. However, the views expressed in this exchange are not, from my experience, exceptional in that I believe they are commonly held amongst much of the student body, certainly within the institution at which I work. What is perhaps unusual in this instance is the force and eloquence of their expression.
3 Presumably, although one cannot be sure, funded by the family of the student. It is worth noting in this context the Law Society *Law Student Cohort Research Studies* (see further n 17, below) which suggest that the applicants for training contracts to the large commercial firms who do enjoy particularly high levels of success tend to be; young, white and not disabled; independent-school educated and from a privileged social-class background; to have a professionally qualified parent and, of particular importance, to be more likely to have attended an 'old' university as a law undergraduate, or the College of Law as a CPE student. As a young, white male attending a Russell Group 'old' university Peter's profile is thus not dissimilar to the above and, for all the well-documented levels of student-debt, such debt is recognized as not impacting on all students in the same way; it is not unknown for the more affluent law students, across universities, to have considerable levels of expendable income relative to many of their peers. More generally, as Shiner puts it, '. . . if certain communities face discrimination in the process by which the legal profession recruits its members, then how legitimate are any claims that the profession may make in terms of *representing* these communities?': M. Shiner 'Young, Gifted and Blocked! Entry to the Solicitor's Profession' in P. Thomas (ed.)

Discriminating Lawyers (London, Cavendish, 2000) pp. 87–120 (at p. 87, my emphasis). For all their elite status within the profession, it is precisely the large City and, to a lesser degree, large provincial firms which, to quote Shiner, '...appear ... to be the *driving force* behind ... institutional and social class biases' in the profession: Ibid.

4 Perhaps more sobering for a student such as Peter at a 'middle-tier' UK university is the fact that research suggests the larger City firms, in particular, continue to have a '...strong bias in favour of Oxbridge graduates and trainees from privileged class backgrounds': M. Shiner, Ibid., p. 118. It is estimated that Oxbridge graduates are roughly 10 times as likely as a 'new university' law graduate to be working in the City firms: M. Shiner, Ibid.

5 'Whoever dies with the most toys wins' is a well-known corporate slogan: see, alternatively: http://www.weathergraphics.com/tim/economy.htm. In keeping with this spirit, the phrase 'kill what you eat' has found common currency as a description of income and billing practices within some firms in this sector of the profession: e.g. 'Lockstep v. Kill What You Eat', http://blogs.law.harvard.edu/waddle/2003/09/25.

6 On which see further A. Bradney *Conversations, Choices and Chances: The Liberal Law School in the Twenty-First Century* (Oxford, Hart, 2003). C.f. J. Newman, *The Idea of a University* (New York, Holt, Rinehart and Winston, 1960).

7 A defence of which can be found in A. Bradney, Ibid.

8 See further, for example, the work listed at n 42, n 43 below.

9 The term is itself, of course, mediated by socio-economic assumptions: c.f. 'Career opportunities are the ones that never knock/Every job they offer you is to keep you out the dock/Career opportunity the ones that never knock...': The Clash, *Career Opportunities* (1977) (J. Strummer, M. Jones).

10 These firms have been described as exerting an almost '...magnetic quality in attracting new recruits': R.G. Lee (2000) '"Up or out" – Means or Ends? Staff Retention in Large Law Firms' in P. Thomas (ed.) *Discriminating Lawyers* p. 183. In the 1999 intake of trainee solicitors, for example, the top ten firms by size sought to recruit 930 trainees, accounting for over 20 per cent of all training contracts offered that year: calculated from *The Lawyer Student Special* (2000), quoted in R.G. Lee, Ibid. These firms pay high salaries and, Shiner suggests, '...are able to cream off the best qualified candidates' as a result of their greater ability to finance trainees through the LPC and, where relevant, the CPE: op. cit. n 3.

11 Issues explored in a series of conference and workshop presentations to the Socio-Legal Studies Association Annual Conference (2002), the Annual Meeting of the International Working Group for the Comparative Study of the Legal Profession (2002) and the Institute for Advanced Legal Studies (2002): copy of papers with author. The materials considered in the broader study are, I argue, replete with powerful messages about what it means to achieve social and economic success as a lawyer. These ideas, however, are, on closer examination, bound up with assumptions about codes of social, cultural and economic capital which are mediated by beliefs about social class, gender, sexuality, race and ethnicity. Such an interrogation of images does not seek to engage with an 'image of legality', in the sense of exploring the representation of legal doctrines (by tracing, say, a fragmentation in the form of or enhanced visibility of policy in law: c.f. B. Carlsson and M. Baier, 'A Visual Self-Image of Legal Authority: 'The Temple of Law' (2002) 11 (2) *Social and Legal Studies* pp. 185–211); nor, from a different perspective, the question of how images of legality are understood in relation to the legal consciousness of 'ordinary people': see further D. Curtis and J. Resnik 'Images of Justice' *Yale Law*

Journal 96 pp. 1726–1771: R. Cotterrell *Law's Community* (Oxford, Clarendon Press, 1995). P. Ewick and S. Silbey *The Common Place of Law: Stories From Everyday Life* (Chicago, Chicago University Press, 1998). See further n 25, below.

12 On the connections between texts, individuals and social formation see further, e.g. A. Tudor, 'Culture, Mass Communication and Social Agency' (1995) 12 *Theory, Culture and Society* pp. 81–107: E. Chaplin *Sociology and Visual Representation* (London, Routledge, 1994): M. Emmison and P. Smith *Researching the Visual* (London, Sage, 2000): G. Rose *Visual Methodologies* (London, Sage, 2000). Amongst the now vast literature on the relation between law and popular culture note, R.K. Sherwin *When Law Goes Pop: The Vanishing Line Between Law and Popular Culture* (Chicago, Chicago University Press, 2000): A. Chase 'Toward a Legal Theory of Popular Culture' (1986) *Wisconsin Law Review* pp. 527–569: A. Sarat and J. Simon (eds) *Cultural Analysis, Cultural Studies and the Law* (Duke University Press, 2003): P.W. Kahn, *The Cultural Study of Law: Reconstructing Legal Scholarship* (Chicago, University of Chicago Press, 1999): D.L. Gunn, *The Lawyer and Popular Culture* (Texas, Willa. S. Hein, 1993): A. Sarat and T. Kearns (eds) *Law in the Domains of Culture* (Michigan, University of Michigan Press, 2000): L.C. Bower, T. Goldberg and M. Musheno (eds) *Between Law and Culture: Relocating Legal Studies* (University of Minnesota Press, 2001). More generally, J. Leonard (ed.) *Cultural Studies: A Reader in Postmodern Critical Theory* (New York, State University of New York Press, 1995).

13 Again, this literature is voluminous. On the development of the UK profession see further: R.L. Abel, *English Lawyers Between Market and State: The Politics of Professionalism* (Oxford, Oxford University Press 2003): R.L. Abel *The Legal Profession in England and Wales* (Oxford, Basil Blackwell, 1988): C. Glasser 'The Legal Profession in the 1990s – Images of Change' (1990) *Legal Studies* p. 1; J. Flood 'Megalaw in the UK: Professionalism or corporatism? A preliminary report' 64 *Indiana Law Journal* at p. 569: J. Flood 'Megalawyering in the global order: the cultural, social and economic transformation of global legal practice' 3 *International Journal of the Legal Profession* p. 169: A. Boon and J. Levin, *The Ethics and Conduct of Lawyers in England and Wales* (Oxford, Hart, 1999): M. Burrage 'From a gentleman's to a public profession: status and politics in the history of English Solicitors' (1996) 3 *International Journal of the Legal Profession* at p. 45: B. Cole *Trends in the Solicitors Profession: Annual Statistical Report 2000* (London, Law Society, 2000): B. Cole, *Solicitors in Private Practice – Their Work and Expectations Research Study No. 26* (Research and Policy Planning Unit, London, Law Society, 1997): A. Sherr, 'Superheroes and Slaves: Images and Work of the Legal Professional' (1995) 48 (2) *Current Legal Problems.*

14 Following on from a recognition of the diversity of the terms 'law student' and 'law school', I will in what follows make a number of assumptions about the age profile of trainee solicitors generally. However, it is important to recognize the presence of a relatively small, but significant, number of trainee solicitors who are what Shiner (op. cit. n 3) has termed 'late starters' to the profession. These individuals, research suggests, can have distinctive experiences of both the training contract and future career progression: G. Walker, 'Born Again Lawyers' *The Lawyer* 5 March 2001 p. 35. Shiner has classified the 'conventional student' as being 23 years or younger during the final year of degree, the 'late starter' as between 24 and 28 and the 'mature starter' as 29 or older. See further M. Shiner, op. cit. n 3, p. 91. Many texts under consideration in what follows are nonetheless framed by and seek to address a shift away from late adolescence/university life into what will be the (at least for some) the independent adulthood of life during the training contract: on the wider

context of such transition see F.K. Goldscheider and C. Goldscheider, *The Changing Transition to Adulthood: Leaving and Returning Home* (London, Sage, 1999). Interestingly, the decision to apply to such firms is itself presented as a key life stage, with the law firm as an organization sensitive to the importance of helping an individual 'Bridge the Gap' successfully: 'From university to the profession is a big step. At Berwin Leighton we try that bit harder to ensure the transition is a smooth one': also 'To Gap or Not To Gap: The Pros and Cons' *Plum*, 5th edn (London, S.J. Berwin, 2003) p. 22.

15 Itself, of course, a problematic term: D. Goleman, *Emotional Intelligence: Why it Can Matter More Than IQ* (London, Bloomsbury, 1996): H. Gardner, *Frames of Mind: The Theory of Multiple Intelligences* (New York, Basic Books, 1993).

16 See further the argument of P. Thomas and A. Rees 'Law Students – Getting in and getting on' in P. Thomas (ed.) op. cit. n 3, pp. 33–37.

17 On which note the studies based on the experiences of a cohort of law students who were due to complete the academic stage of legal training (law degree or CPE) in 1993: D. Halpern *Entry into the Legal Professions – The Law Student Cohort Study Years 1 and 2* (London, Law Society, 1994): M. Shiner and T. Newburn *Entry into the Legal Professions: The Law Student Cohort Study Year 3* (London, Law Society, 1995): M. Shiner *Entry into the Legal Professions: The Law Student Cohort Study Year 4* (London, Law Society, 1997): M. Shiner *Entry into the Legal Professions – The Law Student Cohort Study Year 5* (London, Law Society, 1999). Shiner's research (1999) points to a complex but nonetheless 'discernible bias' in relation to the way in which ethnicity, gender, social class and education (school, university) impact on the chances of securing a training contract and progressing in law firms; M. Shiner, *Law Student Cohort Study* Year 5 Ibid. 1999 Table 4: also M. Shiner, op. cit. n 3, p. 99.

18 The following argument relates to images and social and cultural changes which, I suggest, have a particular resonance for understanding these firms. This argument does not necessarily (although it might) relate to student perceptions of the legal profession in any more general sense.

19 A. Bradney, op. cit. n 6: M. Thornton, 'The demise of diversity in legal education: Globalisation and the new knowledge economy' (2001) 8 (1) *International Journal of the Legal Profession* pp. 37–56.

20 The idea of choice must itself, of course, be treat with caution; for example, access to economic, cultural and symbolic capital itself structures the 'choice' an individual such as Peter, above, might make in relation to a decision as whether or not to enter the legal profession (and, if so, what part of the profession to practice in). Integrating wider issues of personal background, disposition and personality, biography and so forth into any analysis of such choice remains a notoriously complex problem. Any such discussion can itself be located in the context of the 'complex diversity of choices' facing the individual in late modernity: A. Giddens, *Modernity and Self-Identity: Self and Society in the Late Modern Age* (Cambridge, Polity, 1991) p. 80. Note, e.g. 'Where you can be exceptional': Reynolds, Porter, Chamberlin, 2001: Masons, 1999/2000.

21 Allen and Overy, 2001, my emphasis.

22 M. Thornton, op. cit. n 19. These firms are widely seen as organizations going from strength to strength, outstripping the growth in other areas of the profession to the point 'where the top ten firms are producing about the same percentage of turnover of fee income for all firms in England and Wales': R.G. Lee (2000), op. cit. n 10 at p. 183. See also A. Freeman, 'A Critical Look at Corporate Practice' (1987) 37 *Journal of Legal Education* p. 315, cited in M. Thornton op. cit. n 19.

23 The need for research is itself particularly important in this area where, as

Bradney and Cownie observe, important as information about the background to obtaining a position as a trainee solicitor is '. . . it is less important than *what happens* during the process of training itself. It is at this stage that we would expect the most intense period of acculturation to take place as the law student becomes absorbed into the community of solicitors. However it is precisely at this point that we know least': A. Bradney and F. Cownie *The English Legal System in Context* (London, Butterworths, 1998) p. 142, my emphasis.

24 On the changing nature of the 'large firm' more generally: M. Galanter and T. Palay *Tournament of Lawyers: Growth and Transformation of the Big Law Firm* (Chicago, Chicago University Press, 1991): R.G. Lee (1992) 'From Profession to Business: The Rise and Rise of the City Law Firm' 19 *Journal of Law and Society* at p. 31: R.G. Lee, op. cit. n 10: R.G. Lee *Firm Views: Work of and Work in the Largest Law Firms: Research Study No 35* (London, Law Society, 1999).

25 The research referred to at n 11 is based on a study of 35 brochures and 41 advertisements produced by a range of City of London and large regional firms in the UK, drawn from over a period of five years and targeted at those individuals considering a career in (broadly) corporate commercial, 'blue-chip' City work. Although the brochures vary in size and content they seek to convey, taken together, an essential core of information to the 'would-be' lawyer. The majority of these derive from the 'Top 20' firms, as listed in *Chambers Guide to the Legal Profession* (London, Chambers, 1999).

26 According to *Chambers Student Guide to the Legal Profession 2003* (London, Chambers, 2002) post-qualification salaries in these firms are now regularly in excess of £50,000.

27 According to Shiner, op. cit. n 3, p. 117, while 75 per cent of City trainees in the Law Society Cohort Studies (n 17, above) received professional sponsorship to pay their fees and/or maintenance costs, this compares with less than 5 per cent of high street trainees.

28 There is, of course, no 'one' type of university law school. Law schools vary in terms of their institutional contexts, academic standing and broader function within the distinctive legal, political and wider communities in which they exist. See further, and generally, A. Bradney, op. cit. n 6: A. Bradney 'Law as a Parasitic Discipline' (1998) 25 *Journal of Law and Society* 71: A. Bradney 'Legal Education in the 21st Century' in Grant *et al. Legal Education 2000* (Aldershot: Gower, 1988): A. Bradney 'Ivory Towers or Satanic Mills: Choices for University Law Schools' (1992) 17 *Studies in Higher Education*: R. Brownsword 'Where are all the law schools going?' (1996) The Law Teacher 1: F. Cownie (ed.) *The Law School: Global Issues, Local Problems* (Aldershot: Gower, 1999): R. Brownsword 'Law schools for lawyers, citizens and people' in F. Cownie, Ibid.: A. Bradney and F. Cownie 'Transformative Visions of Legal education' (1998) 25 *Journal of Law and Society* 1: A. Bradney and F. Cownie 'Working on the Chain Gang?' (1996) 2 (2) *Contemporary Issues in Law* 15: P. Harris and M. Jones 'A Survey of Law Schools in the UK' (1996) 3 *Law Teacher* 91: W.L. Twining 'Thinking About Law schools: Rutland Reviewed' (1998) 25 *Journal of Law and Society* 1: W.L. Twining *Blackstone's Tower: The English Law School* (1994). UK law teachers are equally diverse (although, it would appear, a relatively homogeneous employment grouping in terms of ethnicity and socio-economic background): 'Readers of [the journal *Legal Studies*] are most likely male, pale, middle-class and able-bodied. True, there is more chance that they are female than there would have been 20 years ago, but those women will almost invariably be fit and white': C. Wells, 'Working Out Women in Law Schools' 21 (1) *Legal Studies* at p. 116.

29 The law student population across UK law schools itself varies considerably in

terms of entry age, educational (dis)advantage, wealth, by, for example, the need to work long hours during their degree, in the need to meet family responsibilities and so forth; 'There can be little, any, doubt that that law students tend to be recruited from well-qualified families with a tradition of employment and high-status occupations'. M. Shiner, op. cit. n 3, p. 92. In view of the fact most lawyers are graduates, it is unsurprising that social imbalance at the academic stage of qualification should then help maintain the social imbalance of the profession: Law Society, *Annual Statistical Report 2000* (Law Society, London, 2001) chs 6 and 7.

30 N 10, above.

31 An issue of growing concern in the profession, notably in relation to issues of gender, race and ethnicity: on the latter see, for example, S. Vignaendra, M. Williams and J. Gavey, 'Hearing Black and Asian Voices – An Exploration of Identity' in P. Thomas, op. cit. n 3: Law Society, *The Guide to Professional Conduct of Solicitors* 1999 (London, Law Society, 1999): H. Carr and E. Tunnah (2002) 'Opportunities or Deterrent: Black Caribbean students experience of the LLB', paper presented at the Institute for Advanced Legal Studies, January 2002 (copy with author). It is estimated that a little less than one quarter of African Caribbean applicants tend to secure a position as a trainee compared with almost three quarters of white candidates: M. Shiner, op. cit. n 3 at p. 99. According to the *Annual Statistical Report: Trends in the Solicitor's Profession 2000* (London, Law Society, 2001), in 1999–2000 solicitors from ethnic minorities accounted for 7.6 per cent of solicitors on the Roll, 6.1 per cent of solicitors with practising certificates and 5.8 per cent of solicitors in private practice. Nine per cent of solicitors in London are estimated to be of BEM background: Source: H. Carr and E. Tunnah, Ibid.

32 That both the Law Society and the Bar Council take equal opportunities and diversity with increasing seriousness is beyond doubt. The Law Society has a principle of professional conduct outlawing discrimination and the 1995 Anti-Discrimination Rules require every firm to have an anti-discrimination policy, with the Law Society's model Anti-Discrimination Policy applying in lieu: *The Guide to Professional Conduct of Solicitors* (London, Law Society, 1997, ch 7). On the distinction between *difference* and *disadvantage* in this context, and how this relates to discrimination, see further M. Shiner, op. cit. n 3, pp. 90–91.

33 See further R.G. Lee *Firm Views: Work of and Work in the Largest Law Firms: Research Study No 35* (London, Law Society, 1999).

34 R.G. Lee, Ibid. Many of these issues are themselves, interestingly, discussed in the student legal press: e.g. 'My City Hell: The Pain Barrier' (of the ex-'magic circle' trainee) *Lex* Issue 15 Spring 2003, pp. 86–88: J. Currie 'Walking Away' *Lawyer 2B* December 2002, p. 45: J. Currie 'Dead End' *Lawyer 2B* March 2003 pp. 24–25. Lee notes, op. cit. n 3 at p. 183) there are now '. . . serious quality of life issues facing such firms, and that staff retention is a major headache'. To a degree at least, the insecurities of the employment within the corporate financial sector has become a recurring theme within the published material aimed at law students and well as in the media more generally.

35 R.G. Lee, op. cit. n 10, 2000, at p. 200.

36 Data does suggest that the traditional characterization of the legal profession generally as 'being made up of white, middle-aged, public school, Oxbridge educated men' is, increasingly, simplistic: M. Shiner, n 3, op. cit., p. 91. Women have for some time constituted the majority of those studying law and entering the profession. By 1993 the majority (57 per cent) of those due to complete the academic stage of training were women: *Factsheet Number 2* 'Women in the Legal Profession' (London, Law Society, 1999). In 1999–2000,

53.1 per cent of all admissions to the Solicitor's Roll were women: *Law Society Annual Statistical Report 2000* (London, Law Society, 2001 Table 10.5). In 1996–1997 47 per cent of the traineeships registered with the Law Society were held by men and 53 per cent were held by women: see further C. McGlynn *The Woman Lawyer: Making the Difference* (London: Butterworths, 1998) Table 3.1. See further, on the wider context of such data, S. Walby, *Gender Transformation* (London, Routledge, 1997): R. Crompton, D. Gallie and K. Purcell. *Changing Forms of Employment: Organisation, Skills and Gender* (London: Routledge, 1996): S. Walby (ed.) *Gender Segregation at Work* (Milton Keynes: Open University Press, 1988). Notwithstanding the above, at the same time evidence indicates that women within the legal profession as a whole continue to be less well-paid than men (C. McGlynn, Ibid., p. 83), under-represented in the upper echelons of the profession (in 1997 women accounted for 16 per cent of partners in solicitors firms: Ibid.. p. 95) and more likely than men to remain at assistant solicitor level (*Annual Statistical Report 2000*: Law Society, London, 2001), para 2.9–2.10 and Tables 2.9 and 2.10). It is reported that 84 per cent of men make partner level but only 58 per cent of women: *The Solicitors Profession in England and Wales* (London, Law Society, 2001) p. 65: B. Cole, *Annual Statistical Report* 2000, n 13, Table 2.9. The related literature on women and the legal profession, exploring these and many other issues, is itself now voluminous: see: H. Sommerlad and P. Sanderson *Gender Choice and Commitment: Women Solicitors in England and Wales and the Struggle for Equal Status* (Aldershot: Ashgate, 1998): U. Schultz and G. Shaw (eds) *Women in the World's Legal Professions* (Oxford, Hart, 2003): J. Brockman *Gender in the Legal Profession: Fitting or Breaking the Mould?* (British Columbia, UBC Press 2001): C. McGlynn 'The Business of Equality in the Solicitors' Profession' (2000) 63 *Modern Law Review* p. 442: J. Hagan and F. Kay *Gender in Practice: A Study of Lawyers' Lives* (New York: OUP, 1995): K. Hull and R. Nelson 'Gender Inequality in Law: Problems in Structure and Agency in Recent Studies of Gender in Anglo-American Legal Professions' (1998) *Law and Social Inquiry* p. 681: D. Ross *Bridging the Gap: A Report on Women in Law* (London: Quarry Douglas Consulting Group, 1990): D. Podmore and A. Spencer 'Gender in the Labour Process – the case of women and men lawyers' in D. Knights and H. Wilmott (eds) *Gender and Labour Process* (Aldershot: Gower, 1986): M. Harrington *Women Lawyers: ReWriting the Rules* (New York: Alfred Knopf, 1992): E. Skordaki 'Glass Slippers and Glass Ceilings: Women in the Legal Profession' (1996) 3 *International Journal of the Legal Profession* at p. 7: H. Sommerlad 'The Myth of Feminisation: women and cultural change in the legal profession' (1994) 1 *International Journal of the Legal Profession* pp. 31–53.

37 E.g. M. Thornton, op. cit. n 19.

38 J. Farrar 'Law departments attack the profession's meddling' (2003) 2 (5) *Lawyer 2B* p. 1: L. Bibbings (2003) 'The Future of Higher Education: "Sustainable Research Businesses" and "Exploitable Knowledge"' *Socio-Legal Studies Association Newsletter* 40, Summer, p. 1: J. Currie 'Legal Education Locks Horns with Regulators' (2002) 2 (2) *Lawyer 2B* p. 1: L. Bibbings (2003, on behalf of the SLSA), *SLSA Response to the Joint Academic Stage Board Consultation on the Relationship of Foundation Degrees to the Law Qualifying Degree* (copy with author): R. Collier (2003) 'The Uncertain Future of (Critical) Socio-Legal Studies' *Socio-Legal Studies Association Newsletter* 39, Spring, p. 3.

39 That is, income beyond the research/teaching streams. This phrase has come to encompass a range of income generating entrepreneurial activities such as Continuing Professional Development, 'spin-off' companies, consultancies and so forth.

40 It is notable that the very kinds of marketing under consideration here have increasingly come to pervade the higher education sector, with UK law schools marketing themselves in ways not dissimilar to the private sector firms: J. Bodoh and R. Mighall, 'Brand New Image' *Guardian* 29 January 2002 ('One of the significant factors of the perpetual "crisis" in higher education ... has been the increasingly sophisticated way in which institutions have begun to market themselves ... in a crowded marketplace many universities have got to grips with the harsh realities of commercial life, and are strutting their promotional stuff with the best of the private sector'). Or, as Thornton observes (op. cit. n 19, p. 47), 'For universities to survive, university managers have accepted that they must enter the market. The movement in favour of academic capitalism has occurred with remarkable rapidity ... as a corollary of neo-liberalism'. Of course, adopting the language of corporate enterprise and innovation is one thing: encouraging genuine innovation, creativity and critical thinking on the part of legal academics and law students quite another: see T. Blacker, 'A Degree of Dangerous Philosophy' *Independent* 22 November 2002.

41 M. Thornton op. cit. n 19. at p. 43. This is particularly clear in terms of how the perceived graduate employment needs of the corporate firms can feed through to considerations of law school staffing. It has become notoriously difficult for some institutions, for example, to appoint in the commercial law field, particularly at senior positions, even though these are areas in which there appears to be considerable student demand.

42 The literature on which is now vast. See generally A. Brooks and A. Mackinnon (eds) *Gender and the Restructured University: Changing Management and Culture in Higher Education* (Buckingham, The Society for Research into Higher Education and Open University Press, 2001): S. Slaughter and L. Leslie, *Academic Capitalism: Politics, Policies and the Entrepreneurial University*, Baltimore, MD: Johns Hopkins University Press: J. Currie and J. Newson (eds) *Universities and Globalization: Critical Perspectives* (London, Sage, 1998): M. Thornton, op. cit. n 19.

43 M. Thornton op. cit. n 19 at p. 43. Note, e.g. the issues raised in the WG Hart Legal Workshop 2001, 'The Changing Work and Organisation of Lawyers and its Educational Implications', Institute for Advanced Legal Studies, 26–28 June 2001 (Call for Papers: 'Does legal education keep pace with legal practice? Should it? What should legal education do?'). See also: M. Thornton 'Among the Ruins: Law in the Neo-Liberal Academy' (2001) 20 *Windsor Yearbook of Access to Justice* pp. 3–23: H.W. Arthurs 'Globalization of the Mind: Canadian Elites and the Restructuring of Legal Fields' (1997) 12 (2) *Canadian Journal of Law and Society* p. 219: J. Flood, 'Legal Education, Globalization, and the New Imperialism' in F. Cownie (ed.) *The Law School: Global issues, Local Questions* (Aldershot, UK and Brookfield, VT, Dartmouth/Ashgate, 1999), p. 128: R. Collier, 'The Changing University and the (Legal) Academic Career – Rethinking the 'Private Life' of the Law School' (2002) 22 (1) *Legal Studies* pp. 1–32.

44 M. Thornton op. cit. n 19 at p. 43, my emphasis.

45 S. Slaughter and L. Leslie, op. cit. n 42.

46 See the work cited above, n 42, n 43.

47 In repositioning academics as 'knowledge workers' within a market economy – individuals for whom knowledge is not seen as something valuable in and of itself but as, rather, a commodity, a *resource* to help create wealth and competitive advantage – the idea of 'useful knowledge' has become a leitmotif of New Labour's present Higher Education policy: C. Clarke, *Times Higher Education Supplement* 16 May 2003 p. 1.

48 See, for example, n 42, above.
49 On which, and although pre-dating recent developments, see further: P. Hill-
    yard and J. Sim, 'The Political Economy of Socio-Legal Research' in P. Thomas
    (ed.) *Socio-Legal Studies* (Aldershot, Dartmouth, 1997) pp. 45–75. Compare P.
    Hillyard, 'Invoking Indignation: Reflection on Future Directions of Socio-
    Legal Studies' (2002) 29 (4) *Journal of Law and Society* pp. 645–656.
50 T. Blacker, op. cit. n 40: A. Brooks 'Restructuring Bodies of Knowledge' in A.
    Brooks and A. Mackinnon, op. cit. n 42, pp. 15–45.
51 'Higher Education used to be a profession where you traded off a high level of
    personal autonomy against reasonable financial rewards. Now, rewards have
    collapsed from the merely inadequate to the truly ludicrous.' M. Kleinman,
    'Why I have no regrets about having left academe' *Times Higher Education Sup-
    plement* 14 November 2003 p. 16.
52 Herbert Smith, 2002.
53 D. Chaney, *Lifestyles* (London, Routledge, 1996) p. 37.
54 Ibid., p. 4.
55 Ibid., p. 37, my emphasis. On the relation between consumption, lifestyle and
    identity see more generally: G. McCracken, *Culture and Consumption* (Bloom-
    ington, Indiana University Press, 1990): S. Edgell, K. Hetherington and A.
    Warde (eds) *Consumption Matters: The Production and Experience of Consumption*
    (Oxford, Blackwell, 1997). S. Brown, 'What's Love Got To Do With It?' Sex,
    Shopping and Subjective Personal Introspection' in S. Brown, A.M. Doherty
    and B. Clarke (eds) *Romancing the Market* (London, Routledge, 1998) pp.
    137–171: J. Baudrillard, *The Consumer Society* (London, Sage, 1998): C. Camp-
    bell, *The Romantic Ethic and the Spirit of Modern Consumerism* (Oxford, Blackwell,
    1989). Also P. Falk and C. Campbell (eds) *The Shopping Experience* (London,
    Sage, 1997): G. Ritzer, *The McDonaldization of Society: An Investigation into the
    Changing Character of Contemporary Social Life* (London, Sage, 1995).
56 See further n 11.
57 Ibid.
58 Pannone and Partners, 2002.
59 In this respect facilities aimed at 'body servicing' the corporate lawyer should
    not be seen as mere benefits; they are essential elements which facilitate and
    make possible the kinds of physical and psychological investments and social
    practices being demanded by the firm. Thus, it is commonplace to find, along-
    side details of the salary to be expected, reference to the extensive range of
    facilities such as (a far from comprehensive list): travel season ticket loan;
    private medical scheme; annual health screening; free membership of a gym
    and sports club (some on-site and with professional instruction); a subsidized
    food bar; ticket schemes for selected theatres; in-house consultation and treat-
    ment with a doctor and dentist; dry cleaning collection and delivery service;
    and the provision, when required, of serviced apartments.
60 See n 3, above, regarding the social class background of recruits to these firms.
61 Ashurst Morris Crisp, 2002, p. 22.
62 Publications, for example, such as *Lex: For the Lawyer of the Future* (published
    three times a year by Legalese London): *Target Law* (published by London, GTI
    Specialist Publishers): *The Trainee*, the magazine of the Trainee Solicitors
    Group (Harrogate, Barker Brooks Media Ltd): *LegalWeek Magazine* (Student
    Specials) (London, Global Professional Media Ltd: www.legalweekstudent.net):
    and *The Hobson's Law Guide* (Cambridge, CRAC Publications/Hobsons PLC).
    Note also, although from a different perspective, *www.rollonfriday.com*. Many of
    the themes discussed below in relation to consumption and space pervade this
    website aiming to '. . . provide news, views and gossip on the legal profession':

http://www.rollonfriday.com/index_freetime.htm (e.g. sections dedicated to 'Food and Drink', 'Free Time' and the 'Glamorous Solicitor'). *Rollonfriday.com* has itself featured in publicity material produced by the firms: e.g. Bristows, 2003. The significance of these texts is especially interesting given that many students get their (initial) ideas of law from popular culture.

63 See, for example, from 1998 (considered by many to be the high point of 'Brit Pop' and 'new laddism') the use of an image of two men, without trousers and sitting on washing machines: 'Suits You Sir' *Lex* Summer Term, 1998 Issue 1 p. 1. The playful nature of much of the student legal press itself cross-refers to aspects of other products: e.g. *Viz Comic* (London, John Brown Publishing).

64 The corporate firms have turned, in particular, to aspects of both the style and content of contemporary youth magazines One of the most interesting examples of this trend raises a number of broader issues about how consumption practices are presented as a key part of the lawyers lifestyle. The following is from a piece entitled 'Beer and Bonding in the Boardroom', taken from *Plum*, 4th edition, published by S.J. Berwin as an adjunct to the communication of core information about the training contract contained elsewhere:

> Although the phrase 'the Boardroom' conjures up images of pinstriped old goats smoking cigars and congratulating themselves on being masters of the universe, this is not the case at SJB. Well, at least not on the last Friday of every month, for that is the firm drinks evening. The Boardroom's exotic flower arrangements are booted out to make way for much more interesting items – namely glasses and alcohol. As the noise level increases the Boardroom is transformed into the Gray's Inn Road branch of *All-Bar-One* (well, almost) ... For trainees the evenings are a perfect opportunity to ... indulge in some alcohol fuelled bonding with people from all over the firm – though it has to be said that it is not the right time to test whether your new boss has a good sense of humour! It is a popular and highly recommended start to the week end.
>
> S.J. Berwin, *Plum 4th Edn* (London, SJ Berwin, 2002) p. 16

Compare, in style and content, aspects of magazines aimed at a predominantly male market (the 'lad mags' such as FHM, Loaded, Maxim): see further N. Stevenson, P. Jackson and K. Brooks, *Making Sense of Men's Magazines* (Cambridge, Polity, 2001): B. Benwell (ed.) *Masculinity and Men's Lifestyle Magazines: Sociological Review Monographs* (Oxford, Blackwell, 2003). Also B. Crewe, *Representing Men: Cultural Production and Producers in the Men's Magazine Market* (London, Berg, forthcoming).

65 Covering information essential to the 'would-be' lawyer such as the nature of the firm and range of work undertaken; the experience of the trainee solicitor during the traineeship and/or vacation placement (the opportunities that would be offered, the demands that would be made and, on occasion, the salary); the nature of life after qualification (the future promotion prospects, available areas of employment within the firm and so forth); and, of course, the basics of contact details and how to apply.

66 'This Life is about Friends', above an image of ten trainees [six women, four men], playing on the titles of two popular television programmes. D.J. Freeman, 2001/2, an explicit reference to *This Life* (BBC TV) and *Friends* (Channel 4), the latter an iconic text concerned with youth friendships in transition, the former a well-received drama set in legal practice. I am grateful to Richard Mullender for pointing this out.

67 One firm brands its brochure 'Unplugged and Uncovered' (Wragge and Co., 2001), utilizing a texture and style similar to the work of the designer Peter

Saville for Factory Records, Manchester, during the 1980s and 1990s: P. Saville, *Designed by Peter Saville* (Princeton, Princeton Arch, 2003).

68 Firms are increasingly utilizing the work of modern artists to denote what is presented as the 'distinctive' 'cutting-edge' character of the firm. E.g. Laurence Graham, 'Car Tyres, Containers and Career Opportunities', 2002/3, a series of postcards of modern art works with information on the reverse covering aspects of training offered by the firm.

69 This is a recurring theme within many of the trainee profiles: E.g. 'After dinner (which itself included an unlimited supply of wine) . . . the alcohol had already robbed me of all sense of sight and sound . . . This is when it gets hazy . . .': Kevin Cook, Trainee: Weil, Gotshal and Manger, 2003, quoted in *Target* 7th edn (London, GTI Specialist Publishers, London). Alcohol consumption also features significantly in lifestyle articles within the general legal press: e.g. 'London Barfly: Jacqui Walker bends her elbow at some of the capital's finest watering holes' *The Trainee*, Spring 2001 p. 14. Intriguingly, there are (albeit understandably) no mentions of other drugs of choice, notwithstanding what is known about the range and prevalence of drug use amongst the youth population in general, the student community as well as within the City of London: see further T. Newburn and M. Shiner, *Teenage Kicks?: Young People and Alcohol – A Review of the Literature* (York, Joseph Rowntree Foundation, 2001): B. Malbon, *Clubbing: Dancing, Ecstasy and Vitality* (London, Routledge, 1995): K. Brain, *Youth, Alcohol and the Emergence of the Post-Modern Alcohol Order* (London, Institute of Alcohol Studies, Occasional Paper, 2000): N. Dorn, *Alcohol, Youth and the State* (London, Croom Helm, 1983): S. Morgan, 'Cheap Drinks, Heavy Costs: Students and Alcohol' 56 *Youth and Policy* pp. 42–55: F. Coffield and L. Gofton, *Drugs and Young People* (London, IPPR, 1994).

70 At times the references to alcohol, as above, are light-hearted and playful, hinting at the existence of a life beyond the hard work in the firm: 'We Often Go out Drinking', Wragge and Co., 2000. See further M. Adler 'From Symbolic Exchange to Commodity Consumption: Anthropological Notes on Drinking as a Symbolic Practice' in S. Barrows and R. Room (eds) *Drinking Behaviour and Belief in Modern History* (Berkley, University of California Press) at pp. 376–389 Alcohol is, nonetheless, widely recognized as a key feature in the lifestyle of the City lawyer, a depiction in keeping with the research suggesting that mainstream night-life culture is itself 'awash on a sea of alcohol': D. Hobbs, S. Lister, P. Hadfield and S. Hall, 'Receiving Shadows: Governance, Liminality in the Night-Time Economy' (2000) 53 (1) *British Journal of Sociology* pp. 89–105, cited in P. Chatterton and R. Hollands, 'Theorising Urban Playscapes: Producing, Regulating and Consuming Youthful Nightlife City Spaces' (2002) 39 (1) *Urban Studies* pp. 95–116 at p. 102 How such images might be read by trainees whose backgrounds mean alcohol will not be a part of 'firm life' (for example, because of religious or other beliefs) is, of course, a different question.

71 See the work cited n 55, above.

72 P. Chatterton and R. Hollands, op. cit. n 70, p. 96. This argument is explored in more depth in P. Chatterton and R. Hollands, *Urban Nightscapes: Youth Cultures, Pleasure Spaces and Corporate Power* (London, Routledge, 2003). See also P. Willis, *Common Culture* (Milton Keynes, Open University Press, 1996): P. Williams, P. Hubbard, D. Clark and N. Berkley, 'Consumption, Exclusion and Emotion: The Social Geographies of Shopping' (2001) 2 (2) *Social and Cultural Geography* pp. 202–220: D. Slater, *Consumer Culture* (Oxford, Polity Press, 1997): R. Bocock, *Consumption* (London, Routledge, 1993): K. Roberts 'Same

activities, different meanings: British Youth Cultures in the 1990s' (1997) 16 *Leisure Studies* pp. 1–15: K. Roberts and G. Parsell 'Youth Cultures in Britain: The Middle Class Takeover' 13 *Leisure Studies* pp. 33–48. R. Hollands, *Friday Night, Saturday Night: Youth Identification in the Post-Industrial City* (Newcastle, University of Newcastle Upon Tyne Department of Sociology, 1995): T. Edwards, *Contradictions of Consumption: Concepts, Practices and Politics in Consumer Society* (Buckingham, Open University Press, 2000): B. Fine, 'From Political Economy to Consumption' in D. Miller (ed.) *Acknowledging Consumption* (London, Routledge, 1995): C. Campbell, 'The Sociology of Consumption' in D. Miller, Ibid.

73 Ibid. Also P. Chatterton, 'Governing Nightlife: Profit, Fun and (Dis)Order in the Contemporary City' 1 (2) *Entertainment Law* pp. 23–49.

74 P. Chatterton and R. Hollands, op. cit. n 70, p. 96: also D. Wynne and J. O'Connor, 'Consumption and the Postmodern City' (1998) 35 (5–6) *Urban Studies* pp. 841–864. The literature on contemporary youth lifestyles and cultures more generally is voluminous. See, by way of illustration: S. Miles, *Youth Lifestyles in a Changing World* (Buckingham, Open University Press, 2000): S. Redhead, *Subculture to Clubcultures* (Oxford, Blackwell, 1997): S. Redhead (ed.) *Rave Off: Politics and Deviance in Contemporary Youth Culture* (Aldershot, Avebury, 1993): S. Redhead, D. Wynne and J. O'Connor (eds) *The Clubcultures Reader* (London, Blackwell, 1998): S. Thornton, *Club-Cultures – Music, Media and Subcultural Capital* (Cambridge, Polity Press, 1995): A. Bennett, *Popular Music and Youth Culture: Music, Identity and Place* (Basingstoke, Macmillan, 2000).

75 P. Chatterton and R. Hollands, op. cit. n 70, pp. 108–109 my emphasis: also D. Slater, op. cit. n 72 R. Bocock, op. cit. n 72.

76 The reference to *All Bar One*, above, n 64, is itself significant in this regard: see P. Chatterton and R. Hollands, 2003, op. cit. n 72, pp. 122, 156–157. This is not simply a 'mainstream' bar par excellence, owned by the same company as the student-oriented *It's a Scream* chain; it is also marketed specifically (if not exclusively) at a young professional market and with a particular focus on attracting women: see further J.C. Everett and I.R. Bowler 'Bittersweet Conversions: Changing Times for the British Pub' 30 (2) *Journal of Popular Culture* pp. 101–122.

77 *Lex*, Spring Term, 2002 pp. 42–43: see D. Wynne, 'Leisure, Lifestyle and the Construction of Social Position' (1990) 9 *Leisure Studies* pp. 21–34.

78 *Lex*, Ibid., exemplifying themes in R. Shields (ed.) *Lifestyle Shopping: The Subject of Consumption* (London, Routledge, 1992).

79 Ibid.

80 S. Miles, op. cit. n 72: F. Stewart, 'The adolescent as consumer' in J. Coleman and C. Warren (eds) *Youth Policy in the 1990s: The Way Forward* (London, Routledge, 1992). Also, by way of introduction: G. Valentine, T. Skelton and D. Chambers, *Cool Places: An Introduction to Youth and Youth Cultures* (London, Routledge, 1998). 'Going out/drinking' has been identified as the third most important spending priority amongst 16–24-year-olds in the UK: Mintel, *Nightclubs and Discotheques* (London, Leisure Intelligence September, Mintel, 1998): Mintel, *Pre-Family Leisure Trends* (London, Leisure Intelligence January, 2000): Note, e.g. 'Thrill-seeking men lost out to women in degree results' *Sunday Times* 16 November 2003: J. Parkinson 'Students 'focus on social lives' *BBC News* 13 November 2003.

81 P. Bordieu, *Distinction: A Social Critique of the Judgement of Taste* (London, Routledge and Kegan Paul, 1984): 'Like every sort of taste [distinction] unites and separates. Being the product of the conditioning associated with a particular

class of conditions of existence, it unites all those who are the product of similar conditions while distinguishing them from all others. And it distinguishes in an essential way, since taste is the basis of all that one has – people and things – and all that one is for others, whereby one classifies oneself and is classified by others': Ibid., p. 56. See also B. Longhurst and M. Savage, 'Social Class, Consumption and the Influence of Bordieu: Some Critical Issues' in S. Edgell, K. Hetherington and A. Warde (eds) *Consumption Matters: The Production and Experience of Consumption* (Oxford, Blackwell, 1996).

82 P. Chatterton and R. Hollands, op. cit. n 70, at p. 95.

83 E.g., D. Harvey, *The Urban Experience* (Oxford, Basil Blackwell, 1989): D. Karp, G. Stone and W. Yoels, *Being Urban: A Sociology of City Life* (London, Greenwood Press, 1991): D. Ley, *The New Middle-Class and the Remaking of the Central City* (New York, Oxford University Press, 1996): M. Featherstone and S. Lash (eds) *Spaces of Culture: City-Nation-World* (London, Sage, 1999): D. Clarke, 'Consumption and the City, Modern and Postmodern' (1997) 21 (2) *International Journal of Urban and Regional Research* pp. 18–37.

84 P. Chatterton and R. Hollands, op. cit. n 70, p. 97 my emphasis.

85 A. Scott, *The Cultural Economy of Cities* (London, Sage, 2000).

86 P. Chatterton and R. Hollands, op. cit. n 70, p. 97. See further work cited n 83. Also: B. Jessop, 'The Entrepreneurial City: Reimagining Localities, Redesigning Economic Governance or Restructuring Capital' in N. Jewson and S. McGregor (eds) *Transforming Cities* (London, Routledge, 1997): N. Blomley, The Properties of Space: History, Geography and Gentrification (1997) 18 (4) *Urban Geographer* pp. 286–295: S. Zukin, 'Socio-Spatial Prototypes of a new organization of consumption: the role of real cultural capital' (1990) 24 *Sociology* pp. 37–56: P. Hall, 'Creative Cities and Economic Development' 37 (4) *Urban Studies* pp. 639–649: S. Zukin, *The Cultures of Cities* (Oxford, Blackwell, 1995): S. Zukin, 'Postmodern Urban Landscapes: Mapping Culture and Power' in S. Lash and J. Friedman (eds) *Modernity and Identity* (Oxford, Blackwell, 1992): J. Hannigan, *Fantasy City: Pleasure and Profit in the Postmodern Metropolis* (London, Routledge, 1998).

87 Enmeshed with the appeal to developing this up-market identity, the selling of the corporate lifestyle has been marked, in particular, by a culture of the 'groomed' body and an interest in 'body culture' which reflects what sociological work suggests to be a heightened reflexivity about the self within the social conditions of late-modernity: A. Giddens, op. cit. n 20: M. Featherstone, *Consumer Culture and Postmodernism* (London, Sage, 1991). This is not to argue that the lifestyle depicted here is in any sense necessarily 'healthy', notwithstanding the provision of facilities aimed at body maintenance (n 59, above). It is to suggest, however, that the body and self-presentation within this employment context demands *maintenance*, not simply in the face of disease and the deterioration accompanying the ageing process, but also in such a way as to accord with the cultural norms around what is to constitute 'acceptable' appearance. The practices of grooming, dressing and the activity of shopping are, more generally, widely seen as important practices through which the attributes and characteristics of images are accorded such meaning. See the work cited at n 55, above. On the transformation of the male body in this context see S. Nixon *Hard Looks: Masculinities, Spectatorship and Contemporary Consumption* (London, UCL Press, 1996) at p. 11. See also F. Mort *Cultures of Consumption* (London, Routledge, 1996). Also S. Bordo *The Male Body: A New Look at Men in Public and in Private* (New York, Farrar, Straus and Giroux, 1994). As such, a concern with the management of impressions and the presentation of a groomed (acceptable) body appear as pivotal concerns.

'Becoming', presenting and experiencing oneself as a successful City solicitor involves a process of subjectivization in which these techniques of care, consumption and self-policing are central.

88 Compare A.T. Kronman, *The Lost Lawyer: Failing Ideals of the Legal Profession* (Cambridge, MA, Belknap, 1993). Although the idea of public service does appear in the occasional references to *pro bono* work and, to a lesser degree, via reference to desirable activities to be undertaken via the 'gap year': '[The work camp] shows Kay is willing to roll up her sleeves and get stuck in' (Graham Stoddart, Graduate Recruitment Officer, Macfarlanes, quoted in *Target* 7th edn 2003 p. 12: P. Hall, 'Creative Cities and Economic Development' 37 (4) *Urban Studies* pp. 639–649:.

89 P. Chatterton and R. Hollands, op. cit. n 70, p. 97.

90 P. Chatterton and R. Hollands, op. cit. n 70. See further M. Featherstone, op. cit. n 87: R. Imrie, H. Thomas and T. Marshall, 'Business Organisations, local dependence and the politics of urban renewal in Britain' 32 (1) *Urban Studies* pp. 31–47: S. Lash and J. Urry, *The End of Organised Capitalism* (Cambridge, Polity, 1987).

91 Herbert Smith, 2002. See further N. Wrigley and M. Lowe, *Retailing, Consumption and Capital: Towards the New Retail Geography* (Harlow, Longman, 1996). The representation of the 'Other' here is intriguingly associated with history, ethnicity, with what is 'trendy': a world of cheap curries and (in contrast to the City?) an ethnically diverse population. The text exemplifies the targeting of corporate leisure activities (e.g. commercially provided bars, gyms, pubs and so forth) at '. . . cash-rich groups such as professionals and high level service sector workers (the 'suits')': P. Chatterton and R. Hollands op. cit. n 70. p. 99. Of course, for many the use of such private provision (e.g. in the form of the use of private health clubs and gyms) will already be a well-established practice established during undergraduate studies.

92 The dominant representation of the urban within many of these texts continues to be that of the City of London, understandably given that London remains the base for the principal offices of many of these firms. Here, the historical landmarks of the square mile routinely combine with the architecture of the tower-block and skyscraper in such a way as to depict an appealing blend of tradition and modernity: E.g., Ince and Co., 2001. Increasingly over the past decade, however, other world centres of corporate activity now feature heavily, reflecting both the transnational nature of corporate legal work and the importance of the global market in which the firms operate.

93 D. Wynne and J. O'Connor, op. cit. n 74.

94 M. Featherstone, op. cit. n 87, p. 101. See also J. Hannigan, op. cit. n 86: J. Urry, *Consuming Places* (London, Routledge, 1995): S. Lash and J. Urry *Economies of Signs and Space* (London, Sage, 194): K. Hetherington, 'Identity Formation, Space and Social Centrality' (1996) 13 (4) *Theory, Culture and Society* pp. 33–52: K. Hetherington, *Expressions of Identity: Space, Performance, Politics* (London, Sage, 1998). The images of the city at night are often blurred in such a way as to depict the city 'on the go: note, e.g. the imaging of Hong Kong, Paris, London and Singapore: Herbert Smith, 2002. Also B. Clarke and M.G. Bradford 'Public and Private Consumption and the City' 35 (5–6) *Urban Studies* pp. 858–888.

95 The large regional firms explicitly seek to appeal to trainees who may wish to resist the allure of the City of London for (it is suggested) reasons of personal lifestyle, maintenance of family ties and friendship networks by highlighting the 'quality of life' agenda. The reasons for joining regional firms are, nonetheless, explicitly linked to the possibilities for having 'fun': 'Newcastle has some-

thing of a reputation for enjoying itself. We should know. But the nightlife isn't all you'll enjoy at Dickinson Dees' (Dickinson Dees, 2001). Also Watson Burton, 2003. For a rather different view of the re-imaging of the city of Newcastle Upon Tyne as 'cultural city' c.f. R. Hollands, 'From shipyards to nightclubs: restructuring young adults' employment, household and consumption identities in the north-east of England' (1997) 41 *Berkley Journal of Sociology* pp. 41–66: P. Chatterton and R. Hollands, *Changing Our Toon: Youth, Nightlife and Urban Change* in Newcastle (Newcastle, University of Newcastle, 2001): R. Hollands and P. Chatterton 'Changing Times for an old industrial city: hard times, hedonism and corporate power in Newcastle nightlife' 6 (3) *City* pp. 291–315. Note 'Bar Fly': http://www.tsg.org.uk/localBarfly.asp. Common to the representation of UK cities such as Leeds, Sheffield, Manchester, Birmingham and Newcastle, the cultural characteristics of an urban centre – as, let us say, lively, exciting, friendly – are drawn on so as to present the firm itself as similarly small but manageable: 'Birmingham has a bit of a bad reputation, Spaghetti junction and all ... so what is it really like for the ... employees who live and work there? ... People who have been away for a few years are quite shocked at all the new bars, pubs and clubs that have sprung up' Wragge and Co., 2003. C.f. 'Second to None' *The Trainee* Issue 14 2003 pp. 20–21. Compare I. Taylor, K. Evans and P. Fraser, *A Tale of Two Cities: Global Change, Local feeling and Everyday Life in the North of England: A Study in Manchester and Sheffield* (London, Routledge, 1996).

96 From memory, the exact words said to me by Peter. This may be indicative of what might be termed a lack of respect between student and lecturer. The comment is, however, given the material aspirations of the individual, a not inaccurate statement.

97 M. Savage, P. Dickens and T. Fielding, *Property, Bureaucracy and Culture: Middle Class Formation in Contemporary Britain* (London, Routledge, 1992). See also M. Savage and T. Butler (eds) *Social Change and the Middle Classes* (London, UCL Press, 1995): R. Crompton, 'Consumption and class analysis' in S. Edgell, K. Hetherington and A. Warde (eds) *Consumption Matters: The Production and Experience of Consumption* (Oxford, Blackwell, 1996): T. Butler, *Gentrification and the Middle-Classes* (Aldershot, Ashgate, 1997).

98 D. Chaney, op. cit. n 53, p. 38, my emphasis.

99 That is, over the post-war period university academics can be seen as – notwithstanding the processes of marketization, outlined above – the embodiment of an 'ascetic non-commercial middle class': see, generally, A.H. Halsey and M.A. Trow, *The British Academics* (London, Faber and Faber, 1971). This can be seen, for example, in various aspects of the 'University Novel': e.g. Amis's *Lucky Jim* (1954), *Snow's* The Masters (1951), Bradbury's *The History Man* (1975), and *Lodge's* three novels *Small World* (1985), *Changing Places* (1978) and *Nice Work* (1989). If the latter work, in particular, sought to address aspects of the processes marketization then underway, compare, a decade on, A. Oakley's *Overheads* (2000). See, generally, M. Proctor and W. Metzger, *The English University Novel* (Ayer, Ca, University of California Press, 1977).

100 M. Savage *et al.*, op. cit. n 97, p. 127.

101 'Countdown to more opportunities ... Number 10: Sexy Deals', Cadwalder, 2001: S.J. Berwin, *Plum 5th edn* front page.

102 N 64, above.

103 For a historical analysis of which see P. Goodall, *High Culture, Popular Culture: The Long Debate*, St Leonards, Allen and Unwin, 1995).

104 I. Welsh 'Merchandising Men or Marketing Masculinity?' (1994) Paper pre-

sented to the BSA Annual Conference *Sexualities in Social Context*, Preston, 28–31 March 1994 (Copy of paper with author).

105 A theme particularly marked in the general legal press but also evident in the materials produced by the corporate law firms: Also 'Lisa was really glad she hadn't worn a skirt that day' *Lex* Issue 15 Spring term 2003, p. 1. 'Glittering Prizes' *Lex* Issue 12 Spring term 2002, front cover.

106 M. Savage *et al.*, n 97, p. 214. See also S. Munt (ed.) *Cultural Studies and the Working Class* (London, Cassells, 2000): 'While we certainly work hard, we play hard too . . .': Freshfields, Bruckhaus Deringer, 2003. Thrift has observed how the purchase of a substantial country house in the southern half of England became during the 1980s (and has continued to the present day to be) a 'reasonably common element' of a postmodern lifestyle practices by private sector young(ish) professionals in the later 1980s: N. Thrift, 'Images of Social Change' in C.V. Hamnett, L. McDowell and P. Sarre (eds) *The Changing Social Structure* (London, Sage, 1989).

107 This is not to argue, however, that insecurity is not endemic in this sector, particularly at times of economic downturn. It is to claim that, within the discursive context outlined above, the kind of distinctive positioning outlined in this paper is occurring.

108 This is not, of course, to deny the presence of some, or indeed, many wealthy and financially secure individuals within the legal academy; individuals for example, who may have entered universities at an earlier moment (and, say, invested in property accordingly); or, perhaps, individuals who have inherited, or will inherit, considerable sums of money and/or property and for whom, ultimately, relatively low academic salaries may be offset by the presence or promise of other income. It *is* to argue that, compared to many public and private sector employees, there are many academics, especially at early career level, who face real and pressing financial difficulties: n 126, below. For an alternative argument see A. Bradney, op. cit. n 6.

109 There is an argument to be made, indeed, that it does not 'pay' to be 'too bright', if such intelligence were to signal an 'otherworldliness' associated with a disinterest in or disinclination towards commerce and 'making money': c.f. 'Make Money Not Love' – T-shirts worn by trainee solicitors at S.J. Berwin (*Plum* 4th Edition, S.J. Berwin, 2002).

110 See, for example, the argument of A. Bradney, op. cit. n 6, above.

111 'Successful' is, of course a problematic term. See further R. Pahl *After Success* (Oxford. Blackwell, 1995). Compare I. Craib, *The Importance of Disappointment* (London, Routledge, 1994). A rather different issue is the psychological ramifications of achieving success with in a particular field of employment: see further R. Pahl, Ibid. ch 4 'Styles of Success in Business' pp. 56–77: Also M.E.P. Seligman, P.R. Verkuil and T.H. Kang, 'Why Lawyers Are Unhappy' (2002) 23 (1) *Cardozo Law Review* pp. 33–53: P.J. Schiltz, 'On Being a Happy, Healthy and Ethical Member of an Unhappy, Unhealthy and Unethical Profession' (1999) 52 *Vand Law Review* at p. 871.

112 C. Handy, *The Empty Raincoat*, 1994, quoted in R. Pahl, Ibid., p. 181.

113 On issues of retention generally, see R.G. Lee, op. cit. n 10.

114 Although there is some acceptance that this transition from the profession to law teaching can itself be gendered: E. Cruickshank 'Careers for Women in Law' in *Women and the Law* (London, Law Society, 2003).

115 P. Chatterton and R. Hollands, op. cit. n 70, p. 109. It is important to remember that the associated 'acceptable workplace performance' is itself gendered in a number of ways: L. McDowell, 'Body Work: Heterosexual Gender Performances in City Workplaces' in D. Bell and G. Valentine (eds) *Mapping*

Desire (London, Routledge, 1995).

116 P. Chatterton and R. Hollands, op. cit. n 70, p. 97, my emphasis.

117 A. Sherr and J. Webb, 'Law Students, the External Market and Socialization: Do we make them turn to the City?'(1989) 16 (2) *Journal of Law and Society* pp. 225–249.

118 P. Chatterton and R. Hollands, op. cit. n 70.

119 M. Keith and S. Pile, *Place and the Politics of Identity* (London, Routledge, 1993).

120 P. Chatterton and R. Hollands, op. cit. n 70, p. 109. See further A. Hollander, *Sex and Suits: The Evolution of Modern Dress* (New York, Alfred A. Knopf, 1994). Also F. Davies *Fashion, Culture and Identity* (Chicago, University of Chicago Press, 1992): 'With the new freedom of personal choice unfettered by strict social codes, the individual psyche can privately illustrate itself in some detail for its own satisfaction using the modern visual vocabulary of dress'. A. Hollander, Ibid., p. 187. The imaging described above meshes with the kinds of representations of 'success' and 'fun' to be found in many university law school student publications: e.g. *All Rise: The Legal Journal of Newcastle Law School* Spring 2003 (Newcastle, The Eldon Society, 2003). See also R. Collier, "Nutty professors', 'Men in Suits' and 'New Entrepreneurs': Corporeality, Subjectivity and Change in the Law School and Legal Practice' (1998) 7 (1) *Social and Legal Studies* pp. 27–53.

121 C.f. U. Beck and E. Beck-Gensheim, *Individualization: Institutionalized Individualism and its Social and Political Consequences* (London, Sage, 2002) esp ch 3 'Beyond Status and Class?' pp. 30–42.

122 P. Chatterton and R. Hollands, op. cit. n 70, p. 109.

123 As R.G. Lee, op. cit. n 10, makes all too clear. See, generally, R. Abel, 2003, op. cit. n 13. On wider changes relating to the profession see M. Cain, 'The Symbol Traders' in M. Cain and C. Harrington (eds) *Lawyers in a Postmodern World* (Milton Keynes: Open University Press, 1996): J. Hagan and F. Kay *Gender in Practice: A Study of Lawyers Lives* (New York, Oxford University Press., 1995): D. Sugarman 'Blurred Boundaries: The Overlapping Worlds of Law, Business and Politics' in M. Cain and C. Harrington, Ibid.

124 A recent survey of academics in the UK found that 25 per cent had suffered from a stress-related illness during the last twelve months, which was serious enough to warrant taking time off work. Fifty-three per cent of academics reported poor psychological health, including stress, sleeplessness and depression, while 44 per cent of university lecturers had seriously considered leaving higher education and 49 per cent had considered early retirement over the past few years: G. Kinman *Pressure Points: A survey into the causes and consequences of occupational stress in UK academic and related staff* (London: AUT, 1998). Kinman also found that, on average, more women academics than men reported that the pressure to publish had increased significantly (para 9.11.2); and that women, rather than men, reported the difficulty balancing family and workplace commitments as a source of stress (para 9.11.12). See also I. McNay *The impact of the 1992 RAE on Institutional and Individual Behaviour in English Higher Education: The Evidence from a research project* (1997). The AUT itself runs a 24-hour Stressline for members: Tel: (08705) 234533: c.f. M. Tytherleigh and C. Cooper, 'Lives on the Rocks' *Times Higher Education Supplement* 3 October 2003 p. 16.

125 In the climate outlined in this paper, and in a context in which a corporate need for learning and knowledge is in many respects driving reform of the higher education sector, it is notable that law is a discipline experiencing particular problems around the recruitment and retention of academic staff:

J. Hurstfield and F. Neathy *Recruitment and Retention of Staff in UK Higher Education 2001* (London, IRS Research, 2002) – 'Pay levels were cited by many as the main reason for . . . problems. Higher pay offered by the private sector was viewed as a key factor impacting upon institutions' ability to attract and retain . . . some groups of academic staff – *notably those in law, IT and engineering*' (p 10, my emphasis): 'The subjects that were particularly problematic were accountancy, law and economics' (p 57). See also *Recruitment and Retention in UK Higher Education*, London, CVCP Publications, 2000).

126 An issue which relates to questions of recruitment and retention, above. Many early career legal academics, for example, are not, at current salary levels in the UK, in a position to afford 'first rung' housing in a context of spiralling house prices which have forced many public sector workers out of the market. It is, we have seen, private sector professionals who are in many ways best placed to benefit from the cultural provision associated with the new urbanism. These issues may seem minor to the 'committed' academic for whom such lifestyle choices may be secondary: c.f. A. Bradney, op. cit. n 6. However, they would appear to be factors which do frame the future career choices of many graduates: on the 'coming crisis' of socio-legal research, e.g. S. Witherspoon, 'Research Capacity: A Crisis in Waiting?' *Socio-Legal Newsletter* No 37 Summer 2002 p. 1: R. Collier, op. cit. n 38: L. Bibbings, n 38.

127 A.H. Halsey *Decline of Donnish Dominion: The British Academic Professions in the Twentieth Century* (Oxford: Oxford University Press, 1995).

128 Compare B. Wilson, *The Youth Culture and the Universities* (London, Faber and Faber, 1970): 'The point of studying has largely ceased to be the end of becoming the cultivated, educated man (sic): it has become the acquisition of a good job (or the experience of a good time in the free environment of the university)': B. Wilson, 'Social Values and Education' in B. Wilson, 1970, Ibid.

129 See A. Adonis and S. Pollard, *A Class Act: The Myth of Britain's Classless Society* (London, Penguin, 1998) ch 3 'The Super-Class'.

130 On this culture of 'up or out' see R.G. Lee, op. cit. n 10.

4 The media and public understanding of the law

Lieve Gies

Introduction: the limitations of content analysis

Textual critique and other forms of content analysis represent the method that is most commonly used in research on law, media and popular culture. Such an approach has been successfully deployed to examine the way in which law is portrayed in the media and in popular culture more generally. It has undoubtedly assisted legal scholars in developing a better understanding of the differences and similarities between the narrative conventions operated by law, on the one hand, and those of the media and popular culture, on the other. The study of media texts has also made it possible to shed light on law's ability to act as an enduring source of fascination and inspiration in popular culture.[1]

In spite of its obvious attractions, the study of media-as-text has some important shortcomings. These become particularly apparent when content analysis is used as a basis for making claims about the extent to which the media influence their audiences. As similar debates in criminology and media studies have highlighted, it is notoriously difficult to establish the effect which film, television and other media have on audiences' thoughts and behaviour.[2] However, there appears to be a consensus that the meaning which people generate when reading or 'decoding' a movie or a newspaper cannot be simply 'read off' the texts which they consume.[3] The issue of media effects, although generally considered to be very elusive, has been approached using a variety of statistical, qualitative and experiment-based methods, all of which centre on audiences, or segments of media audiences, rather than exclusively focusing on media content. Audience research in the study of law and popular culture is comparatively rare,[4] but there is nevertheless intense speculation about the power of the media to shape people's understanding of the law. Central to such speculation is the idea that, generally speaking, people have very little first-hand legal experience, making them instead almost entirely dependent on unreliable mass media, which are in the habit of routinely misrepresenting and distorting the law. This in turn raises the spectre of such inaccuracies making people unduly pessimistic about the effectiveness of the law to tackle major social problems or, by contrast, inflating public expectations as to the type of redress law can offer.[5]

These concerns raise important issues, revealing the anxiety which popular culture is able to generate inside academia.[6] The issue of distortion hints at a positivist perspective and begs the question of where we can find an undistorted version of law, considering that law predominantly exists in some discursive form, be it in the shape of legal codes, textbooks, legislation or judgements, and that legal truth is therefore invariably a matter of representation and interpretation.[7] The accusation of distortion also suggests that there is considerable unease about the media becoming a major source of legal socialization which is capable of eroding law's authority. The theme of 'trial by the media', i.e. the idea that the media are increasingly encroaching upon the exclusive domain of the law and undermine basic legal safeguards, represents a familiar undercurrent in the study of law and the media.[8] Margaret Thornton concurs:[9]

> Popular culture, as the embodiment of non-rationality – emotion, corporeality, tactility, aestheticism and the spectacular – is corrosive of the authority of law. (. . .) Fear of the effect of popular culture on law today would seem to be analogous to Plato's fear of the corrupting effect of profane poetry on philosophy in Classical Athens.

However, the effect of popular culture on the authority of law is not the immediate concern of this chapter: instead, my focus will predominantly be on the idea that people lack first-hand experience of law, making them almost entirely dependent on the media for their legal knowledge.[10] My main aim is to explore and elucidate a methodological framework which would make it possible to form a better understanding of the extent to which the media are important in providing people with 'surrogate' or vicarious legal experience. Textual analysis alone is insufficient to achieve this: the focus has to be wide enough to include some form of audience research. Moreover, the suggestion that people when going about their everyday business have little direct legal experience ultimately requires a perspective that is not exclusively media-focused but concerns itself more generally with the presence of law in everyday life. In what follows, I first draw a brief historical sketch of audience research, charting its evolution from a behaviourist perspective to an ethnographic approach. While behaviourism regards media audiences as impressionable and passive, ethnographic analyses construct the audience as actively engaged in the production of meaning, highlighting the diversity of resources and experiences which people bring to bear upon media texts.

Second, I discuss the significance of socio-legal research that has provided some useful insights into the crucial relationship between law and everyday life. Looking at the role of the media in determining people's familiarity with law from this particular angle has the advantage of highlighting law's ubiquitous presence in everyday life, an omnipresence which cannot always be exclusively attributed to the influence of the media. In the final section of this chapter, I combine ideas from audience research and socio-legal research on everyday legal experience to consider the specific role of the media in accounting for people's familiarity with the law. Law's ability to disrupt everyday life and the resonance of media portrayals with first-hand legal experience will be highlighted as potentially important factors which determine the role that the media are able to play in shaping people's understanding of the law.

Establishing the media's influence: the view from media studies and socio-legal analysis

Three perspectives on audience research

In assessing the place of the media in people's understanding of law, it is useful to distinguish between three possible approaches which may be taken when explaining how audiences relate to media texts. These approaches are underpinned by different research traditions in media studies, each of which is characterized by specific assumptions and distinct methodologies.

From a historical perspective, the tap on the knee or behaviourist approach to media effects is the oldest tradition which has shaped the idea – prevalent at times not only in media studies but also in other disciplines, for example in criminology – that the media are able to exert an influence on their audiences which these find somehow both irresistible and inescapable. The notion of choice or free will, that is the possibility that audiences have some discretion as to the role which media products play in structuring their worldviews and thoughts, does not enter the equation in classic media effects research. As Stuart Hall[11] puts it: 'Though we know the television programme is not a behavioural input, like a tap on the kneecap, it seems to have been almost impossible for traditional researchers to conceptualize the communicative process without lapsing into one or other variant of low-flying behaviourism'.

This preference for the 'stimulus/response' or 'hypodermic syringe' model in explaining the relationship between media products and audiences can be attributed to early media research at the beginning of the 20th century which was predominantly rooted in psychology and social psychology, disciplines which preferred to focus on determinants of individual behaviour through the prism of methodogies derived from the natural sciences.[12] Moreover, the political climate of that age also provided support for a strong media effects hypothesis. The period between the First and the Second World War was the age of propaganda in which governments discovered the media's potential as a weapon of persuasion which could be used to manipulate public opinion. The Frankfurt School, for example, which was influential in European and North American media research, explained the descent of German society into fascism through the influence of the media functioning as a potent agent of mass propaganda. In unravelling the media's extraordinary powers, much emphasis was placed upon the atomization of industrial societies which meant that their fabric had disintegrated to such an extent that the individual's only meaningful social relationship was with the mass media, thus eliminating intermediary levels of interaction which would otherwise be provided by interpersonal relations.[13]

Although the hypodermic syringe model was challenged and refined after the Second World War, it was not until the late 1970s that audience research witnessed the kind of methodological and epistemological shift that was necessary to dethrone behaviourism and to break the spell which the question of media effects had had on generations of researchers.[14] Even today, the tap on the knee metaphor is unmistakably present in contemporary efforts to locate and explain the importance of the media.[15]

Research into law and popular culture is by no means an exception. Despite there being an extensive body of research that examines the relationship between crime and the media, little is known about the way in which we use the media in making sense of issues of law and justice in general. Instead, it is often taken for granted that the media must play an extremely important role in shaping people's understanding of the law.[16] As is the case with behaviourist media research, socio-legal analysis tends to ignore the distinction between the content of a media text and audiences' reading of that text.[17] Audiences' responses are all too often inferred from the text, creating the impression that the media indeed act as a hypodermic syringe injecting people with distorted representations of the law. When Sherwin, determined to establish the (negative) impact which popular culture has on lawyers' conduct in the courtroom, asks the question 'What stories, what recurring images and metaphors, what stock scripts and popular stereotypes help us through the day? And where do they come from?', he does not hesitate: 'For most people, the source is not difficult to ascertain. It is the visual mass media: film, video, television, and to an increasing degree computerized images (...). In a sense, we "see" reality the way we have been trained to watch film and TV'.[18]

The hypodermic syringe is clearly implied here: the media train us in seeing things in a specific way and they have 'conditioned' us, eliminating other factors which may influence our perception mechanisms. There is an atomist dimension underpinning Sherwin's confident assertions which is similar to behaviourism: he argues that the effect of the media is pervasive suggesting that these have almost become the only possible source of human experience today, thereby ignoring other sources of influence in our lives, such as the vital interpersonal contact most of us have with friends or relatives in everyday conversations.

Another striking parallel between socio-legal analysis and behaviourist media research is the emphasis on negative influence. The media often stand accused of inculcating people with a flawed and distorted version of the law, making it difficult to envisage the possibility that the media may actually make a positive contribution to people's understanding of the law, for example by acting as a source of legal knowledge, by stimulating public debate on issues of justice and by making specific struggles visible.[19] In short, the media's 'pro-social effects', are routinely ignored in socio-legal analysis.[20] The preoccupation is with negative effects, not with potential benefits which may be derived from media exposure.[21] Research which is specifically concerned with the mass media and perceptions of law, especially crime, has been struggling to detach itself from behaviourism.[22] Important debates, for example on pornography, continue to be premised upon the assumption of a decisive and predominantly negative influence of the media on behaviour and attitudes, despite the fact that some authors now believe that consuming pornography has no impact on sex crimes,[23] prompting Sparks[24] to remark that 'much of the work that exists on screen violence [is] very unconvincing'.[25]

In the light of this enduring preoccupation with negative media effects, one might be forgiven for thinking that the behaviourist model is still the undisputed and only possible way of conceptualizing the relationship between the media and their audiences. This, however, flies in the face of evidence suggesting that other areas of audience research have evolved enormously since the early days of studies of media effects. The work of the Centre for Contemporary Cultural Studies at Birmingham University (UK) in the late 1970s and early 1980s – representing the second approach to audience research I wish to discuss here – provided the breakthrough which proved to be decisive in transforming audience analysis. The question to be asked was no longer 'what do the media do to people?', but 'what do people do with the media?'. As Curran points out, this change in emphasis was in itself not new: as early as the 1930s more 'liberal' voices in media research emphasized the idea that 'audiences [were] not empty vessels waiting to be filled'.[26] Moreover, the notion of the active audience can be traced back to a much earlier tradition, which is known as 'uses and gratifications' because of its focus on the uses which audiences make of the media for the purpose of 'gratifying' or fulfilling specific needs, for example, the need for information, companionship and entertainment.[27]

However, whereas the uses and gratification tradition from the late 1950s onwards was unable to sever its link with psychology and lab experiments, the Birmingham School can be credited for promoting a radically different methodology which disposed of the idea that media audiences could be treated as lab specimens to be isolated from their everyday social context.[28] It became clear that an experimental setting was inadequate in exploring the relationship between the media and their audiences because it overlooked the vital link with everyday life. The living room, not the psychologist's lab, became the focus of attention as a result of the intervention by the Birmingham School. Audiences' relationship with television, a medium heavily embedded in domesticity, could not be studied in isolation: domestic rituals, family relations and even the interior design of people's living room were treated as relevant factors in explaining audiences' interpretation and

use of television.[29] The preferred methodology for uncovering the importance of the domestic in media use was ethnography. 'Clinical empiricism'
was out, field research became the preferred method.[30]

From a conceptual point of view, the change in focus from effects to
meaning, or from behaviourism to semiotics, was as important as the change
in setting from laboratorium to the living room. This paradigmatic shift is
largely attributed to Stuart Hall's[31] model of encoding and decoding, signalling a new dawn in qualitative audience research, which has become
known as 'reception analysis'. What was at issue was more than just the
question of whether media audiences either passively or actively engaged
with media texts. The emphasis in Hall's paper was on the possibility of
audience resistance in the process of making sense of the media. The audience was not only active, it was also potentially involved in a subversive
pattern of unseating the hegemonic subtext of media products.

Hall's model is very simple, but as Alasuutari observes, it is this very
simplicity which makes it one of the key references in contemporary reception analysis.[32] The basis of this model is that encoding (the way in which
media professionals shape a text) and decoding (the way in which encoded
messages are subsequently interpreted and understood by audiences) are seen
as two separate moments in the production of meaning which do not
necessarily coincide. A media text on its own is a half-finished semiotic
product which reveals little about the way in which audiences actually interpret it. In Hall's model, audiences might partly ignore the meanings
embedded in encoded texts by producing an 'oppositional' reading, which
means that the ideological underpinnings of a text are read 'against the
grain'. Although the model also includes the possibility of a dominant-
hegemonic reading in which the decoder faithfully reproduces the encoded
message, its significance lies in the fact that it envisages a scenario in which
media influence is not inescapable, but actively resisted by the audience.
This has inspired an entire generation of researchers in media and cultural
studies to examine the significance of class,[33] gender[34] and ethnicity[35] – to
name just a few factors – in subverting dominant meanings embedded in
media texts.

The emphasis on the active audience in reception analysis renders it
hugely problematic to judge the reactions of an audience by the media texts
it consumes. To cite an example used by Hall,[36] the media generate images
of violence but these images are not violent in themselves.[37] They are
representations to be decoded by audiences whose interventions are crucial
in making these images meaningful. The pessimism underpinning traditional research into media effects thus disappeared: a particular media text,
when looked at in isolation, may not be the most refined cultural artefact,
but thanks to the creativity of its readers, it may acquire a level of sophisti-
cation one could not envisage on the basis of the text alone. The liberating
potential of reception analysis was most strongly felt in relation to media
texts which are typically consumed by women, for example, soaps, women's

magazines and romance novels.[38–40] The traditional feminist stance was strongly reminiscent of classic research into media effects: early feminist analyses portrayed women as victims of patriarchal media whose inescapable influence served to reinforce gender stereotypes and to reconcile women with their subordination.[41] However, in the 1980s, there was a remarkable turning point: the stigma attached to women's media, it seemed, had been lifted thanks to the new insights into audience research offered by reception analysis. Even feminist academics confessed to liking soaps and women's magazines.[42] Pleasure was an amorphous but widely used term in describing women's experiences of media texts, emphasizing the non-judgemental philosophy underpinning reception analysis. Women's media were not something to be despised or dismissed. Reading *Cosmopolitan* or watching *Eastenders* was taken seriously by a new wave of feminist researchers who sought to identify ways in which female audiences subverted the patriarchal subtext of media products.[43]

However, the celebratory and optimistic undertone of reception analysis became a target for fierce criticism in the 1990s.[44] The politics of some strands of reception analysis was openly questioned. Some detected an anti-public service media agenda: the traditional justification for public service television is its mission to deliver high quality programmes. Placing too much emphasis on audience resistance could pull the rug from under the feet of those in favour of a quality conscious public-service media landscape. Hence, it was argued that reception analysis played an ideological role in justifying the neo-liberal project of deregulation and commercialization of the media because, after all, audiences would concoct their own meanings and interpretations irrespective of the intrinsic qualities of the original media products beamed into their living rooms.[45] What argument, for example, would be left to challenge the corporate dominance of a few media giants and press magnates, if it is the prevailing belief that the decision on the value and meaning of cultural products ultimately lies with the audience? To be criticized for supporting a populist version of neo-liberalism is undoubtedly an ironic fate for a research tradition firmly rooted in the kind of neo-Marxist analysis which clearly underpinned Hall's seminal encoding/decoding model.

However, the criticism of reception studies goes much wider than an interrogation of its political credentials. From a conceptual viewpoint, the main limitation of the encoding/decoding model is that it is still very much media-centred, in the sense that a strong emphasis is placed upon the way in which the media structure people's understanding of reality. Audiences respond to media texts, either to resist or to accommodate their dominant meanings, but the encoding/decoding model tells us little about the way in which people's constructions of reality encompass a wider catalogue of experiences in which the media are sometimes of little or no importance. Reception analysis, like research into media effects, is fairly narrowly focused on the interrelations between media and audiences, despite its incorporation of everyday life as a central category in explaining this relationship. What is less obvious from such a media-centred analysis is that people, in making sense of the world, rely on a potentially unlimited range of experiences and narratives, only a limited proportion of which may be located in the media. The potential blind spot in reception analysis is that it may still end up giving the media too much preponderance and ignore other influential sources of knowledge.

In correcting this media bias, it is worth considering a third perspective on the role which the media play in audiences' lives. The emergence of a constructionist model in studies of media use and public opinion offers the possibility of placing the media in a much broader framework by exploring their place in a wide range of everyday experiences.[46] In this approach, media discourse is treated as one of many cultural resources on which people draw when constructing meaning. The underlying concept is that when people engage with the media, they bring to the equation a certain amount of cultural, social and psychological baggage which exists independently of any media influence. Motivation, for example, is a crucial, yet often ignored factor which determines whether or not individuals are willing to consider specific media texts. As Schrøder points out: 'If people are not somehow motivated to read a media text they encounter, the reception process is arrested right there'.[47] The consumption of media products is therefore not an unquestionable given: there are many different factors which determine whether or not individuals indeed select a media text and what they eventually make of their selection. The starting point of constructionist audience research is not a specific media text or media genre; instead the focus is on interpretive communities which act as a mixed and varied pool of knowledge, values and ideas.[48] In constructionist analyses of media culture, it is the socio-cultural background of people, and not the media products they consume, which is seen as a more reliable predictor of how individuals construct social meaning.

It is perhaps unsurprising that such insights are most likely to come to the fore in research in which the media are not a primary concern. Thus, for example, Gamson and Modigliani's first and most important question was to establish how people understand the issue of nuclear energy, a process in which media discourse is only one of several ingredients to make up the 'cultural toolkits' of individuals.[49] Hence, they argue that 'however dependent the audience may be on media discourse, they actively use it to construct meaning and are not a passive object on which the media work their magic'. In a larger study of the way in which people make sense of politics, Gamson treats the media as one of several 'frames' which are used to construct political meaning.[50] His conclusion is that even in relation to issues for which the media seem to be the only available frame of reference (e.g. environmental issues in relation to which there is likely to be a lack of first-hand experience), people will still draw on other resources to supplement media discourse.[51] Gamson emphasizes that this does not rule out the possibility that the media may have powerful effects: it only serves to highlight that media influence is dependent on other socio-cultural factors.

The constructionist approach, unlike classic effects research and reception studies, is a clear invitation to understand the media as one of many frames which people use to make sense of the world. Such an approach has clear potential when it comes to studying the way in which people make sense of the law. Constructionism could provide an antidote for blunt and generalizing statements about media influence. Can we indeed assume that 'for much of what we think we know, it is a good bet that it comes in the form of popular culture'?[52] Can we maintain that '[m]any people learn about law from exposure to television and other media of popular culture, not from direct experience in the legal system'?[53] It seems more plausible that the media interact with notions of law which are subtly woven into the fabric of everyday life, in the form of minute and almost invisible encounters: paying bills on time, driving on the right side of the street, observing rules and regulations when using public amenities, refraining from undesirable behaviour when in the company of other people, and so on.

In relation to discussions of media and crime, the constructionist perspective has already proved fruitful. For example, Sasson situates the media among a wider pool of resources (both cultural and experiential) which people use when asked to discuss crime-related problems.[54] Hence, he argues: 'Attributing popular constructions of crime to media influence exclusively is particularly problematic'.[55] He does not dispute the relevance of media-oriented frames to have come to the fore in his discussions with research participants: he merely draws attention to the fact that the media alone are insufficient for understanding how people construct crime as a social problem. People consciously weave direct experience and cultural images of crime together in such a way that they are able to generate a persuasive account of their take on crime. This means that we must be prepared to accept that individuals are sufficiently 'media-savvy' to be aware that newspapers and television cannot always be regarded as the most reliable or authoritative sources of knowledge. People are capable of detecting the media's deceptions and distortions which means that they are not prepared to put all their eggs in the media's basket.[56] In keeping themselves informed of the world around them they also rely on other sources, including direct or personal experience.

There seems little reason to assume that the same observation would not also apply to media images of law: why would a lay audience not be discerning enough to realize that the average courtroom drama or detective series is not entirely representative of the actual operations of a court or a police station? Karpin in a particularly incisive analysis of the way in which the Australian judiciary 'reads' popular culture comments on the tendency of judges to portray themselves as discerning consumers of the media while treating the general public as 'glassy eyed dupes'.[57] A similar observation comes from Buckingham who argues that 'discourses about media effects carry a considerable social charge: they provide a powerful means of defining oneself in relation to others, not least in terms of maturity and emotional "health" '.[58] Hence, we need to recognize that people prefer to see themselves as discerning consumers of the media, while often identifying others as victims of media manipulation and distortion. However, if we all tend to see ourselves as immune from bad media influence, this begs the question of who exactly are those glassy eyed dupes whom we believe fall so easily prey to the media's pernicious effects.

Adopting a constructionist approach allows for a foregrounding of media literacy and a redressing of the balance by locating the media in a wider set of social experiences: answering the question 'where do most people get their legal knowledge from?' is not as straightforward as saying: 'the media, of course'. Socio-legal analysis is not a stranger to such an approach. It has the natural advantage of not being media-centred, thus making it all the more surprising for relevant research not to have paid more attention to the potentially large repertoire of experience and knowledge which people activate in arriving at a specific interpretation of legal issues. As I argue in the next section, research on legal consciousness, which firmly situates law at the heart of everyday life, could provide a very useful connection between constructionist audience analysis and the question of where we should place the media in people's understanding of the law.

Law's ubiquitous presence in everyday life

The notion that law is constitutive, instead of external, to everyday life has in recent years emerged as a central theme in the law in everyday life movement. Sarat and Kearns identify two main orientations in studies of law and society.[59] The instrumental perspective typically regards law as a set of distinct norms which somehow are situated outside society and which can be deployed as an external instrument for introducing important societal changes. Much of the research in this tradition is concerned with studying how effective law is in shaping and regulating social life. By contrast, the constitutive perspective focuses not on how law influences society from outside, but on ways in which law is active in processes of meaning and self-understanding. Instead of looking at how law 'as an external, normative missile'[60] changes people's behaviour and attitudes, the constitutive approach is interested in how notions of legality form part of the way in which people see themselves and interpret the world around them. In the words of Ewick and Silbey, law 'has a commonplace materiality pervading the here and now of our social landscape'.[61]

The idea that the media can exert a strong influence on their audiences due to a lack of first-hand experience of law seems to fit into the instrumental perspective: here, law is seen as somehow apart from society, with the media playing an important role in generating a knowledge of aspects of law, and crime in particular, which are largely unknown in the sphere of everyday life. By contrast, the ethnographic tradition of law in everyday life, which clearly adopts a constitutive approach, regards law as something that is deeply embedded in people's consciousness. Consciousness, not knowledge, seems to be the crucial issue. Thus, Sarat, in his study of the legal consciousness of welfare recipients, does not aim to find out what the participants in his research know about welfare services and social laws. Instead, he is interested in what law means to them.[62] Similarly, ethnographic studies of small-claims courts and local courts aim to uncover an ideological struggle, focusing on the way in which litigants challenge the hegemony of one particular legal ideology by appealing to alternative systems of meanings and beliefs.[63] The theme of struggle and resistance runs as a central thread through these studies. Hegemony and resistance are seen as two sides of the same coin: on the one hand, people, in particular those at the margins of society, accept dominant ideas of law and justice, while on the other hand, they also constantly seem to challenge these ideas through some form of resistance.

The concept of legal consciousness is important for grasping this ambivalence of domination and resistance. According to Trubek:[64] 'Legal consciousness is that aspect of consciousness of any society which explains and helps justify its legal institutions', while Sarat sees legal consciousness as synonymous with ideology.[65] In the case of the welfare recipients he interviewed, this consists of a mixture of ideas confirming and contesting dominant legal principles. In spite of repeated disappointments when appealing to the welfare system, those seeking assistance somehow manage to remain hopeful that one day they will be successful in obtaining effective redress for their never-ending housing and debt problems. Legal consciousness is therefore much more than the reflection of individual experience. It is law's mythical and ideological qualities which keep individuals' hope alive. As Engel points out, 'There is an individual aspect to consciousness (. . .) but an individual's consciousness is shaped by the structures and relationships of which she or he is part',[66] something that is also reflected in Ewick's and Silbey's definition of legal consciousness as neither a set of conscious attitudes nor an entirely 'epiphenomenal' by-product of structural conditions.[67] Instead, they see it as a cultural practice in which individuals activate a set of cultural codes and schemas when making sense of the world around them. Legality, in its structural sense 'consists of cultural schemas and resources that operate to define and pattern social life',[68] but at the same time, it is dependent on individual action for its reproduction and application. These various codes of legality are not exclusively legal. Instead, they comprise a wide and diverse set of rules and principles which are not limited to law alone. Some of the examples which Ewick and Silbey cite include notions of competition and fair play which emanate from a variety of social contexts.

Law from a constitutive perspective is seen as ubiquitous in everyday life. The schemas reproduced in legal consciousness can be found everywhere, although law may also be hardly visible because it shares many of its interpretive codes with other areas of social activity. The question that is of particular interest here is: where do we situate the role of popular culture and the media in this 'commonplace' conception of law and legal consciousness? It seems obvious that the media play an active part in providing the interpretive schemes of legal consciousness, while also imposing limitations on the cultural resources that are made available to audiences, for example because of the way in which gatekeepers in the media control information flows.[69] The problem with studies of legal consciousness – and this in marked contrast with research traditions, which take the issue of media influence as their primary concern – is that the role of the media tends to be ignored, not because media input is seen as unimportant, but because it is treated as self-evident. It is striking that, for example, in the stories which Ewick and Silbey collected, the media seldom explicitly come to the fore.[70] In fact, this seems to be the case for the majority of studies of legal consciousness and law in everyday life. In a review article, Hirsch[71] has highlighted this failure to examine the role of popular culture in shaping legal consciousness, and the same void continues to exist, making it seem as if the importance of the media and popular culture is taken as a given which does not warrant further examination.

The challenge for the study of law and media culture is to generate a more critical awareness of the role which the media might (or might not) play in furnishing and sustaining various codes of legality without slipping into a media-deterministic account in which legal consciousness would be entirely explained through the media. As Vine argues, it is a truism to say that the media are influential.[72] The issue is not whether they are important, but the extent to which they are important and the manner in which their influence is felt. We seem to know relatively little about the relationship between the interpretive schemes routinely supplied and reproduced by the media, and other resources used by individuals to construct legal meaning. For example, how compatible are media and non-media sources of legal consciousness? In their research on violence, Schlesinger and his colleagues suggest that women who have themselves been victims of violence are able to criticize non-realistic media representations of violence by drawing a contrast with their own experiences.[73] Similarly, as I have already noted, Sasson's research indicates that experience-based knowledge and popular wisdom operate alongside media schemes in constructions of crime.[74] These studies suggest that there is sometimes a clear difference, even conflict, between the various resources with which people construct reality.

Another very important reason why we cannot just take for granted that the media and popular culture are important as indirect sources of legal consciousness is that in some cases they might be less significant than we think they are. There are a number of explanations as to why the media might not be prominent or, even, may be completely absent in individuals' accounts of legal meaning. As I argue below, in some situations, non-media schemes could outweigh the media as a resource of legal consciousness because of an influential form of personal experience of law, which might in turn be attributed to a specific social positioning on the class, race and gender axis. There might even be a methodological factor at work, in the sense that the role of the media only becomes visible when they are the focal point of research. If this were the case, it would indeed suggest that a media-centred focus tends to exaggerate the media's significance, another reason why it cannot be simply assumed that the media are necessarily an overriding source of legal meaning.

Social identity and the interplay between media and non-media related sources of legal consciousness

Two themes have emerged in my discussion so far. The first theme concerns the idea that audiences make active choices when interpreting media texts and draw on a large repertoire of resources when making sense of the world around them. The second theme is that, contrary to the view that the media can strongly influence people's legal knowledge and attitudes towards law because many are believed to lack relevant first-hand experience, it could be argued that law is ubiquitous in everyday life, partly, but not exclusively, thanks to the media. This makes the focus less media-centred. However, a drawback, as I have emphasized, is that the media tend to fade too much into the background, explaining why their interaction with legal consciousness has seldom been examined.

In examining the interplay between media-based and first-hand experiences of law, the interpretive community (or communities) to which someone belongs would appear to be a crucial factor. Social identity is likely to determine how much first-hand legal experience an individual has, which in turn could influence the extent to which media sources are able to shape a person's legal consciousness.[75] The question is: what kind of balance is there likely to be between media and personal experience? Which factors determine the media's relevance in resourcing the legal consciousness of individuals of different social and cultural backgrounds? Two elements that are potentially relevant in addressing these questions will be considered in this section: first, the extent to which law is experienced as a disruptive presence in everyday life and, second, the extent to which media are able to resonate with first-hand legal experience.

In their analysis, Ewick and Silbey distinguish between three patterns of legal consciousness.[76] A first way of experiencing the presence of law in everyday practices is what Ewick and Silbey define as 'before the law'. This emerges when people see law as something that is removed from ordinary social interaction whilst simultaneously acknowledging the law's authority. Here, law has a role in daily life, but it never seems to form an integral part of the everyday because it remains an independent entity that has its place elsewhere. Law is typically experienced as a parallel universe which overlaps very little with everyday life. The emphasis in the 'before the law' stance is on law as something distant, making people feel that legal remedies and procedures are beyond their reach, leaving them powerless. The second dimension of legal consciousness in the classification which Ewick and Silbey suggest is 'with the law' and it refers to the belief that law is a kind of game which individuals might deploy in their daily activities. From this perspective, law operates as a strategic resource: it is something that is there to help people to look after their interests in their interactions with others. This suggests that individuals would feel, to a large extent, able to control the presence of law in their lives, even though Ewick and Silbey emphasize the importance of contingency and unpredictability in the perception of 'law as a game'.[77] Finally, there is what Ewick and Silbey call the 'against the law' dimension of legal consciousness, in which the emphasis is on people's resistance, often in the form of 'make-do' tactics[78] and usually involving small gestures of subversion. The main purpose of such resistance is, as Ewick and Silbey point out, to 'forge moments of respite from the power of law'.[79]

Social identity is seen as an important determinant of variations in legal consciousness: research suggests that underprivileged groups are most likely to have a legal consciousness which is characterized by a 'before the law' perception or a feeling of being up against the law.[80] Law for them can become the overwhelming web-like enclosure that Sarat describes in his work on the legal consciousness of welfare recipients,[81] while for ethnic minorities in urban areas, simply venturing out onto the street can be sufficient to expose them to the law's suffocating potential, for example, by being subjected to vexing stop-and-search procedures.[82] This suggests that, depending on their social status, people will have a more or less confident attitude to the law, which would explain why some perceive the law to be on their side while others experience it as a constant hindrance. Race, class, gender and the mere fact of residing in a suburb as opposed to the inner city, therefore, tend to give rise to different legal experiences and, hence, a different form of legal consciousness. Furthermore, negative experiences which take the form of an 'against the law' type of legal consciousness may also impact on the way in which different social groups use the media as a resource for making sense of the law. Although Dowler's analysis was not concerned with legal consciousness, his survey of perceptions of police effectiveness in the US underscores the importance of first-hand experience: his main conclusion is that people's satisfaction regarding their own personal contact with the police outweighs media influence and constitutes the overriding factor in accounting for public confidence in the police.[83] Thus, it could be argued that when people have predominantly negative personal experiences of the law, such as a perception that the police is unhelpful and uncooperative, this will somehow have a much greater impact on people's legal consciousness than does any media exposure. The extent to which law is seen as a disruptive force in everyday life, as illustrated by an 'against the law' type of legal consciousness, may therefore be an important element in accounting for possible differences in the way in which interpretive communities with different social and cultural characteristics make sense of the law.

A related factor which potentially determines the significance of the media as a source of legal consciousness is the extent to which media representations resonate with first-hand legal experience. In my discussion above, I have already mentioned the relevance of motivation in audience reception: media texts that fail to appeal to audiences will only make a limited impact. Hence, for example, Dowler suggests that audiences may seek out media messages which are consistent with preconceived views which they hold of a specific issue such as police effectiveness. Audience preferences represent particular difficulties in correlation studies, yet they are also potentially of vital importance in interpreting media effects: for example, having established a correlation between the type of newspapers which respondents prefer to read and their perceptions of crime, O'Connell, Invernizzi and Fuller were subsequently unable to exclude the possibility of this being a bottom-up (readers' perceptions of crime guide their choice of newspaper) rather than a top-down phenomenon (newspapers determine readers' perceptions of crime).[84] Furthermore, there is evidence to suggest that social identity is responsible for what Sasson calls a 'differential attentiveness to media discourse' which was evident from the different accounts (stories, anecdotes, theories, etc.) which individuals of various social backgrounds produced in the context of his research.[85]

It is therefore not inconceivable for a sharp contradiction between media images and personal experience to result in the media being discounted as a source of legal consciousness. Someone from a minority background might be relatively indifferent towards mainstream media representations of law. Gross comments that for minority groups ignoring the mass media is the most difficult form of resistance because of the media's omnipresence in everyday life, notwithstanding the existence of alternative media.[86] He is right to a certain extent: it is hard to avoid the presence of media images and mainstream media usually outweigh what Fraser[87] terms 'subaltern counterpublics', media of communication which provide minorities with positive self-images and which consciously challenge media representations which prevail in the dominant public sphere.[88] However, the omnipresence of the images promoted by mainstream media does not exclude the possibility that individuals are able to bracket these images, or at least sideline them, to a significant degree. Conversely, individuals may be motivated to specifically seek out media contents which resonate with their own first-hand legal experiences. Schrøder highlights the vital role of the 'link of relevance' between the personal sphere of a reader/viewer and the sphere represented by media texts, suggesting that the overlap between text and experience is extremely important.[89] Thus it could be argued that what people see on television or in other media has to relate to their own experiences in order to be relevant as a resource with which they can make sense of law. As Thompson points out:[90]

> Non-local knowledge is always appropriated by individuals in specific locales and the practical significance of this knowledge – what it means to individuals and how it is used by them – is always dependent on the interests of recipients and on the resources they bring to bear on the process of appropriation.

For example, it is difficult to imagine that a high profile case such as that of Stephen Lawrence would not constitute a potentially relevant framework for individuals seeking to make sense of their own personal experiences of institutional racism in their contact with law enforcement agencies. The murder of the black teenager Stephen Lawrence, especially the failure of the police to bring his alleged (white) killers to justice and the subsequent public inquiry into the case, is undoubtedly one of the most significant turning points in race relations in Britain of the last decade.[91] The story received intense media coverage and came to symbolize police racism in a gripping manner. The way in which mainstream media largely embraced the findings of the Lawrence Inquiry remains a fairly exceptional situation, but it is one that ethnic minorities, especially those of Afro-Caribbean origin, are likely to consider to be of great symbolic importance. Significantly, for example, the Stephen Lawrence case was mentioned by ethnic minority participants in Genn's survey of people's experiences and perceptions of the legal system.[92]

There are undoubtedly numerous inescapable media events, which John Fiske defines as 'sites of maximum visibility and maximum turbulence'[93] to which virtually every member of a society is exposed. The Stephen Lawrence case had such moments of intensity. The fall of the Berlin Wall, the attacks on the World Trade Centre and the Pentagon in the US on September 11 2001, the Monica Lewinsky affair, the trial of O.J. Simpson and the Gulf Wars are other examples of cataclysmic media events, some with global impact, producing an endless stream of stories and anecdotes that highlight a diversity of legal issues. Even individuals who try to avoid these major media events, for example through a conscious decision not to watch television or read any newspapers, may find these somehow inescapable because they have become a talking point in virtually every context of social interaction. Short of isolating themselves completely from society, people may have very little choice but to take notice of these major events.

It is tempting to argue, in analogy with Gerbner's theory of the distorting effect that prolonged and intense exposure to television has on perceptions of crime, that media events portraying a major upheaval within the legal or political system are bound to impact upon everyone's legal consciousness.[94] While there is evidence to suggest that, regardless of social position, members of a society tend to share some important cultural resources (some of which are media-related), factors such as class, race and gender may still affect the level of attentiveness that individuals display towards cataclysmic media events.[95] If the link of relevance between media discourse and experience is absent or very weak, the potential of these omnipresent media stories to act as a decisive political resource may be negligible. That explains, for example, why big media events may be not relevant at all to the legal consciousness of some social groups while being overwhelmingly present in that of others. For example, Sasson found that, despite significant media coverage of the incident, the story of the beating of Rodney King by LAPD Police was rarely referred to by white participants in his research while it figured prominently in the accounts of black participants.[96]

Conclusion

In this chapter, I have argued for more attention to be focused on audiences in the study of law, media and popular culture, in particular when the aim is to establish how exposure to various cultural representations impacts on people's understanding of the law. An important criticism I developed is that content analysis alone is inadequate as a method for examining the interrelations between the way in which people perceive law and the way in which the media represent law. For legal scholars to simply observe their own likes and dislikes of specific media texts is insufficient. Qualitative methods of audience research would seem to be an obvious alternative, but to date such methods have only been occasionally applied in research on law and the media.[97] Within audience research there has been an enormous evolution, from an effects-based tradition in which media audiences were treated as lab specimens that could be isolated from their social background, to an ethnography-led tradition in which audiences are seen as active participants in the production of meaning. Moreover, in recent years a constructionist approach, premised upon the belief that people have some choice as to the cultural resources which they rely upon to make sense of the world, has emerged to constitute a less media-centred focus.

Within the socio-legal tradition, I emphasized the importance of the study of law in everyday life which provides a basis for challenging the notion that law only plays a marginal role in the lives of ordinary people. Law is situated at the very heart of everyday life and it is rooted in an aspect of ideological awareness that is called 'legal consciousness'. Such a perspective has the potential to significantly weaken the automatic presumption that people are bound to be strongly influenced by the media because they lack any relevant first-hand experience of law with which to offset or to correct 'distorted' media images. I also highlighted another crucial factor, social identity, which has a decisive impact on direct legal experience. I explored the impact that law's ability to disrupt everyday life and the availability of first-hand legal experience may have on the level of attentiveness to media discourse likely to be displayed by different social groups. Although there is some research to support the significance of social identity, there is undoubtedly scope for a further deepening of our understanding of the way in which race, gender, class and other identity traits act as mediating factors in the relationship between legal consciousness and media consumption. Making sense of the complex interplay between the consumption of 'legal' media texts and audience perceptions is a tall order, but it is foremost a task which is almost certain to further enhance the burgeoning study of law, media and popular culture.

Notes

1 It would be impossible to give an overview of the literature here. Recent work includes: R. Nobles and D. Schiff, *Understanding Miscarriages of Justice: Law, the Media, and the Inevitability of Crisis* (Oxford: Oxford University Press, 2000); R.K. Sherwin, *When Law Goes Pop: The Vanishing line between Law and Popular Culture* (Chicago: University of Chicago Press, 2000); S. Greenfield, G. Osborn and P. Robson, *Film and the Law* (London: Cavendish, 2001); M. Thornton (ed.) *Romancing the Tomes: Popular Culture, Law and Feminism* (London: Cavendish, 2002); S. Brown, *Crime and Law in Media Culture* (Buckingham: Open University Press, 2003).

2 See, for example, D. Gauntlet, *Moving Experiences* (London: John Libbey, 1995) and D. Howitt, *Crime, the Media and the Law* (Chichester: John Wiley & Sons, 1998).

3 Certeau argues: 'In any case, the consumer cannot be identified or qualified by the newspapers or commercial products he assimilates: between the person (who uses them) and these products (indexes of the "order" which is imposed on him), there is a gap of varying proportions opened by the use that he makes of them'. See M. de Certeau, *The Practice of Everyday Life* (Berkeley: University of California Press, 1984), p. 32.

4 For example, Greenfield *et al.* regard both production and consumption as important areas for future development in the study of law and film. See S. Greenfield, G. Osborn and P. Robson, *Film and the Law*, pp. 190–192.

5 For example, Browne comments in relation to the rise of 'Court TV' in the US in the 1990s: '"TV-izing" legal proceedings might well increase the amount of individual vigilantism and violence on the streets because people will see that in order to get "justice", as they define it, they will have to take the law into their own hands – they cannot count on a legal system that is virtually self-paralyzed, expensive, and moves at an intolerable snail's pace'. See R.B. Browne, 'Why Should Lawyers Study Popular Culture', in D.L. Gunn (ed.) *The Lawyer and Popular Culture: Proceedings of a Conference* (Littleton, CO: Fred B. Rothmann & Co., 1993), pp. 7–22, p. 14.

6 Legal academics are not alone in their concerns about the effects of media distortion: the medical profession is equally concerned about the way in which the media portray health-related issues. See C. Seale, *Media and Health* (London: Sage, 2002).

7 See M. Thornton, 'Law and Popular Culture: Engendering Legal Vertigo', in M. Thornton (ed.) *Romancing the Tomes*, pp. 3–19, p. 11: 'Positivism seeks to deny the subjectivity of the interpretive process, a process that necessarily disturbs the rigidity of a technocratic legal system'.

8 See A. Garapon, 'Justice out of Court: The Dangers of Trial by the Media', in D. Nelken (ed.) *Law as Communication* (Aldershot: Dartmouth, 1996), pp. 231–245.

9 M. Thornton, 'Law and Popular Culture: Engendering Legal Vertigo', p. 15.

10 Empirical research has produced contradictory results. For example, Hans claims

that: '[b]ecause a relatively small proportion of the public has direct experience with the justice system, public knowledge and views of law are largely dependent on media representations'. See V.P. Hans, 'Law and the Media: An Overview and Introduction', *Law and Human Behavior*, 15, 5 (1990), pp. 399–407, at 399. Genn, in her British survey of people's perceptions of the legal system concludes that most people's expectations of courts, judges and lawyers are shaped by the media. See H. Genn, *Paths to Justice: What People Do and Think about Going to the Law* (Oxford: Hart Publishing, 1999), pp. 246–247. However, Dowler's statistical analysis of attitudes towards policing in the US contradicts the notion that a lack of first-hand experience makes people dependent on the media for their information. His study suggests that there is a correlation between direct experience of policing and heavy television viewing, in that individuals who watch a lot of television and who have had previous contact with the police are more likely to have a negative image of police effectiveness. See K. Dowler, 'Media Influence on Citizen Attitudes toward Police Effectiveness', *Policing and Society*, 12, 3 (2002), pp. 227–238.

11 S. Hall, 'Encoding/Decoding', in S. Hall, D. Hobson, A. Lowe and P. Willis (eds) *Culture, Media, Language* (London: Hutchinson, 1980), pp. 128–138.

12 D. Gauntlet, *Moving Experiences* (London: John Libbey, 1995), p. 9.

13 D. Morley, *Television, Audiences and Cultural Studies* (London: Routledge, 1992), p. 45.

14 D. McQuail, *Mass Communication Theory* (London, Sage, 1994), pp. 331–332.

15 See for example M. Heins and J.E. Bertin, 'The St. Louis Court Brief: Debating Audience "Effects" in Public', *Participations* 1, 1 (2003), available at http://www.participations.org.

16 See for example Friedman: 'The ceaseless flow [of media images] puts ideas into people's heads. These are the basic stuff of legal culture, and legal culture is the architect and the mechanic of law'. See L.M. Friedman, *The Republic of Choice* (Cambridge, MA: Harvard University Press, 1990), p. 129.

17 Macaulay warns that '[a]rmchair self-analysis of our own reaction is not enough'. See S. Macaulay, 'Popular Legal Culture: An Introduction', *Yale Law Journal*, 98, 8 (1989), pp. 1545–1558 at 1552.

18 R.K. Sherwin, *When Law goes Pop*, p. 21.

19 Ibid. See also S. Macaulay, 'Images of law in everyday life: the lessons of school, entertainment, and spectator sports', *Law & Society Review*, 21, 1 (1987), pp. 185–218.

20 See S. Livingstone, 'On the Continuing Problem of Media Effects', in J. Curran and M. Gurevitch (eds) *Mass Media and Society*, 2nd edn (London: Arnold, 1996), pp. 305–324 and P. Mason, 'Watching the Invisible: Television Portrayal of the British Prison 1980–1990', *International Journal of the Sociology of Law* 28 (2000), pp. 33–44.

21 I. Ang, *Living Room Wars: Rethinking Media Audiences for a Postmodern World* (London: Routledge, 1996).

22 For example, this seems to be the thrust of a study of school shootings in the US in which it is argued that the media are responsible for cultivating a public fear that is disproportionate to the actual incidence of school shootings. See R. Burns and C. Crawford, 'School shootings, the media, and public fear: Ingredients for a moral panic', *Crime, Law & Social Change* 32 (1999), pp. 147–168. See also D. Kidd-Hewitt and R. Osborne, 'Preface', in D. Kidd-Hewitt and R. Osborne (eds) *Crime and the Media: The Post-modern Spectacle* (London: Pluto, 1995), pp. ix–x, p. ix: '[T]he theoretical debate about the relationships between crime and the media remain locked in paradigms of effects and quantification'.

23 D. Howitt, *Crime, the Media and the Law*.

24 R. Sparks, 'Masculinity and Heroism in the Hollywood "Blockbuster"', *British Journal of Criminology* 36 (1996), pp. 348–360 at 350.

25 Having said this, it has to be emphasized that there is some excellent audience research which examines a range of issues from a non-behaviourist perspective. For example, Schlesinger and his co-authors resolutely turned their backs on the behaviourist tradition by examining not how the media might cause women to fear violence, but by asking what women who have been physically abused think of media images of violence. The traditional perspective is, thus, completely reversed in this research. Instead of assuming that the media influence women's views on violence, the focus is on how personal experiences of domestic violence interact with women's readings of the media. See P. Schlesinger, R.E. Dobash, R.P. Dobash and C.K. Weaver, *Women Viewing Violence* (London: BFI, 1992).

26 J. Curran, 'Rethinking Mass Communications', in J. Curran, D. Morley and V. Walkerdine (eds) *Cultural Studies and Communications* (London: Arnold, 1996), pp. 119–165.

27 K.C. Schrøder, 'The Best of both Worlds? Media Audience Research between Rival Paradigms', in P. Alasuutari (ed.) *Rethinking the Media Audience* (London: Sage, 1999), pp. 38–68.

28 I. Vine, 'The dangerous psycho-logic of media "effects"', in M. Barker and J. Petley (eds) *Ill Effects: The Media/Violence debate* (London: Routledge, 1997), pp. 125–146.

29 R. Silverstone, *Television and Everyday Life* (London: Routledge, 1994).

30 See D. Morley, *Television, Audiences and Cultural Studies*, p. 174.

31 See S. Hall, 'Encoding/Decoding'.

32 P. Alasuutari, 'Introduction: Three Phases of Reception Studies', in P. Alasuutari (ed.) *Rethinking the Media Audience* (London: Sage, 1999), pp. 1–21.

33 D. Morley, *The 'Nationwide' Audience: Structure and Decoding* (London: BFI, 1980).

34 J. Radway, *Reading the Romance* (Chapel Hill NC: University of North Carolina Press, 1984).

35 T. Liebes and E. Katz, *The Export of Meaning: Cross-cultural Readings of Dallas*, 2nd edn (Cambridge: Polity Press, 1993).

36 S. Hall, 'Encoding/Decoding', p. 131.

37 D. Gauntlet, *Moving Experiences*, p. 17.

38 For example, C. Geraghty, *Women and Soap Opera* (Oxford: Polity, 1991) and M.E. Brown, *Soap Opera and Women's Talk* (London: Sage, 1994).

39 For example, J. Winship, *Inside Women's Magazines* (London: Pandora, 1987) and J. Hermes, *Reading Women's Magazines* (Cambridge: Polity, 1995).

40 J. Radway, *Reading the Romance*.

41 I. Ang and J. Hermes, 'Gender and/in Media Consumption', in J. Curran and M. Gurevitch (eds) *Mass Media and Society*, pp. 325–347.

42 L. Van Zoonen, *Feminist Media Studies* (London: Sage, 1994), 106.

43 Ibid.

44 P. Alasuutari, 'Introduction: Three Phases of Reception Studies', p. 10.

45 J. Corner, 'Reappraising Reception: Aims, Concepts and Methods' in J. Curran and M. Gurevitch (eds) *Mass Media and Society*, pp. 280–304; D. Morley, 'Populism, Revisionism, and the "New" Audience Research', in J. Curran, D. Morley and V. Walkerdine (eds) *Cultural Studies and Communications*, pp. 279–293.

46 See D. McQuail, *Mass Communication Theory*, p. 331.

47 K.C. Schrøder, 'Making sense of audience discourses', *European Journal of Cultural Studies* 3, 2 (2000), pp. 233–258 at 244.

48 P. Alasatuuri, 'Introduction: Three Phases of Reception Studies', p. 6.

49 W.A. Gamson and A. Modigliani, 'Media Discourse and Public Opinion on

Nuclear Power: A Constructionist Approach', *American Journal of Sociology* 95/1 (1989), pp. 1–37 at 10.

50 W.A. Gamson, *Talking Politics* (Cambridge: Cambridge University Press, 1992).

51 Ibid., p. 178.

52 L.M. Friedman, 'Law, Lawyers and Popular Culture', *Yale Law Journal* 98, 8 (1989), pp. 1579–1606 at 1593.

53 R.V. Ericson, P.M. Baranek and J.B.L. Chan, *Representing Order: Crime, Law, and Justice in the News Media* (Milton Keynes: OUP, 1991), p. 17.

54 T. Sasson, *Crime Talk: How Citizens Construct a Social Problem* (New York: Aldine de Gruyter, 1995).

55 Ibid., pp. 162–163.

56 Schrøder notes that empirical research has shown that media audiences are capable of criticizing the aesthetics of media texts, which includes an awareness of the 'constructedness' of specific media messages, i.e. an awareness that the latter are not a transparent representation of reality. See K.C. Schrøder, 'Making Sense of Audience Discourses', at p. 247.

57 I. Karpin, 'She's Watching the Judges: Media Feedback Loops and What Judges Notice, in M. Thornton (ed.) *Romancing the Tomes*, pp. 47–65, p. 58.

58 D. Buckingham, 'Electronic Child Abuse? Rethinking the Media's Effects on Children', in M. Barker and J. Petley (eds) *Ill Effects: The Media/Violence Debate* (2001, second edition), pp. 63–77, p. 69.

59 A. Sarat and T.R. Kearns, 'Beyond the Great Divide: Forms of Legal Scholarship and Everyday Life', in A. Sarat and T.R. Kearns (eds) *Law in Everyday Life* (Ann Arbor, Michigan: University of Michigan Press, 1993), pp. 21–61 and B.G. Garth and A. Sarat, 'Studying How Law Matters: An Introduction', in B.G. Garth and A. Sarat (eds) *How Does Law Matter?* (Evanston, Illinois: Northwestern University Press, 1998), pp. 1–14.

60 A. Sarat and T.R. Kearns, 'Beyond the Great Divide', p. 29.

61 P. Ewick and S.S. Silbey, *The Common Place of Law: Stories from Everyday Life* (Chicago: University of Chicago Press), p. 16.

62 A. Sarat, 'The Law is All Over: Power, Resistance and the Legal Consciousness of the Welfare Poor', *Yale Journal of Law and Humanities*, 2 (1990), pp. 343–379.

63 S.E. Merry, 'Everyday Understandings of Law in Working-Class America', *American Ethnologist*, 13 (1986), pp. 253–270. See also B. Yngvesson, 'Inventing Law in Local Settings: Rethinking Popular Legal Culture', *Yale Law Journal* 98/8 (1989), pp. 1689–1708.

64 D.M. Trubek, 'Where the Action Is: Critical Legal Studies and Empiricism', *Stanford Law Review* 36 (1984), pp. 575–622 at 592.

65 A. Sarat, 'The Law is All Over'.

66 D. Engel, 'How Does Law Matter in the Constitution of Legal Consciousness?', in B.G. Garth and A. Sarat (eds) *How does Law matter?*, pp, 109–144, p. 112.

67 P. Ewick and S.S. Silbey, *The Common Place of Law*, p. 36.

68 Ibid., p. 43.

69 P. Golding and G. Murdock, 'Culture, Communications, and Political Economy', in J. Curran and M. Gurevitch (eds) *Mass Media and Society*, pp. 11–30.

70 P. Ewick and S.S. Silbey, *The Common Place of Law*.

71 S.F. Hirsch, 'Subjects in Spite of Themselves: Legal Consciousness among Working-Class New Englanders', *Law and Social Inquiry* 17, 4 (1992), pp. 839–857 at 854.

72 I. Vine, 'The Dangerous Psycho-Logic of Media "Effects"', p. 125.

73 P. Schlesinger *et al.*, *Women Viewing Violence*.

74 T. Sasson, *Crime Talk*.
75 Ibid., p. 154: 'Class and race contribute to the pool of resources for making sense of crime by providing subcultural popular wisdom and by shaping typical life experiences. They also influence attentiveness to media discourse and hence its availability as an ideational resource'.
76 P. Ewick and S.S. Silbey, *The Common Place of Law: Stories from Everyday Life*.
77 Ibid., p. 135.
78 M. de Certeau, *The Practice of Everyday Life*.
79 P. Ewick and S.S. Silbey, *The Common Place of Law*, p. 48.
80 Ibid., pp. 234–235. See also L.B. Nielsen, 'Situating Legal Consciousness: Experiences and Attitudes of Ordinary Citizens about Law and Street Harassment', *Law & Society Review* 34, 4 (2000), 1055–1090.
81 A. Sarat, 'The Law is All Over'.
82 A. Clancy, R. Aust and C. Kershaw, *Crime, Policing and Justice: The Experience of Ethnic Minorities Findings from the 2000 British Crime Survey* (London: Home Office Research, Developments and Statistics Directorate, 2001).
83 K. Dowler, 'Media Influence on Citizen Attitudes toward Police Effectiveness', p. 236.
84 M. O'Connell, F. Invernizzi and R. Fuller, 'Newspaper Readership and the Perception of Crime: Testing an Assumed Relationship Through a Triangulation of Methods', *Legal and Criminal Psychology* 3 (1998), 29–57.
85 T. Sasson, *Crime Talk*, p. 156.
86 L. Gross, 'Out of the Mainstream: Sexual Minorities and Mass Media', in G. Dines and J.M. Humez (eds) *Gender, Race and Class in Media* (London: Sage, 1995), pp. 61–69, p. 67.
87 N. Fraser, *Justice Interruptus: Critical Reflections on the 'Postsocialist' Condition* (London: Routledge, 1997).
88 For example, Bradley notes in his research findings that women of Afro-Caribbean origin often criticized mainstream British media for offering distorted representations of black people and that they expressed a preference for reading the alternative black press. See R. Bradley, *Public Expectations and Perceptions of Policing* (London: Home Office Research, Development and Statistics Directorate, 1998).
89 K.C. Schrøder, 'Making sense of audience discourses', p. 245.
90 J.B. Thompson, *The Media and Modernity: A Social Theory of the Media* (Cambridge: Polity, 1995), p. 207.
91 The campaign to bring the killers of Stephen Lawrence to justice enjoyed huge support from all mainstream media. The tabloid newspaper, *The Daily Mail*, in particular, took the extraordinary step of publicly naming the five suspects in the case. As Yuval-Davis points out, public support for the case partly reflected a genuine shift in awareness on matters of race and multiculturalism. However, the middle-class background of the Lawrence family, in her view, also made the media particularly sensible to their plight. Other less 'deserving' groups may not be so fortunate, and their quest for visibility often has to do without the support of media and public opinion. See N. Yuval-Davis, 'Institutional Racism, Cultural Diversity and Citizenship: Some Reflections on Reading The Stephen Lawrence Inquiry Report', *Sociological Research Online* 4 (1999). Available at http://www.socresonline.org.uk/socresonline/4/lawrence/yuval-davis.html (last visited 5 February 2003); L. Bridges, 'The Lawrence Inquiry-Incompetence, Corruption, and Institutional Racism', *Journal of Law and Society* 26/3 (1999), 298–322.
92 See H. Genn, *Paths to Justice*, p. 243. This is also consistent with Sasson's findings. See T. Sasson, *Crime Talk*, p. 156.

93 T. Sasson, *Crime Talk*, p. 7.
94 See G. Gerbner, 'The Hidden Side of Television Viewing', in G. Gerbner, H. Mowlana and H.I. Schiller (eds) *Invisible Crises: What Conglomerate Control of the Media Means for America and the World* (Oxford: Westview Press, 1996), pp. 27–34.
95 T. Sasson, *Crime Talk*.
96 Ibid., p. 156.
97 A noteworthy piece of research is Turnbull's study in which she aimed to establish what readers thought of crime fiction. See S. Turnbull, ' "The Mystery of the Missing Discourse": Crime Fiction Readerships and Questions of Taste', in M. Thornton (ed.) *Romancing the Tomes*, pp. 241–256.

Part III
Sport

5   Contextualizing the Football Disorder Act

Proportionality under the hammer

Geoff Pearson

Introduction

It is now over 30 years since the first reported death of a British football fan as a result of so-called 'football hooliganism'. Fan fatalities as a result of crowd violence, disorder and poor stadium management in particular were nothing new to the sport of football, but a popular press-driven awareness of the supposedly new phenomenon, combined with the nature of the death itself, meant that this was seen as a watershed. Blackpool fan Kevin Olsson was stabbed to death during a match against Bolton Wanderers on 24 August 1974, at a time when – in terms of incidents of disorder, the number of arrests and the extent of media coverage – football hooliganism was only starting to approach its peak.[1]

Considering the media and legal reaction to football-crowd violence since this time, it might naturally be assumed that fatalities and serious injuries resulting from crowd disorder were commonplace. However, the first football fatality remains one of very few resulting directly from violence involving British supporters. Armstrong and Hobbs note that even during the supposed 'peak' of football hooliganism, there were no more than two 'hooliganism-related' deaths a year,[2] and in more recent times the number of fatalities caused by football disorder have dropped even further, making headline news on the rare occasion they do occur.[3] Indeed, whilst football hooliganism remains prominent in the public's consciousness, even after the dramatic reduction in reported incidents and arrests that followed the Heysel and Hillsborough disasters of the mid to late 1980s, the actual physical and economic damage of domestic football-related disorder remains comparatively low.[4-6] In the last decade, it can be argued that the impact of crowd disorder upon domestic professional football has been nominal;[7] the football industry in the UK has generated more income than ever before;[8] stadiums have become safer and crowds, comprising an increasing number of women and families, have continued to rise.[9]

By comparison, at the end of the 1970s, football was in a much less healthy state, and the machinery of the law was in full operation at a number of levels to respond to what was perceived as an increasing threat to the game itself. Sensationalized media reporting of incidents of disorder involving football fans[10] put pressure upon the government, judiciary and police authorities to take firm action to combat what was now commonly referred to as 'football hooliganism'. The Safety at Sports Grounds Act 1975 included provisions granting the police extra powers to insist upon certain crowd control measures inside stadiums, whilst judges started to impose high deterrent sentences upon those who were convicted of offences defined to fall within the accepted boundaries of 'football hooliganism'.[11] Meanwhile the numbers of police at the football grounds and railway stations serving them increased in an attempt to control unruly crowds and prevent disorder.[12]

In the 30 years following the first football hooligan killing, the law's attempt to break the link between football matches and disorder has taken place on three levels; continued judicial attempts in the higher courts to impose deterrent sentences,[13] often supported by political intervention;[14] a plethora of legislation criminalizing acts perceived to form or encourage hooliganism,[15] and in the 1980s, a shift in policing tactics towards 'intelligence based' policing that saw the establishment of the Football Intelligence Unit branch of NCIS.[16] The combined use of sustained anti-hooligan legislation and police 'intelligence' to combat the phenomenon culminated in the introduction of Banning Orders under the Football Disorder Act, which will form the main focus of this chapter. The 2000 Football Disorder Act ('the Act') will be placed in the historical context of political and legal responses to football hooliganism, especially that involving English football fans travelling abroad to watch club sides or the England National Team. In particular, this contextual analysis will focus on the legal principle of proportionality; that is, arguments relating to the necessity and reasonableness of a particular legal response in relation to the actual nature, scale and extent of a social problem.

Construction and response: legal overreaction to football hooliganism

Legal reaction to the phenomenon of 'football hooliganism' has been both extensive and controversial. Ground breaking and rights-infringing legislation has been introduced, deterrent sentences at the expense of justice in the individual case have been imposed and the police have resorted to extreme tactics of surveillance and filing of suspects that appear more appropriate for the likes of international terrorists. However, popular criticism of these measures is generally muted, with Parliament and the media more likely to call for even tighter control of football fans rather than express concern for the civil liberties and fundamental freedoms of innocent fans under the Rule of Law, the European Convention and Treaty on the European Union.

The unwillingness to criticize such draconian state responses has been surprising, especially in the light of the 1989 Hillsborough disaster. The tragedy, which resulted in 96 football supporters being crushed to death on a football terrace, was caused not by 'football hooliganism', but by measures introduced to try and control it, coupled with attitudes and actions resulting from an obsession with the problem that overrode more pressing safety issues.[17] However, despite this paradox, legal reactions to football-crowd disorder, especially that involving England fans abroad, grew even more drastic and out-of-proportion to the scale and extent of the problem following the tragedy.

Such policies were allowed to proceed despite their infringing of fundamental civil rights as a result of the way in which the phenomenon of 'football hooliganism' had been constructed by both the media and the law in the previous 40 years. From the late 1960s,[18] newspapers started reporting incidents of football-crowd disorder under a new label – 'football hooliganism'. Before this time, incidents of crowd disorder at football had attracted no such overreaching label. In the case of *Munday* v. *Metropolitan Police District Receiver* for example, a crowd of 40–50 football fans who broke into a garden, threatened and struck the gardener with a bottle and then pinned the plaintiff's daughter against a wall while they damaged property and stole ladders in order to gain entry to a sold out match were referred to by the judge merely as 'excited' and 'enterprising'![19]

Many authors, for example Cohen and Hall, have noted the impact of media reporting of hooliganism upon the perceived extent and seriousness of the problem and Redhead rightly describes the phenomenon as one, '...which has no precise legal definition and remains more or less historical (and hysterical) mass media construction'.[20] The reaction to the 'teddy boys' and 'mods and rockers' had already set a precedent for a so-called *moral panic*[21] over juvenile delinquency that the press fuelled by over-reporting in sensational language incidents of football disorder. By the 1970s, press reporting had established football hooliganism as a new, coherent and distinctive type of disorder and firmly entrenched it into the minds of readers. As the moral panic over football hooligans grew, the media reported more incidents, in increased prominence, and in more sensational terms. This, in turn, fuelled the obsession with the phenomenon and created an 'amplification spiral' of moral panic and media reporting.[22]

The demand for a response to the perceived problem inevitably fed through to the legislature, the judiciary and the police. By now the problem of football-crowd disorder was being labelled the 'The English Disease' by the media, apparently after the phrase had been coined by the foreign press who were worried about football supporters in their own countries becoming 'infected'. Later, the disease metaphor was adopted by politicians, police and even judges in trials of the hooligans, with striking results. Its application to football-related violence emphasized the apparently threatening, contagious and damaging characteristics of the phenomenon, allowing it to be used to justify action against the 'hooligans'. It was hardly surprising that the moral panic fuelled by a combination of the extensive use of the disease metaphor and – more importantly – the continued sensational over-reporting of incidents of football-crowd disorder, led to a dramatic response by the law in an attempt to control the situation. The continuous *re-activation* of the disease metaphor was used to legitimate 'tough action' against the football hooligans, including new legislation, deterrent sentences, oppressive and civil-liberties infringing police tactics and media condemnation.[23] This construction, by both the media and the organs of law, of the phenomenon of 'football hooliganism' is therefore essential to any understanding of the subsequent legal response.

It has been argued that overly constructive approaches to football hooliganism have missed the point that there exists 'a highly complex and serious social phenomenon' that has to be faced up to and managed in some way.[24] However, if the incidents of violence and disorder that occasionally occur in connection with a football game were constructed as, for example, 'over-enthusiastic boisterous behaviour by tipsy sports fans', or even 'rough and tumble between consenting adults', then legal responses to the constructed phenomenon would be entirely different and would almost certainly not infringe, to the same extent, the civil liberties of those *suspected* of seeing 'aggro' as part of the essential match-day experience. It has even been suggested that the manner in which football hooliganism has been constructed is class-based; during the Parliamentary debate on the Sporting Events (Control of Alcohol) Act 1985 it was contended that:

> People cannot expect to go to a football match and not be a little bois-terous. If they were all public school boys they would be described as high-spirited, but when working-class youngsters engage in boisterous behaviour, it becomes hooliganism.[25]

Whether there is any truth in this or not, the current socio-legal construction of football-crowd violence by the media and the law has had a direct practical effect on how all football fans are treated. Wildly differing incidents ranging from end-of-season pitch invasions, drunken disorder in town squares to meticulously planned incidents of violent disorder between 'firms' have been agglomerated to construct a single label of 'football hooliganism'. Meanings have then been attached to this label identifying it as bringing 'shame' upon the nation and at the extremes even suggesting that it is in some way a sickness that threatens to destroy the very fabric of civilized life in the UK.[26] This understanding has then been reflected in the legal reaction to the constructed phenomenon. Unsurprisingly, such a construction has led to a 'blunderbuss approach'[27] by government, police and judiciary that has been out of all proportion to the actual seriousness and threat posed by violence and disorder caused by football supporters, in terms of physical damage, economic cost, personal injury and death.

The social problems posed by incidents of disorder connected in some way with football matches, in the media-constructed contagious and malignant form of 'football hooliganism', were therefore well-known to the legislature and judiciary by the late 1970s; 'All of us are now well aware of the problems which arise from the misconduct of football supporters...' noted Lawton LJ during a sentencing appeal of one such hooligan.[28] The judiciary in the higher courts were keen to adopt the media construction of hooliganism – disease metaphor included – when they were ruling on cases of football-related crime, particularly when it came to passing sentence. Constructing an individual's offence as part of a wider malignant trend, disease or conspiracy that threatens the very fabric of society inevitably had a serious impact upon the type of sentence handed down. Certainly constructing football hooliganism as a disease spreading through the body (whether that 'body' be society or football) meant that tough action against the hooligans could be metaphorically justified in terms of protecting the rest of society. Defeating the disease must be the overriding aim, often requiring sacrifice. The body may have to undergo the pains of chemotherapy if the spread of the cancer is to be prevented, or the limb of the victim may need to be amputated in order to protect the rest of the body from the spread of infection.[29]

Deterrent sentences were seen as a way of tackling hooliganism, often at the expense of justice in the individual case and usually following a judicial construction of football-related disorder following the lines of the media construction of hooliganism. In the trials of the fans involved in the Channel ferry disorder of 1985, Russel LJ stated that:

> This affray ... involved football hooligans whose violence and particular form of violence is a particular scourge at this time ... the reputation of this country and of every person in it has been brought into contempt, certainly in Europe if not in the rest of the world. I know of my own knowledge that the foreign press call this particular form of mindless violence 'The English Sickness'.[30]

The judge then imposed severe custodial sentences upon the defendants, including an eight-year sentence upon the eldest. Similarly, a five-year sentence had been handed down to the Cambridge United 'Hooligan General',[31] and ten-year sentences were given to the alleged ringleaders of the 'Chelsea Headhunters' following the appropriately named undercover police operation 'Operation Own-Goal'.[32] '...The courts have come to the conclusion that this disorderly conduct at football matches has got to stop and the courts are going to do their best to ensure that it does stop', stated Lawton LJ in *Motley*, adding that, 'We are confident that if the courts impose a policy of this kind for the rest of this football season, there may be an improvement next year'.[33] Trivizas' research into sentences for football-crowd offences in comparison with other crowd offences identified that '...persons committing offences in football crowd disorders were punished more severely than persons committing similar offences in other circumstances.'[34] Therefore, those committing acts of violence that the judges did not consider 'football hooliganism' could expect more lenient sentences, even where the definition of what is and what is not football hooliganism is narrow. A spectator at a school match who injured a linesman in a violent and unprovoked attack, for example, had his sentence reduced from nine months to seven weeks on appeal when the judge ruled that there was 'no question of football hooliganism' in the defendant's actions.[35]

Until the late 1980s, the legislature were considerably less assuming of the media construction of hooliganism, at least in a specific sense. However, new statutes provided the police with more means to control football grounds (e.g. by insisting that grounds had control rooms and segregation),[36] banned alcohol on designated football transport and within sight of a football pitch[37] and introduced exclusion orders to prevent those convicted of 'football-related' crimes of disorder from attending live matches.[38] However, appeals for knee-jerk legislation to try and stamp out football hooliganism amounted to little until the revolutionary Football Spectators Act 1989 provided for a National ID Card Scheme for all those who wished to attend football matches. The aim of the scheme was to 'break the link' between football and violence by preventing those who had committed offences from being able to obtain the cards and therefore attend matches. However, the ID Card Scheme was never implemented, after Taylor LJ's Hillsborough Stadium Disaster Report criticized it as unworkable.

The Taylor Report's criticisms of the ID Card Scheme were based mainly on arguments of proportionality and departed from the previous vulnerability of many of the judiciary to the exaggerated media construction of football hooliganism. In reality, and despite the moral panic, Taylor considered that hooliganism was not a big enough problem to require such a dramatic (and practically problematic) new law that would infringe the civil liberties of many innocent fans and would seriously damage the national game.[39] Taylor agreed with critics that '. . . the scheme proposes a sledgehammer to crack a nut; a sledgehammer which may not swing at all but, if it does, may not swing safely or even reach the nut',[40] instead suggesting more limited legislation to deal with specific forms of disorder that had proved difficult to prosecute in the courts.[41] However, this kind of proportionality did not stand up to the pressures placed on the government by incidents of crowd disorder from English football fans abroad. Here pressure from the British media and the police was compounded by demands from foreign governments for the UK to prevent the 'hooligans' travelling, pressure that ultimately resulted in the Football Disorder Act 2000.

The Stone Island invasion: English fans abroad

It is difficult to gauge the exact impact of the legal attempts to control hooliganism in domestic football, but in the late 1980s and early 1990s it was perceived that football-crowd disorder in and around football stadia had decreased. Reports of serious incidents became less frequent and arrests for football-related offences started dropping sharply and this continued as attendances post *Italia 90* were rising.[42,43] This perceived drop in hooliganism was almost certainly not as dramatic as it was claimed at the time, and was as much a result of a change in the nature of the violence (and where it took place), combined with a reduction in the sensationalist press reporting of incidents as a reduction in the actual amount of disorder. Indeed, the nature of the disorder and the reporting of it are linked. As incidents of serious violence started taking place further from the stadiums, and became more discriminate in terms of those who were caught up in them, the media was no longer present to witness them and fewer incidents were reported. The media panic about hooliganism started to dissipate and football grounds seemed safer places to visit than before. How much this was a result of legal attempts to control the phenomenon is debatable; it is likely that such a drop as occurred in and around football stadiums was more a result of stadium redevelopment following the Taylor Report (newer all-seater grounds more easily covered by Closed Circuit Television (CCTV)), the changing nature of football support as ticket prices rose, and socio-cultural changes essentially making hooliganism – certainly in its old manifestation – less 'fashionable'.

With the exception of the creation of Restriction Orders under Section 15 of the Football Spectators Act 1989, legal attempts to control hooliganism had been focused exclusively on football violence in the domestic game. However, another problem was that of violence caused by English football fans travelling abroad to watch either their club team in the European club competitions or the English national team. Two of the first widely reported incidents involving English fans abroad occurred when Tottenham Hotspur travelled to Rotterdam for the 1974 UEFA Cup Final, and then when trouble broke out on Manchester United's visit to St Etienne in the European Cup-Winners' Cup in 1977. By the time of United's next Cup-Winners' Cup campaign, in 1983/4, their fans had been banned from travelling with the team because of disorder they had become involved in abroad.[44] The following season, there were 39 fatalities in the build up to a Liverpool v. Juventus European Cup Final when a wall collapsed under the pressure of Italian fans trying to escape a terrace 'charge' by Liverpool fans. The large number of deaths means that the so-called 'Heysel disaster' of 1985 remains seen as the most serious incident of football-related disorder in Europe. However, although the role of disorderly English fans in the tragedy should not be discounted, the fatalities were not deliberate, and in part a consequence of the dilapidated state of the stadium rather than merely as a direct result of football violence. Trouble abroad was also frequently occurring involving supporters of the English national team, most notably in Italy during the 1980 European Championships, and games in Switzerland in 1981 and Luxembourg in 1983. English club sides were banned from European Competitions for five years following the Heysel tragedy, but large-scale disorder continued to break out, during England's 1988 European Championship campaign in Germany and, to a lesser extent, at the start of the 1990 World Cup in Italy.

By now, the decrease in hooliganism in and around British football stadiums made the continuing disorder involving England fans abroad more pronounced. It was suggested that with police and stewards[45] now in relative control of domestic football stadiums, and with CCTV and the impact and threat of exclusion orders[46] making wide-scale trouble more difficult, the hooligans were turning their attention to games abroad, where it was felt the police were less capable of dealing with disorder, and where if caught, the most severe punishment was likely to be mere deportation back to England. In addition, the power to impose Restriction Orders under the Football Spectators Act upon those convicted of football-related offences in order to prevent them travelling abroad to watch England was not being used by the courts: when the England team travelled to the Republic of Ireland for a high-risk friendly match in 1995, one that saw serious rioting by England fans inside the stadium and resulted in the game being abandoned, only two fans were subject to restriction orders.[47]

The potential for disorder abroad was also escalating as the number of fans wanting to travel abroad with England – and the re-admitted English club sides – increased. As many as 40,000 England fans travelled to Marseilles for England's opening World Cup 1998 match against Tunisia;[48] and in 2000, approximately 20,000 managed to squeeze into the small Belgium town of Charleroi for an England v. Germany game during the European Championships.[49] Large numbers of club supporters were also travelling; the Portuguese authorities were caught totally off-guard by the reported 10,000 Manchester United supporters who travelled for a 1997 European Champions Cup Quarter-Final game in Oporto, and the number that travelled to Barcelona for Manchester United's 1999 European Cup Final was probably nearer 60,000, at least double that which had made the shorter trip to Heysel on the previous occasion that an English side reached the final. The huge numbers of travelling fans were perceived by both the UK and host authorities as creating a massive potential for disorder. Three factors in particular had been identified by the authorities, media and the fans themselves as making this potential for disorder a reality: high consumption of alcohol by English fans before matches, a minority of 'troublemakers' who were able to encourage disorder from drunken fans, and overreaction by local police forces that could turn minor disorder into a full-scale riot.

At the World Cup in Marseilles in 1998, the 'worst case scenario' occurred, when large numbers of drunken England fans, gathered in the old port the day before the match, became involved in widespread disorder with local North Africans and the police. TV cameras relayed back to the UK scenes of police firing tear-gas and baton-charging English fans. In Charleroi at *Euro2000*, similar scenes occurred, when Belgium police used water-cannons to try and control English supporters. On this occasion, nearly

1,000 English supporters were arrested,[50] although an overreaction by the authorities undoubtedly made the disorder appear more severe and widespread than it otherwise would have been. In both cases, blanket coverage by the media saw the disturbances on the front page of almost every newspaper and the first item on the television news, with journalists and commentators condemning the hooligans and demanding further controls on fans travelling abroad.

Banning orders in the making: responses to hooliganism abroad 1997–2000

The legislative response to the events in Marseilles and Charleroi was swift. It was already clear that Restriction Orders had made little impact in preventing those involved in disorder from travelling. By 1997, only nine such orders had been made, approximately one for every year the Football Spectators Act 1989 had been in force. Following disorder in Rome as England qualified for the World Cup, the then Home Secretary admitted that, 'Restriction Orders haven't really worked',[51] and issued guidelines to the judiciary to impose orders on everyone convicted of a football-related offence in the run-up to the World Cup.[52] The final setback for Restriction Orders was the revelation that not one of the English fans arrested in the rioting in Marseilles had been served with an order; those fans who were serving bans had stayed at home, but the violence was as bad as anything witnessed involving supporters of the national team.

However, despite the failure of the Football Spectators Act, banning the 'hooligans' from travelling was still considered by the authorities to be the best way to prevent disorder. In the week following the Marseilles violence, British police prevented 363 English fans from leaving the country to attend the World Cup, turning them back at ports and airports. This restriction on movement was based purely on the grounds of police 'intelligence', suggesting that the fans were intent on causing disorder at future matches. These restrictions were not a result of lawful banning orders, and there was no right to challenge or appeal against the decisions of officers to turn back certain fans. The impromptu bans for suspected hooligans were a knee-jerk reaction to government embarrassment and pressure from both the media and the French authorities and were combined with emergency French legislation providing the French police (advised by British police 'spotters') with the power to expel any suspected hooligans already in France. The week between the Marseilles riot and the England v. Colombia match in Lens turned into a witch-hunt, both at home and abroad, for these 'known hooligans'. One 34-year-old fan, it appeared, was expelled from France because of a single football-related offence committed when he was 17.[53] Under such vague parameters for selection, and without the need for serious evidence of guilt or any significant accountability, it is likely that totally innocent fans were being unlawfully refused entry to France or deported back to the UK.[54]

Despite the remainder of England's World Cup passing off relatively quietly, the tournament had proved once again that Restriction Orders were having little effect in preventing football violence by English fans abroad, and there were further demands for the introduction of legislation that would allow bans to be imposed upon those continually referred to by the police and Home Office as 'known hooligans'. The phrase 'known hooligans' is misleading, as this implied that there was already some proof that such individuals had been involved in criminal acts. Instead, the 'known hooligans' were actually 'suspected hooligans' – those suspected by the Football Intelligence Unit of involvement in disorder but without sufficient evidence against them to enable a successful prosecution in a criminal court. As a result of this confusion, pressure started to be applied to allow the imposition of bans upon those whom the police suspected of committing acts of criminal disorder, but against whom they had little evidence, which prevented them pursuing the conventional route of requesting a Section 15 Restriction Order as a result of a 'football-related' conviction.

An attempt to introduce such legislation was set in motion immediately following the World Cup in the shape of a private members bill, which eventually became the 1999 Football (Offences and Disorder) Act.[55] Along with plugging various loopholes in the previous legislation,[56] the bill originally intended to give the police power to confiscate the passports of those identified on Football Intelligence Unit files as being 'known hooligans' (or 'prominents') even if they did not possess previous convictions. It was only due to a shortage of parliamentary time – combined with the contentiousness of the move in terms of civil liberties meaning the bill was unlikely to be given royal assent in time – that this aspect of the bill was dropped. However, by this stage the government was promising to return to the issue of International Banning Orders (as Restriction Orders were now renamed)[57] for unconvicted fans as a way to try and prevent football-related disorder abroad by English supporters.[58]

The response of the mass media to the disorder, and expected disorder, at *France 98* and *Euro2000* was a throwback to the sensationalized over-reporting of football-crowd violence in the UK. Harry Harris of *The Mirror* for example echoed FIFA's demand that the British Government should prevent any fans who did not have tickets from leaving the shores of the UK for the duration of the 1998 World Cup. His attempt to apply a tabloid version of the doctrine of proportionality demonstrated that the principle can only work if there is a serious attempt to balance the infringements of civil liberties on one hand with an actual analysis of the nature and seriousness of the social problem on the other. 'If anyone tells me that this is a restriction on civil liberties', Harris explained, 'they should go to France. Where our country will be disgraced.' The behaviour that apparently warranted such drastic action included England fans '...baring their backsides ... the Union Jacks and the T-Shirts ... the drunkenness ... the foul language. . .'[59] The responses to the 1998 and 2000 disorder by both the mass media and the House of Commons indicated that football hooliganism – in this guise disorder abroad involving groups of English football fans – was not perceived to be the 'nut' of a problem as suggested by Lord Justice Taylor. Restriction Orders had failed and a sledgehammer was going to be required if the 'shame and menace' of football hooliganism was to be curtailed.

A sledgehammer to crack a nut? The Football Disorder Act

Supporters of the original Football (Offences and Disorder) Bill did not have to wait long for the government to deliver on its promise. Following the disorder in Charleroi at *Euro2000*, the Football (Disorder) Act 2000 was introduced. The Act, which through Schedule 1 amended Part II and Schedule 1 of the Football Spectators Act 1989 (Restriction Orders), drastically increased police and court powers to prevent suspected hooligans leaving the UK when the English national team, or their own club side, was playing abroad. First, the amended Section 14B now allows International Banning Orders to be imposed as a result of a 'complaint' to the Magistrates' Court by the chief officer of police. An application for such a ban can be made if, '. . . the respondent has at any time caused or contributed to any violence or disorder in the United Kingdom or elsewhere.'[60] It will be successful if the police are able to prove to the court that the individual has contributed to violence or disorder and if 'the court is satisfied that there are reasonable grounds to believe that making a banning order would help to prevent violence or disorder at or in connection with any regulated football matches'.[61] In addition, Section 14C extends the type of 'relevant' disorder to include that which has no connection with football, moving away from the previous law which had only allowed banning orders to be imposed upon those who had committed a fairly narrow band of 'football-related' offences. Sections 21A–B go even further than this, allowing any constable in uniform (during the 'control period' surrounding a regulated football match or tournament) who has reasonable grounds for suspecting that an individual, (a) has previously caused or contributed to disorder and, (b) might be intending to cause disorder at the match/tournament in question, to detain the suspected hooligan pending a Magistrates' Court hearing to determine whether a Section 14 Banning Order should be imposed.

Unlike the original Restriction Orders, the new banning orders have been widely used. By the time of the first major international tournament following the introduction of the legislation – the 2002 World Cup in Japan and Korea – 1,014 banning orders were in force,[62] which had risen to approximately 2,100 by the time of the 2004 European Championships.[63] In addition, the banning orders were in some quarters credited with the lack of disorder that occurred at the World Cup,[64] although it is likely that other factors were far more influential in this.[65] It was no surprise then, when the 2002 Football Disorder (Amendment) Act extended the lifespan of the 2000 Act for a further five years, meaning that banning orders of this nature were not only still in effect for the European Championships in Portugal in 2004, but will also be used for the World Cup in Germany in 2006 (assuming of course that one of the home nations qualifies!).

The imposition of banning orders upon those who have not been convicted of an offence raises very serious civil libertarian questions. Primarily, it can result in a situation where individuals who have not been convicted of any criminal offence, and therefore under the presumption of innocence cannot be punished by the criminal law, are having fundamental rights of freedom of movement being taken away from them. Such a move challenges the fundamental liberal rights provided by the Rule of Law upon which the UK constitution is based, and against which it still legitimates itself, the general principle that individuals should not have their freedoms infringed unless they have been found guilty of a criminal offence by an independent judiciary. As we will see, questions must also be raised as to the legislation's legality under the United Nations and European Declarations of Human Rights and under the Treaty on the European Union.

Gough and Smith v. Chief Constable of Derbyshire

Unsurprisingly, the imposition of banning orders on complaint by the Magistrates' Courts was soon challenged at the higher courts under both EU law and the Human Rights Act 1998 (which is meant to enshrine the European Convention of Human Rights within domestic law). In 2002, an appeal by two Derby County fans, Carl Gough and Gary Smith, against the decision of the Magistrates' Court to impose International Banning Orders on them under the 2000 Act reached the Court of Appeal (Civil Division).[66] The bans had been served upon Gough and Smith as a result of police 'profiles' compiled by the Football Intelligence Unit, which suggested they were active members of a hooligan 'firm' known as the 'Derby Lunatic Fringe'. The appellants contended that the orders were unlawful because they breached the Human Rights Act and the right of citizens to leave their territory under the EU Treaty.

Although Gough and Smith were ultimately unsuccessful in their appeals at both the Divisional Court and the Court of Appeal, the judgments in both cases provide an interesting analysis of the legality of the 2000 legislation, particularly regarding the questions:

1   Is a banning order a 'criminal penalty'?
2   What is the standard of proof under which a Section 14B Banning Order can be imposed?
3   Is the 2000 Act a proportionate response under EU law to the problem posed by football-crowd disorder abroad?

It is contended that with regard to question 3 in particular, both the Divisional Court and Court of Appeal failed to adequately balance the risk of the loss of the fundamental rights of innocent fans on the one hand, and the seriousness of football-crowd violence – combined with the effectiveness of banning orders in preventing it – on the other. Instead, the judgments indicated once again an inability on the part of the courts to go beyond the 'common sense' and reactionary construction of football hooliganism, an inability that, as we have seen, has characterized judicial responses to the phenomenon from the mid-1970s to the present day.

Gough and Smith contended that in allowing magistrates to impose banning orders as a result of a complaint rather than a conviction for a relevant offence, the statute breached Article 6 of Schedule 1 of the Human Rights Act – which provides amongst other things for the right to a fair and public hearing for any criminal charge. Article 6(2) also protects the presumption of innocence: 'Everyone charged with a criminal offence shall be presumed innocent until proved guilty according to law'. The appellants argued that a banning order was a criminal penalty but that it was being imposed under a standard of proof that was much lower than for any other criminal charge, where a penalty could only be imposed where guilt was established *beyond reasonable doubt*. The Divisional Court held that guilt for the purposes of a banning order could be established by a burden of proof more akin to the civil 'balance of probabilities', and this, the appellants argued, precluded a fair hearing.

The issues of the burden of proof required for banning orders, the type of evidence relied upon and how this relates to the presumption of innocence has been discussed in more detail elsewhere.[67] To summarize, both the Divisional Court and the Court of Appeal in *Gough and Smith* ruled that banning orders were *not* criminal penalties and thus did not need to follow the criminal burden of proof.[68] This, it can be argued, thereby interpreted and applied the Human Rights Act in a way that prevented its provisions forming a practical and effective safeguard and therefore failed '. . . to give effect to the Act as a constitutional instrument'.[69] The Appeal Court did, however, accept that because banning orders placed 'serious restraints on freedom that the citizen normally enjoys', in deciding whether to impose a banning order, the Magistrates' Court should 'apply an exacting standard of proof that will, in practice, be hard to distinguish from the criminal standard'.[70] If the Magistrates' Courts follow this lead and only impose banning orders when they are convinced beyond reasonable doubt that they are necessary to prevent the individual in question from committing acts of football violence abroad, then many of the concerns relating to Article 6, and Article 6(2) in particular will be alleviated.[71]

However, the type of evidence accepted in the Court of Appeal hearing of *Gough and Smith* seemed to suggest that such a strict burden of proof is not likely to be followed in the Higher Courts, never mind at Magistrates' Courts level. Much of the evidence contained in the FIU files on the defendants was of questionable value in determining whether Gough and Smith had committed football-related offences. Their profiles enclosed entries including: '7/8/99. Leeds v. Derby, Gough seen leaving stadium with three other males', and '11/12/99. Smith seen sitting in the southeast corner of the ground during the Derby v. Burnley FA Cup game'. Additional evidence that was used to try and convince the court of Gough and Smith's involvement in disorder was the fact that they had been spotted in a group of fans apparently known as 'The Derby Lunatic Fringe', a group which, the police revealed, sometimes became involved in disorder with other 'firms'. This evidence is merely 'guilt by association' rather than anything pertaining to a standard of proof that would be necessary for conviction in a criminal trial. It is concerning that despite the court's claims that the standard of proof for the imposition of a banning order should be 'hard to distinguish from the criminal standard', no evidence was noted in the judgment of the Divisional Court or Court of Appeal that actually pointed to either defendant actually committing a specific criminal offence.[72]

Section 14C of the 2000 Act also allows the court to take into account issues such as deportation from a foreign country and ejection from a football ground. This is despite substantial evidence of this occurring regularly to fans who simply happen to be 'in the wrong place at the wrong time' without any real evidence of the committal of a specific criminal offence.[73]

Gough and Smith: an application of the doctrine of proportionality?

In terms of European Union law, the appellants argued that the Act contravened Articles 1 and 2 of the 1973 EC Directive, which provides that Member States shall grant their nationals '...the right to leave their territory.'[74] They argued that *even if* it was acceptable to prevent this freedom of movement on public policy grounds, such restrictions would only be permitted under EU law, if they could be justified under the principle of proportionality. The doctrine of proportionality is one that is relevant not just for EU law but throughout both civil law and common law systems – a fundamental principle that aims to balance the rights of the individual on the one hand and the interests of the state on the other. The doctrine of proportionality is also essential in Human Rights law, and has been used at length by the European Court of Human Rights in determining whether state breaches of the Articles are justifiable:

> ...the Court must determine whether a fair balance was struck between the demands of the general interest of the community and the requirements of the protection of the individual's fundamental rights. The search for this balance is inherent in the whole of the Convention...[75]

It is accepted that although there are several *absolute* civil rights (i.e. rights that cannot be infringed by the state under any circumstances, the right not to be tortured[76] would be one example), most individual rights can be lawfully breached by the state where it is absolutely necessary. The Right to Liberty and Security, for example, can be taken away where an individual is found guilty of any offence and imprisoned in line with existing criminal law.[77] Similarly, most commentators agree that the EU right to leave a Member State can be lawfully curtailed by the state in the interests of national security or public health.[78] Therefore, where a real need exists for the state to curtail individual freedoms in order to protect its own interests it is generally considered that the doctrine of proportionality makes these infringements lawful, so long as they go no further than are absolutely necessary to achieve the legitimate aim. As Lord Diplock explains, the doctrine of proportionality should be concerned with the 'gravity of the mischiefs' against which the legislative provision was aimed: 'In plain English it means, "You must not use a steam hammer to crack a nut, if a nutcracker would do"'.[79] The relevance of the doctrine was accepted by both courts in *Gough and Smith*: 'In my judgment, this difficult trade between private right and public good is regulated by the idea of proportionality', stated Laws LJ at the Divisional Court.[80]

In *Gough and Smith*, the proportionality argument was used by the appellants in relation to EU Law to argue that the Football Disorder Act's banning orders went beyond a lawful infringement of their rights under the EC Directive.[81] The test of proportionality relied upon by the appellants was from *de Freitas* v. *Permanent Secretary of Ministry of Agriculture*,[82] a test that was accepted by the court as an appropriate way of balancing up the needs of the state with the rights of the suspected 'hooligans'. According to *de Freitas*, the court needed to ask whether:

(i) the legislative objective is sufficiently important to justify limiting a fundamental right;
(ii) the measures designed to meet the legislative objective are rationally connected to it; and
(iii) the means used to impair the right or freedom are no more than is necessary to accomplish the objective.[83]

The appellants accepted that preventing crowd disorder was a legitimate public policy aim, but contended that it did not justify prohibiting UK nationals – who had committed no football-related offence – from exercising their freedom to move from one Member State to another. Therefore, they claimed that the provisions of the Act permitting this provided a *disproportionate response to the public policy aim*. The appellants backed this up by pointing out that, 'there are classes of persons capable of doing much more damage than football hooligans who are free, under domestic law, to leave the country, including drug dealers and paedophiles', and persons suspected of being international terrorists.[84]

One of the most significant aspects of the *Gough and Smith* appeals were the courts' attempts to address the issue of whether banning orders for unconvicted fans were a proportionate response to football-related disorder abroad. The question of whether 'the legislative objective was sufficiently important to justify limiting (the right to leave the UK)' (test i) required the courts to look at the seriousness of football violence abroad; an analysis that could have looked in detail at issues such deaths and injuries caused in football disorder abroad, as well as any economic or social cost to the countries involved. The question whether 'the means used to impair the right or freedom are no more than is necessary to accomplish the objective' (test iii) needed a study of the effectiveness of banning orders in limiting hooliganism abroad. Was there any evidence that banning orders actually prevented disorder? Were there similar – or even better – ways of preventing and controlling disorder that did not require such a restriction on the fundamental rights of EU citizens?

However, both the Divisional Court and the Court of Appeal failed to seriously address either of these questions. Instead, and in common with their predecessors in the 1970s and 1980s, the courts focused on a pre-established construction of football-crowd disorder emphasizing its threatening and malignant qualities. From the very outset of the first appeal at the Divisional Court, Laws LJ had already established some 'facts' about the phenomenon. It was a 'rising spectre',[85] and a 'shame and a menace',[86] and the purpose of banning orders was '...to protect the public, here and abroad, from the evil of football violence and the threat of it.'[87] When ruling that the bans had been lawfully imposed under the doctrine of proportionality at first instance, Laws LJ reverted back to the disease metaphor in order to support his decision, stating that, 'the State was entitled to conclude that very firm measures were justified to confront the various sickening ills of football violence'.[88] This was far from the serious and objective step-by-step analysis required by the *de Freitas* test. The rhetoric from *Gough and Smith* indicates once again the importance of the un-reflexive and 'common sense' construction of football hooliganism that has been accepted by the judiciary in the same way it was accepted throughout the media. At first instance in particular, sensationalized language and the recurring disease metaphor was used in an attempt to establish the need for the legislation without looking at questions such as the damage caused by the phenomenon or the actual effectiveness of the banning orders in preventing disorder.

The Court of Appeal made a more serious attempt to actually consider the extent and seriousness of football violence abroad, with Lord Phillips stating early on in the case that, 'As questions of proportionality are an important feature of this appeal, we propose to say a little about this phenomenon at the outset.'[89] Furthermore, he accepted that,

> We have found the issue less easy to resolve than did Laws LJ. The fact that previous measures had not prevented football hooliganism by

English fans abroad does not demonstrate that the more radical measures introduced by the 2000 Act were necessary or proportionate.[90]

In establishing whether a legal response is 'proportionate' to a phenomenon under the test set out in *de Freitas* v. *Permanent Secretary of Ministry of Agriculture*, it is vital to understand exactly what this phenomenon is, looking at issues such as its extent, severity and the 'harm' caused by it. Such an analysis would need to be impartial and unprejudiced, providing as objective an evaluation of football-crowd disorder abroad as is possible. In this ideal appraisal, evidence from a number of sources, from the police dealing with incidents of disorder, to those bar owners whose establishments are in effect 'taken over' by English supporters abroad and, of course, from the football supporters themselves could have been taken into account. However, such a wide-ranging evaluation with the objective of providing an accurate and impartial picture of the phenomenon abroad did not take place at either appeal.

Instead, what analysis did take place was based entirely on the statements made by the police and Home Office, inter-subjective opinions from those who had requested the bans in the first place rather than a genuine attempt to identify in any material terms the seriousness and threat of the phenomenon. A witness statement from Superintendent John Wright was used in support of the case against the appellants as a supposedly motive-free objective account of football-crowd violence in this country:

It has been common for groups of males to associate themselves with football clubs as a vehicle for them to become involved in violence and disorder. This has developed to the stage where this has become extremely organised. These groups will often make use of mobile phones and the Internet [to] arrange fights with other like-minded individuals. These fights often involve the use of weapons, e.g, knives, bottles and CS gas. They usually occur away from football grounds at railway stations or in or around city centre public houses.[91]

The statement led Lord Phillips to conclude that, 'To describe what takes place by the word "warfare" is hardly too strong'.[92]

Evidence as to the seriousness of football-crowd violence involving English fans abroad was taken from a summary provided to the court by David Bohannan of the Home Office, who had responsibility for controlling football-related disorder:

In most cases, the disorder has occurred in streets and bars rather than in the grounds and often during the period leading up to match day. Each incident has brought shame on our national reputation and also resulted in very many arrests and expulsions of English supporters by host nations. Acts of disorder by English supporters receive wide media coverage both in the UK and abroad.[93]

These statements were presented by the court as objective and unprejudiced despite the fact that the Act was proposed and supported by these parties who, therefore, may have had a vested interest in exaggerating the problem. The acceptance of these statements as uncontestable fact was even more astonishing bearing in mind that the Chief Constable of Derbyshire was the respondent in the case before the court. If the judiciary truly intended to apply the yardstick of the test of proportionality to state-backed practices, then it would be hoped they would be circumspect when taking such statements from interested parties into account, in the same way in which they would have presumably responded to statements from the appellants to the effect that football hooliganism was not a serious problem at all!

Later, the court used statements by then Home Secretary Jack Straw – another advocate of the legislation – to try to establish the seriousness of football-crowd violence abroad.[94] Here, at least, the court attempted to bring in evidence that, prima facie could shed some light on the extent of the problem, by referring to the 'appalling scenes' (Jack Straw's quote)[95] at Charleroi and noting that 965 English fans were arrested during the *Euro2000* tournament.[96] This evidence was used by the court to indicate the extent and severity of hooliganism abroad, which would need to be taken into account when assessing whether banning orders for fans who are not convicted of football-related offences was a proportionate response to the problem (it is '. . . relevant, not by way of interpretation of the Act, but to inform the debate on proportionality that arises on this appeal').[97]

Unfortunately the value of even this evidence is highly contentious. The observations carried out at *Euro2000* by the author and other academics suggested that the 'appalling scenes' beamed over television from Charleroi's main square before the England v. Germany game started actually demonstrated to a greater extent the inappropriateness of the police response to the crowd rather than the extent of any 'hooliganism'.[98] The reaction of the Belgian police to some minor acts of vandalism and disorder by a small minority was to corral large groups of fans together (both offenders and innocent fans) and indiscriminately fire water-cannons into a large crowd of English fans, German fans and locals present for a pre-match concert. The author was one of those corralled outside a bar by Belgian police, and only allowed to leave near kick-off time upon producing a ticket for the match. Gary Smith was caught in the same incident, and the mere fact that he was the wrong side of the police cordon was used as evidence to suggest he should be served with a banning order (Lord Phillips considered this profile to be 'of particular relevance'):

> Smith was seen in the square in Charleroi after the disorder had occurred corralled by the Belgium police with around 15 other Derby prominents and 1,500 other England supporters.[99]

Certainly a police response targeted on individuals committing offences rather than against an entire crowd would have not resulted in the 'appalling scenes' perceived by Jack Straw and others.[100]

In addition to an uncritical acceptance of the government's interpretation of the TV pictures from Charleroi, the court also failed to scrutinize the large number of arrests made at the tournament in sufficient detail. Whilst Lord Phillips noted the high number of arrests, he failed to mention that only *one* of these fans was actually convicted by the Belgian authorities of a criminal offence.[101] Following the presumption of innocence, which it is still claimed remains the 'golden thread' of English criminal law,[102] this should mean that the other 99.9 per cent were not guilty of an offence – an astonishing statistic that is mentioned at no stage in the judgment. This is a crucial issue, with evidence of the Belgian police corralling large groups of fans who had committed no offence in a response to minor incidents and arresting and deporting those fans who were simply in the wrong place at the wrong time. In one incident, as a reaction to a minor disturbance occurring in a Brussels bar (reported by some present as being no more than a fan falling off his stool and breaking a glass), Belgian police fired tear gas inside and then arrested everyone coming outside in order to escape the fumes.[103] Even the Belgian police were forced to accept that a significant number of *innocent fans* were arrested at the tournament as a result of this style of policing.[104]

These factors are highly important in casting doubt over the Court of Appeal's view that football-crowd disorder abroad was a problem so serious that Section 14 Banning Orders were a proportionate response. In addition, they also raise serious questions as to the reliability and relevance of police intelligence files upon which banning orders are being imposed. Should we assume that all those arrested at *Euro2000* were 'blacklisted' as 'prominents' by NCIS (as happened to those deported from *Italia 90*)?[105] Since one of Smith's 'profiles' included him being one of 1,500 fans corralled by Belgian police in Charleroi, it is likely a number of these fans have been.

In finally ruling 'that preventing football hooligans from taking part in violence and disorder in foreign countries is an imperative reason of public interest which is capable of justifying restrictions on their freedom of movement',[106] therefore meaning that banning orders for unconvicted fans were a proportionate response, the Court of Appeal gave three reasons that were less than convincing. The court ruled the orders were necessary because: (a) other nations had requested the UK to act to prevent English supporters causing disorder on their own territory; (b) future disorder could lead to a ban on English clubs competing in Europe which in turn would have serious financial implications for the game; and (c) 'hooliganism by English and Welsh supporters abroad tarnishes the reputation of this country'.[107] Whether requests from other nations to act, and the fear about the 'reputation' of the UK, would count as a legislative objective sufficiently serious to justify the infringements of the fundamental rights of citizens is highly doubtful.

Furthermore, the claim that English clubs could be banned from Europe is both unrealistic and irrelevant; the disorder that led to both the Act and the *Gough and Smith* case centred around the English National Team and not English club sides, whose supporters have, with only a few exceptions,[108] conducted themselves well since the return of English club sides to European Competitions.[109] At the time of the Appeal hearing there had been no serious threats by UEFA to exclude one, never mind all, English sides from European Competitions since their re-introduction in 1990.

The sledgehammer that might not reach the nut: do banning orders actually work?

By June 2004, 2,100 football banning orders were in force, with the police believing that more were needed.[110] However, even if we were to assume that football violence abroad was a serious enough phenomenon to necessitate such measures, can we be sure that the costs to the civil liberties of those serving such orders are actually justified in terms of the effectiveness of banning orders in preventing football violence abroad? Again, this was an issue that should have been raised during the proportionality arguments in *Gough and Smith*. The second element of the *de Freitas* test talks broadly of the measures needing to be merely 'rationally connected' with the legislative objective which surely should include the fundamental question of whether the measures are likely to have a positive, significant and material impact upon that objective.

There is certainly evidence suggesting that banning orders do not bring the objective of limiting football violence involving English fans abroad significantly closer. First, other methods of banning English fans from travelling to matches have failed to reduce disorder. Banning orders may have legitimized the actions of UK police and foreign immigration officials in turning back 'suspected hooligans', but these actions had been widely used prior to the Act to prevent disorder, and with little effect. Preventing 363 'known hooligans' crossing into France for the 1998 World Cup failed to avert the violence witnessed in Lille and Lens, and similar tactics used before *Euro2000* had little impact in reducing disorder in Charleroi.[111] Even more significant is the problem facing the police that many of the fans involved in football-related disorder abroad are unknown to them. It was not just the 'known hooligans' that were causing the problems – the police had been preventing those travelling abroad or had kept them under close scrutiny long before the Act was introduced – but large numbers of fans whom the police had not suspected would become involved in disorder. The disturbances in Belgium at *Euro2000* demonstrated this problem at its worst, with the vast majority of the 965 arrested fans being unknown to the UK police as potential troublemakers. Football Intelligence Officers considered only 35 of those arrested to be 'prominent football hooligans'. In addition, only 40 per cent of those arrested had any kind of criminal conviction, the vast majority of which were unrelated to football.

This evidence provides a serious problem for those justifying the legislation under the second leg of the *de Frietas* test. Even assuming that these 965 arrested fans were involved in disorder of some sort (and, as has already been noted, the numbers of innocent supporters arrested at the tournament was high), what impact would banning orders have had upon the behaviour of fans had they been in force? Even if all the 'prominents' had been served with banning orders and remained in the UK, it appears that a high level of disturbance and arrests would have occurred regardless. If hooliganism is still taking place at an unacceptable level despite a high number of banning orders, how can it be claimed that the Act is 'rationally connected' with a reduction in the disorder and that the limits on the fundamental freedoms of potentially innocent fans are justifiable under the principle of proportionality? Therefore even the argument that the infringement to civil liberties resulting from the imposition of banning orders is justified on the pragmatic grounds that 'the end justifies the means' could be flawed.

Conclusion

From the deterrent sentences of the 1970s, the Ferry Port blockades and the 70-mile long 'alcohol-free corridor' of *France98*, to the imposition of football banning orders upon fans convicted of no offence, many of the legal responses to football-crowd disorder breach important fundamental freedoms and civil liberties of often totally innocent football fans. As with all legal reaction to social problems, the question of what measures are appropriate is one based on the internal objectives and legitimating aims of the law itself. Common law, Supra-national and International Human Rights law and EU law all make reference to the doctrine of proportionality; that measures infringing the rights of individuals must only be taken by the state in exceptional circumstances when a social problem (be it national security, public health or public safety) needs to be dealt with, and the best or only way to manage the problem also infringes the said rights. The principle asserts that such infringements must be limited to those that are absolutely necessary to confront that problem, with anything above and beyond this being disproportionate. The end should justify the means, a sledgehammer must not be used to crack a nut.

Banning orders imposed under the 2000 Football Disorder Act infringe many important civil liberties. They restrict the right of EU citizens to leave their nation state, allow detention of 'suspected hooligans' on the whim of a senior officer and impose a quasi-criminal penalty upon individuals without adhering to the safeguards present under criminal law – most notably the presumption of innocence and the burden of proof of guilt beyond reasonable doubt. Even the Court of Appeal, in *Gough and Smith*, has allowed banning orders to stand on evidence that was little more than guilt by association. A piece of legislation providing such widespread, arbitrary and draconian powers has been accepted as legitimate despite its total disregard for the protections supposedly granted by the likes of the doctrine of proportionality, the European Convention of Human Rights and the Rule of Law. This is as a direct result of the way that football-crowd violence abroad has been constructed by the media and how this construction has influenced successive governments and the courts.

This popular understanding of football-crowd disorder has been fashioned by the uncritical use of the 'football hooligan' label, sensational mass media over-reporting from the late 1960s onwards (including the coverage of the *France98* and *Euro2000* disorder) leading to a 'moral panic', and the widespread appropriation of the disease metaphor by the legislature, police and judiciary. Such an entrenched socio-legal construction curtails the possibility of the doctrine of proportionality acting as a protection against over-the-top criminal-legal responses to incidents of football disorder abroad involving English fans. Opportunities to step away from the exaggerated construction of football hooliganism and embark in a critical re-evaluation have been missed by the judiciary, even in cases such as *Gough and Smith*, where the aim of the court has been to apply the doctrine of proportionality in order to judge the legality of banning orders for unconvicted fans. Instead, the *Gough and Smith* judgments did little more than reactivate the 'common-sense' understanding of the menace posed by the disease of football hooliganism, in the light of which it is difficult to claim that the wide-ranging restrictions on civil liberties are anything but necessary and justifiable.

However, a thorough application of the doctrine of proportionality to Section 14 Banning Orders, taking into account the wide-ranging infringements of fundamental freedoms in comparison to the relatively small scale of disorder involving English fans of both the national team and club sides abroad, exposes the radical provisions of the 2000 Act as being the proverbial sledgehammer to crack the nut. Even against the relatively wide test of proportionality under EU law provided by *de Frietas* (which allows far more legislative discretion than under the European Convention of Human Rights), banning orders are found wanting.

The first question *de Freitas* asks is whether the legislative objective is sufficiently important to justify limiting a fundamental right. Football-crowd disorder abroad is clearly a social problem, and undoubtedly can be an embarrassment for the British Government, but the actual threat and damage caused by it is minimal in comparison with other pan-European crime. With up to seven English club sides playing in Europe on a fortnightly basis at times (not including the engagements of the English national team), incidents are few and far between. Even when they do occur, they result in relatively little damage and few, if any, serious injuries.[112] Even the 'appalling scenes' in Charleroi were little more than evidence of a police over-reaction in a square packed with thousands of fans to a few criminals throwing plastic chairs. The mass deaths and serious injuries directly caused by football violence that might have been expected in the 30 years following the murder on the Kop at Bloomfield Road in 1974 simply have not occurred. When compared with the more immediate threats posed by the likes of drug trafficking, major fraud and more recently international terrorism it should be asked whether the government, courts and intelligence services have got their priorities right.

Second, whether 'the measures (i.e. banning orders) designed to meet the legislative objective are rationally connected to it' is also questionable. With the majority of those arrested at *Euro2000* being unknown to police, it is difficult to accurately claim that banning orders would have prevented this disorder. As with the abandoned I.D. Card Scheme, the sledgehammer might not actually be capable of cracking the nut. Finally, whether 'the means used to impair the right or freedom are no more than is necessary to accomplish the objective' is also in doubt. There are many other ways to prevent football disorder abroad that do not result in the likely trampling on fundamental rights of innocent football fans; for example, improved policing from certain Member State police forces[113] and support for 'fan embassy' and fan self-policing schemes. These type of measures may prove to be not only more acceptable responses to incidents of disorder around football matches in terms of civil liberties, but are also likely to have a greater positive impact upon the behaviour of the tens of thousands of English football fans that travel abroad to watch their teams every year.

Notes

1 This is a popular understanding of football hooliganism, for example expressed by Butler who claims that, '. . . during the 1960s the number of disturbances – and the media and public consciousness of the problem – steadily increased', Butler, B., 'The Official History of the Football Association' (1991) Queen Anne Press: London, p. 197). Pratt, J. and Salter, M. ('A Fresh Look a Football Hooliganism', *Leisure Studies* 3/2 1984 201–230, p. 201) write that, 'Since the late 1960s, violence and the expectation of violence at football matches would appear to have become something of a permanent fixture in their own right'. The Leicester school note an increase in incidence of football hooliganism from the mid-1950s onwards (e.g. Murphy, P., Williams, J. and Dunning, E., 'Football on Trial' (1990) Routledge: London, p. 73) but that this was certainly exaggerated by the 'media orchestrated moral panic' from the mid-1960s (ibid. See also Dunning, E., Murphy, P. and Williams, J., 'The Roots of Football Hooliganism' (1988) Routledge: London).
2 Armstrong, G. and Hobbs, D., 'Tackled from Behind', in Giulianotti, R. *et al.* (eds) *Football Violence and Social Identity* 1994, London: Routledge: 196–228, at p. 196 (the time period in question was 1979–1982).
3 E.g. those of Matthew Fox in 1998 and Nathan Shaw in 2002.
4 In the ten years between 1992 and 2002, arrests for 'football related' offences dropped by 30 per cent (Home Office Statistics on Football-Related Arrests and banning orders).
5 Although the deaths of 39 Italian supporters at Heysel in 1985 was linked to crowd disorder, they were actually more the direct result of the inability of an internal wall to cope with the pressure of a crowd surge by fans trying to escape disorder. Despite initial attempts to blame the Hillsborough disaster on

drunken and ticket-less fans, the Taylor Report found that bad policing and an unsafe stadium was the real cause of the deaths of the 96 fans.

6 A comparison with 'alcohol-related' violence, for example, demonstrates the relatively low numbers of serious incidents arising from 'football hooliganism'. 1.2 million alcohol-related assaults were reported in 1999, one in six of which resulted in medical attention, meaning that 2 per cent of the UK population were victims of such attacks in that year alone ('Alcohol-related assault: findings from the British Crime Survey'. Home Office Report 35/03). However, despite the numbers and seriousness of the attacks, alcohol-related violence appears to receive no more media stigmatization than has been attached to 'football hooliganism'.

7 Although there have been recent calls by the police for clubs to foot the bill for policing football matches away from the stadium as a result of the cost of such operations.

8 Deloitte & Touche Annual Review of Football Finance, June 2002.

9 In 1989, 18,457,691 attended Football League matches in all four divisions. By 2002, this had risen to 27,907,983.

10 See Hall, S., 'The Treatment of 'Football Hooligans' in the Press', in Ingham, R., *Football Hooliganism: The Wider Context* (1978) London: Inter-Action Inprint.

11 E.g. *R* v. *Bruce* 65 Cr App Rep 148 (1977), *R* v. *Motley* 66 Cr App Rep 278 (1978), *R* v. *Dunphy* 3 Cr App R (S) 309 (1981).

12 By the 1983/4 season, the cost of policing football matches had reached 9.5 per cent of gate receipts (Butler 1991, p. 205).

13 However, research carried out by the author at Preston Magistrates' Court suggested that this 'lead' by the higher courts was not being pursued by the Magistrates' Courts even following high-profile disturbances. This trend had earlier been noted by Magistrates' Court research by Salter, M. ('Judicial Responses to Football Hooliganism' (1986) Northern Ireland Legal Quarterly 37/3: 280).

14 For example, Home Secretary David Blunkett stating that he wanted to 'nail' an alleged 'hooligan ringleader' arrested at the 2004 European Championships (BBC 5Live 20/06/04). In addition, during France 98, Tony Blair demanded in the Commons that employers of those arrested for 'hooliganism' took 'very strong action' against them (BBC News, 17/6/98).

15 Including the Sporting Events (Control of Alcohol) Act 1985, the Public Order Act 1986, the Football Spectators Act 1989, the Football Offences Act 1991 and the Criminal Justice and Public Order Act 1995. For more on this see Pearson, G., 'Legislating for the Football Hooligan: A Case For Reform' in Greenfield, S. and Osborn, G. (eds) *Law and Sport in Contemporary Society* (2000), London: Frank Cass.

16 See Armstrong and Hobbs (1994) for more on the Football Intelligence Unit and the undercover operations intended to gather 'intelligence' against the hooligan firms.

17 Hillsborough Stadium Disaster Interim Report, HMSO 15/4/89, especially para 182.

18 Dunning *et al.* (1988) note that, 'As far as we have been able to ascertain . . . it was the start of the 1966–7 League programme which saw the first references in the national press to the activities of "hooligan gangs"' (p. 165).

19 (1949) 1 All ER 337 at p. 339.

20 Redhead, S., 'Always Look on the Bright Side of Life' in *The Passion and the Fashion* (1993) Avebury: Aldershot p. 3.

21 Cohen, S., *Folk Devils and Moral Panics* (2002), London: Routledge.

22 See Hall, S. (1978), especially pp. 15–26.

23 Pearson, G., 'The English Disease? The Socio-Legal Construction of Football

Hooliganism' *Youth and Policy – The Journal of Critical Analysis* No. 60, Summer 1998: 1–15, p. 12.

24 Williams, J., 'The Cost of Risk Societies' *The Journal of Forensic Psychiatry* Vol. 12 No. 1 April 2001 1–7, p. 2.

25 Hansard [Commons] 3/7/85, Col. 398.

26 As the judge in the case of *R* v. *Rogers-Hinks* constructed it (11 Cr App R (S) 234 at p. 237).

27 For example the legislative response to the problem of ticket touting (Greenfield, S. and Osborn, G., 'After the Act: The (Re)Construction and Regulation of Football Fandom', *Journal of Civil Liberties* 1996 Vol. 1: 7–28, p. 28).

28 *R* v. *Motley* (1978) 66 Cr App R 274 at p. 277.

29 See Pearson (1998), p. 13.

30 *R* v. *Rogers-Hinks* 11 Cr App R (S) 234 at p. 237.

31 *R* v. *Muranyi* 8 Cr App R (S) 176.

32 The convictions were quashed on appeal when it was revealed that that much of the evidence had been fabricated.

33 *R* v. *Motley* (1978) at 278.

34 Trivizas, E., 'Sentencing the Football Hooligan', *British Journal of Criminology*, 1981 21: 342–349, p. 346.

35 *R* v. *Squibbs* C.A. (Cr) 17/5/82 Unreported.

36 Safety at Sports Grounds Act 1975.

37 Sporting Events (Control of Alcohol) Act 1985.

38 Public Order Act 1986.

39 The Report also identified safety concerns with the scheme, most notably congestion at computerized turnstiles and had doubts as to whether the technology to run the system was sufficiently developed.

40 Hillsborough Stadium Disaster Final Report HMSO 15/5/89, paras 377 and 424.

41 The result was the Football (Offences) Act 1991, which criminalized invading the pitch, indecent and racist chanting and throwing missiles inside a stadium.

42 There were 6,147 arrests during the 1987/88 season, dropping to only 4,119 in the season following *Italia 90*.

43 The total attendance for the 1987/8 season was 17,968,965, which had increased to 19,027,390 by 1990/91.

44 Although Bufford chronicles that they still travelled regardless (Bufford, B., *Among the Thugs*, 1995, Mandarin: London Part 1, pp. 35–106).

45 Many clubs employed increasing numbers of stewards and private security firm employees following the ruling in *Harris* v. *Sheffield United FC Ltd* [1987] 3 WLR 305 that clubs should foot the bill for police officers stationed inside their stadiums (even when extra officers were deemed necessary by the police themselves but not the club in question).

46 Under Section 30 of the Public Order Act 1986. By 1996, there were 400 (Domestic) Exclusion Orders in force preventing convicted 'hooligans' from attending football matches.

47 The *Guardian* 27/2/95. However, the Football Intelligence Unit claimed that they knew of at least 30 'known hooligans' making the trip.

48 Author's own estimation from Participant Observation. The *Telegraph* (16/6/98) conservatively estimated that only 25,000 English fans were present inside the stadium for the match with another 2,000 watching on a Giant Screen on the beach.

49 The *Guardian* 28/6/00, *The Telegraph* 18/6/00, 17/6/00.

50 Although only one was charged with an offence.

51 The *Guardian* 22/10/97.

52 This saw the number of Restriction Orders soar to 70 (*Express* 31/8/98).

53 *The Times*, 26/6/98.

54 For more on the responses of British and French authorities to the disorder in Marseilles, see Pearson, G., 'Legitimate Targets? The Civil Liberties of Football Fans', *Journal of Civil Liberties*, 1999, Vol. 04/1, 28–47, pp. 41–47.

55 For more on this, see Osborn, G. (2002) 'Football Hooliganism and Human Rights', *Journal of Civil Liberties*.

56 Such as extending the definitions of illegal chanting to include that carried out by an individual and extending the definition of 'football-related' for the imposition of banning orders.

57 Exclusion Orders were renamed Domestic Banning Orders (Football (Offences and Disorder) Act 1999 s. 6(1).

58 Kate Hoey (then Sports Minister) Standing Committee D, 5/5/99.

59 The *Mirror*, 31/3/98.

60 Schedule 1, Section 14B(2).

61 Schedule 1, Section 14B(2)(b).

62 www.nds.coi.gov.uk/.

63 Lord Bassam, Lords Hansard, 4/5/04 Col.: 1104.

64 E.g. http://www.cjsonline.gov.uk, 8/8/02.

65 The cost of travel and accommodation combined with an expectation amongst many of England's followers that there would be little opportunity for trouble, both as a result of few of the 'hooligans' travelling and a lack of opportunity for confrontation with rival fans or locals.

66 *Gough and Smith* v. *Chief Constable of Derbyshire* [2001] 4 All ER 289 (DC) and *Gough and Smith* v. *Chief Constable of Derbyshire* [2002] EWCA Civ 251 (CA). See Pearson, G., 'A Cure Worse than the Disease? Reflections on *Gough and Smith* v. *Chief Constable of Derbyshire*' in *Entertainment Law* 2002 Vol. 1 No. 2: 292–102.

67 Ibid. See also 'Football Banning Orders' Current Survey, *Public Law* Autumn 2002: 576–577 and Taylor, N., 'Football Banning Orders do not violate Community or Convention law' (2002) *Journal of Criminal Law* 66(4), 309–311.

68 This is a contrasting decision to that in *Lauko* v. *Slovakia* [1999] 1 EHRLR 105, where it was held that an anti-social behaviour fine under the Minor Offences Act 1990 *was* a criminal charge and should only be imposed following the correct criminal procedure required by Article 6. The fact that a state classified an act or a penalty as 'non criminal' does not mean that the European Court of Human Rights is precluded from ruling that the act or penalty *is* in fact criminal in nature (see *Benham* v. *UK* (1996) 22 EHRR 293).

69 Clayton, R., 'Regaining a Sense of Proportion: The Human Rights Act and the Proportionality Principle' EHRLR 2001, 5: 12.

70 *Gough and Smith* v. *Chief Constable of Derbyshire* [2002] EWCA Civ 251 para 90.

71 Although questions must then be asked as to the effectiveness of the Act, which was introduced to impose banning orders upon those whom the police did not have sufficient evidence to lead to a criminal conviction for football-related violence.

72 Pearson (2002), p. 98.

73 At the World Cup in Italy in 1990, for example, over 300 English fans were deported, but only 60 of these had officially been arrested (Armstrong and Hobbs 1994, pp. 221–222).

74 Council Directive 73/148/EEC, Article 2(1).

75 *Sporrong and Lonnroth* v. *Sweden* [1983] 5 EHRR 35, p. 52.

76 ECHR Article 3.
77 ECHR Article 5.
78 *Gough and Smith* v. *Chief Constable of Derbyshire* [2002] QB 1213, para 46.
79 *R* v. *Goldstein* [1983] 1 WLR 151 at p. 155.
80 *Gough and Smith* v. *Chief Constable of Derbyshire* [2002] QB 1213, para 76.
81 Council Directive 73/148/EEC, Article 2(1).
82 *de Freitas* v. *Permanent Secretary of Ministry of Agriculture, Fisheries, Lands and Housing* [1999] 1 AC 69.
83 Ibid., para 63.
84 *Gough and Smith* v. *Chief Constable of Derbyshire* [2002] EWCA Civ 25, para 57.
85 *Gough and Another* v. *Chief Constable of The Derbyshire Constabulary, Regina (Miller)* v. *Leeds Magistrates' Court, Lilley* v. *Director of Public Prosecutions* [2001] 3 CMLR 29 Heading 3.
86 Ibid., para 1.
87 Ibid., para 42.
88 Ibid., para 81.
89 *Gough and Smith* v. *Chief Constable of Derbyshire* [2002] EWCA Civ 25, para 3.
90 Ibid., para 82.
91 Ibid., para 6.
92 Ibid.
93 Ibid., para 7.
94 Ibid., para 25.
95 Hansard (HC Debates), 13 July 2000, Col.: 1181.
96 *Gough and Smith* v. *Chief Constable of Derbyshire* [2002] EWCA Civ 25 para 25.
97 Ibid., para 24.
98 See, for example, Stott, C.J. (2003) 'Police expectations and the control of English soccer fans at "Euro2000"'. *Policing: An International Journal of Police Strategies and Management.* 26, 640–655.
99 Ibid., para 35.
100 The more targeted style of policing was used by the Dutch with great success before England's first game of the tournament.
101 Even this conviction is highly suspect. Ironically, British intelligence officers have not insisted on a banning order being served on the individual because they are convinced the conviction is unjust (Mark Forrester 01/09/02).
102 Per Viscount Sankley L.C. in *Woolmington* v. *Director of Public Prosecutions* [1935] A.C. 462 at 481, affirmed in *Attorney-General of Hong Kong* v. *Lee Kwong-Kut* [1993] 3 WLR 329 at 339–340.
103 Including an American businessman detained for 22 hours before being released without charge (*Telegraph* 19/6/00).
104 'Hooligan' Part II, BBC Television, BBC 2, 19/5/02.
105 Armstrong and Hobbs (1994) at p. 221.
106 *Gough and Smith* v. *Chief Constable of Derbyshire* [2002] EWCA Civ 25 para 62.
107 Ibid., para 62(ii).
108 The disorder in Copenhagen between Arsenal and Galatasaray fans in 2000 is the most obvious example. Other incidents of disorder affecting fans of English club sides, for example involving Manchester United fans in Istanbul in 1993, Leeds fans in the same city in 2000 and Manchester United fans in Oporto in 1997 have been more the result of violence by home supporters and/or bad policing than 'hooliganism' by English fans.
109 In this period, Manchester United alone have played 60 matches away from home in Europe (including the 2002/03 season). In the 2002–2003 season alone, English club sides played 39 matches abroad in European competitions.
110 Lords Hansard, 4/5/04 Col.: 1104.

111 The names of 300 'known hooligans' were passed onto Dutch police ahead of England's match in Eindhoven with this intention (*Telegraph* 11/6/00).

112 The two days of reported 'rioting' in Albufeira, Portugal, by English supporters during the 2004 European Championships, for example, led to no major injuries; the BBC reported that despite up to 200 fans being involved on the first night, only ten individuals, including one police office, required medical treatment for minor injuries.

113 E.g. the 'staged intervention' policy of Portuguese police at the 2004 European Championships.

6 Sports and the countryside in the twenty-first century[1]

Andrew Blake

Country sports, and the question of their potential futures (if any), raise a number of profound and complex issues about local identity and political agency, and their regulation, in the contemporary world of globalizing capitalism and commodified leisure practices. To most of their supporters, traditional country sports involving hunting, shooting and fishing are claimed to be the participant expression of a social group and its agriculturally related mode of life in the countryside itself. Without the supporting apparatus of the rest of rural life, its proponents argue, the notion of country sports would have no meaning. They are therefore conceptually as well as spatially a world away from the hyper-commodified and globalized mercenary trade of urban sports such as professional league football, in which the highest-paying professional teams asset-strip the developing world to provide a form of circus-entertainment for a paying public, most of whom access the resulting entertainment on screen. All the circus needs is a big top, which could be anywhere – so new stadia are built where convenient, whatever the traditions of the clubs which play in them. Country sports, on the other hand – the argument runs – are crafted in relation to landscape and community, and cannot survive without both.

Against this well-defended position, however, run a number of counter-positions which define both countryside and sport rather differently. The countryside is also the site for a number of long-established sporting activities which do not involve the torture and killing of fish, birds or animals – activities such as fell running, rock climbing and mountaineering. In their turn these relatively well-established pursuits have recently been joined by 'extreme' activities such as bungee-jumping, white-water canoeing and snowboarding. To the proponents of these activities, questions of community and tradition, or even of the countryside as the *location* of community and tradition, are less relevant. The countryside is the location, and for some of these activities needs preparation as such, but need not necessarily have any sustaining local culture; in particular, the existence of agriculture (the sustaining modus operandi of most extant British landscapes) is irrelevant to these pursuits.

For many users, meanwhile, the countryside is idealized as the location of a very unsporting peace and quiet, of afternoon teas and short walks: in the definition below to achieve remoteness, a sense of nature, and to 'get away from it all' means setting aside large tracts of land specifically for the purpose. In this definition most land, containing forms of contemporary agriculture such as intensively sewn crops and battery produced animals, is not really 'countryside' at all:

> The essence of the concept of national parks lies in the striking quality and remoteness of much of the scenery, along with the harmony between man and nature which it displays, and the opportunities it offers for suitable (quiet, open-air) recreation. The qualities do not necessarily depend on altitude: lowland areas might also qualify if, for example, they contained extensive areas of semi-natural vegetation, such as forest, heathland or downland, and if they provided opportunities to 'get away from it all'.[2]

Official policy has tended to support the latter position, designating some areas as of 'natural beauty', and allowing the rest to function as intensive agricultural land, subject to the whims of the EU's Common Agricultural Policy. In this sense only a few areas of land are 'countryside'; the rest is merely a farm.

It became common in the early twenty-first century to attack the UK's New Labour government as a proponent of consumer capitalism, individual wealth and the private ownership of actual and virtual space – in other words, this particular government was accused of hanging on to the coat tails of Thatcherism, without an ideology of its own. While such an accusation is not without foundation, the New Labour government's legislation on rural issues has gone against this tendency and included a number of measures designed to go against the wishes of landowners and the ways in which country people claim, collectively, to wish to use the land. In doing so, according to the landowners' representatives, the legislators are imperilling the traditional social communities which are held together by these uses of the land. Symbolic of these debates were the questions of access to open land for walkers, and the future of hunting sports. The devolved Scottish parliament, also run by a Labour administration, both confirmed the general public's right to access to land and, in 2002, after fierce debate in and outside parliament, banned hunting with dogs.[3] Meanwhile for England and Wales the 2000 Wildlife and Countryside act included a limited 'right to roam' over land not used for intensive agriculture, and anti-hunting bills like that for Scotland were three times passed by the House of Commons with very large majorities. However, opposition in the House of Lords had on each occasion prevented these bills from becoming law, and the issue remained unresolved despite a commitment in the Labour government's 2001 manifesto to 'enable Parliament to reach a conclusion on this issue' until February 2005 when under the provisions of the Hunting Act 2004 hunting with dogs was banned in England and Wales.[4]

In opposing the will of the House of Commons the movement for the preservation of hunting, shooting and fishing sports, led by the broad-based coalition the Countryside Alliance, deployed a politics of identity and of alienation, in which the 'right' has taken on much of the apparatus of popular protest which has been associated with movements of the left and the indigenous poor. The Countryside Alliance claimed that traditional rural dwellers are being denied the right to preserve their culture by an oppressive urban majority (including those who have moved from town to country 'looking for peace and quiet' rather than becoming part of the indigenous lifestyle); furthermore that this oppressive majority is driven not only by the discourse of animal rights but also by class hatred.

As a component of this articulate and aware minority politics, a 2003 poster advertising campaign by the Countryside Alliance used images of black female farmer's wife and restaurateur Sarah Lake and slim young white female nurse Sarah Bell – each of whom is an enthusiastic huntswoman, and each was photographed both in pinks and workwear. This campaign laid the questions of stereotyping and minority discrimination firmly on the table, though these shocking images also underlined the quotidian rural whiteness and masculinity of these activities as they are more generally represented. The Countryside Alliance pressed home its egalitarian claims with a picket of the 2003 Labour Party conference led by pro-hunting bikers, and another led by 'miners, nurses, teachers, lollipop ladies, undertakers, dinner ladies'.[5] Adopting the Alliance's discourse and supporting the freedom to practise animal-centred countryside sports as a fundamental 'human right', the conservative broadsheet newspaper the *Daily Telegraph* argued from a position of libertarianism informed once again by an adopted politics of the minority – whose associated positions include anti-identity-card campaigns.

At stake here, then, are a number of competing definitions both of the countryside and of sport; these have emerged and been fought over a long period of intense historical change. The employment opportunities produced by the Industrial Revolution of the 1780s and after began to transfer most people to large towns and cities, where urban sports were developed as country ways were lost. This helped to produce a collective town-dwellers' notion of the countryside not as a place of farm labour, food production and class conflict, but as a green haven of peace and tranquillity. During the later nineteenth century the railways, and during the twentieth century a strange combination of communist agitation against aristocratic privilege, and the increasing prevalence of the motor car, opened up the furthest reaches of the British countryside to the urban population.[6] National Parks, created by the National Parks and Access to the Countryside Act 1949, are the apex of the systematic post-war development of significant tranches of land as opportunities for leisure and tourism – chiefly for the use of people who do not live and work in the country themselves – which includes mapped foot and cycle paths and bridleways for horse riding, regulated by local authorities; but also country hotels, and walking, camping, climbing and mountaineering goods. There has been, then, both a regulatory *classification* and a general *commodification* of the great outdoors, in order for people to consume the countryside as walking or climbing observers rather than as resident hunters or farmers.

Such use has increased since the first National Parks were designated. The increasing pressure to self-produce the fit body – in the early twenty-first century associated with a moral panic over 'obesity'[7] – has coincided with the marketing of the country as the repository of health-giving fresh air and exercise, which in turn has led to acute pressure on areas of the greatest perceived natural beauty. The first Parks were all upland areas remote from London, rather than the chalk downland or open heath and forest in the south-east of England – areas of perceived beauty which were, nonetheless, the site of intense tourist pressure. The South Downs has an estimated 39 million person-day-visits per year,[8] and the (smaller) New Forest 22 million,[9] and for this reason among others there has been continuing pressure since the 1940s to re-create both these areas as National Parks, announced by Government in 1999 as a 'millennium gift to the nation', At the time of writing the planning of the South Downs park was underway, while the boundary of the New Forest National Park, meanwhile, was announced in June 2004; under the New Forest National Park Designation Order 2005, the Park was to become fully operational on 1 April 2006.

National Parks are subject to complex legislative frameworks, their shape controlled by boundary commissions; development within them is strictly limited. While there was much popular support for these proposals, there was also opposition from local individuals committed to a view of the countryside closer to that of the Countryside Alliance, and who see the incursion of walkers, cyclists and campers as a threat to their way of life – as here in evidence to the New Forest public enquiry:

> Commoners are individuals who possess rights of common. They exercise their grazing rights by 'depasturing' their stock on the open forest. Only a small number are able to make a complete living from commoning. Most are part-time commoners supplementing their income from other sources; others simply keep one or two animals on the forest to maintain the age-old tradition. 'Backup grazing' is important to commoners to support their commoning activities. This is the enclosed pasture land, ideally located close to a commoner's holding, which is used for over wintering stock, raising store cattle, making hay or silage, tending sick animals and young stock, and preparing stock for market. This land may be owned or rented. In addition to the land that is presently in use as backup grazing, there is a wider pool of land currently used for other purposes that might be capable of use as backup grazing for future generations of commoners, subject to availability and

cost. In recent years, commoners have found it increasingly difficult to purchase suitable properties and smallholdings due to very high prices – reflecting the area's popularity with commuters and holidaymakers. In addition, it has become very difficult to purchase or rent suitable paddocks or fields because of the premium values that such land can achieve for more intensive forms of agriculture, for recreational horsekeeping, and in some cases for mineral extraction and urban development.[10]

It is worth noting that none of these spaces are seen by farmer, commoner, walker or horse rider alike as suitable for the noisier, and/or more 'extreme' postmodern country sports such as mountain biking or 4×4 driving.

The commoners present their way of life as under threat from the incursion of market forces. Capitalism – which forces up house prices and encourages unsympathetic in-migration – is seen to impinge on 'tradition'. The Countryside Alliance tries to occupy a similar position: but can it? Hunting on horseback can still be seen as 'traditional', and even as locally democratic, though access to horse and hound still requires both capital and training. However, whatever their supporters argue, fishing and shooting have left the boundaries of 'tradition' and become contracted *rights*, an aspect of the more general regulation, commodification and corporatization of contemporary sport through the legal realizations of time and opportunity as property. Buying an afternoon's trout fishing or a day on a grouse moor, in other words, involves a similar limited-access and limited-use agreement to that involved in buying an afternoon's use of an executive box at a Premiership soccer match or in subscribing to a television sports channel. Both the 'right to roam' established in 2000, and the creation of the new National Parks, are a denial of this web of contemporary capitalist economic and spatial relations, and without a synchronous, profound, rethinking of what 'the countryside' is, and how it is currently operated upon by the forces of capital and class, such legislation is arguably an anachronism in a world of commodified agriculture, leisure and tourism services in which the 'right' to access and use any commodity is *always* paid for.

Thatcherism (re)established the bourgeois values of individual ownership and the primacy of capital partly through modernizing the countryside, both through 'heritage' (commodified leisure forms such as country house visits) and through new forms of enclosure – the selling of land owned by privatized corporations such as British Gas and BT, and the creeping privatization of the Forestry Commission. The 1980s, in other words, established a view of property and right which is closer to that held in the eighteenth century than the semi-nationalized public sphere of the post-war settlement, which includes the National Parks. The icing on this particular cake was the 1994 Criminal Justice Act, whose draconian new views of criminal trespass reinvigorated the sense of genuinely private and/or corporate land-ownership, and which in turn meant yet more bourgeois pursuit of the dream of country life. This is one example of something common in contemporary Britain, a 'retrolution', in which the future (of ownership, in this instance) is presented in the past's terms.[11]

Again, it would appear in this light that the right to roam, however welcome in itself, seems ideologically absurd, given the intensification of ownership rights during and after the 1980s. Nonetheless, the idea of the right to roam is conducive to those participatory country sports facilitated by the creation of National Parks – not hunting, shooting or fishing but orienteering, fell running, hill walking, mountaineering and perhaps even (a particular landowners' bugbear, shared by many walkers) mountain biking. Though these activities could be said to belong in the widest sense to 'heritage culture' – they are inheritors of the practices of nineteenth century aristocratic masculinity, which include the origins of mountaineering – they are also in their turn deeply commodified, served by dedicated clothing firms such as Rohan, Berghaus, and the Brasher Boot Company, and magazines like *The Great Outdoors*, which celebrate both in concept and commodity the public availability of recreational landscape. Anyone wishing to see a more fully realized, democratic, version of this notion might visit Sweden or Finland, and examine (or better, use!) those countries' cross-country skiing networks and hiking trails. But Britain is not Scandinavia (or even the USA, whose magnificent national and state parks offset the otherwise hyper-individualized view of landownership in that country); and activities such as hiking or skiing are emphatically not what the Countryside Alliance wishes to preserve.

The Countryside Alliance started by deploying its range of contemporary political techniques against its opponents to stunning, if not quite lethal effect. One of the first actions of the 1997 Parliament was a private member's bill to ban hunting with dogs, passed at first reading by a massive Commons majority which the Bill's opponents countered not just by lobbying, but by a well-calculated use of the politics of mass opposition. The Alliance's campaign adopted wholesale the leftish traditions of CND/ Greenham/Ecological activism which had become increasingly 'respectable' partly thanks to mass protests over the export of live animals. These protests, and public horror and anger at police intervention on behalf of animal traders, were one aspect of a very widespread public unrest about the unaccountable practices of industrial farming, which had produced BSE and subsequently the foot and mouth disease epidemic of 2001, and was later echoed by concerns (and again mass protests) over genetically modified crops. The 1998 Countryside March saw over a quarter of a million people in the biggest central London demonstration since the heyday of the Campaign for Nuclear Disarmament; this was followed in short order by the abandonment of the Fox-hunting Bill through the fiction of lack of parliamentary time. However, this success for the Countryside Alliance was followed by an organizational crisis comparable to that within the Conservative Party, and driven by similar, interconnected inner tensions; which is probably why Tony Blair considered it safe to return to the issue, in June 1999 promising that hunting would be banned during the lifetime of the subsequent Parliament – the promise was then, as we have seen, repeated in the manifesto. Despite the lukewarm conclusions of an enquiry chaired by Lord Burns which reported to Parliament in 2000 that the ending of hunting would not have the claimed devastating effects on rural economies, a new Bill to ban hunting with dogs was introduced in March 2002.[12]

The renewed threat, however, revived the Countryside Alliance, and there was an even bigger Countryside 'Liberty and Livelihood' March in central London in March 2002, with some estimating the turnout on this occasion as half a million, and most agreeing it was over four hundred thousand; at any rate it rewrote the record books once more as the largest British public demonstration (though it was arguably superseded in size by the march against the Iraq war in early 2003). Again, the new Bill was held up in the House of Lords, and effectively blocked by the time Parliament broke up for its summer recession in June 2003. But the context of the opposition was different, as the word 'livelihood' implies; the mass support for the Country-side Alliance now reflected the widespread view not just that rural sporting activities were under threat but that farming itself was in crisis, with knock-on effects on the countryside, its communities and way of life as a whole. Farmers were reportedly leaving the land at the rate of 200 per week in the summer of 2003; their (small) farms were being bought by wealthy incom-ers who wished to own country houses with pleasant rural views, and were happy for any actual farming to be outsourced to local contractors (often using illegal, temporary, immigrant labour on very low wages, rather than people who could be described as part of a local rural community).

This situation strongly echoes that of the 1880s: the very similar crisis over agriculture and land use in a time of declining prices which arose at the end of the nineteenth century remained unresolved until the land sales which fol-lowed the First World War began to remove the aristocracy from their natural habitat, and created a large number of medium-sized family owned farms, many of which did well from the subsidy regimes of the 1940s and after, but had by the turn of the century become unviable in their turn, thanks both to horrendous waves of animal disease and the continuing market control of a small cartel of supermarkets. There is a set of problems in agriculture, which should be obvious to all who have tasted the 'ripe' but tasteless tomatoes pro-vided by supermarkets that have abolished seasonality by global import strat-egies. Indeed, these issues are addressed by the Countryside Alliance and its satellite organizations, which for example promote Farmers' Markets as an alternative to the supermarket cartel.[13] There is another strong echo of the politics of the left here: the provision of local food for local people is also, of course, a key strategic aim for the anti-capitalist movement.

Nonetheless the Countryside Alliance remained *principally* concerned not with the general rural crisis but with the defence of rural sporting practices, and here the representational disjuncture is at its widest. After all, whatever our concerns about quality and safety, most of us recognize that food is pro-duced in the countryside and that farmers (if not their subsidies) are therefore a good thing. But we do not value a distinctive rural sporting culture, partly because we tend to recognize as 'sport' only the games which were codified in or around the 1860s – urban contests with restricted playing times and enclosed areas, involving human performance. The football and rugby codes, representative county cricket, lawn tennis and so on were (re)invented during the decade of the 1851 census, which revealed that for the first time the majority of Britons lived in towns and cities; a process of urbanization which the rest of the world has followed. By the 1880s most of the new codes were undergoing professionalization, and/or debates about its extent. These 30 years were a very important moment in world history, as the subsequent globalization of these sports has shown.

But – and here the traditionalists' argument is, again, on very shaky ground – the same processes which aided urbanization, and the creation of urban sport, also helped to create what we now know as country sports. Even as they were in most eyes being 'replaced' by urban time- and arena-based sports, country sports became more accessible to (wealthy) town dwellers. The railways facilitated the transport of horses, and so in both racing and fox hunting, national circuits were developed – in just the same way that the national railway network made the Football League possible. Urban dwellers such as Londoner Anthony Trollope used railways to attend hunting meets in the Midlands. Grouse shooting on the moors of Yorkshire, and deerstalking in the Highlands of Scotland, also became pursuits nationally available (to the wealthy) thanks to the railway. And from this point on the countryside, its culture and its sports, were increasingly seen as part of a sanitized and pseudo-timeless natural environment. This was a sweeping change. Even early in the nineteenth century, field sports were an acknowledged aspect of the class war whose countryside manifestations included the Captain Swing riots of the 1820s.[14] Only the revision of the game laws in the Game Act of 1831 allowed tenant farmers to shoot 'game' animals and birds, the property of the landowner, which were causing damage to their crops. But a generation on, following various adjustments to the Parliamentary franchise, field sports were seen as archaisms. An attack on fox hunting by historian E.A. Freeman, published by the liberal *Fortnightly Review* in 1869, simply dismissed it as aristocratic barbarism.[15]

Freeman's attack led to a spirited debate involving two of the founders of the *Review*, the enthusiastic huntsman Anthony Trollope, and Helen Taylor, an opponent of hunting; Freeman and Taylor are usually taken to have won the argument. They are therefore among the early proponents of the position that defines 'sport' positively only when it is derived from that moment of relatively comfortable bourgeois hegemony in the 1850s, which produced the urban, time-based and professional sporting world which we now take for granted – for example the National Portrait Gallery's exhibition of Sporting Heroes, held in 1999, excluded field sports altogether, and represented few amateurs.[16] 'Sport' today, then, is urban and professional, and is represented as such.

Television follows this agenda: there have been a few fishing programmes, but the closest terrestrial television comes to hunting is through coverage of that vestigial relative of fox hunting, National Hunt racing. In 1998, despite vigorous complaint, BBC2 even dropped the popular (and one assumes relatively cheap) sheepdog-trialling contest 'One Man and his Dog'. Sky Sports' voracious multi-channel appetite for sporting contests has led to coverage of sporting clay shoots, and 1999 saw a clay-target simulacrum of rough shooting, 'Man and Dog', but there is little coverage of actual hunting with dogs, or the shooting of game – certainly no televised 'Glorious 12th' of August (the opening day of the grouse-shooting season). Television represents the countryside as the place townies go for a quiet weekend, or to move to for a quiet life, indeed as 'natural', rather than the man-made food factory which most of it is. Some aspects of meat production (i.e. the killing of purpose-bred animals) have been represented through programmes such as *Country Hour*, and tangentially, and only implicitly, through the massive number of infotainment cookery programmes; but animals are usually seen more sentimentally, through vet programmes such as *Pet Rescue*. Television casually and routinely, in both fictional and non-fictional forms, displays violence against the person; but it never shows human violence against animals.

Of course field sports and country living are more generously represented in print: there are dedicated magazines, upmarket glossies like *Country Living* and *The Field* and downmarket, male-hobbyist weeklies such as *Coarse Fishing* or *Sporting Gun*. Across all these publications the discourse of country sport inhabits and reworks the discourse of all contemporary, commodified participation sports: describing the activity, how to do it well, and what to buy in order to be able to do it. Since the object for most country sports enthusiasts is participation rather than spectatorship, the coverage is, therefore, directly comparable with that for contemporary 'extreme' adrenaline sports such as snowboarding and hang gliding, and field journalism represents its 'timeless' pursuits through a set of contemporary commodities and commodified practices. In all sports, including field pursuits, capital flows into leisure: through catering for corporate entertainment, and through sports clothing and equipment such as saddles and safety hats, rods and lines, guns and cartridges. And through the trade in, precisely, estates: not the superior cottages of the faux-rural *Country Life* and its televised equivalents but fully fitted hunting estates with some or all of farms, tied cottages, big houses and/or hunting lodges, grouse moors, salmon or trout streams, and enough woodland and cover crops to hide pheasants, partridges and foxes. Reading such material, anyone with the money can learn how to take part in traditional rural sports – how to become part of an oppressed minority.

Alongside the appeal to tradition and the deployment of minority politics, the other chief parameter of hunting/shooting/fishing discourse is a strongly argued relationship between field sports and conservation. The umbrella over this position is the truism that hunting requires the preservation of air, land and water game in woodland, scrub, and relatively clean water, and the consequent argument that this activity should therefore be encouraged because it prevents the reversion of the countryside to pesticide-poisoned prairies in which, as in parts of East Anglia, streams have turned to nitrogenous drains, with dangerous consequences for the human water supply as well as the fish, and the birds which feed on them. The most prominent national game-shooting organization, doubtless with an eye to lobbying tactics, calls itself the British Association for Shooting and Conservation; it helps to fund the Game Conservancy, which conducts £1.5 million of research annually into topics such as the type of ground cover and crops suitable for the raising of game, which can aid cash-strapped farmers' diversification by encouraging them to farm with a more ecosensitive and biodiverse approach, and then make money from the selling of shooting and fishing rights. The organization has collaborated with English Nature and other quangos in producing plans for the game-friendly conservation of areas such as the Somerset Levels.[17]

We end with a closer look at this ecologically sensitive activity. Although the government has explicitly stated that it is not under threat,[18] shooting enthusiasts assume that since hunting has been banned, shooting will be top of the agenda for the class warriors who in their view are the leading opponents of bloodsports. Furthermore, since the Dunblane massacre (on 14 March 1996, frustrated would-be paedophile Thomas Hamilton shot and killed 16 children with a legally held handgun) handgun ownership was banned in the Firearms Amendment Act 1997, and subsequently there has been an increasingly vocal lobby against all gun ownership. Meanwhile crimes involving the use of illegally held guns have risen sharply; and the Home Office continues to propose tighter gun control legislation. The Campaign for Shooting, an associate campaign of the Countryside Alliance, is one result of these twin pressures.

There were some 560,000 shotgun licence holders in the UK in mid-2003,[19] a figure which has been in gradual decline for two decades thanks in part to the lack of police enthusiasm for private ownership of such weapons. Many licence holders shoot clay targets only; most shoot game as well, using clays to keep their eyes in during the close season. Shooting is striated by the class differences signalled by the shotgun itself: new or used, a matched pair of handmade game guns by the likes of Purdey can cost as much as a new Porsche (i.e. in excess of £60,000), while equally efficient factory made guns by say Browning or Beretta can be bought new for less than £1,000 each. Similarly, while opportunities for shooting pheasant, partridge or grouse during the season, when available, retail at several hundred pounds per day upwards, wildfowling (the shooting of wild duck or geese) can be far cheaper, and pheasants are often bred and shot by syndicates which are cheaper to join, if more exacting in their requirements of members. Common estimates are that over 25 million pheasants per year are bred, released and shot (at – many escape) in Britain.[20]

Clay pigeon shooting is a more democratic (though, again, mainly masculine) pursuit. The real popularity of this activity dates from the Captive Birds Act of 1922, when the semi-rural working-class pursuit of live-trap pigeon shooting was banned (despite a petition in the sport's favour, organized by the *Daily Express* newspaper, with over a million signatures). This ban was among the last vestiges of the puritanical anti-popular-sporting movement which had banned bull running and dog fighting in the 1840s, but – until recently – had not turned its attention to the cruel sports of the upper classes.

Deerstalking and other rifle-based pursuits are the preserve of a smaller group, again partly thanks to the draconian views of the licensing authorities, and partly thanks to the costs of opportunities for using rifles, which range from the very expensive – such as deerstalking in the Scottish Highlands – to the cheap but still comparatively rare – e.g. 'lamping' to 'control' foxes. There are some 131,000 rifle licence holders in the UK.[21]

Shooting has only a shadow existence as a sporting activity within recognized public discourse. A keyword search for 'shooting' in the online archives of magazines and newspapers will reveal first references to warfare and political dispute; second to crime; third to computer games; and fourth to sporting shooting – and only then with any frequency during the Olympic Games. There was, for example, an unusual amount of media coverage in the aftermath of the British success in clay target shooting at the 2000 games. But coverage even of this relatively uncontroversial moment of national triumph has to be seen in the context of the coverage of shooting issues during that year:

> 31 January 2000 the *Daily Telegraph* reported rural-incomer disquiet at Richard Faulds' clay-target practise (they didn't like the noise); the article predicted an Olympic medal for Faulds despite this opposition.

> 4 April a Home Office Select Committee report on air gun, rifle and shot gun ownership recommended tighter controls on licensing and the ending of licenses, indeed any use of shotguns and rifles, for the under-14s. A common viewpoint given in evidence to the Committee, most prominently by Scots, was that no-one who is not directly involved in vermin control should ever be allowed legal possession of any projectile weapon for any purpose.

> 31 July a *Guardian* feature on sporting clay-shooting world champion George Digweed also predicted a medal for Faulds.

> 20 September Faulds duly won his Olympic gold medal, and was praised by then Sports Minister (and enthusiastic clay shooter, and, I fear, Arsenal fan) Kate Hoey; there was a brief press debate about Faulds's right to practise and the nature of the 'local' opposition thereto. A reported increase in enquiries about taking up shooting was glossed by the *Daily Telegraph* as 'the sport's emergence from the shadow of the Dunblane massacre'.

29 September charity Animal Aid revealed what it claimed was the truth about pheasant shooting in a report entitled 'The Killing Fields'. Animal Aid's report was a deliberate political intervention, released to coincide with this revival of interest in shooting – the 'truth' being both that a very large number of birds are slaughtered, and, worse, that many of them are only wounded and therefore die slowly and in pain; the *Telegraph*, the only paper to feature the story on this day, predictably rubbished Animal Aid's views in a leading article.

4 October the *Guardian* replayed the Animal Aid position more or less verbatim, though without acknowledgement, in a report about an anti-pheasant-shooting protest by 'local inhabitants' (none of whom claimed to work on the land) of Cwm nant-y-Meichiaid valley, mid-Wales.

4 October Home Office Minister Charles Clarke, responding to the Home Office Select Committee report into gun ownership which had been published in April, announced new controls on shotgun ownership. License applicants will have to demonstrate 'good reason' to own and keep a gun (a phrase which still at the time of writing awaits cogent definition). The Minister rejected the recommendation that under-14s should be banned from having shotguns, explicitly because Faulds had shot from an early age.

Throughout October and November, *Clarissa and the Countryman* represented country sports, including game shooting (and the resulting food) on prime time BBC2 television.

19 and 20 November. Queen Elizabeth II was criticised by the middle-market tabloids. She had been photographed while (apparently expertly) wringing the neck of a pheasant which had been wounded but not killed outright during a shoot at Sandringham (which the monarchy has always run as a sporting estate). There was general tabloid support for the League Against Cruel Sports' subsequent condemnation of pheasant shooting, and the tabloids also presented much sexist comment on the allegedly unfeminine cruelty of Her Majesty's participation in country sports.

It is worth noting that exactly the same range of discourses was in play four years later as the Athens Olympics drew near. A Prince, William, had been attacked in the popular press for shooting, in Africa, a deer from an endangered species (the paper eventually apologized in June 2004 for what was in fact an unfounded allegation);[22] the Home Office was carrying out yet another consultation on further proposed limitations on gun ownership;[23] and Richard Faulds's neighbours were still complaining about the noise as he practised for the forthcoming Games.[24]

It is all too easy to see from the above how and why those defending country sports – whether lords and ladies, wealthy businessmen or small farmers – can and do represent themselves as an oppressed minority, suborned by tyrannical townies who want a countryside in which nothing and no one gets hurt, or makes a noise, and there aren't any unpleasant smells. Because in a way they are. The Home Office Select Committee's recommendations for more stringent controls on the ownership of shotguns, in the alleged interests of public safety, were made despite common recognition, reported by the Committee and repeatedly agreed by government, that almost all gun-related crime is carried out with illegally held handguns, submachine guns, pump-action shotguns (which are illegal in the UK) and assault rifles. There was no acknowledged sense either in the Committee's report or government response of how any or all of their recommendations might affect the countryside, or its future. Meanwhile the incoming middle class who opposed Richard Faulds's right to shoot are now an entrenched part of the semi-rural, semi-suburban South East of England.

The shooting industry is held to be worth at least £650m per year to the UK economy[25] – this is probably a little *more* than the meat export industry which was 'protected' during 2001 through a claimed £9bn worth of responses to foot and mouth disease, which included the mass public slaughter and burning of millions of animals that were not particularly sick. These included controls under the Foot and Mouth Disease Order 1983 which closed almost all hunting, and most shooting sports, down altogether for several months, and therefore put an end to many of the relevant businesses. Unlike the farmers and livestock dealers who had caused the spread of foot and mouth disease in the first place, the owners of these businesses (like others engaged in rural leisure and tourism) were not able to claim compensation for loss of earnings. In 2001 the Government gave priority to a few thousand (at most) exporters of meat, as its predecessor had done in the mid-1990s controversy over live exports.

All this raises the meta-issue which has been addressed implicitly throughout this chapter: what is land for, and where is the countryside? Principally, it seems, land is for the manufacture and export of food, whatever the cost to British industry and the taxpayer, to existing small farmers, or to unsubsidized production in the developing world, while the countryside is a few small areas of land set aside for recreation. We might think of the first as an aspect of globalization (which it is), but as it happens the tourism and leisure promoted in the development of national parks, and all manner of traditional and innovative activities in the rest of the designated countryside – including hunting, shooting and fishing – could be, and perhaps already are, just as important to the UK's engagement with globalization. The legal status of the countryside and those who work and play within it does not yet fully reflect this fact.

Notes

1 I'm grateful for the opportunity to contribute this chapter, which updates and develops my article 'Field Sports: the Pursuit of the Right?' in *Soundings* no. 13, Autumn 1999, pp. 141–152.

2 *The Report of the National Park Review Panel* (sometimes referred to as the Edwards Report), the Countryside Commission, London, 1991, p. 135.

3 The Protection of Wild Mammals (Scotland) Bill received royal assent on 15 March 2002.

4 Labour Party Manifesto 2001, *Ambitions for Britain*, p. 23.

5 www.countryside-alliance.org accessed 14.02.04.

6 For a significant example of the growing relationship between the car and countryside as recreation see H.V. Morton, *In Search of England*, first published 1927, and seldom out of print since: currently Da Capo Press 2002.

7 See e.g. House of Commons Health Committee, *Obesity*, third report of session 2003–2004, 2 vols, Stationery Office Ltd 2004.

8 South Downs Campaign, *Recreation in the South Downs National Park*, paper in evidence to the Public Inquiry into the Proposed South Downs national Park, inquiry document number WR/3275/9A, 2004.

9 Council for National Parks, *Fifteen Forest Facts*, press release, June 2004, p. 3.

10 New Forest National Park (designation) order 2002 Inquiry Position paper 1, *Reasons for designation and the New Forest national park boundary*, The Countryside Agency 2002, p. 31.

11 For discussion of the idea of retrolution see A. Blake, 'Retrolution: Culture and Heritage in a Young Country', in A. Coddington and M. Perryman, eds, *The Modernisers' Dilemma. Radical Politics in the Age of Blair*, Lawrence & Wishart 1998; and Blake, *The Irresistible Rise of Harry Potter*, Verso 2002, pp. 8–9, 15–17.

12 Lord Burns *et al.*, *Final Report of the Committee of Inquiry into Hunting with Dogs in England and Wales*, Stationery Office Ltd 2000.

13 www.countryside-alliance.org accessed 10.04.04.

14 See E. Hobsbawm and G. Rudé, *Captain Swing*, Pimlico 1993.

15 E.A. Freeman, 'The Morality of Field Sports', *The Fortnightly Review* vol. XII no. 3, Sep. 1869, pp. 353–385.

16 See James Huntington-Whiteley and Richard Holt, *The Book of British Sporting Heroes*, National Portrait Gallery 1999, pp. 18–21.

17 British Association for Shooting and Conservation, *Shooting Facts*, 2003 p. 57.

18 'We have no intention whatsoever of placing restrictions on the sports of angling or shooting', *Ambitions for Britain*, p. 23; on 17th July 2004 the Party announced that it was in process of drafting Charters for both angling and shooting.

19 Home Office figure reported on its website www.homeoffice.org.uk, accessed 23.07.04.

20 *Shooting Facts*, p. 35.

21 Ibid.

22 Matt Wells, 'Prince William forces Press Apology', the Guardian 17.6.04.

23 *Controls on Firearms. A Consultation Paper*. Home Office Communications Directorate, May 2004.

24 The BBC reported in its build-up to the 2004 Olympics that Faulds 'still gets complaints from the neighbours about noise from the family shooting range'. Andrew Fraser, 'Road to Athens', BBC.co.uk/sport/hi/Olympics accessed 23.7.04.

25 *Shooting Facts*, preliminary p. 3.

7 Virtually foul or virtually fair?

FIFA, fair play and video gaming

Mark James

Introduction

The computer and video games sector is currently one of the fastest growing and dynamic forms of popular entertainment in the world.[1] The biggest grossing DVD of 2002 was, for the first time, not a film but a video game. 'Grand Theft Auto: Vice City' sold over 1 million copies on its opening day of sales in the USA. If 'Vice City' had been a film, this would have represented takings equivalent to its being the thirty-fifth highest grossing opening weekend ever.[2] It sold over 1 million copies in the UK in the eight weeks between its release and Christmas 2002[3] and to date has sold around 5 million copies worldwide, adding to the 11 million copies sold of its three predecessors.[4]

Outside of video games, football is still the most popular spectator and participation sport in the world.[5] Therefore, it is not surprising to find that football-based video games are amongst the biggest selling titles on all games consoles. By far the biggest selling football simulation franchise is the range of games endorsed by FIFA, the world governing body of football, and produced annually by US-based company Electronic Arts. FIFA 2003 features club and national teams and is available worldwide, avoiding the need for country-specific titles. EA also produced a specialist title, FIFA World Cup 2002 to coincide with the FIFA World Cup in Korea and Japan.

The game is updated each year, not just to improve its gameplay but also to improve the 'reality' of the game. The graphical likenesses of the players are improved, their transfer values and skills are updated and teams' squads are altered to reflect closed-season transfers. These games all carry the FIFA logo, and now also the logos of most major professional leagues such as the FA Premier League, La Liga and Major League Soccer, and are the only video games to be officially licensed by FIFA and FIFPRO, the International Federation of Professional Footballers, which endorses the game on behalf of the players. About five million copies of the game are sold worldwide each year, of which 2.5 million are sold in Europe.[6] There is no recommended retail price for games, which retail for £30–£45, the price fluctuation depending on which shop and in which country they are bought.

In 1993, two years before Sony's launch of the PlayStation console that heralded a new growth in home video gaming, FIFA launched its Code of Conduct for Football. The Code of Conduct encourages fair play and ethical conduct in football to ensure that players play not only by the letter of the Laws of Football but also in accordance with their spirit. The Code of Conduct, with its emphasis on sporting conduct and respect for one's opponents has sought to reinforce FIFA's position as the moral guardian of the game of football. To underline its commitment to the spirit of fair play, FIFA presents special awards for sporting conduct and rewards teams that finish highest in its fair play competitions. Codes of Conduct are of increasing legal importance as they can be referred to by courts when determining liability in negligence for personal injury. The Code of Conduct is referred to when determining whether or not an injury causing challenge was an acceptable means of playing the game and therefore within its playing culture.[7]

During this period, FIFA has also introduced a series of rule changes to ensure that football is a safer game for its participants to play. To this end, for example, the tackle from behind was outlawed in 1996 and deliberate foul play should now result in at least a caution, or where it denies a clear goal-scoring opportunity, then the player should be sent off.[8] These initiatives and rule changes have been introduced to try to change the playing culture of football and make it a safer, fairer game to play.

However, at the same time that FIFA has been encouraging fair play, it can also be seen, tacitly at least, to have been encouraging cheating and the use of violent play through its licensed video games. In direct contradiction to the stated aims of the Code of Conduct, these games allow for a range of deliberate foul play strategies whilst failing to make any reference to the ideals of the Code of Conduct itself. This chapter examines whether the playing culture of virtual football games can, potentially, have any impact on the playing culture of 'real' football.

The current explosion in the popularity of video games has led to a burgeoning academic study of games and gaming.[9] To date, the majority of empirical research has focused on the social and psychological effects of gaming, whilst the textual and narrative analyses of specific games and games genres have drawn on the techniques more often associated with critical film and literature studies.[10]

This chapter uses totally different techniques to analyse football video games and gaming. It draws on legal theory and notions of rule obedience to explore some possible problems that could be associated with the range of FIFA licensed video games in their current form. It focuses, in particular, on the ability to cheat in the virtual world of the video game and the lack of any reference in these FIFA licensed products to the Code of Conduct, the Laws of Football or indeed to any contextualizing of fair play at all. This is contrasted with FIFA's ever-growing emphasis on fair play and sporting conduct and its grandiose visions for the sporting enlightenment of footballers. The symbolic impact on FIFA's fair play drive is analysed in the light of its most popular licensed product, seemingly encouraging the use of instrumental violence to achieve victory when FIFA itself is attempting to punish more severely these precise forms of conduct when perpetrated in 'real' games.

Underpinning this discussion is the continual prospect of litigation for sports injuries and whether a failure to promote or enforce adequately a Code of Conduct such as FIFA's could lead to a governing body's liability for injuries caused during participation. Post *Watson* v. *British Boxing Board of Control*,[11] this could now be a point of more than mere academic interest as governing bodies can, in certain circumstances, find themselves legally responsible for the safety of those playing their sport.

The playing culture of sport

The playing culture of a sport can be defined as including all conduct that is accepted as being an integral part of playing the particular game as it is expected to be played by its participants. It will include, but not be limited to, conduct that is within the rules of a game. It will also include violations of the rules of the game that are considered to be an inevitable concomitant to the normal playing of the game.[12] Playing culture is, therefore, a normative standard of behaviour. It identifies the norms that are followed by players and others involved with the playing and running of a sport, such as the coaches. In football, there are three main sets of norms that can be used to determine appropriate behaviour; the official norms or rules of the game, the informal player norms, or the rules as they are interpreted by the players, and the fair play norms as found in the Code of Conduct. All must be taken into consideration when determining the seriousness of a player's conduct, or misconduct, and whether or not it was within the playing culture of football.

This is reflected by the differing attitudes towards the same rule violation by players, referees and the courts. Thus, for example, each of the following is in breach of the Laws of Football and the Code of Conduct but all result in different outcomes:

> Pushing or tripping, minor breach of the rules, within the playing culture, in game penalty only.

> Late tackle, serious breach of the rules, within the playing culture, in game penalty and possible disciplinary tribunal penalty.

> High late tackle, serious breach of the rules, breach of the playing culture, in game and disciplinary tribunal penalties, possible action in negligence.

> Fighting, serious breach of the rules and of the playing culture, in game and disciplinary tribunal penalties and possible criminal prosecution.

Therefore, commonly occurring, predominantly non-injurious conduct falls within the playing culture of football, whereas conduct outside of the normative structure of the game is treated severely by the governing body of the game and potentially also by the courts.

Although there are some conflicts surrounding who should provide the definition of playing culture, the obvious choice appears to be the governing body of the particular sport.[13] Thus, FIFA, through UEFA in Europe and the FA in England, is the body best placed to determine what is and what is not acceptable normative behaviour within the playing culture of football. Specific rule changes, the interpretations of offences under the Laws of Football and amendments to the Code of Conduct are undertaken at world level by FIFA and implemented by the subsidiary regional and national bodies. What FIFA decrees, the rest of the world should follow.

One of the aims of football video game simulations is to make playing the video game approximate as much as is possible to the real game. A number of techniques are utilized by software manufacturers to try to achieve this. Some are reflected in the actual gameplay of the game, whilst others are a part of the design, artwork or look of the game. Into the latter category falls the use of close facial and visual likenesses of the players and stadiums to their real-world counterparts, realistic kit reproductions including colours and team sponsors, TV-style camera angles, real time commentaries recorded by well-known commentators, action replays, goal celebrations and the cheering and singing of the crowd.

Those that fall into the former category constitute the virtual playing culture of the video game. These include the rules of the game and their enforcement, the use of tactics and substitutions, ball skills and tricks and the ability to tackle an opponent both within and outside of the rules of the game.

To achieve the highest level of simulation, the video game's playing culture must approach, as far as is possible, that of the real game. For example, mistimed challenges should result in a free kick but those that are late or deliberate should be punished with a caution or a dismissal. This is, to some extent, what does happen in the FIFA/EA games. However, the punishments do not reflect accurately those that would occur in the real games, in terms of length of ban, nor are there commensurate rewards for playing according to both the letter and the spirit of the rules as there is no reference to the Code of Conduct or to fair play awards. Instead, violence can be used in a purely instrumental way, either to break down play or to cause injury to an opponent. The lack of any reference to the Code of Conduct, or of any contextualizing of violent conduct, or fair play, therefore means that a significantly more violent virtual playing culture is established than FIFA is seeking to promote in real games of football.

The FIFA Code of Conduct

The FIFA Code of Conduct was relaunched in 1993 to demonstrate the commitment of the world governing body of football to sporting conduct and fair play.[14] The idea behind the Code was that the playing culture of football should develop in a way that emphasized playing the game within the spirit of the rules rather than promoting a win-at-all-costs culture. The ten-point Code calls for players to win and lose gracefully, to avoid causing injury to one's opponents and to have respect for the rules, traditions and players of the game.[15] These include:

> 2. Play Fair . . . Winning is without value if victory is achieved unfairly or dishonestly. Playing fair earns you respect, while cheats are detested.
> 3. Observe the Laws of the Game . . . It is important to understand the spirit of the rules. They are designed to make the game fun to play and fun to watch.
> 7. Reject . . . Violence . . . Show that football does not want violence . . . sport is peace.
> 9. Denounce Those who Attempt to Discredit our Sport . . . Don't be ashamed to show up anybody who you are sure is trying to make others cheat. Denounce the culprits who are trying to spoil our sport.

Although many criticisms can be made of these overly prosaic manifesto-style pronouncements, the Code has been designed to encourage sporting conduct and to reduce cheating, violent play and arguing with referees. Taken together with the various rule changes that have been implemented in recent seasons, FIFA can be seen, at least on the face of it, to be attempting proactively to change and regulate the playing culture of football worldwide. If the Laws of Football and the Code of Conduct are complied with, then players would no longer attempt to injure others, nor fight with them, nor argue with the referees, nor try to dive to win penalties and get their opponents cautioned or sent off.

FIFA has also introduced a number of non-playing-based measures that are supposed to diffuse antagonism and encourage a friendly rapport between players. For example, child mascots accompany players onto the pitch, especially at big games. Players must shake hands with their opponents prior to kick off and, as from 2004, at all FIFA-sponsored finals tournaments, they will have to partake in an official post-match handshake after the final whistle.[16] This gesture is supposed to be one of mutual respect and to demonstrate the true spirit of the game as it should have been played.

At FIFA organized competitions, such as the World Cup, the team with the best disciplinary record wins the Fair Play Trophy. For this, the players receive commemorative medals and the national association receives $50,000 of sports equipment for youth team development.[17] UEFA grant entry to the UEFA Cup for three Fair Play representatives. These three representatives are nominated by the three leagues that finish top of UEFA's fair play rankings. The nominees are usually the winners of that league's own fair play competition or the next best placed side in the fair play competition that has not already qualified for either the Champions' League or UEFA Cup.[18] Thus, there is often quite some incentive, whether financial or sporting, to winning a fair play competition.

FIFA is quite determined to impose its own standards of conduct on those who play football. These extend beyond playing the game in the spirit that FIFA would like to see the game played to ensuring that the players shake hands and have the necessary regard and respect for their opponents. Not all of these measures are appropriate for replication in a football simulation video game, though all could be represented in some form in the course of the game itself or in the simulated video montages, or cut scenes, that start and finish the playing section of each game. It would also be possible to incorporate the Fair Play logo into the perimeter hoardings of the virtual stadiums, as occurs in real tournaments; however, all of these are currently given over to adverts for FIFA's commercial partners. Further, it would be possible to include a link to the Code of Conduct itself from, for example, the start up menu. However, in contrast to the efforts of FIFA in the real world of football, none of these fair play initiatives are replicated in the virtual world of the game.

The FIFA/Electronic Arts football games

The FIFA/EA football games are consistently amongst the best selling titles on all games consoles and PC's.[19] The games pride themselves on being as realistic as is possible in a video game. Players are instantly recognizable and have personalized characteristics such as speed, tackling ability, skill, fitness and aggression. In-game tactics have developed over the years, so that gamers can play the offside trap or one-two's, or play a more defensive or attacking strategy to fit the style of each gamer.[20] These developments ensure that the look and feel of the game and the game play improve year-on-year.

The series of games began in 1993 with the release of FIFA International Soccer. FIFA Soccer 1996 was launched two years later and then from 1997, with the release of FIFA 98, EA has brought out an updated version of the game every year. In 2002, an additional game, 2002 FIFA World Cup was released to coincide with the FIFA World Cup Finals series in Korea and Japan. The first three titles saw the gradual improvement of game play and graphical depictions of the players. However, it was FIFA 99 that saw the groundbreaking improvements to graphical qualities and controversial additions to the game.

In FIFA 99, player likenesses were much improved, the real time commentary was revolutionary and the game play was enhanced by the ability of a gamer to utilize sliding and standing tackles, special player moves, ball skills and tactics. Controversially, the virtual players could also be made to cheat by committing deliberate fouls and diving. If a gamer chooses to use the intentional foul tactic, his player will either lunge at, kick, elbow or push the virtual opponent, causing injuries to opponents that can be sufficient to require them to be substituted. Although a gamer can be punished by having a free kick or penalty awarded against him, or by having his player cautioned or sent off, this is by no means guaranteed. This can be made especially unlikely if the gamer reduces the severity of the refereeing so that such challenges can be made with near impunity. The ability to impose a lower, self-referential and violent standard of conduct on the game that is at odds with FIFA's official version of how football ought to be played is clearly against the ethos of the Code of Conduct.

During the game, if a player is sent off, he is banned for one game only, regardless of how many times he has been sent off previously. In the English Premier League, a player would be automatically banned for a minimum of three games for being sent off for deliberate foul play or violent conduct. There is no mention anywhere in the game, whether in the player's manual or from one of the start up menus, of the Laws of Football, the Code of Conduct or that the use of foul play can lead to the injury of opponents. Further, after a foul has been committed in the game, during the replay of the incident, the offending players appear to dispute the referee's decision, by gesturing either their exasperation at the decision or that the fouled player dived. Again, this is 'conduct' that is actively discouraged by the FIFA Code.

From FIFA 2000 to date, deliberate fouling and diving have been removed as in-game moves. The former has been replaced by the ability to perform an aggressive tackle. An 'ordinary' tackle, is where the defender tries to dispossess the ball carrier with a challenge made whilst standing up and will never result in the conceding of a foul. The new 'aggressive' tackle is always a sliding challenge. A well-timed challenge results in the defender coming away with possession of the ball. A mistimed challenge will usually result in a free-kick being given away. There is no distinction between a deliberately or accidentally mistimed challenge, though the later the contact is made with the ball carrier, the more likely that the defending player will also receive either a caution or be sent off. These challenges can also result in the tackled player being injured and requiring substitution. From FIFA 2000, the 'aggressive' tackle comes with a warning that if mistimed, a foul could result. However, there is no warning that injuries may be caused. Again, if the severity of the refereeing is reduced, injuries can be inflicted on star opponents without conceding anything more than a free kick, thereby allowing violent conduct to be used instrumentally as a tactic, instead of resulting in a sending off. In the tournament modes of both FIFA World Cup 2002 and FIFA 2003, if a player is booked twice in different games, he is banned for one game and if sent off, he is banned for the following two games. Although this is a closer representation of what occurs at the FIFA

World Cup Finals, it does not reflect the increased penalties that domestic leagues hand down to repeat offenders. Where the virtual players are disciplined, they still occasionally dispute the decisions of the referees, with impunity, demonstrating a level of dissent that would in a real game result in a booking.

Such an addition to the game of the ability to foul certainly adds a new dimension to the authenticity of the video games. However, there is still no mention of either the Laws of Football or the Code of Conduct. Further, there are still no fair play logos around the ground, though the commercial advertisements are becoming more sophisticated. Nor are there bonuses for fair play. As punishment, particularly the awarding of red and/or yellow cards, is not automatic, a gamer is able to use in-game violence in a much more instrumental manner than is possible in reality. Yet again, by adjusting the severity of the refereeing, or even switching it off, gamers can ensure that violence becomes an integral part of the game as virtual injuries can be inflicted without the consequential punishment of a sending off resulting. It must be noted that not everybody plays the FIFA games in this manner. However, the game enables violence to be used in an instrumental manner that is not possible in the real game, where such conduct would result in fouls being conceded and often automatic bans being imposed.

In the light of the ability of a gamer to use violence instrumentally for the purpose of achieving victory, the question arises of whether the lack of emphasis on fair play in FIFA's video games can have any impact upon a participant's adherence to the Code of Conduct in real football matches. This analysis is purely theoretical drawing upon much that has been found and discussed on similar issues of violence promotion in other contexts. It is not seeking to prove definitively that playing video games will make gamers use foul play or violence in real sport.

Do virtual fouls cause real fouls?

The impact of playing video games on the behaviour of gamers has as yet not been greatly explored.[21] However, there are distinct similarities between the empirical research that has been carried out to date and the theories that are relied upon to explain such a link and similar studies on the effects of violent videos, films and television programmes on viewers' behaviour.[22] If such a link can be proven to exist, then it could be assumed that deviant behaviour in football simulation games, such as cheating and the use of violence, would lead to changes in the normative behaviour and attitudes of gamers when they play in real football matches. This would lead to a change in the playing culture of football making cheating, foul play and the use of instrumental violence more acceptable. If such a connection cannot be proven, then an alternative analysis is needed to establish whether such a link is possible.

In 2000, Craig Anderson and Karen Dill undertook two studies based on playing and watching violent video games to establish whether such games made the subjects more aggressive. They explained the reasons behind carrying out this study as being because,

> Entertainment media affects our lives. What behaviors children and adults consider appropriate comes, in part from the lessons we learn from television and the movies. There are good theoretical reasons to expect that violent video games will have similar, and possibly larger, effects on aggression.[23]

Their studies established that there was such a link; however, they do warn that their methodology may be partly undermined as violent people may be drawn to playing violent video games. Their conclusion is that,

> When combined with what is known about other types of media violence effects, most notably TV violence, we believe that the present results confirm that parents, educators, and society in general should be concerned about the prevalence of violent video games in modern society, especially given recent advances in the realism of video game violence.[24]

If translated to football simulations by analogy, then if, hypothetically, it could be assumed that there is a link between in-game behaviour and behaviour outside of the context of video games, then the use of violence in football simulations would lead to the use of violence in real football games.

Anderson and Dill go on to explain why they think that exposure to violent video games makes gamers more aggressive. First, gamers identify with the in-game aggressors, the characters that gamers use to play the game, thus heightening the impact of the in-game violence. Second, because there is active participation, where the gamer interacts with the game and the violent situations that he/she encounters rather than simply viewing violent images, gamers will learn to react more aggressively in all situations in which they find themselves. Finally, the addictive nature of video gaming reinforces the inherent characteristics of violent video games and this may lead gamers to learn and use aggression more readily.

> When the choice and action components of video games is coupled with the games' reinforcing properties, a strong learning experience results. In a sense, violent video games provide a complete learning environment for aggression, with simultaneous exposure to modeling, reinforcement, and rehearsal of behaviors. This combination of learning strategies has been shown to be more powerful than any of these methods used singly.[25]

If the findings of this study were replicated in respect of football simulation video games, then it would be expected that those who learn the advantages of using instrumental violence in video games would replicate its use in real football games. Conversely, if video games create such effective learning environments, then it should also be possible to encourage fair play were the necessary incentives present.

However, it must be noted that the authors of this study themselves are at pains to point out that such a link is only possible and not yet definitively proven. Other studies have come to quite different conclusions.

In respect of gamers identifying with the characters within a game, whether aggressive or not, Kinder has found a different rationale behind the gamer's choice of character with which to play.[26] During a study of the characters chosen by players of Nintendo's 'Super Mario Brothers 2', she found that boys were just as likely to choose 'Princess Toadstool', a character designed specifically for young female gamers, as their character because of her special powers, rather than 'Mario' or 'Luigi' who were designed more specifically with the young male gamer in mind. Their reasons for such a choice were driven mainly by the character's potential in-game performance; they thought that they were more likely to do better in that particular game with that particular character.[27] Gamers were therefore choosing their characters instrumentally on the basis of in-game ability rather than identifying with the characters themselves.

If this line of argument is translated into football simulation video games, then gamers should be more likely to pick the most skilful teams and utilize their ball skills and tackling abilities rather than the most aggressive teams as the use of the former are more likely to result in victory. Although not invalidating Anderson and Dill's research, it may mean that the application of their identification theory has to be restricted to first person shooting games rather than sports games where the gamer is able to choose with which team to play.

Further, Newman hypothesizes that gamers actually identify with the capabilities of the characters, not the characters themselves.[28] Thus, in football simulations, the choice of a skilled team playing fairly could encourage the gamer to replicate such ball skills and tactics in a real game of football. Therefore, in terms of the gamer's identification with aggressive characters leading them to act aggressively outside of the gaming environment, there is an equally persuasive theoretical and empirical basis that suggests that gamers behave instrumentally in their choice and use of characters in an attempt to achieve victory and act only with respect to playing the video game.

Anderson and Dill's second point, that the active participation in violent video games causes increased aggression, can also be countered. Squire acknowledges that there can be a high level of learning achieved through gaming and that this is at least in part attributable to the active participation of the gamers in the game.[29] However, he goes on to state that there is nothing to suggest that such in-game learning is applied anywhere but in the context of the video game itself.

> While pundits and theorists suggest that game-playing might be increasing kids' critical thinking or problem solving skills, research on transfer gives very little reason to believe that players are developing skills that are useful in anything but very similar contexts. A skilled *Half-Life* player might develop skills that are useful in playing *Unreal Tournament* (a very similar game), but this does not mean that players necessarily develop generalizable ... skills. Just because a player can plan an attack or develop lightening quick reactions in *Half-Life* does not mean that she can plan her life effectively, or think quickly in other contexts ... one of the main reasons being that these are two entirely different contexts and demand very different social practices.[30]

Again by analogy, according to this line of argument, even if a gamer does cheat or use violence within the context of a football simulation, there is nothing to suggest that this learned behaviour will be put in to practice on the football field. There is not even any evidence to suggest that gamers connect playing video games with playing football. Further, the behaviour and skills learned in the video game, involving the movement of a digitally created simulacra by means of a handheld controller are so different from those required to play football that the learning acquired from the former context will not, and perhaps even cannot, be translated in to practice in the latter.

Finally, where Anderson and Dill highlight that around one in five gamers exhibit signs of addiction and that this can lead to a heightening of the learned aggression, the converse, that at least 80 per cent of people are not addicted to gaming and therefore are unlikely to be made more aggressive by playing such games, must also be highlighted. As there is not yet evidence to link addiction to violent video games with increased aggressive tendencies, this point seems to be rather hyperbolic.

Thus, the very nature of football simulations and the endless range of choices that must be made by gamers may have some impact on changing attitudes towards cheating and the instrumental use of violence. The intense level of interaction with video games goes beyond the mere ludic attraction of playing football or the emotional interaction with watching live sport. The choices to be made in video games are constant and rapid, potentially leading to distorted views about the use of cheating and violence as a legitimate tactic. However, there is little evidence to support the hypothesis that any such attitudes will, as a matter of course, be taken beyond the confines of the video game itself.

Learning from video games must be contrasted with learning about the video games. The former means that lessons learned in the game will be imported into real life actions. There is little evidence to support this transfer of learned skills and attitudinal norms from the virtual world of the video game to the real football pitch. The latter means that lessons learned within the video game will be used instrumentally only within the video game, or other similar games. This is much more likely to happen, though the long-term effect on attitudes to cheating is as yet unknown. Thus, if it cannot be proven that the ability to cheat and use instrumental violence in football simulations does lead automatically to violence in real games, can the ability to use instrumental violence inform gamers' attitudes as to the use of violence in real games?

The importance of obeying the rules of the game

The major concern of the empirical researchers in this area is whether the playing of particular games does lead to a change in the behaviour of the subject. The concern here is not with proving that alterations in behaviour do occur, but with analyzing whether the development of consistent portrayals and usages of instrumental violence can change how its use is perceived by the viewing/gaming public. Put simply, can the ability to use violent play in football simulation video games contribute to a change in the attitudinal norms that a gamer has towards cheating and the use of violence in real sports?[31]

Before examining this question in detail, it is first necessary to establish briefly why sports' rules should be obeyed by sports participants. Only if there is a reason for obeying the rules of a game will acts that are outside of those rules be worthy of scrutiny.[32]

The constitutive rules of a sport define what the sport is and how it should be played. If all of the participants in a game know the constitutive rules and agree to be bound by and play by them, then a sports contest can take place. This usually occurs when the participants simply agree to play a particular sport as all involved in the potential contest will know the rules of the game and will expect to be bound by them. Thus, observance of the rules or laws of a sport is essential for the contest to take place.

The effect on a sports contest of rule violations will depend upon the nature of the violation and, in legal terms, its *mens rea*. Accidental, or unintentional, rule violations are an integral part of most sports. They are accounted for usually by either a participant's lack of understanding of the rules, for example picking up the ball in football, or their lack of skill, for example a mistimed tackle. When these occur in the game a penalty of some kind will normally be incurred. To avoid their recurrence, the participant will have to acquire a better understanding of the rules or to practise tackling and become more skilful, as appropriate.

Intentional rule violations are more complex and can again be broken into two categories; those where the perpetrator seeks both to break the rules of the game and to avoid punishment and those where the perpetrator expects to be punished and accepts such punishment as the necessary concomitant of the rule violation. The former is clearly cheating as, according to Delattre,

> Competing, winning and losing ... are intelligible only within the framework of rules which define a specific competitive sport. A person

may cheat at a game or compete at it, but it is logically impossible for him to do both. To cheat is to cease to compete.[33]

By this reasoning, a unilateral reforming of the constitutive rules of a game by one participant results in that participant no longer playing the same sport as their opponent. Therefore, the contest can no longer take place as the opponents are playing different games by different rules. Thus, the rules of a sport must be obeyed by all participants otherwise the sports contest cannot take place. This reasoning also applies to those who expect to be punished for their rule violations.

An alternative line of argument claims that a participant deliberately breaking the rules of a sport and expecting to be punished for it is a legitimate tactic of the sport or game as it is open to use, or abuse, by all willing to run the risk of being punished.[34] However, unless such a tactic is universally accepted by all participants, for example the acceptance of the forward pass and blocking in rugby in the US, which paved the way for the evolution of American Football, any player unilaterally playing outside of the constitutive rules of the game cannot be said to be playing that game. Although playing practice may differ from this ideological basis, it explains why those who play sport should, ideally, do so by the known constitutive rules of the game.

FIFA's Code of Conduct agrees with this philosophy. In particular, Articles 2 and 3 require observance of the rules of the game, respect for others involved in the game and the avoidance of cheating. Therefore, there appears to be a sound logical and moral basis for obeying the rules of a sport.

However, this same philosophy does not automatically underpin the FIFA/EA video games. By allowing gamers to use instrumental violence, vary the severity of the refereeing and by failing to draw their attention to either the Laws of Football or the Code of Conduct, deliberate rule violations, or cheating, can become an integral part of the playing of the game. Thus, can a failure to play within the Laws of Football and the Code of Conduct in football simulation video games change the attitudinal norms that a gamer has towards cheating and the use of violence in real sports?

The importance of rule dis/obedience

Sport has the potential to shape views on such diverse subjects as authority, obedience of the law, conduct and attitudes towards societal values.[35] Of all forms of popular culture, sport is particularly well-placed to perform this role, as it has a similar procedural and punishment structure to the law.[36] It has a government/governing body, that passes laws/rules, that are enforced by the police/referees, the breach of which results in punishment, whether a prison sentence or a playing ban respectively. Playing a sport according to its rules has many similarities to the notions of obedience to the law that are found in social contractarianism.[37] The former requires obedience to its rules, otherwise you cannot be said to be playing the game. The latter requires obedience of the law, otherwise you can no longer be said to be a citizen of that state. Therefore, jurisprudential techniques more often associated with legal analysis can also be used to examine what influences a person's attitudes towards obeying the rules of sports and video games.

Further, sport and the law do not act in isolation from each other. Whilst FIFA tries to promote a playing culture that reduces the risk of cheating and consequential injury to football players, the law in the UK has been expanding to encompass acts of participator violence.[38] Where sport was once seen as a fabricated reality and participator violence as not real violence, sport is now very much a site of real and actionable injuries.[39]

If sport can influence people's perceptions of law, authority and obedience, there would appear to be no reason why video games, in particular football simulations, could not also be such an influence. The football simulations seek to replicate as accurately as possible the action, abilities and playing culture of real football to give gamers as authentic an experience as possible. To maximize that authenticity then, the ability to violate the rules, both accidentally and deliberately, must be incorporated into the game. The former is necessary, as not all gamers will have perfected the skills needed to play the game so that accidental fouls will naturally occur from time to time. The latter is also a necessary part of the video game, as deliberate foul play, or cheating, is sometimes seen as an integral part of normal playing practice, regardless of whether or not it should be. As the ideal of rule obedience is not achieved in reality, the more authentic video games will incorporate cheating into their own virtuality. If video games thus mirror the choices and playing culture of the real game of football, there is little reason to doubt that they too *could* play a role in influencing gamers' attitudes to rule obedience in the same way that other media portrayals of sport could similarly influence them.

The problem arises, however, that when football simulation video games influence gamers' perceptions of attitudinal norms or behaviour, they are not necessarily teaching the same messages as the real sport teaches its participants. The difference is in the existence of an effective punishment and reward structure. In football, a failure to obey the Laws of Football will result in a foul being called. If the foul is serious enough, not only will a free kick or penalty be awarded, but the player may also be cautioned, sent off and/or banned from playing. With the FA now having the ability to punish a player on the basis of video evidence alone, the symbolic effect of rule breaking is high and is strongly enforced by the fines and playing bans that the governing body can and does impose.[40] This leads to a very real psychological impulse to obey the Laws of Football, or at least to play the game within its playing culture, in the future.[41]

In video games, however, the symbolic impact of the punishment is low to non-existent. First, the gamer is not punished personally, as he or she is neither fined nor banned from playing the video game. Second, the punishment that is inflicted neither reflects the seriousness of the foul committed nor is it imposed on the gamer as an individual. Even if a virtual player is sent off, the 'ban' imposed is shorter than would be the case in real football competitions. Further, the bans do not get cumulatively longer the more regularly that a gamer's players are punished as they do under the current FA administered scheme. Third, the severity of the referee can be reduced or switched off, thereby ensuring that no penalties will be imposed for foul play at all. In stark contrast to this, FIFA regularly hands down edicts to referees to ensure that they are imposing the Laws of Football ever more strictly.[42] Finally, as an opponent gamer's players can be injured by the acts of foul play, violence can be used instrumentally to an extreme that is not possible in real football matches.

Thus, the minor nature of the virtual punishments does not act as either an actual or symbolic punishment and therefore does not provide the necessary psychological impulse to the gamers to obey the rules of the game. If gamers learn from all of their surroundings, including the media, sport and video games, then the lessons being taken away from video games are substantially different from those that are learned when playing or watching real sport. The enforcement of the rules in the video games lacks any real ceremonial force that can act symbolically as a deterrent to gamers.[43]

This is reinforced by the lack of any reward structure for playing the game according to the Laws of Football. A gamer is not rewarded with a 'fair play bonus' for completing a tournament without one of his players being cautioned or sent off. Extra prize money is not awarded to fund transfers, extra points are not awarded and bonus competitions are not unlocked. Thus, with the pain of sanctions for breach of the rules not guaranteed and with rewards for obeying the rules non-existent,[44] the scene is set for the use of deliberate instrumental rule infractions for the purpose of securing victory. If such rule violations then become institutionalized, then the whole playing culture of the game becomes more violent by accepting and integrating forms of violence that would otherwise be banned.[45]

The Code of Conduct can be considered to be an interpretative, or secondary, legal norm, where the Laws of Football, as the constitutive rules of the game, are the primary norms. Such secondary norms add force to the primary norms by providing further explanation for the existence of the primary norms or by being part of the ritual that conditions responses to a rule or law. Where football is concerned, it promotes fair play and respect for the rules and other players and explains why cheating and the use of violence should not be tolerated.

The failure to refer to the Code of Conduct in the FIFA/EA games removes one of the psychological impulsions that create responses to a rule or law, leaving only the largely ineffective coercive or punitive element.[46] Part of the ritual that conditions obedience to the Laws of Football, the explanation of the spirit in which the game ought to be played, is missing, thereby allowing a greater emphasis on winning and/or getting away with cheating instead of encouraging playing within the Laws and fair play to develop.

Policing a virtual Code of Conduct in the FIFA/EA games would be almost impossible because the games console could not check the state of mind of the gamer to ascertain whether or not they were cheating deliberately. In terms of game play, a virtual Code of Conduct would add little or nothing. However, because this element of how law is defined and why it is obeyed is lacking in the FIFA/EA games, the Code of Conduct loses the ability to influence a gamer's conduct in the video game, either because the terms of the Code are unknown to the gamer, or because it is seen as inapplicable because it is not referred to in the video game, or because it is seen as irrelevant because nobody is charged with breaching it when a foul is committed.

By marginalizing the effectiveness of the Code as a secondary or interpretative norm, gamers no longer find it obligatory and instead its ethos is replaced by a focus on winning and the use of instrumental violence. Thus, the Code has no imperative force in the video game leading to a lack of psychological conditioning to obey its terms within the game. Further, it cannot help to teach gamers about fair play and the need to obey the Laws and the Code when playing real games of football as its existence is not brought to their attention.

In this scenario, gamers could fail to learn the value of fair play and instead learn that instrumental violence can be used to achieve success in the games. Although it may not cause gamers to act violently towards another participant in a real game of football, a lack of understanding of the Code could lead to a lack of understanding of the spirit of the Laws of Football. Gamers will understand that the fouls that they commit are fouls but not why they should not commit them as they could rationalize the use of instrumental violence as a necessary, if not legitimate, tool to achieve victory. As discussed by Suits, gamers may become willing to justify the use of violence as an effective in-game tactic whilst accepting that it is in fact contrary to the rules of the game.[47] Thus, it is possible that the overall normative structure of football could change through exposure to the playing culture of football simulation video games through a process whereby the use of instrumental violence is rationalized as a legitimate in-game tactic, despite its being contrary to the rules of the game.

Conclusion

It is possible that football simulation video games may have the capability to influence people's attitudes towards the use of violence in football matches. Although it cannot be conclusively proven that such a link exists, the lack of an effective coercive impulse to obey the Laws of Football and the lack of reference to FIFA's Code of Conduct provides a sound basis from which a claim that video games may help gamers to rationalize the use of instrumental violence as a legitimate tactic can be developed. What these video games have the potential to do is present violence as being a natural and inherent part of the playing of football.[48]

If the development of a more violent virtual playing culture does influence the playing culture of real football matches, then this could pose significant legal problems for FIFA. In *Watson* v. *British Boxing Board of Control*, it was held that one of the main roles that must be fulfilled by the governing body of a sport is to ensure the safety of those who are playing their game. In *Watson*, the Board of Control were held liable for failing to have in place a set of up-to-date guidelines for establishing a procedure in accordance with current best practice for treating boxers who had suffered traumatic brain injury during the course of a bout. By failing to require adequate medical cover at the bout and failing to require their immediate transportation to a neurosurgical unit, the Board of Control were in breach of their duty to take reasonable care of the safety of boxers fighting in bouts that it had licensed. The court held that as the Board was best placed to conduct research into such injuries and procedures and was the only means of ensuring a consistent approach to these matters across the UK, that it should be held liable for the exacerbation of Watson's injuries caused by the failure to treat his brain haemorrhage with sufficient speed.

By analogy to the reasoning in *Watson* and other sports negligence cases, a governing body may now also be liable for a failure to ensure the reasonable safety of the participants who are playing its sport.[49] This would require of the governing body that it ensured that its safety rules were regularly reviewed and that it developed and maintained a reasonably safe playing culture within its sport. To date, FIFA has achieved this through regular rule changes and its emphasis on the Code of Conduct. However, if a link can be proven to exist between the tacit encouragement of violent conduct in the FIFA/EA games and violent play in football matches, then FIFA could be found to be liable for injuries caused by failing to provide a safe environment in which to play football or by failing to encourage or enforce a reasonably safe playing culture for football. Injuries are a foreseeable outcome of allowing a violent playing culture to develop. FIFA encourages and controls football and is therefore in a position to enforce the Laws of Football and the Code of Conduct. Should it fail to do this, and the game can be proven to have become more violent, then the risk of being sued for injuries caused through the use of instrumental violence becomes more real.

At present such an action could not succeed, as it would be impossible to prove a causal link between the use of instrumental violence in video games and an increase in the use of violence in real football matches. However, as research continues to be conducted in this area, and with the theoretical possibility that such a link may one day be proven to exist, FIFA should ensure that its biggest selling licensed product cannot be used against it in the future.

This discussion also brings into question the nature of the role of the governing body of a sport. Is its purpose to make the rules of the game and administer the various competitions, or to enforce the moral code of the game, or to exploit commercial revenue streams, or a combination of all three? There can be little doubt that the first of these is an integral part of the role of a governing body. Without an official rule-making body and organizer, the sport would not be able to exist in its current form. FIFA has claimed for itself the role of the moral guardian of the game; therefore, it has instituted the Fair Play Campaign in an effort to encourage sporting conduct. Finally, it exploits its revenue-earning capacity so that it can fund the development of football throughout the world, particularly at youth level and in developing countries. Alternatively, it can be seen as a self-serving capitalist financier of a massive worldwide industry, making profits of itself and for itself. Thus, it would appear that all three are elements of the role of FIFA as the world governing body of football.

The difficulty for FIFA is that these three roles must be managed very carefully to avoid creating an unsustainable internal conflict. In the case of licensed video games, a revenue stream is being exploited that appears to promote values that are in conflict with its role as moral guardian of the game. If the role as moral guardian of the game has precedence, then it cannot justify the endorsing of the commercial product, unless that product is developed to make at least some reference to the Code of Conduct. If the exploitation of the revenue stream is to take priority, then it calls into question the legitimacy of FIFA to rule on the game's moral standards if these can be discarded so easily when a multi-million dollar product endorsement is at issue.

Alternatively, it calls into question the need for FIFA to have a Code of Conduct. The pronouncements that are in the Code are either important to FIFA's vision of the game, in which case they should be elevated to the status of primary norms, integrated into the Laws of Football and enforced as such, or they are not, in which case there is no need for them to exist as anything other than a preamble to the Laws of Football. Instead, by promoting a product that makes no reference to the Code of Conduct, doubts are raised about the role of FIFA as the governing body of football, its governance of the game and its need to be there for anything other than to produce the rules of the game and organize the competitions.

Perhaps of greater importance here is that this is an opportunity missed by FIFA to reinforce its commitment to fair play and sporting conduct. Instead it is sending out mixed messages through different media. Through its fair play competitions, Code of Conduct and general pronouncements on sporting behaviour, FIFA denounces cheating, the use of violence and arguing with referees, whilst in the FIFA/EA video games the first two are available as in-game moves to the gamer and the latter appears to occur during the story telling sequences of the game. If nothing else, the video games are at least symbolically undermining FIFA's commitment to fair play.

If video games are to replicate more accurately the 'authenticity' of the game, then some reference to fair play and/or the Code of Conduct could be used as an important educative tool to reinforce FIFA's preferred ethos of sporting conduct, mutual respect and injury reduction. Not all aspects of their fair-play initiatives would translate easily into video games. Nor would all of them be necessary to draw a gamer's attention to the Code. For example, the Code could be accessed through the main start up menu and the Fair Play logo could be incorporated into the perimeter hoardings in the virtual stadiums. To provide the necessary encouragement to play fairly, a gamer who completes a tournament or season without his team recording a red or yellow card could be rewarded with a bonus competition or team only accessible by winning a fair play award. This would not interfere with the current playing format but would simply add a fair play dimension.

There is no need to remove the ability to commit fouls from video games; first, it is impossible to eliminate accidental foul play and errors of judgement so fouls will continue to be committed by gamers. Second, the lack of any empirical data linking violence in football video games with violence in football renders such removal an unnecessary overreaction. Instead, the game should be balanced by some reference to fair play, the Laws of Football and/or the Code of Conduct. This then leaves gamers with a genuine choice within a recognized punishment and reward structure of whether to play the game in accordance with the Code and receive the additional in-game bonuses, or to rely on the use of instrumental violence and risk the in-game punishment that goes with it. If FIFA do not incorporate some aspect of their fair play drive into their licensed football simulation video games, then they will have missed a big opportunity to educate gamers about sporting behaviour. Such a failure runs the risk that lessons about how and when to use instrumental violence may instead be learned.

Thus, the potential impact of the Code of Conduct is reduced dramatically by its failure to be incorporated in the FIFA/EA video games. The most that is normally seen of the Code in action is when the child mascots run out with the players for the pre-match warm up and when the players shake hands just before the start of the game. By failing to reinforce the message of the Code of Conduct in the video games, FIFA runs the risk that those playing in real football matches will also be less interested in playing football in the spirit in which the guardians of the game intend and more like they do when they play the video game.

Unless, or until, football achieves a state of hyperreality, where the video game is more real that the sport itself, or it can be proven that gamers' behaviour in video games does influence their attitudinal norms in real football matches, then much of this remains only hypothetical possibility. The fabricated reality of the football simulation video game is not yet more real than the reality of playing football itself. However, what this analysis does demonstrate is the possibility that a move toward this situation could happen and that the behaviour exhibited by video gamers when playing video games could be replicated in real football matches.

The ability to cheat in the FIFA/EA football games, coupled with the lack of any reference to FIFA's Code of Conduct exemplifies a symbolic undermining of the concept of fair play and the tacit promotion of instrumental violence and cheating in real football matches by football's world governing body. There is nothing inherently objectionable to allowing a gamer to choose to utilize a cheat, or aggressive tackle, or foul tackle action in the video game as part of attempting to recreate as authentic a reproduction in the game play as possible. However, without the concomitant commitment to the Code of Conduct an important component in the construction of 'right actions' in sport is missing. The primary norms of the game, as contained in the constitutive rules of football, lack the rationalized explanation, contained in the Code as secondary or interpretative norms, of what acts should or should not be performed and why such conduct is or is not penalized.

This failure to contextualize fair play sacrifices the actual and symbolic effect of the Code of Conduct at the expense of playability and supposedly authentic in-game choices about whether or not to commit a foul. At present, it is unknown whether exposure to the different normative framework capable of being established in video games does influence gamers' attitudes towards violence and cheating in real football matches. However, FIFA's failure to use their most successful licensed product as an effective educative tool in their fair play initiatives should give rise to a cause for some concern. By failing to educate video gamers about playing fair and the Code of Conduct, there is a chance that they may become football players who are more ambivalent about sporting conduct, fair play and instrumental violence. Where this results in increased injury levels amongst footballers, FIFA could find itself having to answer for this in court.

Notes

1 For convenience, referred to as video games in this chapter.
2 http://www.gta-vice.com, accessed 14 May 2003.
3 http://news.bbc.co.uk/cbbcnews/hi/sci-tech/newsid_2840000/2840929.stm, accessed 14 May 2003.
4 http://www.3davenue.com/gta3vce32002.shtml, accessed 14 May 2003.
5 For further analysis of this phenomenon see, Giulianotti, R., *Football: a sociology of the global game* (1999) Oxford: Polity.
6 http://www.psextreme.com/scripts/news2/new.asp?newid=1609, accessed 14 May 2003.
7 See for example the skiing case, *Lyon* v. *Maidment* [2002] EWHC 1227, where the International Skiing Federation's Rules of Conduct were referred to when determining liability following an on-piste collision.
8 Law 12, Laws of Football, http://www.fifa.com/fifa/handbook/laws/2004/LOTG2004_e.pdf, accessed 28 July 2004.
9 See for example the online journal Game Studies, http://www.gamestudies.org and the research database http://www.ludology.org.

10 Ibid.

11 [2001] QB 1134.

12 See further, Williams, G., 'Consent and Public Policy' [1962] Crim LR 74, Gardiner, S., 'Not playing the game: is it a crime?' (1993) 137 (27) Sol J 693 and James, M., 'The Trouble with Roy Keane' (2002) 1(3) *Entertainment Law* 72.

13 For counterargument see, Grayson, E., 'Making foul play a crime' (1993) 137 (26) 628, who argues that the courts should define what constitutes acceptable conduct on the field of play.

14 See further, http://www.fifa.com/en/media/index/0,00,37246,00.html?articleid =37246, accessed 28–07–04.

15 Ibid., for the full text of the Code.

16 http://www.fifa.com/en/display/article,53661.html, accessed 15 May 2003.

17 http://www.fifa.com/en/display/article,40907.html, accessed 15 May 2003.

18 http://www.uefa.com/competitions/uefacup/CompetitionInfo/index.html, accessed 28 July 2004.

19 See for example the charts and reviews features at http://www.ps2home. co.uk/games_chart.htm and http://www.gamestracker.co.uk/pc/chart.htm, accessed 28 July 2004.

20 Video and computer games players refer to themselves as gamers.

21 See for example, Anderson, C. and Dill, K., 'Video Games and Aggressive Thoughts, Feelings, and Behavior in the Laboratory and in Life' (2000) 78 (4) *Journal of Personality and Social Psychology* 772, discussed below.

22 See for example, Huesmann, L., 'Psychological processes promoting the relation between exposure to media violence and aggressive behavior by the viewer' (1986) 42 *Journal of Social Issues* 125, and Bibbings, L., 'The things they make you do: researching violence in television and cinema – a review of publications' (1998) 3(3) *Comms Law* 103.

23 Anderson and Gill (2000).

24 Ibid.

25 Ibid.

26 Kinder, M., *Playing with Power in Movies, Television and Video Games: From Muppet Babies to Teenage Mutant Ninja Turtles* (1993) London: University of California Press.

27 Ibid., p. 107.

28 Newman, J., 'The Myth of the Ergodic Videogame' (2002) 2(1) Game Studies, http://www.gamestudies.org/0102/newman, accessed 22 May 2003.

29 Squire, K., 'Cultural Framing of Computer/Video Games' (2002) 2(1) Game Studies, http://www.gamestudies.org/0102/squire, accessed 22 May 2003.

30 Ibid.

31 For a similar approach in a different context see, Greenfield, Osborn and Robson, *Film and the Law* (2001) London: Cavendish Publications, p. 27.

32 See further Morgan and Meier (eds) *Philosophic Inquiry in Sport*, 2nd edn (1995) Leeds: Human Kinetics, particularly chs 18–26 and Fraleigh, *Right Actions in Sport* (1984) Leeds: Human Kinetics, particularly ch 5.

33 E. Delattre, 'Some Reflections on Success and Failure in Competitive Athletics' (1975) 2 *Journal of Philosophy of Sport* 136.

34 B. Suits, 'The Elements of Sport' in R Osterhoudt (ed.) *The Philosophy of Sport* (1973) Springfield: CC Thomas, p. 50.

35 Carlsson, B., *Excitement, Fair Play, and Instrumental Attitudes* (2000) Lund: Lund University, p. 16.

36 For an alternative view that the importance of sport's influence on society is generally overlooked see, Blake, A., *The Body Language – the meaning of modern sport* (1996) London: Lawrence and Wishart, ch 1.

37 See further, Freeman, M., *Lloyd's Introduction to Jurisprudence*, 7th edn (2001) London: Sweet and Maxwell, pp. 111–118 and 146–154.

38 For example, in tort *Condon* v. *Basi* [1985] 1 WLR 866 and in the criminal law, *Attorney-General's Reference (no 27 of 1983)* (1994) 15 Cr App R (S) 737. For more detailed discussion see Gardiner, S., James, M., *et al.*, *Sports Law*, 3rd edn (2004) London: Cavendish Publishing, chs 15 and 16.

39 Carlsson (2000) p. 12.

40 http://news.bbc.co.uk/sport1/hi/football/teams/e/everton/2959434.stm, accessed 3 June 2003.

41 The theory of psychological impulses causing obedience to the law is based on the Scandinavian Realist school of jurisprudence. See Freeman, M. (2001) ch 10 and McCoubrey, H. and White, N., *Jurisprudence*, 3rd edn (1999) Oxford: OUP ch 10, particularly the work of Axel Hagerstrom.

42 See http://www.fifa.com/en/regulations/regulation/0,1584,3,00.html, accessed 28 July 2004.

43 Macaulay, S., 'Images of Law in Everyday Life: The Lessons of School, Entertainment and Spectator Sports' (1987) *Law and Society Rev* 21(2) 185, p. 209.

44 See further the discussion of the work of J. Bentham and H.L.A. Hart in McCoubrey and White (1999), ch 2.

45 Macauley (1987), p. 205.

46 McCoubrey and White (1999), ch 10.

47 B. Suits, 'The Elements of Sport' in R Osterhoudt (ed.) *The Philosophy of Sport* (1973) Springfield: CC Thomas, p. 50.

48 See also Carlsson (2000) p. 73.

49 See particularly *Smoldon* v. *Whitworth* [1997] PIQR 133 and *Vowles* v. *Welsh Rugby Union* [2003] EWCA Civ 318.

8 The juridification of sport

Ken Foster

Introduction

Law in liberal democracies is increasingly invasive. The realm of what is outside legal regulation annually grows smaller. Law now regulates many areas of social life that historically have appeared immune from law. The household, the workplace, the army, the prison and the hospital have all come under the gaze and surveillance of law. Few areas of social life have escaped invasion by law and the substitution of social norms by legal norms. Where can this invasion of the organic sphere of voluntary rule creation and enforcement, and its infection by law, be best studied? The sporting field currently provides the best example. Sports law uniquely offers a field in which the constitutive power of regulation and law is easily studied, and where the arguments over legal intervention are not yet closed. Sport can still be seen as an autonomous social field, a separate sphere, outside the normal assumptions of everyday practices, in which the law should have no place. This very apartness makes the issue of regulation in sport interesting to legal theorists. Law deals with the pathological not the normal. It concentrates on the frontier; it lives at the boundaries not at the core. To track where law is invading new social fields, such as sport, is to see the constitutive power of law at work as well as marking the movement of the legal frontier.

Yet the invasion is not only about conquering, about replacing a social norm with a legal norm. Conquering is the easy task if the invading army is strong enough; and few can deny the power of law. To rebuild the conquered territory, so that it has its own legitimacy and autonomy is more difficult. External law cannot solely coerce the internal field into submission to its norms. Readjusting to the gaze of law is more complex. What I want to explore in this chapter is juridification, as a process of interaction between internal regulation and external law, and to study the way in which an internal regime of autonomy is altered by legal intervention.

Juridification as a concept

Juridification as a concept is used to transcend the dichotomy of internal, voluntary, self-regulation and external, compulsory, legal regulation. It concentrates on the way in which law, without necessarily invading a social field directly, can still reconstitute that field in its image. So the social field begins to become more 'legal', to ape the form of law, to have its own 'internal law', and to introduce the 'rule of law' into its practices. In short, the social field is both passive and active. It is juridified and it juridifies itself.

However, many other authors have used 'juridification' in a more limited one-dimensional sense to describe the increasing intervention by law into a social field. This usage emphasizes three principal factors prior to juridification:

1   that the social field is little regulated other than by its own voluntary norms;
2   that actors are orientated to social obligations rather than legal duties;
3   that it has dispute mechanisms that are not legally enforceable.

As a concept, juridification seems to have entered English legal scholarship in the early 1980s during the debate over the increasing legal intervention in British industrial relations. In a definitive article in 1985, Jon Clark reviewed the use of the term by Spiros Simitis, who saw it 'as an inevitable consequence of industrialization, involving the gradual replacement of a society based on contractual agreement by a "law-driven society"'.[1,2] His use of the term describes an activist state intervening in industrial relations by legislation at the expense of voluntary collective bargaining, with the aim of steering economic life in a particular direction. He concluded 'juridification is thus tied irrevocably to state intervention'.[3] This is a narrow definition but it expands somewhat on the crude notion of legal intervention. It captures the displacement of voluntary norms, created through collective bargaining, by state created norms. It thus becomes for Simitis a descriptive term for increasing state intervention in industrial relations. However, it does not suggest that there is an interactive process between law and the social field that it is invading.

In a more recent article, Rubin has applied juridification to the changes occurring in military law.[4] He argues that military law has been transformed from an autonomous legal system, which was 'strongly characterized by a policy of absentionism', into a system that has adopted civilian norms, especially from the criminal law.[5] This has been followed more recently, Rubin continues, by a process of juridification, as areas such as military discipline have been subject to externally imposed legal regulation. This process has been accelerated by equal opportunities legislation and by the Human Rights Act. Rubin defines juridification as 'external legal norms ... being *imposed* on the armed forces in situations where such legal norms had hitherto been absent'.[6]

He identifies three key elements in this process of juridification. One, that disputes are resolved by an independent judicial process. Two, that juridification displaces 'normative systems or folkways which possess law-like characteristics'.[7] Three, that juridification is imposed law 'as distinct from having been (consensually) adopted by the military law system'.[8] Rubin specifically draws an analogy between military law and industrial relations in the 1970s and, like Simitis, he sees the imposition of external norms as central to the process. Rubin's use of the concept is more sophistic-ated, but he nevertheless treats it as a synonym for legal intervention into social relations previously regulated in non-legal ways. This is reflected in Rubin's adoption of Scott's definition; 'juridification describes a process by which relations hitherto governed by other values and expectations come to be subject to legal values and rules'.[9] This again suggests a simple one-way process rather than a more complex interaction.

Likewise, the use of juridification as an idea in the sports law literature mainly describes a simple process of legal intervention into a private realm. For example, in 1995 Gardiner and Felix, using as their example the increas-ing litigation by football players for injuries inflicted on them by fellow players, began their article thus:

> There is increasingly a view that the law should be involved more prominently in the regulation of sport . . . This juridification of an area that has traditionally been seen as essentially of a private nature raises issues concerning the legitimacy of legal involvement.[10]

Similarly, writing in 1998, Morris and Little speak of 'the remorseless commercialization and finance domination of ever greater areas of profes-sional sport inevitably brings in its wake creeping juridification in the form of legislative and judicial colonization of sports administration'.[11] The image of 'colonization' suggests the imposition of external norms although Morris and Little do recognize the importance of judicial, as well as legislative, intervention on the sporting field.

Juridification as used in sport

I want to argue for a more complex definition, in particular not to limit 'juridification' solely to an imposition of external norms. There is also a process of voluntary adoption, where the external norm is integrated into the social field. For example, juridification limits the autonomy of sporting bodies; but not necessarily by direct prescription. Sporting bodies 'learn' to follow basic principles of fairness, and to act in a judicial way. This is more domestication rather than colonization.

I attempted a definition of juridification in 1993 thus:

> a viewpoint [that] would emphasize the 'internal law' of sport, the way in which it creates its own legislation and rules, its own administrative regulation and its own procedures or processes for judgement. This

'internal law' is only influenced by external law in a weak sense. The emphasis is on the ability of internal law to be self-regulating and create the power to control its own system. External law is limited to providing a facilitative framework that allows voluntary autonomy within fixed boundaries, which are often procedural. Any greater degree of intervention that interferes with the internal law may be subject to a process of readjustment or even denial of the external imposed norms that allows the internal law to re-assert its own relative autonomy. This process is also described by legal theorists as juridification, which refers to the process by which social norms are transformed into legal norms. At a simple level, it merely reproduces the traditional idea of private and public realms, with private areas increasingly being subject to public or judicial control, a move from voluntarism to legalism. However, it offers also a more complex version that stresses the interaction as legal norms are used to reorder the power relations within the social arena.[12]

Whilst not wishing to defend every word of my original attempt at a definition, it emphasizes several points that are missing from simple models of legal intervention.

First, the internal regulatory regime may already have many elements of 'law' in a legal pluralist sense. A regulating sports body will have a constitutive document, the rulebook, a disciplinary regime to enforce the rules, and often a private system of dispute resolution that is legalistic, in that it is procedurally protective of the 'defendant' and administered by a lawyer. In other words, the internal regime of sport is not anarchic and free to operate entirely as it wishes. The internal regime may already mimic external legal standards by having formal written rules and a private system of justice, which prevents arbitrary decision-making and respects due process in its disciplinary functions. Different parts of the sporting organization act as lawmaker, prosecutor, judge and jury; again mimicking the separation of powers.

Second, the process of juridification alters this internal regulatory regime. Litigation becomes an ever-present threat; the threat alone can modify rules and practice. Decisions are legally challenged; rulebooks are judicially criticized. The internal rules and procedures will then reorient themselves to external norms.

Third, the mechanism for settling disputes changes with juridification. Rubin stresses that disputes are resolved by an independent judicial process and sees this as an important element of juridification. I would widen 'judicial' to include any third-party dispute-settlement mechanism that takes decision-making away from the administrators of sport and gives it to impartial outsiders. Juridification also alters perceptions of how sporting disputes are settled. Players increasingly see disputes as being resolvable through the law as well as through social or sporting mechanisms; you mean I can sue them over this!

Fourth, external law does not always intervene in the sense of imposing a norm but often creates a 'facilitative framework that allows voluntary autonomy within fixed boundaries'. This framework is frequently procedural rather than substantive; in other words, justice must be done by the rules and be seen to be done without prejudicing the basic rights of individuals.

Fifth, whereas previously social actors feel that duties are obligatory according to the rules of the semi-autonomous realm and not because they are imposed by an external legal order, they come to see obligations and advantages as legal duties and rights. I must do this because the law requires it: not I should do it because the social order calls for it to be done. Juridification in this dimension describes an internalization of the legal norm as the basis of action.

Sixth, the 'intervention' of law is not self-operative. There can be a complex process of integration. The external norm may be ignored, modified or reinterpreted. There is a symbiotic interaction between the internal and the external. Indeed, it is possible that there is a feedback loop by which the external law is modified by the altered internal norms.

Seventh, juridification is not only about the interaction of the formal rules of an internal legal order with an external law but is also a process that can alter the power relations within the internal regime.

Juridificaton as process

In this section, I want to expand and illustrate the main characteristics of juridification in sport.

Rules are codified

One of the chief characteristics of juridification is codification. It is the essence of sport that it has a set of codified rules to play the game. There has been academic discussion of what criteria identify a sport as opposed to other types of competitive physical activity. One way of answering this question is to conclude that sport is constituted by its rules. Without rules, and therefore the possibility of cheating, what is being done is not a sport.

The rules of major sports are codes. Lawyers often originally drafted them and they named them the *laws* of cricket or whatever. They have the characteristics of formal legal rules; they appear precise, clear and unambiguous. A rule, in its formal sense if not necessarily in its interpretation, must be clear to all participants in a game. Otherwise, the game will be constantly disrupted by disputes as to the existence of the rules, as opposed to the application or interpretation of the rules.

The codification of rules is reflected, albeit indistinctly, in the rules that apply to the administration of sport. These are often formal documents, written in legal language, and aping the character of formal rules. They aspire to be precise, clear and consistent.

The rulebook of any major sport in 2005 now reads like a legal document and parts of it will indeed have normally been drafted by lawyers. For example, the rules that govern the Zurich Premiership in Rugby Union begin with a definition section that includes the following:

1.2 Interpretation
(a) Where the context so admits:
(i) words importing the singular shall include the plural and vice versa;
(ii) words importing the masculine gender shall include the feminine gender; and
(iii) words importing persons shall include firms, corporations and unincorporated associations.
(b) Reference to any Act, Statute or statutory provision shall include a reference to that Act, Statute or statutory provision as amended, re-enacted or replaced from time to time, whether before or after the date of adoption of these Regulations, and any former Act, Statute or statutory provision replaced (with or without modification) by the Act, Statute or statutory provision referred to and any subordinate legislation made there under respectively.

This is direct plagiarism; its source is the Interpretation Act.

As well as precision, a codified rulebook will strive to be clear. However, the need for formal precise powers is counterbalanced by the need to retain discretion. This latter need in turn leads to wide and vague expressions being used. The disciplinary powers of the governing body are often deliberately opaque. They contain discretionary powers, such as penalties for 'bringing the game into disrepute'. For example, the Jockey Club's Licensing Committee can refuse to grant a licence. Rule 60 of the Club states that 'The Stewards of the Jockey Club may refuse to issue a rider's licence or permit to a person who, in their opinion, is not a fit and proper person to hold such a licence or permit'. Likewise, under Rule 2(v) of the Rules of Racing, the Stewards of the Jockey Club can exclude individuals, regardless of whether or not they are subject to the Rules of Racing, from any premises owned, licensed or controlled by the Jockey Club. They may do this at their 'absolute discretion' if 'they consider the presence of such a person on such premises undesirable in the interest of racing'. Phrases such as 'undesirable' and 'fit and proper' are capable of wide interpretation and may be retained on the advice of lawyers who lack the knowledge or foresight to specify precise conditions, such as a criminal record, that define 'undesirable'.

Consistency in the interpretation of rules is a further key element in the formalization and codification of rules. Nevertheless, the structure of many sporting bodies makes this difficult to achieve. The process of amending rules by committees can lead to inconsistent provisions appearing in the rulebook that make an unambiguous interpretation of the rules difficult. Increasingly, the rulebooks of governing bodies incorporate other documents, particularly from international sporting federations. Such inconsistencies can tax the best legal minds. For example, in *Korda* v. *ITF*[13] there was a dispute as to whether the ITF, as the governing body of tennis, was allowed an appeal from its own Appeals Committee to the Court of Arbitration for Sport. The ITF had its own anti-doping rules but had also introduced an explicit appeal for players to the Court of Arbitration for Sport. The ITF felt that a too lax sanction had been imposed on a tennis player who had been found guilty of taking drugs. Mr Justice Lightman found at first instance that the rules did not allow such an appeal by the governing body, as opposed to the player. The Court of Appeal disagreed. But all the judges in the litigation struggled to reconcile the resulting meld of documentation. Lord Justice Auld spoke of his 'considerable hesitation because of the seemingly internal inconsistencies in the ITF [rules] and the CAS Code'. Inconsistency can also arise from other factors. Governing bodies tend to decide issues on a case-by-case basis with very little use of precedents and frequently without publishing their reasons. Such *ad hoc* decision-making can lead to inconsistent results in similar cases.

A final characteristic of formal rulebooks is that they aim to be complete and gapless, thus anticipating all possible outcomes. However, such completeness is illusory. For example in the 1997–1998 football season, Middlesbrough were demoted from the Premier League because of the deduction of three points for failing to fulfil a fixture when they were unable to raise a full team because of illness in the squad. The FA committee that heard their appeal confirmed the deduction despite the absence of any rule governing the postponement of matches.

In summary, the process of juridification has led to rulebooks becoming more codified, especially as to the disciplinary powers of governing bodies. The language used is more formal and legal, discretion is circumscribed and its exercise governed by clear criteria, and vague powers have sometimes been removed.

Internal regulation adapts by changing rules

One of the most interesting aspects of juridification is the way in which the internal micro-regulatory system adjusts to external pressure. Unlike a crude model of intervention, the changing external environment of law and litigation can produce important internal adjustments without the need for direct legal intervention. Intervention by judges through litigation, or even just the threat of it, can force governing bodies to rethink their rules and practices. The threat of regulatory intervention by the state can have the same effect.

One example of a change in sporting rules caused partly by fear of litigation has been the changing rules relating to scrums in rugby union. There is a known risk of injury, especially neck and spinal injuries, in scrummaging. This is especially so with younger players, who have not developed the physique to withstand the impact of contact within scrums. These dangers led the governing bodies to adapt their rules in order to minimize such injuries. This nevertheless did not prevent the injury in *Smoldon* v. *Whitworth*, where an injured youth player sued a referee for negligence because of his failure to prevent collapsing scrums.[14] In the Court of Appeal Lord Justice Bingham remarked:

> It is not in doubt that the authorities responsible for the government of rugby football introduced a number of new rules specifically designed to protect young players against the risk of spinal injuries caused by excessive impact on engagement and by collapsed scrums. It would seem clear that one of the reasons for affording this special protection was the belief that younger players were particularly susceptible to injuries sustained in this way.

Similarly, in *Watson* v. *British Boxing Board of Control*, the governing body's regulations on medical care for boxers at the ringside were held not to be sufficient, in the light of good medical practice, to prevent a finding of negligence.[15] On appeal it was argued that the judge had failed to have due regard to the fact that there was no evidence that any boxing authority anywhere in the world had made rules imposing requirements such as those he held the board to have been negligent in failing to impose. The Court of Appeal dismissed this argument summarily:

> The next ground advanced by the board in support of the contention that the judge applied too high a standard was that there was no evidence that any other boxing authority in the world imposed more rigorous requirements than those of the board's rules. The judge accepted that this was the case but ruled that ultimately it was for the court to determine whether even the most widely followed practice was acceptable. In this, the judge was correct.[16]

In other words, the judge had effectively laid down requirements that a non-negligent board must have, and these were higher than any currently been used. The consequence of the judge's finding of negligence was that the British Boxing Board of Control (BBBC) changed its rules so that, as a minimum, they matched up to the standards laid down by the judge. This was in effect a judicial rewriting of the rules.

Additionally, the decision in *Watson* also rejects the idea that the current practice within a sports governing body was privileged and unchallengeable. This 'internal law' was overruled by external standards derived from a broader morality. The same argument was aired expressly in *Jones* v. *Welsh Rugby Union*.[17] The defendants argued that custom and practice validated their existing disciplinary procedures. As summarized by the judge, the Rugby Union argued that 'the best indicator of what procedure is reasonable and fair is that which members of the unincorporated association have voluntarily accepted and applied over many years'. The judge was not convinced by this argument. The present rules were clearly defective and unlawful in her view.

Conversely, a rule book may survive judicial scrutiny and so gain an added legitimacy. In *Gasser* v. *Stinson*, Mr Justice Scott held that a disciplinary rule of the International Association of Athletics Federations (IAAF) that imposed strict liability for doping offences and gave a fixed sentence for such offences was not unfair or unreasonable.[18] This judgment gave the green light to IAAF to retain these provisions in their rules. This is what could be termed the other side of juridification – the implicit approval of an existing rulebook as opposed to the re-writing implied by the decision in *Watson*. However, there has continued unease that fixed sentences in particular were not certain to survive legal challenge. The current rules of the IAAF provide for two levels of offences, and of penalties that are 'a minimum of two years'.[19] Strict liability is still retained; 'athletes ... are responsible for all or any substance present in their body'.[20]

Dispute mechanisms changed

Litigation threats

The most visible sign of juridification in sport is the greatly increased frequency with which litigation is threatened as a method of dispute settlement. Most sporting disputes, and not only those that have an economic dimension, seem to be accompanied by a threat of legal action. Indeed the threat of litigation can even prevent sport being played.[21]

These threats reflect a changing ideology. The sporting and social mechanisms for settling disputes are being displaced by legal ones. Those involved in sport speak more and more of rights and of suing. This threat of litigation is sometimes derided as not being sportsman-like. This expresses a nostalgic view that disputes are best settled on the field or in the dressing room. As Mr Justice Drake pointed out in the litigation between Paul Elliott and Dean Saunders over an injury that finished Elliott's career:

> I will, first, make a few general observations about the relationship of the law and sport. I have no doubt that there is a lot of popular support for the view that the law should be kept away from sport. Amateur sport is primarily for the enjoyment of those taking part, professional sport, primarily for the entertainment of spectators. But in both cases there is some natural feeling of repugnance when what happens during a sporting event is made the subject of legal proceedings.[22]

There are limitations to this view and he went on to say:

One witness expressed the view that an incident such as the one with which this action is concerned, should be settled in the dressing room rather than in a court of law. By the term 'in the dressing room', he no doubt meant within the bounds of the appropriate body of the Football Association or League. That would be fine, provided first that the dressing room, or appropriate body, provided a fair and just tribunal to investigate and decide the claim and, second, and at least equally important, that the dressing room should by some means provide the money to meet the injured party's compensation, which might very easily be in the order of, say, a million pounds or more.[23]

A threat of litigation is accompanied by a recasting of social obligations and responsibilities into the legal language of rights. The discourse of sport is interlaced with the discourse of law.

Lawyers and legalism

Juridification does not only occur by resort to the courts. The environment of juridification has changed the nature of other dispute-settlement processes within sport. The use of legally qualified persons to chair appeal tribunals within internal disciplinary procedures has introduced a degree of legalism into the proceedings. This process has clearly been accelerated by the increasing use of legal representation; two teams of lawyers arguing a case before a legally qualified chair are likely to produce a legal discourse, and a restructuring of the 'rights and wrongs' of the sporting issue into legal terms. Administrators in sport increasingly have a legal background, as exemplified by the appointment of Peter Lever QC at the Premier League.

An excellent example of legalism occurred in the Jockey Club's handling of the Graham Bradley appeal. Bradley is an ex-jockey who was banned from the sport for eight years for breaking the rules on association when he was a jockey by passing on information about horses to a known gambler.[24] The ban was wide enough to prevent him continuing his later work as a bloodstock agent. A recently retired High Court judge, Sir Edward Cazalet, chaired the appeal allowed under the Jockey Club's Rules. He is not a member of the Jockey Club and so formally independent.[25] Both sides were legally represented. Both legal teams agreed that Article 6 of the ECHR was applicable and Sir Edward Cazalet began his 'judgment'[26] by saying that it raised 'complex questions of law'.[27]

The clearest illustration of juridification, however, is the language of the decision itself. It is long, 62 pages, and gives detailed reasons. It begins:

It is the usual practice of the Appeal Board to give its Reasons in concise form. However, because of the importance of this case and out of deference to the thorough arguments which have been put before us by counsel on a number of complex questions of law, we have thought it appropriate to set out our reasons more fully than is normal.[28]

Presumably anticipating an appeal to the courts, Sir Edward Cazalt's decision is then indistinguishable from a conventional High Court judgment, especially on the key question as to whether the Jockey Club is sufficiently 'independent and impartial' enough to satisfy the standard of Article 6 as to a 'fair trial'.

The flavour of this decision is best shown by quoting part of it.

9.2 On behalf of Mr. Bradley it is accepted that there has been neither any actual lack of independence or impartiality, nor any actual existence of bias. His case is put on the basis that there has not been a sufficient appearance of independence and impartiality, and that there has been an apparent existence of bias. Both parties are agreed that the correct test for the resolving these questions is whether a fair-minded and informed observer ('the observer') would conclude that there was a real possibility of (i) a lack of independence or impartiality, and/or (ii) the existence of bias (see *In Re Medicaments and Related Classes of Goods (No 2)* (2001) 1 WLR 700 and *Porter* v. *Magill* (2002) 2 WLR 37). In this latter case the House of Lords (see paragraph 102) confirmed the Court of Appeal's test that 'the Court had first to ascertain all the circumstances which had a bearing on the suggestion that the judge was biased and then ask whether those circumstances would lead a fair-minded and informed observer to conclude that there was a real possibility, or a real danger, the two being the same, that the judge was biased'. This further means that a material consideration will be whether there are sufficient guarantees to exclude any legitimate doubt in these respects (see *Piersack* v. *Belgium* (1982) 5 EHRR 169). At para 30 the European Court of Human Rights stated that: 'a distinction can be drawn in this context between a subjective approach, that is endeavouring to ascertain the personal conviction of a given judge in a given case, and an objective approach, that is determining whether he offered guarantees sufficient to exclude any legitimate doubt in this respect'.

9.3 Some further guidance as to the nature of the information which the observer is expected to be in possession of, is to be found in the recent Court of Appeal decision of *Subramanian* v. *General Medical Council* [2002] UKPC 64. This decision has been referred to us in writing by both counsel, with written submissions, since the hearing of the 14th January last.

9.4 The facts, shortly stated, are that during a hearing before the Professional Conduct Committee of the General Medical Council, the press disclosed a previous unrelated finding of misconduct against the doctor in question. The hearing proceeded. Following a finding against the doctor that he had been guilty of misconduct, the doctor appealed to the

Court on the ground, inter alia, that, because of the press disclosure of the earlier finding against him, there was apparent bias on the part of the PCC. In dismissing his appeal, the court emphasized that the fair-minded observer was taken to be well and properly informed, knowing the nature and structure of the system in which the tribunal was operating as well as the protections against miscarriages of justice which were built into the system. The fact that the system was a well established one, operated by persons selected and elected to the task and supported by an appeal system are all matters of weight in this context (see para 14). Emphasis was also placed on the importance of the different functions in the organization being kept separate. Furthermore, statements or acts by other members of the organization who are not members of the Disciplinary Committee will not be attributed to the Committee members (see paras 19–20)...

9.6 We conclude that there is assistance to be gained from the decision in Subramanian. The Jockey Club is a regulatory body, wholly in control of horseracing. Under its well established system it sets up rules for regulating that sport, with clear rules as we have indicated, dividing the different functions, in particular as between the Disciplinary Bodies and the Executive. There is also emphasis on the fact that a statement made by somebody within the organization but outside the disciplinary body can be expected to be attributed by the observer to the member of the disciplinary body in circumstances where there is a separation maintained between the different functions of the organization. We bear these factors in mind, and in determining these issues we apply the criteria as stated.

This long extract is indistinguishable from the language and analytical method used by Sir Edward in his previous role as a High Court judge. It juridifies the internal appeal proceedings of the Jockey Club completely. It responds to detailed legal submissions by counsel. It uses the legal test of apparent impartiality, that of 'a fair-minded and independent observer' derived from a recent House of Lords judgment to determine the issue. It quotes several legal precedents, including a ruling of the European Court of Human Rights. It has a careful analysis of the most relevant precedent, *Subramanian*, which is concerned with the General Medical Council and accepts that this is applicable to a sporting body. From this precedent, it extracts the key elements of 'independence', such as a legal chairman and the 'importance of the different functions in the organization being kept separate'. It then applies these criteria to the instant case. It is as 'good' as a High Court ruling and is clearly intended to be so. It simply could not have been written by anyone without legal training.

The juridification of CAS

Juridification is also manifest with the increasing use of CAS as an external appeal body by many governing bodies of sport. CAS is increasingly legalistic. When it was reformed in 1993, following criticism from a Swiss court that it was not independent, it was hoped that CAS could provide swift and non-legalistic awards to settle sports disputes. It has however become more technical and now expresses its decisions in legal language. For example, in an early award, *S* v. *FEI*,[29] the court considered doping regulations that reversed the normal burden of proof and placed it on the competitor. The award is short, the legal reasoning is contained in one paragraph, and the conclusion is simply that 'the appeal is upheld'.

Compare that decision with a more recent one, *Kabaeva* v. *FIG*[30] where there was a 25-page decision. The award is fully reasoned and heavily dependent on precedent. The following extract, discussing the same issue, that of allocation of the burden of proof in doping cases, gives the flavour of the award:

> Having established the principle that the suspension of an athlete for a doping offence requires fault on his/her part, this does not, in the Panel's view, mean that it is for the relevant federation to provide full proof of every element of the offence, as is necessary in respect of a criminal act for which a presumption of innocence operates in favour of the accused. There is no doubt that the federation has to establish and – if contested – prove the objective elements of the offence, in particular, for example, that the sample was taken properly, that there was a complete chain of custody of the sample on its way to the laboratory and that the analysis of the sample was state-of-the-art. This follows from the accepted basic principle of Swiss Law that a person who alleges a fact bears the burden of proof. (Article 8 Swiss Civil Code; see also CAS 98/208, N. & J. & Y. & W. v/FINA, Award of December 22, 1998, CAS Digest II, pp. 234, 237; CAS 99/A/235, M.M. & M. v/FINA, Award of February 29, 2000, p. 14; CAS 2001/A/317, A. v/FILA, Award of 9 July 2001, p. 19 *et seq.*)

In their excellent study of the work of CAS, Morris and Spink describe CAS as possessing the elements of different forms of dispute resolution institutions.[31] They say:

> CAS possesses a keen appreciation of the need for substantive equity in resolving disputes, and in suitable cases has no qualms in drawing on its own subjective notion of fairness, which appears to have no legal foundation, to achieve an equitable outcome even if this involves overriding legal standards. In doing this, the CAS comes closer to the ombudsman than a court of law model of dispute resolution. On the other hand, the

CAS more closely resembles a court than an arbitral model in terms of its attitude towards precedent.[32]

Morris and Spink also explore briefly juridification of the rulebooks by showing that CAS, like courts, can act as a catalyst for the reform of rule-books. They describe CAS as 'identifying seriously defective regulations' and 'suggesting that the sports body might consider reappraising them in the future', thus 'acting as the catalyst for sports bodies to overhaul their internal regulations and practices.[33] This is the process of 'best practice' described above.

I argue[34] elsewhere that CAS could have different functions; a final review body for sporting federations, an ombudsman correcting poor administrative practice, an IOC organ that resolves disputes arsing from the IOC's regulations, an instrument of self-regulation supporting mandatory arbitration and dispensing unsupervised private justice, an independent arbitration system or a court that displaced national courts. Whilst concluding that it still has hallmarks of private justice, there is an increasing juridification. CAS is striving to act as a judicial tribunal, applying a *lex ludica* or a global sports law, free from constraints of national legal systems.

Framework of procedural justice

An important part of juridification has been the extent to which the principles of natural justice have been incorporated into the procedures of sports-governing bodies. In an important study carried out in 1997, Morris and Little surveyed the rulebooks of eight governing bodies in major sports, including football, cricket, rugby and racing.[35] They assessed these rule-books against eight factors demanded by the principles of natural justice. These were pre-hearing procedures, the nature of the hearing, cross-examination, admission of evidence, legal representation, giving reasons for decisions, rights of appeal, and satisfying the rule against bias by having independent adjudicators. Overall, they concluded that most of the rule-books satisfied, and often exceeded, the legal criteria. However, on arguable issues such as allowing cross-examination of witnesses and permitting legal representation, there was not unanimity. What was clear from the survey was that all the governing bodies had considered the legal issues recently and amended their procedures.

However, in some cases, the impetus for change has not come internally from the governing bodies but has been effectively forced on them from outside. A good example is *Jones* v. *Welsh Rugby Union* where a player challenged his ban from the sport. Mrs Justice Ebsworth initially found the disciplinary procedures of the Welsh RFU lacking in several respects.

What is interesting in the case is the rearguard action by the Welsh RFU to defend their procedures that had been retained when the sport had become professional in 1995. The Welsh RFU, in the judge's words, 'argued that if change is decided upon it should be by the Welsh Rugby Football Union at a meeting of its members and not pursuant to any direction of the Court'. The opposite view was that professionalism had changed the context and that 'the professional game needs a more formalized procedure'. The judge accepted this latter argument:

> The rules of the Welsh Rugby Football Union pre-date the introduction of professionals into the game. There is a respectable argument, in my judgment, that that alters the role of the disciplinary body. There is evidence before me that the rules of the Welsh Rugby Football Union differ in their approach from those of the international game and the rules of other professional sports.

The judge then in essence suggested a review of the procedures. She said:

> I am aware that the Welsh Rugby Football Union has powers to review its own decisions and its procedures. There seems to me to be room here for good sense to prevail. There is no need for the suspension to remain in abeyance if the defendants were to reconvene and were to do so under less restrictive rules. I would have thought, though it is not for me, that it would be in the general interest of the game of rugby in Wales. There are significant differences which are set out in the papers between the rules of discipline operated at national and international level and in different sports. There is much to be said for looking at the rules again.

This also indicates a tendency within juridification to look for best practice elsewhere to indicate what the acceptable standards should be.

That was obviously done in this case for on appeal, the Court of Appeal[36] noted that:

> Mindful of her observations, the Union looked at its Rules again and following such re-examination . . . changes were made whereby in future a player's representative should have the right to question the referee and to call and cross-examine witnesses; video evidence would be viewed in the presence of the parties; and requests for legal representation of players would be considered on their merits.

Another example of the same process of more formalized or altered procedures being encouraged by litigation is use of video evidence by football's disciplinary committees. In *Elliott* v. *Saunders*, Mr Justice Drake discussed whether it was right to use video evidence to assist him.[37] He said:

> Unless and until video is introduced by the governing body of a sport, as an aid to the referee or umpire, his decisions on the field must be final as regards what happens during the game. However, the use of video

after the game to correct a wrong decision of the referee which affects a player's future, must surely come into a quite different category. Referees can and do make mistakes ... Where such a mistake has led, for example, to a player suffering serious disciplinary action affecting his future, it must surely be right to use the video recording to correct an injustice. If it shows a referee made a mistake ... then it would be wholly wrong not to use the video.

This was a clear encouragement to the football authorities to use video. It also set guidelines for its use; to help the referee to make a definitive ruling and to correct an injustice that has affected a professional's future earnings. The English FA now uses video to allow a player to appeal against a sending off or a caution, but it also uses video to charge players with disciplinary offences where the referee has missed them. Internal change to 'correct an injustice', encouraged by judges, represents juridification as much as direct intervention.

Obligations seen as legal

The weakness of the interventionist/non-interventionist model is that it contrasts voluntary anarchic regulation with imposed rules. In fact, there is an important intermediate position, which is often the result of juridification. At one extreme, there is autonomy within a system of self-regulation, where the participants feel free to act as they wish without any orientation towards rules or laws and where their actions are governed only by self-interest. At the other end of the spectrum, there are externally imposed norms, which are obeyed for various reasons including coercion by external authority. In-between, there is what can be termed an internal legalism, where people feel bound to follow a rule because they must. This intermediate position reflects a change of mindset by actors within the sporting field. They feel a sense of obligation, that they must follow certain rules or standards because they must, rather than because they can see personal advantage. The individual changes their mindset. They 'know' what is required of due process in disciplinary proceedings; they 'know' that justice must be seen to be done; they 'know' that rules should be applied impartially by administrators who are disinterested; and they 'know' that those who make judgements should show a judicial attitude. This change of mindset internalizes the external norms and standards, without their necessarily having been imposed. This internalization begins to create the norms as part of the semi-autonomous regulatory system. This does not make the norms any less effective. As long as the internalization of the norms has occurred within the regulatory system, it is unnecessary to ask why the individual feels that they must observe the norms. In this way, much juridification of sport has occurred because the administrators of sport have felt obligated to conform to external standards without the need for direct intervention.

It is this form of juridification that suggests that sport is a classic example of what legal pluralists describe as a semi-autonomous social field. Moore's famous definition was that a field:[38]

> can generate rules … internally, but … is also vulnerable to rules and decisions and other forces emanating from the larger world by which it is surrounded. The semi-autonomous social field has rule-making capacities, and the means to induce or coerce compliance; but it is simultaneously set in a larger social matrix which can, and does, affect and invade it

Likewise in her influential survey of legal pluralism, Merry concluded that 'viewing situations as legally plural leads to an examination of the cultural or ideological nature of law and systems of normative ordering'.[39] So that:

> Law is not simply a set of rules exercising coercive power, but a system of thought by which certain forms of relations come to seem natural and taken for granted, modes of thought that are inscribed in institutions that exercise some coercion.[40]

It is the mindset by which the internal legalism comes to seem natural, and therefore part of an order that must be obeyed, which is the consequence, but also the cause, of juridification.

Private governance

The nature of sporting organizations also mirrors the process of juridification. Within civil society, those institutions that are not formally part of government can have powerful economic and social domination. They operate what Macaulay has termed 'private government'.[41] With the commercialization of sport and the spread of professionalism, sporting bodies have been increasingly challenged when exercising powers of governance over sport. The traditional legal view of sporting bodies was that they are private clubs, admitting whosoever they wish, and autonomous in their administration. This view meant that many legal principles were not applicable. The resulting danger was that power could be exercised, especially over players, in arbitrary and non-accountable ways.

The central legal question here is whether the principles that control the exercise of arbitrary power in public governance can be applied to private associations. The well-known answer in English law is no. The case of *Aga Khan* in 1993 decided that the public law remedy of judicial review was not available against the Jockey Club.[42] It has been assumed since this decision that no governing body of sport can be legally challenged in this way. However, in *Rubython* v. *FIA*, Mr Justice Gray said 'I am prepared to accept

... that the arrival of the Human Rights Act entitles the Court to look with circumspection at the *Aga Khan* case'.[43]

Nevertheless, this is not the end of the matter. Legal standards of fairness in decision-making, and of natural justice in procedural matters, have been imposed upon sporting associations. This reflects a judicial recognition that there is not a clear distinction in law between business associations, which as incorporated associations have to meet many legal criteria, and unincorporated social associations, which are unaccountable private clubs with total autonomy over their own internal affairs.

Sporting associations are increasingly treated as a hybrid between these two models. As Mrs Justice Ebsworth said in 1997,

> There are likely to be many people who take the view that the processes of the law have no place in sport and the bodies which run sport should be able to conduct their own affairs as they see fit and that by and large they have done so successfully and fairly over the years. It is a tempting and attractive view in many ways, particularly to those (and I almost said those of us) who grew up on windy and often half deserted touchlines. However, sport today is big business. Many people earn their living from it in one way or another. It would, I fear, be naive to pretend that the modern world of sport can be conducted as it used to be not very many years ago.[44]

The juridification of the internal affairs of sporting clubs and governing bodies has a long history that cannot be described here in detail. That history, however, raises several key issues.

1   To what extent is the sporting organization legally responsible for its own acts and those of its agents, in other words has it any immunity in law?
2   How can the law take into account the organization's inner 'political order', will it influence whether the internal governance of the organization is structured as a participatory democracy, a representative democracy or an autocratic hierarchy?
3   How shall the rights of members be legally conceptualized and protected as against the organization?
4   Can non-members who are injured or affected by the economic or social power of the organization have recourse against it?

Ideology of management and the basis of authority

The ideology of governance within sport in the past has been that of management. *Management* Committees still govern many sports. Their powers are often vaguely expressed and any 'rules' can be viewed by these committees as merely possible limitations on their unfettered power. Wide discretions under the 'rules' are allowed and frequently there are no appeals from decisions.

In regulating sport, governing bodies traditionally rested their control of the sport solely on power. We are running the game – end of story. There was no felt need for legitimacy other than the fact of power. This ideology of unilaterally imposed norms was reflected in the weakness of collective agreed norms and of players' organizations.

There has been a move towards justifying power by appeals to legitimacy, to rest governance of the sport on authority, that is on power legitimately authorized. This increasing legitimacy has been drawn partly from the impartial application of known rules. To ensure that sporting bodies at the very least follow their rules was one of the earliest forms of judicial intervention in sport. As early as 1954, the courts were ready to intervene for this purpose. In *Baker* v. *Jones*, they said that the rules making the central council of a sports governing body 'the sole interpreter of the rules and their decision in all cases final' was contrary to public policy and void.[45]

Contract from status

One important reflection of the process of juridification is that the legal basis of a governing body's jurisdiction over the participants in the sport has been clarified. The 'obligations' of those subject to the jurisdiction of governing bodies are now legally viewed as the result of contract. In *Korda* v. *ITF*, a tennis player tested positive for drugs at Wimbledon.[46] He had signed an entry form that contained the clause 'any person participating in an event sanctioned by the ITF shall be bound by all the provisions' of a 'guide-book', which included submitting to drug testing. Mr Justice Lightman said that a contractual relationship between the international sporting federation, ITF, and the player could 'plainly be inferred', despite the absence of any direct agreement, because Wimbledon was a tournament sanctioned by the ITF. In addition, the player's submission to a drugs test and then to the jurisdiction of an appeals committee was part of 'an acceptance of a contractual relationship'.

Whether such a contract is created simply by entering a competition under the rules of an international sporting federation without an express clause, as in Korda, was discussed in the Modhal litigation.[47] The Court of Appeal, by a majority, thought that it could. Lord Justice Mance rejected the classic argument that the social relations had not yet been juridified. Faced with the contention by the governing bodies that there was no intention to create legal relations, he dismissed the argument summarily; saying that it was 'unrealistic in relation to the modern sporting scene'.[48]

Social relations restructured and power re-ordered

An important consequence of juridification is that it restructures the social relations within the sporting field. Because the internalization of normative behaviour moves from the social to the legal, the basis of legitimacy can change and litigation, or the threat of it, can be used to challenge the existing power structures. This reordering of power relations is reflected in several ways.

Resources

Litigation costs money. Thus, differential access to resources is important. A rich governing body in sport may be prepared to resist legally justified demands by players. A poor governing body may be less able to do so but may be more willing to adapt its internal procedures and administration to reduce the risk of legal challenge. The British Athletics Federation was bankrupt by its defence of the Diane Modhal litigation and was replaced by UK Athletics as the governing body. Its successor has been much more circumspect about potential litigation since. UK Athletics has refused, for example, to follow IAAF rules and automatically suspend athletes who have tested positive for drugs, fearing that a wrongful suspension may expose them to a damages claim from the athlete. Similarly, UK Athletics refused to condemn or prevent the use by Denise Lewis of the East German coach Dr Ekkart Arbeit, who was allegedly tainted with drug use, for fear of a restraint of trade action if they prevented him working in this country.[49] The lesson of Modhal appears to have been learnt and fear of litigation and its attendant cost has made the governing body much more orientated to rule-of-law principles in dealing with those under its jurisdiction. The cost of litigation to governing bodies has been lamented by judges, who fear that the courts are been used expensively to settle disputes that should have been settled in other ways, and have indirectly encouraged alternative forms of dispute settlement. For example in *Alwyn Treherne and others* v. *Amateur Boxing Association of England Ltd*, which ruled on an attempt to set up a rival organization, Mr Justice Garland concluded his judgment by saying:[50]

> I would add finally an expression of regret that two bodies concerned with the promotion of amateur sport ... should have felt compelled to resolve their differences by litigation rather than a process of mediation or conciliation. At the end of the day, funds which might have otherwise been available for the promotion of amateur boxing, have been expended on litigation and done nothing to bring together the opposing factions in Wales.

Personnel

The commercialization of sport, and its more professional administration, has brought different people into the sport. Clubs are now run as businesses, so that it is much more likely that their executives are business people with experience of other areas of business. They will already be, for example, familiar with the standards of fairness and due process required in the disciplinary procedures of workers demanded by unfair dismissal law. It is thus reasonable to assume that such standards are also felt, as a matter of obligation, to be applicable to the disciplinary procedures of sport. Most governing bodies of sport now have access to legal advice and the richer ones have appointed full-time legal officers. Players in the richer sports usually have agents, many of whom have legal backgrounds. Some of these agents also come from the world of entertainment law, where there is always a contract and always a dispute. All these new participants in sporting world have been agents for juridification.

Insurance

Linked to the issue of resources is the question of insurance. As juridification in sport penetrates, administrators and others become much more aware of the risks to both the governing body and to themselves personally. To guard against the risk of litigation and liability they are increasingly taking out insurance. For example in *Smoldon* v. *Whitworth*, in which a referee was held liable for injuries resulting from poor scrummaging, Lord Justice Bingham at the very end of his judgment said:

> We are caused to wonder whether it would not be beneficial if all players were, as a matter of general practice, to be insured not against negligence but against the risk of catastrophic injury, but that is no doubt a matter to which those responsible for the administration of rugby football have given anxious attention.

This is a clear directive to authorities to insure players. Insurance is needed not only to protect the governing body but also to compensate players who may otherwise sue impoverished officials. The need has been highlighted by two recent cases. In *Watson* v. *British Boxing Board of Control*, a sports governing body was for the first time held liable in negligence for its failure to have adequate regulations to prevent serious injuries to boxers.[51] In *Volwes* v. *Evans*, a governing body was held vicariously liable for a referee's negligence.[52] This extension of liability was justified by Mr Justice Morland by the affordability of insurance and the governing body's ability to spread the risk. He said:

> In my judgment when rugby is funded not only by gate receipts but also by lucrative television contracts I can see no reason why the Welsh Rugby Union should not insure itself and its referees against claims and the risk of a finding of a breach of a duty of care by a referee . . . Insurance cover for referees would be a cost spread across the entire game.[53]

Impartial decision-making

Sport seems particularly open to poor decision-making in its internal gover-nance.[54] There is a history of arbitrary decisions that have adversely affected players. These have in part been caused by an ideology of management based on the submission of players to the unquestioned authority of the governing body. Increasing juridification has seen players and athletes treated as equal contracting parties.

The courts could do more to hasten the process of better decision-making. Two important issues could be addressed. One is the increasing use of 'exclusive jurisdiction' clauses by governing bodies to force players to use internal appeals system, to have an appeal at best to the Court of Arbitration for Sport, and to forego any right to take their case to the courts. The issues of genuine consent, of unfair contracts, and the abuse of superior bargaining power are all avenues that could be explored judicially or legislatively in sports law. The second is the issue of impartial decision-making. This is not solved simply by ensuring that impartial persons hear disciplinary cases. There is a wider issue that is especially evident in sport, which might be called the Rawlsian position. Rawls' theory of justice assumes that the prin-ciples of justice are chosen behind a veil of ignorance where no one knows their future circumstances and that therefore rules are formulated to the maximum advantage of all, and 'no one is able to design principles to favour his particular condition'.[55] It is possible that sporting rules are formulated, and decisions made, that appear to be formally neutral but are motivated by clubs, or others, trying to gain sporting or economic advantage.

For example, many sporting leagues now restrict promotion to higher divisions. Clubs who have won lower leagues on sporting grounds are not automatically promoted but restricted by non-sporting criteria such as ground capacity. The clubs already in the higher league, who have an obvious interest in trying to maintain a closed shop to their economic advantage, often make the rules governing promotion.

One example was the reaction to Leicester City gaining promotion to the FA Premier League in 2003. The club had gone into administration to protect itself financially. By doing so, they were able to keep their better players. Leicester was perceived to have gained an unfair benefit and this angered many other League clubs. An initial meeting of all 72 Football League clubs overwhelmingly, with one exception, endorsed a scheme to deduct points and even to relegate clubs forced into administration. However, the proposal was not endorsed at the League's annual general meeting, presumably after legal advice because it operated retrospectively. It was not surprising that the most vocal complaints came from Sheffield United, who, as the losing playoff finalists, felt that they would gain promo-tion in Leicester's place if the new rule was retrospective. Sheffield United's manager Neil Warnock branded Leicester's revival 'immoral' but 'he would, wouldn't he'.[56] The rules were changed later, following a fair procedure, so that clubs in administration would lose points. Leicester City ironically were relegated straight back after one season in the Premier League.

Counter-tendencies

One of the dangers of describing a process such as juridification is that it can appear to be a one-way process, that it has an historical inevitability. Therefore, it is worth concluding by recognizing that there are counter-tendencies. In so far as juridification is a result of commercialism in sport, as it is in the main, these counter-tendencies are reactions to the over-commercialization of sport.

Winning in court

One of the perennial fears that is expressed about the intervention of law into sport is that it will lead to the ultimate absurdity that one day the result of a sporting competition is decided in the courtroom and not on the playing field. This was described by an American court in 1990 as 'the most distasteful innovation of all – resolution of the competition in court'.[57] Lamenting the litigation, which the court felt was an un-Corinthian attempt by the sporting loser to win on a legal technicality; they said 'If the traditions and ideals of the sport are dependent on judicial coercion, [the] battle is already lost'.[58]

Whilst examples of sporting contests being directly decided by courts are rare, there are nevertheless examples where sporting advancement has been thwarted by a judicial decision. A good example is *Stevenage Borough FC* v. *The Football League*, where the Football league refused entry to the winners of the Vauxhall Conference.[59] Their refusal was based on the club's failure to meet criteria of ground size and of financial soundness. Although these criteria were not meet by many clubs already in the Football League, the judge refused to intervene on the grounds of lateness. Stevenage Borough never recovered from this refusal and although they remain in the Conference, they never seriously challenged for promotion until 2005. This outcome was explicitly recognized on appeal where Lord Justice Millett said:

> The financial advantages to Stevenage of promotion to the League would be very substantial, and will be lost for at least one season if the judgment below stands. Moreover, there is no certainty that Stevenage will win the Conference championship next year, and several seasons may elapse before it gains the promotion which it hopes to obtain immediately by litigation.[60]

However, this example does also show the effects of juridification. The Football League altered their rules relating to promotion from the Conference, ensuring at least that the judicial criticism of their discriminatory practices was eliminated. Coincidentally not one winner of the conference has subsequently been refused promotion, whereas two out of three winners before the litigation had been so refused. Additionally, the Football League allowed two promotions a season from the Conference as from 2003.

Uniqueness of sport

The juridification of sport is also noticeable in the activities of regulatory authorities. Football, in particular, has been much influenced by the activities of the regulatory authorities that enforce competition law, both in the United Kingdom and in the European Union. The European Union's approach has tried to recognize the uniqueness of sport; in particular, that it is a cultural commodity.[61] The explicit criteria used by the Commission to enforce its policy have operated as 'soft law', as a quasi-legislative code. This policy has also been reflected in the approach of the European Court of Justice, which in two leading cases in 2000, tried to indicate that some sporting issues are outside judicial rulings. In *Deliege*,[62] the Court refused to overturn a decision by the sporting federation to select one athlete rather than another and in *Lehtonen*,[63] they accepted that a sports league could legitimately have restrictive rules about who was eligible to play in the play-offs of a basketball league.

Immunity of sport

The degree of intervention in the internal affairs of sporting bodies has led them to devise strategies to try to prevent juridification by this method. There are several strategies employed but the most extreme is to try and preserve 'private justice' by forcing 'exclusive jurisdiction' clauses upon athletes as a precondition of competing. For example in the 2003 Americas Cup, there was a provision in the protocol governing the competition that stated 'Any Challenger who resorts to any court or tribunal, other the Arbitration Panel ... [will] ... be in breach of this Protocol and will accordingly be ineligible ... to be the Challenger for the Match.[64] In a classic example of self-reflexivity, the Americas Cup Arbitration Panel decided that this provision was clear and unambiguous, thus precluding any further appeal to the courts.[65]

Forum shopping

International sporting federations have been particularly sensitive to legal intervention because of their global scope and potential legal challenge in any country.[66] They have tried to argue that their activities are not justiciable before national courts. The English courts have robustly rejected this argument for immunity in several cases. In *Gasser* v. *Stinson*, Mr Justice Scott rejected the argument that English law was inapplicable.[67] It had been:

submitted that the restraint of trade rules of English law should not be applied to the IAAF Rules, which are concerned to regulate the eligibility of athletes of many different nationalities to appear in athletic competitions in many different parts of the world. As a matter of policy, he submitted, the courts of this country should not impose a rule of English public policy, founded on English views of freedom of economic competition, so as to regulate international athletics. I see the force of this submission but I am not prepared to accept it.

Similarly Mr Justice Lightman was not prepared to discuss the so-called international law of sport, as implying immunity from the English courts. In *Wilander* v. *Tobin*, he said that 'One expert, Mr Wise, purports to give evidence as to . . . what is described by Counsel as "the International Law of Sport". This is totally inadmissible as irrelevant to any issue at the trial.'[68] This refusal has had at least one important consequence. It has made international sporting federations reluctant to locate themselves in a jurisdiction that will be legally unfriendly. Not long after the decision in *Gasser* v. *Stinson*, the IAAF moved its headquarters from London to Monte Carlo. This kind of forum shopping has become more common with increasing juridification.

Conclusion

Juridification is a complex concept describing several different strands of a process. It is wider than simpler models of legal intervention in sport, and more sophisticated than a model of increasing legalism in sports administration.

Three key features of juridification have been noted. One, that there is already a rule-orientation within sport. Judicial or legislative intervention does not simply fill a void. It tends to encourage voluntary modification of the internal rules by those that have the power to do so. This could be termed administrating in the shadow of the law. Two, juridification describes a change of mindset; an internalization of obligation. This accepts the notion that 'I must do this because I'm legally obligated to do so', or 'an impartial person would act quasi-judicially in these circumstances'. It also embraces an orientation to use the law as the first choice in settling disputes. Third, juridification alters the balance of power within sport.

Juridification as a concept was first debated in industrial relations in the 1970s. Then it centred on whether workers were better served by voluntary collective bargaining, where they could participate in the autonomous creation of norms, or by externally imposed legal rights, which would replace collective norms rather than build upon them. Increasing juridification will spark a similar debate within sports law. Players now understand that they have rights and are prepared to use them. The game on the field may be the same but the social field of sport has changed forever.

Notes

1 Clark, J. 'The Juridification of Industrial Relations: A review article' 12 Industrial Law Journal 69 (1985).
2 Ibid., p. 70.
3 Ibid., p. 71.
4 Rubin, G.R. 'United Kingdom Military Law: Autonomy, Civilianisation, Juridification' 65 Modern Law Review 36 (2002).
5 Ibid., p. 37.
6 Ibid., p. 37.
7 Ibid., p. 48, quoting Arthurs, H.W. *'Without the Law': Administrative Justice and Legal Pluralism in Nineteenth Century England* (Toronto: University of Toronto Press, 1985) p. 3.
8 Rubin, ibid., p. 48.
9 Ibid., p. 37, quoting Scott, C. 'The Juridification of Regulatory Relations in the UK Utilities Sector' in Black, J., Muchlinski, P. and Walker, P. (eds) *Commercial Regulation and Judicial Review* (Oxford: Hart Publishing, 1998) p. 19. Another use of the concept can be found in Flood, J. and Caiger, A. 'Lawyers and Arbitration: The Juridification of Construction Disputes', 56 *Modern Law Review* 412 (1993). Also see Bourdieu, P. 'The Force of Law: Towards a Sociology of the Juridical Field', 38 *Hastings Law Review* 814 (1987).
10 Gardiner, S. and Felix, A. 'Juridification of the football field: strategies for giving law the elbow' 5 *Marquette Sports Law Journal* 189 (1995).
11 Morris, P. and Little, G. 'Challenging Sports Bodies' Determinations' 17 *Civil Justice Quarterly* 128, 130 (1998).
12 Foster, K. 'Developments in Sporting Law' in Allison, L. (ed.) *The Changing Politics of Sport* (Manchester: Manchester University Press, 1993), pp. 105–124 at p. 108. Reprinted in Dunning, E. and Malcolm, D. (eds) *Sport: Critical Concepts in Sociology* (London: Routledge, 2003).
13 *The Times*, 4 February 1999. On appeal, *Independent*, 21 April 1999.
14 *Smoldon* v. *Whitworth* [1997] ELR 115; [1997] ELR 249 CA.
15 [2001] 2 WLR 1256.
16 Ibid. Phillips L.J. at para 111.
17 *Jones* v. *Welsh RFU*, unreported 27 February 1997. *Jones* v. *Welsh Rugby Union*, *The Times*, 6 March 1997.
18 Unreported 15 June 1988.
19 IAAF Rule 60.2.
20 IAAF Rule 55.4.
21 See Thomson, S. 'Harmless Fun Can Kill Someone' 1 *Entertainment Law* 95 (2002), especially the section 'If In Doubt, Ban It'.
22 Unreported June 10 1994.
23 Ibid.
24 He was convicted on several other charges, including under Rule 220 (iii). 'Having acted in a manner which, in the opinion of the stewards of the Jockey Club, was prejudicial to the integrity, proper conduct and good reputation of horse racing in Great Britain whether or not such conduct should constitute a breach of any of the orders or Rules of Racing.' This is an example of a wide discretionary rule.
25 He is however the son of Peter Cazalet, who was a racehorse trainer for Queen Elizabeth, the Queen Mother.
26 A full version of the Jockey Club's decision is at 3 *International Sports Law Review* 71–89 (2003).
27 Paragraph 1.1 of the decision.
28 Ibid.

29 CAS 91/56, 25 June 1992.
30 TAS2002/A/386.
31 Morris, P. and Spink, P. 'The Court of Arbitration for Sport: A Study of the ExtraJudicial Resolution of Sporting Disputes' in Stewart, W.J. (ed.) *Sport and the Law: the Scots Perspective* (Edinburgh: T&T Clark, 2000).
32 Ibid., pp. 72–73.
33 Ibid., p. 74.
34 Lex Sportiva and Lex Ludica: The Court of Arbitration for Sport's Jurisprudence in Ian Blackshaw (ed.) Twenty Years of CAS.
35 Morris and Little, ibid. at p. 132.
36 *The Times*, 6 January 1998.
37 *Supra* fn 21.
38 Moore, S.F. 'Law and Social Change: The Semi-Autonomous Field as an Appropriate Field of Study', 7 *Law and Society Review* 719 (1973).
39 Merry, S.E. 'Legal Pluralism', 22 *Law and Society Review* 869 (1988).
40 Ibid., p. 889.
41 Macaulay, S. 'Images of Law in Everyday Life: The Lessons of School, Entertainment and Spectator Sports', 21 Law and Society Review 185 (1987).
42 *R*. v. *Disciplinary Committee of the Jockey Club, ex parte Aga Khan* [1993] 2 All ER 853.
43 Unreported 6 March 2003.
44 *Jones* v. *Welsh Rugby Union, The Times* 6 March 1997.
45 [1954] 2 All ER 553.
46 *Supra* fn 13.
47 The litigation lasted several years. Queen's Bench Division, 28 June 1996, Court of Appeal 28 July 1997, House of Lords, *The Times* 23 July 1999; No. 2 Queen's Bench Division, 14 December 2000, Court of Appeal, 12 October 2001. (2002) 1 WLR 1192. The contractual question is discussed at length in the final appeal.
48 Ibid., para 105.
49 See Duncan Mackay, the *Guardian*, Monday, 30 June 2003, at http://sport.guardian.co.uk/athletics/story/0,10082,987605,00.html, accessed 11/08/03.
50 Unreported 27 February 2001.
51 [2001] 2 WLR 1256.
52 Unreported 13 December 2002, confirmed on appeal 11 March 2003.
53 Para 23.
54 For a list of standards to be followed in good governance by sporting bodies, see the papers presented at the first European Conference on the governance of sport in 2001, available at www.governance-in-sport.com, especially Chapter 3.
55 Rawls, J., A Theory of Justice (Oxford: Oxford University Press 1973) p. 12.
56 http://news.bbc.co.uk/sport1/hi/football/teams/l/leicester_city/2974007.stm; http://www.soccerage.com/en/13/n9608.html. Both accessed 11/08/03.
57 *Mercury Bay* v. *San Diego*, 76 NY 2d 256 (1990).
58 Ibid.
59 Unreported, 23 July 1996.
60 *The Times* 9 August 1996.
61 On the approach of the European Union, see Foster, K. 'UEFA Rules OK?: European Law's Impact on Football' (2002) *Soccer Review* pp. 31–37; Weatherill, S. 'Fair Play Please! Recent Developments in the Application of EC Law to Sport', 40 *Common Market Review* 51 (2003); Parrish, R. 'The Politics of Sports Regulation in the European Union, 10 *Journal of European Public Policy* 240 (2003).

62 *Deliege* v. *Liege Francophone de Judo*; cases C-51/96 and C-191/97. (2000) ECR
   I-2681; [2000] All ER (D) 519.
63 *Lehtonen & Castors Canada Dry Namur-Braine* v. *FRBSB* (Belgian Basketball
   Federation); case C-176/96. (2000) ECR I-2549; [2001] All ER (EC) 97.
64 Article 10.2 of the Protocol.
65 Decision ACAP 02/06.
66 For a discussion of some of the tactics, see Foster, K. 'Is There a Global Sports
   Law', 2 *Entertainment Law* 1 (2003).
67 Unreported 25 March 1988.
68 [1997] 1 Lloyd's Rep 197.

Part III

Film, literature and music

9 The justice films of Sidney Lumet

Peter Robson

Introduction

The films of Sidney Lumet encompass a number of issues of interest to scholars of law in film. Looking at Lumet provides three potentially valuable insights within the field of law and film studies. First, his films on the justice system provide an opportunity to look at the question of what amounts to the subject matter of inquiry for law and film studies. Second, it allows for some consideration of the questions raised by the notion of the *auteur* as an element within film. Finally, it allows an exploration of some of the elements involved in interrogating more closely the question of law films and genre. The focus on this work of Lumet emerged from work on the development of law films as a whole. In looking at different approaches to law film it seemed that three distinct typologies of lawyer appear in such films. They are also encountered in the early, middle and later work of the prolific director, Sidney Lumet. In simple terms – the heroic figure; the flawed seeker of justice; the amoral hired hand.

Different approaches and goals in law and film studies

Background

This study of Lumet's justice films needs to be placed into context. Hitherto the emphasis in law and film studies has varied.[1] The aims and goals of writers has ranged from practice enhancement through legal/social theory 'sharpening' to some work situated broadly within film studies. Thus we have work that uses film to demonstrate points of practice ranging from the rules of evidence to more effective defence summations.[2] Other work looks at how the promise of justice in the form of the heroic lawyer has altered over the years, as well as to whether this promise was ever as clearcut as all that.[3] Less frequently there have been essays which look at how law films are constructed, how the portrayal of the location of the justice process operates and how the trial is shot.[4] There does not appear to have been any consideration of the process by which the stuff of law fits into the film production scenario. Precisely how funding has been obtained and why certain projects have been delayed or foundered has yet to be addressed. Most law and film work has taken the products as given and worked to analyse the various kinds of portrayals.[5] The process whereby forensic subjects have attracted funding for film-makers is not directly explored. We note that certain other types of films like Westerns and Musicals have waxed and waned.[6] The coverage in the law films that are made has been contextualized in some instances. For instance there are several pieces which take as their point of departure the 'missing lawyers'. Here the absence of a range of figures in the legal scene has been commented on as part of the cultural hegemony of the straight, white male lawyer.[7] In addition the process whereby different kinds of real life stories have made the transition to the screen has been examined.[8]

Work has been both wide in its sweep[9] as well as concentrating on one area of law[10] or theme within law film scholarship.[11] The majority of the work, however, has tended to look at individual films.[12] This individual film work has also included examinations of the relationship between the real life sources of films[13] and occasionally fictional adaptations.[14]

What has been largely absent has been any consideration of the work of individual directors although one essay does centre on myth in the law-centred work of John Ford.[15] This concentrates on three of Ford's films – *Young Mr Lincoln* (1939), *The Searchers* (1956) and *The Man Who Shot Liberty Valance* (1962). Given the relatively high profile of the director as a focus for film studies especially since the emergence of notions of the *auteur* this absence might be seen as surprising. Of course, in some areas of writings in the broad field of law the opportunities for a strongly director-centred approach is limited.[16] Thus, in private eye films, although a popular and consistent style of film directors from Howard Hawks, John Ford and John Huston to Roman Polanski and Robert Altman have limited themselves to directing no more than one P.I. film.[17] Again the same problem could be said to be present in law-centred films with prominent directors like Robert Altman and Francis Ford Coppola limiting their input to single films.[18] There is one notable exception, however. Whenever important landmarks are mentioned in the portrayal of law, works like *Twelve Angry Men* and *The Verdict* are mentioned as well as *Night Falls on Manhattan*. These films were directed by Sidney Lumet. If one widens the scope of investigation to look at law and justice[19] we find in the work of Sidney Lumet a consistent and wide-spread theme – corruption and the worm of special interests at the heart of the administration of justice. This chapter looks at this work not only because of the persistence of these themes but also their longevity. Lumet's first intervention in this area was in 1957 and he has contributed some 12 films around law, corruption and justice since then. His work covers each decade since and this chapter looks at how the focus in the legal system portrayals has shifted and how this work relates to his other discussions of justice themes.

The rationale for examining the justice films of Sidney Lumet

Sidney Lumet directed 40 feature films between 1957 and 1998. He started with *Twelve Angry Men* and his most recent work was a remake of *Gloria*. Some 30 of these have been made available on video.[20] A recurrent preoccupation during the past 34 years has been the problem of how the justice system operated. The concerns have emerged consistently.

Lumet's range has led to him being discussed in condescending tones as a 'journeyman' director.[21]

> Not a film maker in the true sense but a talented and conscientious technician with a passion for the theater and an ability to handle actors.[22]

He seems to be dismissed as 'worthy' and 'driven by a social conscience' rather than spoken of with the reverence of Scorsese, Ford Coppola or even Spielberg. Capable of good films but somehow lacking originality.

> . . . he's a masterful director of actors who, when given the proper material, can assemble a blistering movie. Consequently, he is only as good as his source material . . . and his cast . . .[23]

The trenchant David Thomson for his part goes beyond condescension to level a series of critiques against Lumet including 'meretricious proficiency'. He assesses *12 Angry Men* thus:

> . . . one of the more glib transpositions from the small screen . . . liberally contrived and deluded into the belief that a band of character actors could restore the conscience to an Eisenhower icebox world. Only someone of dour self-seriousness could have kept the film so high-minded; and only a clever handler could have maintained its sham tension . . . The technical skill and glib liberalism of that film were built around Fonda and he was once more revealed as Hollywood's statue of liberty.[24]

His tone has altered a little over the years.

> . . . an acclaimed picture in its day: it was a model for liberal reason and fellowship in the Eisenhower era; or maybe it was an alarming example of how easily any jury could be swayed.[25]

Others *within* the film business have been rather more generous ranging from David Mamet's description of Lumet as 'the maestro'[26] to Steven Spielberg's view that he is 'one of America's greatest film-makers'.[27] In France, too, he has been described as 'one of the best and most active specialists in realistic drama':[28]

This chapter examines the justice themes which Lumet returns to in a significant number of films throughout his long career. In an interview in 1989 Lumet expressed an element of surprise to discover that he had returned to the theme of 'justice' so frequently. He remarked, 'I've never been aware of it as wanting to do movies about the criminal justice system, and then I look back and there are seven, eight, nine of them involved with it . . .'[29]

He provided his own tentative account of why this had been so in 1990:

> I guess when you're a Depression baby, someone with a typical Lower East Side poor Jewish upbringing, you automatically get involved in social issues. And as soon as you're involved in social issues you're involved in the justice system.[30]

Interestingly, the link for an American director is from social issues into the justice system rather than the world of politics or work as we find in the work of Ken Loach with his canon of social issues work – *Riff Raff* (1992), *Raining Stones* (1993), *Ladybird, Ladybird* (1994), *Carla's Song* (1997), *My Name is Joe* (1998), *Bread and Roses* (2001), *The Navigators* (2001), *Sweet Sixteen* (2002) and *Ae Fond Kiss* (2004). The explanation may well lie in the higher profile hitherto of the world of politics in social struggles in Europe. Contrast this with the focus on the courts in the United States. Lining up with De Toqueville, we have the observation by legal thriller writer Philip Friedman that ultimately all social issues eventually reach the courts in the States.[31]

Some possible problems with looking at Lumet

Whether or not it is reasonable to make a selection of certain films for the specific purpose of constructing a director's portrayal of justice requires some discussion. There are questions of distortion of the overall opus. There may be broader social concerns lurking in other less obvious vehicles. Particularly in the collection of essays edited by John Denvir, *Reel Justice*, there are plenty of cues for legal comment in films which are rather less obvious than, for example, *12 Angry Men*. *It's a Wonderful Life* is not a film you would expect to figure in the panoply of legal films. It is used to provide a version of notions of community in a discussion of individualism and child protection in the Supreme Court.[32]

In some of Lumet's other non-justice work, however, there is often some critical reference to the legal system. Thus in the apparently straightforward 'missing hours' thriller, *The Morning After* (1986) there is a *Chinatown* like fatalism about the way the law can be twisted by the rich and powerful. Fading alcoholic actress Alex Sternbergen (Jane Fonda) has been 'set up' by her hairdresser husband, Joaquin Manero (Raul Julia) to 'take the fall' for the person who actually carried out the murder of a sleazy pornographer, Bobby Korshak. It was in fact the hairdresser's new girlfriend, society lady Isabel Harding (Diane Salinger). Manero's aim has been to protect her after she killed the man who had been blackmailing her for years over some photographs. She announces herself to the police in full confidence that her position will protect her:

> *Isabel Harding*:   My father is Joshua Harding
> *Detective Greenbaum*:   Harding? Is that Judge Harding?

From this we can assume that the gloomy assessment of Alex' protector, ex-cop Turner Randall (Jeff Bridges) is likely to come true when Isabel claims that Manero did the killing.

> Who do you think they're gonna believe? Her or some guy named Joaquin Manero? I think she did it but they'll put him away. I think she'll do a little time or none. That's the way it is.

Just like Noah Cross in *Chinatown* (1974), people like the Hardings do not get caught by the web of the law. Outsiders and *arrivistes* like Manero are available for that.

It could be argued that ignoring certain parts of a director's work distorts any possible overall directorial vision. Given the moral issues involved in so much of Lumet's other work, like *The Pawnbroker* (1965), *Running on Empty* (1988) or *Critical Care* (1997) as well as Lumet's own stated perspective, this seems a small risk in this particular instance.

More worrying perhaps is attachment to the notion of the dominant *auteur* which a detailed coverage of the films of one director might seem to imply.[33] It seems, however, not unreasonable to engage with the work of anyone who has made a major contribution to any field. One would, for instance, want to cover the Westerns of John Ford in any broader discussion of the Western, Hitchcock when examining thrillers or the films of Ken Loach in relation to social critique films. Hence, examining the canon of work of Lumet need not imply that the style of his work is elevated above the general thematic concerns of the legal film category being examined.

The team that goes to make a film, as Lumet is keen to stress in his own writing, comprises a whole range of people. Writers, camera crew, actors and the composer of the score all contribute to how the film ends up. Whilst the director may have the 'final cut' it is part of a collaborative effort. (*Lumet*, passim) Thus we find some stars lifting indifferent material or failing to convince. In this context, critics of Lumet have pointed to the lack of 'star power' of the lead actor, Treat Williams in *Prince of the City*[34] in this respect as well as to the superior playing of Jane Fonda in *The Morning After*.[35] There is more than the actors, of course. Why star-studded films fail commercially like *Family Business*[36] remains a mystery, not least to Lumet.[37]

The changing world of Lumet's lawyers

Three distinct typologies of lawyer appear in the early, middle and later work of this prolific director. In *Twelve Angry Men*, *The Verdict*, *Guilty as Sin* and *Night Falls on Manhattan* Lumet has produced films which centre on the operation of the trial part of the legal process. Over a period of 40 years the representation of the lawyer and the justice process has not remained constant. The changes in Lumet's films seem to mirror those observed across the board from a clear faith in the legal process through to doubts and later downright mistrust of the efficacy of the process.[38]

Legal system dynamics

Although in *12 Angry Men* (1957) he is not technically a lawyer, Davis, Henry Fonda's architect juror number 8, can be taken to represent the seeker for truth which the cinematic lawyer traditionally embodies – the quintessential justice figure. Fonda is the link between older versions of the lawyer justice figure encountered in Fonda's own Abraham Lincoln[39] and Spencer Tracy's Darrow figure, Henry Drummond[40] and subsequent lawyer heroes like Gregory Peck's Atticus Finch,[41] Al Pacino's Arthur Kirkland,[42] Cher's Kathleen Riley[43] and Kelly McGillis' Katheryn Murphy.[44] Juror number 8 stands out against the 11 other jurors who are willing to make their decision about the life of the accused without any discussion. Although by no means arguing that the accused could not have stabbed his father to death, as the witnesses have testified, he wants to weigh up the evidence without rushing to judgment. Gradually, through examination the cast-iron case against the boy begins to look less compelling. The reasons why some have voted guilty are exposed as stemming from lack of a tendency to reflect, blatant racial prejudice, interest in getting home, as well as fear of testing their own ideas against more powerful characters on the jury. In the end all are in their different ways persuaded to return a verdict of not guilty. It has all stemmed from the courage and tenacity of juror number 8. He symbolizes what the jury system should be about – as well as possibly what democracy involves.[45] He performs the role which the defence lawyer should have performed in the courtroom. He is a true justice figure.[46]

The contrast with the alcoholic haunter of Funeral Parlours, Frank Galvin in *The Verdict* (1982) is at first blush remarkable. Here is a man who at the beginning of the film has lost his bearings entirely, seeking clients when they are at their most vulnerable. He is rescued from his own self-destruction by a hush money medical negligence case, which his friend Mickey Morrissey (Jack Warden) offers him as a last chance for rehabilitation. Even in this case he acts unethically by failing to advise his clients of an offer from the hospital authorities in the desperate hope that just compensation can be obtained. He wants to bring out into the open the negligent cover-up by the doctor who operates, which has resulted in a young woman being reduced to a persistent vegetative state, kept breathing in a coma by modern technology. The fact that Galvin does not have a conventional case, according to the rules of evidence, provides the tension. The jury heeds Galvin's plea that justice is what courts are about and that the jury have the possibility of achieving such a just result in the case effectively by overlooking the lack of evidence. Whilst Frank starts in the gutter, by the end of the film he has achieved an element of justified self-esteem by his rediscovering the path to what law can achieve. Even further away from the iconic white-suited Atticus Finch[47] is Rebecca de Mornay's calculating courtroom trickster, Jennifer Haines in *Guilty as Sin* (1993). She starts out in another classic mould – mouthpiece for the mob[48] – and takes on the case of slimy businessman, David Greenhill (Don Johnson). Her motives for accepting this case are far from clear. Information from her own private investigator becomes available, which suggests that Greenhill is a serial wife murderer. As a result, part way through the case, having failed to withdraw from representing Greenhill she opts to frame him for murder by planting evidence. The shift from the ethical code embodied by Atticus Finch at the trial of Tom Robinson is remarkable. By illustration, the shift which has been observed between the 1961 and 1991 versions of lawyer Sam Bowden in *Cape Fear* has been described as reflecting the change in the way lawyers are perceived by the public.[49] This shift is exemplified in the courtroom films of Sidney Lumet from the 1950s through the 1980s to the 1990s.

There is something of a return to the morally centred lawyer with Andy Garcia's Sean Casey in *Night Falls on Manhattan* (1996). There are conflicts between Casey in his role as son and as lawyer. He is selected to prosecute the killer who gunned down Casey's policeman father, Liam (Ian Holm) in a drugs bust. Liam's appearance on the witness stand shortly after his release from hospital helps to secure the public profile and, in due course, the post of District Attorney for his son. Casey Junior is required to evaluate the competing claims of his father's corrupt partner Joey Allegretto (James Gandolfini) and the legal system. This choice of the system over loyalty to friends results in Joey's suicide but Sean secures the forgiveness of Liam. The film closes, as it opened, with the orientation lecture for new Assistant DAs. Instead of the tired cynical formulaic recitation, which Sean Casey was given at the start of the film, we have instead an inspiring affirmation of the value of the public prosecution service – by Casey himself. This may indeed be a more corrupt world than that of Henry Fonda's Juror number 8 or even the one Paul Biegler (James Stewart) inhabited in *Anatomy of a Murder* (1959) but there is more than a glimmer of hope that at least some people are seeking justice for all.

Moral quandaries in law enforcement

There are four Lumet-directed films which centre on the enforcement aspects of the justice system. They all focus on the different ways those involved in operating the legal system have to compromise. They involve distinctive types of police malpractice. In *The Offence* (1972) Detective Sergeant Johnson (Sean Connery) gets over-involved with a case and beats a suspected child molester to death. Lumet has disavowed what he refers to as the 'rubber-ducky' school of drama which he associated with early days of television. 'Someone once took his rubber ducky away from him, and that's why he's a deranged killer'.[50] Johnson, it turns out, is reacting to a long-buried molestation incident from his own childhood which seems to have produced his murderous response. It is, nonetheless, his passion to protect the innocent that drives him to act as he does.

In his three later films the focus is on the endemic corruption by way of payoffs to beat police for turning a blind eye to a range of infractions. The first, *Serpico* (1974), is based on a true-life story of a police officer forced to quit the New York force after being set up by his colleagues to face a gunman without police back-up. His offence was failing to fit in by refusing to be a 'dirty cop'. Frank Serpico (Al Pacino) is out of step with all aspects of police behaviour despite an initial commitment to the force through his family connections. By way of contrast another true-life-based cop, Danny Ciello (Treat Williams) switches, in *Prince of the City* (1981), from being part of the elite Special Investigation Unit, accepting bribes and bending the rules as part of his daily work, to becoming an informant for the anti-corruption Chase Commission. His voyage of self-discovery shifts him away from all that he holds dear at the start of his story, family solidarity and the ethos of fellow officers. The end with him teaching in police college is enigmatic, a close-up on his reaction to one of his class leaving indicating that Ciello – a grass on fellow officers – has nothing to teach him. We are neither clear whether the student who leaves represents the force as a whole or not, nor of the effect on Ciello.

Finally, in *Q & A* (1990), an individually flawed police officer operating in a sea of big money and routine corruption has Lieutenant Mike Brennan (Nick Nolte) opening the film himself with the cold-blooded murder of an informant. The rest of the film involves his attempts to divert a green young Assistant DA, Al Reilly (Timothy Hutton), off the scent and treat this is a gangland killing. His failure to avoid nemesis is really incidental. What is interesting is that he no mere psychopath or greedy chiseller. Rather he is a tragic figure driven to kill for what he rationalizes as the greater good of society. He puts his actions and the allegations against him in context in conversation with young DA, Al Reilly:

> It's all coming apart, Al. I want it the way it used to be. I mean you lose control of this fuckin' jungle and you're finished. You know what we're

fighting out there and they know it. That's why they hate me … they want to set you up (per Mike Brennan, *Nick Nolte*)

Echoing the British police advertisement of the 1980s he argues that without cops like him the elemental forces of the jungle that are gangsters and 'lowlifes' would overwhelm comfortable bourgeois society.

The individual against the 'system'

Whilst the first two categories of Lumet justice films focus clearly on those involved in operating the world of legal practice and law enforcement, there are four films which feature the rather broader moral question of the individual's relationship to society as a whole and their entitlement to resist the 'system'. This is portrayed variously as the punishment regime of the armed forces in *The Hill* (1966); financial, emotional and social pressures on the impoverished outsider in *Dog Day Afternoon* (1975); the power of big business in *Network* (1976) and a cheated gangster's girlfriend challenging the unrestrained power of the mob in *Gloria* (1998). In any full consideration of the understanding of justice and its changing nature in the films of Sidney Lumet one would want to point out that in these peripheral films similar sorts of ethical questions and moral principles arise, albeit in unexpected settings. Trooper Joe Roberts (Sean Connery) and some of his fellow sufferers, at the hands of vindictive Staff Sergeant Harris (Ian Hendry), are in the prisoner category for sound reasons of conscience. It is the abusive use of punishment regime which is immoral and unjust in *The Hill*. It is with Joe Roberts that we empathize and who represents a morally centred human. In the same vein, it seems plausible to argue for the moral principles of concern for his fellows as driving Sonny Wortzik (Al Pacino) to embark on a bank robbery in *Dog Day Afternoon*. Lurking beneath the overblown religious tinge to his rhetoric, *Network*'s Howard Beale (Peter Finch) is providing a critique of the blind immorality and injustice of market forces and how they corrupt new values. Similarly, it is her sense of justice denied that impels Gloria (Sharon Stone) into her confrontation with the mob in *Gloria*. She has kept her mouth shut about gang activities and served time. She feels that she has been cheated out of her share of the profits of the enterprise and has been denied her just reward.

The persistent features in Lumet's world of justice

Looking at these dozen films as a whole, a number of different themes and tropes recur. Most powerfully, policing is portrayed as random and chaotic and the embodiment of the 'cock-up' theory. Lumet talks about this on the basis of his observations of police practice over the years, explaining the reality on which the disastrous attempt to arrest a Harlem drug dealer at the start of *Night Falls On Manhattan*. In it the drug dealer shoots two police officers and a further number are accidentally downed by their own colleagues in the confusion. The dealer calmly leaves the scene driving a police car.

> People never believe these kind of raids, the disorganized mess they are – all the plans go out of the window . . . in a 20 year career in the Police Department the average cop draws his gun maybe five times, maybe ten and shoots it once . . . they're scared . . . the kind of result that you see here happens a lot more often than people would care to admit.[51]

In *Serpico* one theme is the failure of the various branches of the forces of law and order to know who is doing what? Similarly in *Dog Day Afternoon* there are near-fatal results deriving from the competing power structures within the police as well as individual initiative. As indicated there is chaos in *Night Falls on Manhattan* which results in the wounding of police as well as escape of the target in a police car. The role of the SIU in *Prince of the City* confuses and conflicts with that of the City cops with operations aborted through failures in the most basic communications.

At a more general level the individual has to isolate himself or herself against the general conformity of the majority in any system. Henry Fonda (*Twelve Angry Men*) must risk the ridicule of his fellow jurors when he votes not guilty and insists that some discussion take place before they go their separate ways. In a rather more intimate way, when he challenges police corruption, Frank Serpico has to draw on his own resources, finding himself isolated both in his work and socially (*Serpico*). Similarly, Danny Ciello experiences the conflict between fidelity to the law and the group ethos (*Prince of the City*) and, closer to home, Sean Casey faces up to the implications of going against the grain and exposing the corruption of his cop father's partner (*Night Falls on Manhattan*). In a slightly different way the pressures from his extended family drives Sonny to engage in bank robbery to meet the miriad demands on him as father, lover and son (*Dog Day Afternoon*). He does not act for himself but for the benefit of the others who depend on him.

Finally, the induction process – or a version of it – is part of the process of socialization against which people measure their success/failure to meet the ideals of the system and themselves and this trope is found in *Serpico* (1974), *Prince of the City* (1981) and *Night Falls on Manhattan* (1996). It is used as both a framing device to open as well as close the two later films as well as opening *Serpico*. Thus it serves as a point of departure as well as form of closure. It allows the audience to have a set of values against which to assess subsequent actions and developments in values.

Concluding remarks

Lumet's justice films are worthy of detailed reading for a range of reasons. They offer a perspective on the major concerns of writers on law and film in relation to the nature of the field of study, the notion of the *auteur* today and issues around genre.

Law films, justice and the curriculum

If, by his own calculation by the end of the 1980s, Lumet had directed 'seven, eight, nine' films … 'involved in the justice system' we might wonder as to the reason for the lack of clarity. The reason for his ambivalence was not, it is suggested simply a question of precise memory in an interview but a question of classification. His uncertainty about the number of 'justice' films he had been involved in stems from the imprecision of the category. Unlike genres such as the western, the musical or horror film, the film dealing with justice and legal themes tends to be subsumed within other categories, rather than be treated as comprising a genre of its own. The range of Lumet's films calls attention to the debate within law and film studies as to what exactly might be the limit of the field of 'law films'.[52] This debate involves an examination of the question of genre and typology. This has not been a major preoccupation with many law and film scholars due to the particular centre of their work and its rather closer relation to law teaching as opposed to film studies. This issue of genre and attempts to categorize films around law is touched on further below.

Lumet as auteur

The work of Lumet can also be adopted as a site to debate the merits and demerits of centring one's attention on the style of individual directors. On one reading the work of Lumet over a period of 40 years would seem to provide a strong antidote to any lingering notions of the director as the sole focus within film studies. The range of styles and themes which he has employed over this period has been considerable from serious drama [*Long Day's Journey into Night* (1962); *Running on Empty* (1988)] to capers [*The Anderson Tapes* (1971); *Family Business* (1989)] and mystery 'whodunnits' [*Murder on the Orient Express* (1974); *Deathtrap* (1982) and *The Morning After* (1986)].

There are, on the other hand, certain tropes that *do* recur in Lumet's work which are almost signatures of a Lumet film. Although Lumet himself is scornful of the French concept of 'un film de Sidney Lumet'[53] as has been noted one can identify recurring stylistic and substantive features – the police as a frightened disorganized mob barely in control [*Serpico*; *Dog Day Afternoon*; *Prince of the City*; *Night Falls on Manhattan*]; individuals existing within a moral vacuum with little to guide them in reaching solutions as to how to behave when surrounded by the coruscating forces of greed and indifference [*12 Angry Men*; *Serpico*; *Prince of the City*; *Night Falls on Manhattan*]; the family as a site of tension with loyalty requiring to be negotiated rather than taken for granted [*Prince of the City*; *Family Business*; *Night Falls on Manhattan*]. For anyone seeking to organize a seminar on the changing portrayal of American justice between 1950 and 2000 it would be possible to cover most of the crucial changes by simply showing major films directed by Sidney Lumet. This is, however, more of a tribute to Lumet's range and durability than a plea for a resuscitation of a focus on the *auteur*.

The legal film – genre, category or what?

The specific feature that attracts a law and film scholar to Lumet is the persistence of the attraction of *12 Angry Men* and the fact that its director has been involved in other films around the broad area of justice. These include classic courtroom dramas centred around a trial – *12 Angry Men* (1957); *The Verdict* (1982); *Guilty as Sin* (1993) and *Night Falls on Manhattan* (1997). There is in the literature on law and film an explicit and an implicit acceptance that it is possible to identify a group of films with recognizable features. Different writers have taken different views of what this group amount to. In the first book, which examined 'courtroom' films, Thomas B. Harris provided his account of their features. These included the struggle of the small person against all odds winning out by a demonstration of innate honesty in the fight for justice, often using a last-minute surprise.[54] Bergman and Asimow outline their features in their assembly of 'trial movies' with the drama of one-to-one confrontations, the built-in suspense factor of the jury/judge decision, exciting themes like murder and controversial moral issues presented as a clash between good and evil.[55] The Special Issues of the University of San Francisco Law Review in 1996 and the Oklahoma City University Law Review in 1997 were principally centred on trial movies. There were, however, indications that some writers were looking at films which focused on distinct aspects of the pursuit of justice. This meant that one could look far beyond the conventional courtroom for this. Thus we find the films of the *Three Stooges* coming under consideration[56] and *Star Trek* being invoked as a way of securing a better understanding of International Law.[57]

There have, however, been implicit and explicit challenges to a narrow view of what can be usefully examined in law and film scholarship. As noted, the collection of essays edited by John Denvir in 1996[58] contained only a couple of essays on trial movies. The others centred on areas where justice was played out in other ways. These include essays on Westerns, *Thelma and Louise*, Woody Allen's *Crimes and Misdemeanours* and the *Godfather* Trilogy. More recently David A. Black has suggested that in law and film work one is looking at 'all fiction films in which legal processes are depicted'. Given that this covers investigation, detection, trial and punishment, he admits this would include 'just about every imaginable fiction film'.[59] This is a challenging approach, which fits in with the tendency of scholars to select single films on which to construct and inform theory. It does not, however, address very satisfactorily the question as to whether there are shifts in the portrayal of various personnel and phenomena within the justice system which are worth noting. Without any kind of 'core' definition or additional categories such changes cannot be assessed.

A rather more prescriptive approach is adopted by Nicole Rafter[60] in her study of crime films. Her solution to the question of genre in law and film studies is to define crime films as those that 'focus primarily on crime and its consequences'. Rather than comprising a genre they amount, in her view, to a 'category' encompassing a number of genres – detectives movies, gangster films, cop and prison movies, courtroom dramas and crime stories. She excludes such tangential fare as action films even where they have a tenuous base in law and order like *Die Hard*. This is one way of solving the problem identified by Tudor[61] of how to classify by characteristics without first having criteria to determine the bounds of the category.

Greenfield, Osborn and Robson suggest that one way forward is to classify on the basis of the critical purpose of the enquiry.[62] This renders the concept as broad overarching concept redundant. An alternative is to seek to reach a consensus about what is meant by the characteristics of a 'Western' or 'law film'. The main area of interest for law teachers has been around trial or courtroom dramas, although genre criteria have been assumed rather than specified.[63]

Adopting the latter approach, Greenfield, Osborn and Robson have suggested that certain characteristics must be present for a film to qualify as a law film

The geography of law, the language and dress of law, legal personnel and the authority of law. This excludes films where 'justice' is enforced outside of any legal framework, such as, for example, war films, social dramas and family sagas.[64]

Whilst this would limit us to a consideration of only the first two grouping of Lumet's justice films it is clear from looking at their context that the categorization centred around the study by lawyers of law-related film as a distinct enterprise within the law school curriculum. This is not to say that themes and issues within this core set of material cannot usefully be supplemented from cognate areas of interest. In this chapter this would include other aspects of the law's operation such as Lumet's police 'legality v. group ethos' films and the informal codes of ethics in the 'individual v. the system' identified above. The question which these problems of categorization raise is what function they have. They are of value where they organize material with common characteristics. They do not determine what questions one might usefully ask about this material and how helpful such questions are. Law and film scholars have had a range of interests in their work ranging from an exploration of the reflexive nature of law and film[65] to the narrower range of movie lawyers.[66] Lumet's work can be drawn on to provide at the very least a guide to how the industry has portrayed the lawyer differently from one era to another. As this chapter has also sought to demonstrate, there is, however, more to Lumet's justice films than this. The tropes he employs offer a powerful critique of the justice system over a period of over 40 years which is unique and deserves to be taken seriously.

Notes

1 For a full description of the work undertaken in the law and film studies field and its development see Greenfield, Osborn and Robson (2001) *Film and the Law* (Cavendish) and Moran, Leslie, Christie, Ian, Loizidon, Elena and Sandon, Emma (eds) (2004) *Law's Moving Image*.

2 Golden Gate Law School Catalogue 2000–2001, San Francisco.

3 Sherwin (1996) 'Cape Fear: Law's Inversion and Cathartic Justice' *San Francisco University Law Review* 1023; Thain (2001) Thain, 'Cape Fear – Two Versions and Two Visions Separated by Thirty Years' *Journal of Law and Society* 40; Asimow (2000b) 'Bad Lawyers in the Movies' 24 *Nova Law Review* 533–591 Rafter (2001) 'American Criminal Trial Films: An Overview of their Development 1930–2000' *Journal of Law and Society* 9; Greenfield (2001). 'Hero or Villain? Cinematic Lawyers and the Delivery of Justice' *Journal of Law and Society* 25.

4 Bohnke (2001) 'Myth and Law in the Films of John Ford' *Journal of Law and Society* 47; Silbey (2001) 'Patterns of Courtroom Justice' *Journal of Law and Society* 97.

5 Bergman and Asimow (1996) *Reel Justice – The Courtroom Goes to the Movies*, Andrews and McMeel, Kansas, Mo *San Francisco Law Journal* (1996) 30: 4.

6 Pam Cook and Mieke Bernink *The Cinema Book* (2nd edn, 1999) Part 5.

7 Graham and Maschio 'A False Public Sentiment: Narrative and Visual Images of Women Lawyers in Film' (1995/6) 84 *Ky Law J* 1027; Shapiro (1995) 'Women Lawyers in Celluloid: Why Hollywood Skirts the Truth 25' *University of Toledo Law Review* 955; Brooks (1997); Moran (1998) *Will Boys Just be Boyz 'N the Hood? African-American Directors Portray a Crumbling Justice System in Urban America* 22 *Oklahoma City University Law Rev* 1 (1997); 'Heroes and Brothers in Love: The Male Homosexual as Lawyer in Popular Culture' *Studies in Law, Politics and Society* Vol. 18, 3; Greenfield, Osborn and Robson (2001) *Film and the Law* Chapter 5.

8 Shale (1996) 'The Conflicts of Law and the Character of Men: Writing Reversal of Fortune and Judgment at Nuremberg' 30 *San Francisco University Law Review* 991; Greenfield, Osborn and Robson (2001) *Film and the Law* Chapter 3.

9 Bergman and Asimow (1996) *Reel Justice*; Greenfield, Osborn and Robson (2001) *Film and the Law.*

10 Asimow (2000a) 'Divorce in the Movies' 24 *Legal Studies Forum* 221–267.

11 Asimow (2000b) 'Bad Lawyers in the Movies' 24 *Nova Law Review* 533–591.

12 Denvir (1996) passim; San Francisco Law Journal (1996); City of Oklahoma Law Review (1997); Picturing Justice (1997) www.usfca.edu/pj.

13 Greenfield and Osborn (1996) 'Pulped Fiction? Cinematic Parables of (In)Justice' 30 *San Francisco University Law Review* 1167; Shale (1996) *'The Conflicts of War'*.

14 Meyer (2001) 'Why a Jury Trial is More Like a Movie than a Novel' *Journal of Law and Society* 133 Robson (2001a) 'Adapting the Modern Law Novel: Filming John Grisham' *Journal of Law and Society* 147; Robson (2001b)) 'Adapting and Re-Adapting – the case of Twelve Angry Men' (Law and Society Association).

15 Bohnke (2001). (note 4 supra).

16 Greenfield, Osborn and Robson (2001) *Film and the Law*, (Cavendish)

17 Gordon Parks directed the first two Shaft films in 1971 and 1972 (*Shaft* and *Shaft's Big Score*) – but not the third (*Shaft in Africa*) in 1973.

18 Altman directed two 'Grisham' films *The Gingerbread Man* (1997) and Ford Coppola *The Rainmaker* (1997).

19 See Conclusion infra for a discussion of such a shift of emphasis.

20 VideoHounds Golden Movie Retriever 2004; *Radio Times Guide to Films* (2004, BBC Worldwide).

21 The critic Pauline Kael and he did not always enjoy a warm relationship – see Cunningham (1991) Sidney Lumet Film and Literary Vision, University of Kentucky Press, Lexington, Ky 232–234; see Kael's damning view of Lumet, albeit in 1968 after the disappointing *The Group* (1966) – *Kiss Kiss Bang Bang* (Little Brown, 1968) 84–85; she refers to his directing of *12 Angry Men*, however, as 'sure fire' – *5001 Nights at the Movies* (1993, Marion Boyars, New York and London); see also the collection of review extracts in Hochman, Stanley (ed.) (1974) *American Film Directors* (Ungar, New York) 290–297 (none cover *12 Angry Men*, however).

22 Sadoul, George (1972) *Dictionary of Film Makers* (University of California Press, Berkeley and Los Angeles) at 159.

23 Curran, Daniel (1998) *Guide to American Cinema 1965–1995* (Greenwood Press, Westport Connecticut and London) at 203.

24 Thomson, David (1980) *A Biographical Dictionary of the Cinema* (Secker and Warburg, London) at 365 and 198.

25 Thomson, David (1994) *A Biographical Dictionary of the Cinema* (Andre Deutsch, London) at 459.

26 Lumet, Sidney (1995) *Making Movies* (Bloomsbury) back cover.

27 Ibid.

28 Passek, Jean Loup (2000) *Dictionnaire du Cinema* (Larousse, Paris) at volume 2 1366 – '*a partir de 1953, l'un des meilleurs et plus actifs specialistes de la dramatique realiste*'.

29 David Margolick, 'Again, Sidney Lumet Ponders Justice', New York Times Dec 31, 1989, sec H, 9 [quoted in Cunningham, Frank R. (1991) 'Sidney Lumet, Film and Literary Vision' at 1].

30 Ibid.

31 Philip Friedman speaking on Mark Lawson's TV assessment of lawyer writers *The Bestseller Brief* [BBC 2 2 February 1994] as quoted in Robson, Peter (1996) 'Images of Law in the Fiction of John Grisham' [in *Tall Stories: Reading Law and Literature* (Dartmouth) at 204.

32 Denvir, John 'Capra's Constitution' (1996) in Denvir, J (1996a) *Legal Reelism – The Courtroom Goes to the Movies*, University of Illinois Press, Urbana and Chicago ed. Denvir J 118–132.

33 Hillier Jim (ed.) (1985) *Cahiers du Cinema* 126–155 Harvard University Press, Cambridge, Mass.

34 *Radio Times Guide to Films* (2003, BBC Worldwide Ltd, London) at 1117.

35 Which produced an Oscar nomination – *Halliwell's Guide* (2004 Harper Collins, London).

36 Sean Connery, Dustin Hoffman and Matthew Broderick seemed to cover a wide range of target audiences.

37 Lumet *Making Movies* at 198.

38 Rafter, Nicole 'American Criminal Trial Films: An Overview of Their Development 1930–2000' in Machura and Robson (2001) Blackwell, Oxford 9–24.

39 *Young Mr Lincoln* (1939).

40 *Inherit the Wind* (1958).

41 *To Kill a Mockingbird* (1962).

42 ...*And Justice for All* (1979).

43 *Suspect* (1987).

44 *The Accused* (1988).
45 Robson, Peter *Twelve Angry Men – Adapting and Re-adapting* (Law and Society Association, 2001).
46 Rafter, Nicole (2000) *Shots in the Dark* (OUP, Oxford).
47 Cf. different perspectives on Atticus have been put forward including in Steven Lubet (2001) *Nothing but the Truth* New York University Press, New York and London.
48 Asimow, M. (2000) 'Bad Lawyers in the Movies' 24 *Nova Law Review* 533–591.
49 Thain, Gerald 'Cape Fear – Two Versions and Two Visions Separated by Thirty Years' [in *Law and Film* Machura, Stefan and Robson, Peter (eds), (2001), Blackwell, Oxford]; Sherwin, R.K. (1996) 'Cape Fear: Law's Inversion and Cathartic Justice' 30 *University of San Francisco Law Review* 1023.
50 *Making Movies* (Bloomsbury, 1995) p. 37.
51 Director Lumet's comments on *Night Falls on Manhattan* DVD.
52 See Greenfield, Osborn and Robson (2001) *Film and the Law.*
53 Lumet talks of his discomfort in seeing *Douze Hommes en Colere* (*12 Angry Men*) billboarded in this fashion in Paris – *Making Movies* Sidney Lumet (1995) at 1 (Bloomsbury, London) 6 and *passim.*
54 Harris, Thomas J. (1987) *Courtroom's Finest Hour in American Cinema* Rowman and Littlefield.
55 *Legal Reelism* (1996).
56 Coyne, R. (1997) 'Images of Lawyers and the Three Stooges' 22 *Oklahoma City University Law Review* 247.
57 Joseph, P. and Carton, S. (1966) 'The Law of the Federation: Images of Law, Lawyers and the Legal System in "Star Trek: The Next Generation"' 24 *University of Toledo Law Review* 43–85.
58 *Reel Justice* (1996).
59 Black, David A. (1999) *Law in Film* University of Illinois Press, Urbana and Chicago at 5.
60 Rafter, Nicole (2000) *Shots in the Mirror* (Oxford University Press, Oxford).
61 Tudor, A. 'Genre and Critical Methodology' [in Nicols (1976) *Movies and Methods*].
62 *Film and the Law* (2001) at 21.
63 Bergman, P. and Asimow, M. *Reel Justice* (1996) *passim.*
64 *Film and the Law* (2001) at 24.
65 Black (1999) op. cit.
66 Bergman and Asimow (1996) *Reel Justice* Greenfield, Osborn and Robson (2001) *Film and the Law.*

10 Gender, power and law in screwball comedy

Re-viewing *Talk of the Town* and *Adam's Rib*

Peter Sanderson and Hilary Sommerlad

Introduction

'Screwball' was the collective designation of a succession of romantic comedies produced in Hollywood, beginning in the 1930s, and, it is argued in histories of the genre,[1] ending with the advent of war in 1942. The two films which we discuss in this chapter may more appropriately therefore be defined as 'post-screwball', produced as they were after the end of this 'golden age', but, in addition to featuring actors like Cary Grant, Jean Arthur and Katherine Hepburn, who consolidated their reputations in screwball, and directors like Cukor, who had been central to the development of the genre, *Talk of the Town* and *Adam's Rib* share with screwball comedies of the New Deal era the tension generated by uncanny juxtapositions and unexpected behaviour. The textual complexity and pervasive ambiguity which results forms, we will argue, a perfect medium for exploring similar ambiguities in law's status as an authoritative discourse.

In a particularly powerful passage in *Language and Symbolic Power*, Bourdieu argues that legal discourse is a distinctive form of speech because it 'brings into existence that which it utters'.[2] However, although he goes on to argue that in this sense it is 'the word of divine right' he crucially identifies the necessity of collective acknowledgement of the authority of the utterance in its accomplishment:[3]

> One should never forget that language, by virtue of the infinite generative but also *originative* capacity – in the Kantian sense – which it derives from its power to produce existence by producing the collectively recognized, and thus realized, representation of existence, is no doubt the principal support of the dream of absolute power.[4]

Although the capacity of film to transmit images and ideologies intact to their audiences is clearly subject to debate, its potential for supporting the collective recognition of the representation of the Rule of Law as a consensual modality of civil society might be seen as sufficient justification for detailed study. It is the contention of this chapter that 'law films' do not simply attempt this collective recognition through crude hegemonic representations of the law, but through multivocal filmic texts which allow the viewers to internalize those ambiguities central to the Common Law tradition, in particular, before providing them with a resolution which confirms the indispensability of the Rule of Law.

The two films which we use to illustrate this argument have, as we acknowledge above, a contested status as 'screwball comedy': and in fact their particular sharpness derives from the fact that each film represents a purposeful conjunction of genres: *Adam's Rib* blends screwball comedy with a pastiche of the traditional courtroom drama, whilst *Talk of the Town* opens as a conventional noirish 'fugitive' story, develops into a combination of domestic comedy laced with jurisprudential debate before concluding with a courtroom drama (Rosenberg describes it as 'a particularly unstable hybrid'[5]). This combination of genres allows both films to achieve a destabilizing ambiguity of mood. Serious discussion of the practical jurisprudence is embedded in mundane domestic transactions, whilst the dignity of the theatre of the courtroom is undermined by the intrusion of private emotion. The fact that both films appear to conclude by reaffirming a more traditional respect for the authority and impartiality of law can not erase the doubt and ambiguity which pervades them.

The particular treatment of law in screwball comedy should only underline, however, a more general conclusion to be drawn about the appearance of law in film. In the past decade several authors have undertaken readings of 'law films' as if they were legal texts.[6] Except when instantiated in censorship, film does not actually encounter law as law, but rather as a representation: its coercive power is implied yet at the same time subverted, in that audiences are empowered to stand apart from the process of the law, and to judge for themselves the transactions and acts of judgement represented within the film. We can thus position the audience of a film similarly to the reader in what Brandist describes as Bakhtin's 'juridical' theory of the novel. The hero acts ethically in his or her own world, experiencing all boundaries as impediments and striving to overcome those boundaries. The author, however, is able to achieve aesthetic judgement by bestowing boundaries and it is this aesthetic judgement that the reader as external spectator co-creates. The author and reader thereby adopt a position akin to Kant's theoretical reason, sitting in judgement.[7]

The film audience's act of judgement must, however, necessarily be constituted in a more engaged form than that implied in the application of theoretical reason. As noted above, it is through law's capacity to represent itself as collectively recognized that the Rule of Law comes to be accomplished. John Deigh, criticizing the legal formalist position, argues that, 'Law, being essentially a system of government, is more than a system of such rules. Governing is more than officiating'.[8] The tension between law's universalist claims, and the reluctance to grant their allegiance of those with particular disagreements with the law or its officials lies, Deigh argues, in its status as the will of a collective, and in the fact that particular experience of the law is through delegated authority. The fabulous narratives of 'law films' provide for a recognition of the emotional power of the bond with law's collective authority, whilst allowing the simultaneous expression of law's inadequacy in the face of particular interests.

This tension between law's universal claims and the particularity of its instantiation in Common Law results in what Endicott describes as the impossibility of the Rule of Law:[9] whilst the Rule of Law and the absence of arbitrary government appears to demand certainty and precision in specific laws and their enforcement, the infinite complexity and unpredictability of social life necessarily demands laws which are vague, and outcomes which are unpredictable. This engenders the following paradox:

> Vagueness in the law leads to arbitrary government . . . law is necessarily vague. So arbitrary government – the antithesis of the rule of law – is a necessary feature of the rule of law. The rule of law entails both the presence and absence of arbitrary government. It is not just an unattainable ideal. It is a necessarily unattainable ideal. It is incoherent.[10]

This paradox applies not simply to the logical coherence of the Rule of Law, but also to its capacity to elicit the allegiance of the population or 'community' which it is intended to govern. Deigh propounds the thesis that the authority of law is conditioned on the emotional bond between the law and its subjects, rather than, as Dworkin argues, from its status as a coherent system of normative thought about human conduct.[11] This emotional bond, it can be argued, is in turn conditioned by the subjects' need for the law to be both dispassionate and compassionate, to regard both the absolute character of the normative rule, and to be simultaneously capable of comprehending the context in which the rule must be interpreted.

The conflict between legal formalism and its critics is encapsulated in two recent jurisprudential debates, which have a direct bearing on our discussion of *Talk of the Town* and *Adam's Rib*. We find the first of these debates in the strand of feminist jurisprudence which counterposes both legal formalism and Dworkin's position 'rights fetishism' (generally itself recorded as a critique of legal formalism), to the significance of particularist standpoints and the view that feminist jurisprudence should prevent the alienation of women's subjectivity, rather than accomplish it, as legal formalism is said to.[12] Difference Feminist jurisprudence is associated with the work of Carol Gilligan, which posits the existence of a distinctive female morality termed the 'ethic of care', and adapts the long-standing Critical Legal challenge to the Rule of Law's underpinning neutrality by focusing on gendered aspects of legal doctrine and method, calling for a new form of law rooted in the ethic of care. This law, which would speak with 'woman's voice', would emphasize emotion, subjectivity and relationality rather than the rationality, objectivity and autonomy characteristic of rights-based discourse. However, the validity of *Difference Feminism*'s critique has been questioned by authors such as Patricia Williams,[13] who have identified the weakness of a position which fails to recognize the protection afforded by formal rights to those belonging to groups without access to relationships of mutual trust with those in power. Two elements of the Difference Feminist position are of particular interest in our discussion of *Adam's Rib*.

A paradigmatic example of the Difference Feminist contention that the law 'privileges a male view of the universe'[14] is offered by the provocation defence in murder cases. Provocation both instantiates and privileges a 'male' modality of human response to threatened property, and inscribes women as objects of proprietorial relations. Men are therefore granted the autonomous agency by this defence, which it correspondingly denies to women. Feminist lawyers' and jurists' responses to this specific defence to the crime of murder vary widely. On the one hand, in a range of cases in the UK, defence lawyers have attempted to extend this defence to cover women who kill their partners as a consequence of the experience of domestic violence. Since provocation as a defence is predicated on the excusability of a sudden and temporary loss of control, women who have been physically dominated and abused in relationships, and whose loss of control has therefore not been 'sudden or temporary' (*R* v. *Duffy*) have had to seek to modify the defence, or to construct an alternative. One example of the latter course has become known as Battered Woman Syndrome (BWS).[15] One of the principal advantages of BWS has been seen as its capacity to 'challenge criminal law's penchant for the separating of context from agency'.[16] However, whether achieving this form of parity in the law, through extending a defence grounded in a consideration of context, is ultimately in the best interests of women as a category is open to debate. Jeremy Horder, amongst others, argues that the existence of provocation as a defence at all reinforces in the law the 'given' character of men's violence against women,[17] and Noonan argues that 'reinscribing woman as victim constrains not only our understanding of female criminality, but it encodes women as subjectless within law'.[18] Further, the interpolation of context into agency widens the potential range of defences for men's violence against women (the cultural context of male violence being one striking example).[19] The ambivalence of the relationship between law and feminist projects is highlighted by the central plotline in *Adam's Rib*: this concerns the trial of a woman for the attempted murder of her husband. The fact that the film is a comedy precludes the death of the husband, and therefore the defence of provocation could not feature explicitly, though references to the issues raised by provocation are evident throughout the screenplay.

A second question posed by difference feminism is whether, given the gendered character of the law, it can be practised differently by women. Sheffield and Shapiro have traced the way that the portrayal of female attorneys developed in film from the time when their status in the profession was that of pioneer, to the stage when they began to dominate entry to law schools.[20,21] Two associations were established at an early stage: that between women lawyers and comedy, connoting the sheer implausibility of women practising law successfully, and, second, that between women and an idealistic (or naive) approach to the practise of law.[22,23] The development of a distinct 'woman lawyer' genre from the 1980s, rather than developing the idea that women might practise in such a way as to give expression to their greater 'connectedness' tended instead to identify women lawyers as caught on the horns of a dilemma. Successful women lawyers either sacrifice their femininity in their quest for success,[24] or prejudice their right to practise by allowing the private domain into their work. One modern classic plotline combines the two themes, with successful women warming or unbending at risk to their physical safety and their integrity (of which the archetypal example is Glenn Close's Teddy Barnes in *Jagged Edge*). As we argue below, screwball comedy allows for a more complex exploration of the ambiguities and dilemmas confronting the protagonists, particularly Hepburn's woman lawyer, in *Adam's Rib*.

The second contemporary debate of direct relevance to our analysis is the critique of criminal law developed by Alan Norrie.[25] In the course of his broader project of offering a sustained critique of the coherence of criminal law, Norrie addresses the problem posed by the concept of corporate liability in criminal law: the concept of the responsible legal individual on which traditional criminal liability is dependent is incommensurate with the social character of the corporation, and attempts either to differentiate corporate from individual liability, or assimilate it to individual liability expose the historical and political character of the apolitical juridical individual. If the law assimilates, in corporate criminal liability, it reveals the actual sociopolitical control functions that rest behind its individualistic forms, for elite criminality cannot be conceptualized within them. If the law differentiates, in strict liability, the control function is again exposed, for it is impossible to explain in formal terms what the difference is.[26]

As E.P. Thompson argues in his discussion of the development of law in the eighteenth century, this critique of the law needs to be modified by a recognition that the Rule of Law, by virtue of its very universalistic claims, acts as a restraint on those powerful who use the law to bolster their own interests:

> There is a difference between arbitrary power and the rule of law. We ought to expose the shams and inequities which may be concealed beneath this law. But the rule of law itself, the imposing of effective inhibitions upon power and the defence of the citizen from power's all-intrusive claims, seems to me to be an unqualified human good.[27]

From a different political perspective, Sullivan argues that some attachment to a Kantian model of the operation of criminal law is inevitable in an 'atomistic and conflictual society'.[28]

The manner in which the two films under discussion raise issues of gender, class and power in relation not simply to the doctrine of law, but also to its authority could be seen as pre-figuring these very contemporary debates. This would of course be a mistake, as the concerns they raise reflect those of the legal realists in the United States during the New Deal Era.[29] David Sugarman has identified the way in which the scepticism of legal realists about the efficacy of an autonomous legal order was undermined by the fuzziness of the line between the public and the private in legal practice, particularly at the local level, and by the partiality of the American Judiciary in striking down New Deal legislation.[30] However, as we engage in a comparative reading of the two films, we can see the continuity of the jurisprudential debates outlined above, and how they emerged from the daily fabric of people's lives and imaginations in the New Deal Era as much as they do today.

Nevertheless, it is notable that many of the more recent 'law films' which have received critical commentary have not been concerned to explore issues quite as deeply as is the case with *Adam's Rib* and *Talk of the Town*. The classic courtroom drama centres on attributions of guilt (whether the accused is guilty of a crime which the audience is expected to agree deserves punishment) rather than the jurisprudential question of the relationship between justice, crime and punishment. In this sense many law films and law series represent theatres in which the same plot is reiterated, and the distinctive mark of *Talk of the Town* and *Adam's Rib* is that neither film uses the courtroom for this form of drama. Other authors have recognized the particular significance of the two films: in particular, Rosenberg's discussion of *Talk of the Town*[31] and Kamir's reading of *Adam's Rib*[32] each focus attention on the multivocal character of their text and the richness of the thematic material. What has perhaps received insufficient attention is the choice of genre.

Bakhtin argues that 'in the world of carnival the awareness of the people's immortality is combined with the realization that established authority and truth are relative'.[33] In screwball comedy, as in carnival, the chaos of the popular and abject can mingle with the dignity of law, undermining its claims to absolute and universal authority without finally negating its necessity, or its claims to the emotional allegiance of the films' principal protagonists, and through them, the audience. In screwball comedy, the inability to render the law plausibly and accurately in the plot's procedural representation does not undermine the force of the critique of law's pretensions. Rather it is the absurdity of plot and scenario which underscores it, and it is to the working out of this critique in the two films that we shall now turn.

Plotting law and lawyers in screwball comedy: synopses of *Talk of the Town* and *Adam's Rib*

Talk of the Town is built around a classic motif of film noir and the social conscience cinema of the 1940s:[34] the falsely accused fugitive from justice.

Leopold Dilg (Cary Grant), an 'anarchist' factory worker in the New England town of Lochester has persistently criticized Holmes, the owner of the factory in which he works under poor working conditions and safety practices, and as a result has achieved notoriety as a troublemaker. He is arrested and charged with arson and murder when the factory burns down and a foreman, Clyde Bracken, disappears. During his trial before local Judge Grunstadt (who is portrayed as hand in glove with Holmes), he escapes from custody, and on a dark and stormy night, takes refuge in a house owned by the family of his childhood sweetheart, Nora Shelley (Jean Arthur). She is preparing the house for a summer let to a Professor of Law, Michael Lightcap (Ronald Colman), who arrives unexpectedly a day early in the middle of the storm. Nora, or 'Miss Shelley' as the two male principals call her, keeps Dilg concealed in the house, and, in order to remain there and protect Dilg, takes on the job of Professor Lightcap's secretary. The following morning Dilg is overcome by hunger, and descends from his attic hiding place to the kitchen, adjacent to the garden in which Lightcap is beginning to dictate his planned paper to Miss Shelley. Overhearing a section of Lightcap's dictation, Dilg intrudes on Lightcap's space in order to dispute the positivist view of law which the Professor is espousing. Hastily designated as Joseph the gardener by 'Miss' Shelley, he engages Lightcap in a series of debates on the nature of law which extend over the next few days: the incongruity of debating with a gardener is apparent to Lightcap, but 'Joseph's' intrusions on his private space are accepted with exemplary liberal tolerance. Dilg argues that Lightcap's vision of the law is arid, devoid of emotion and out of touch with the reality of everyday life. The debates are interrupted by a series of interludes which move the plot forward in two directions.

First, the local Senator arrives to inform Lightcap that if he avoids unfavourable publicity, he will shortly be elevated to the bench of the Supreme Court. Dilg, noting the possible significance of obtaining the support of an elevated Lightcap, persuades Miss Shelley to take Lightcap into the 'real world' of Lochester's baseball stadium, where the Professor encounters Judge Grunstadt, and hears that the Judge was preparing his opinion before the trial had concluded. He is appalled by Grunstadt's 'ignorance' but interestingly not by the apparent possibility of corrupt and prejudicial judgement.

Lightcap's view of the law is gradually transformed by two parallel processes. First, Miss Shelley and Sam Yates, the attorney appointed to defend Dilg against Dilg's wishes, and who attended law school with Lightcap, attempt to draw Lightcap from the refuge of Sweetwater into the 'real world' of Lochester, and engage him with the facts of the Dilg case rather than the law. Second, Lightcap's initial frosty aloofness is thawed by an emotional attachment both to Miss Shelley and to Dilg, so that when Dilg's identity is finally revealed, he is drawn into an investigation of the case which reveals Holmes as the real culprit but also involves him in actions close to the boundaries of legality. With a new appreciation of the need to ground the practice of law and justice in everyday reality, Lightcap finesses Holmes and Grundstadt with a speech to Dilg's lynch mob in the Lochester courtroom, heralded by a pistol shot in the air. Dilg's release and Holmes' and Grundstadt's conviction are announced through the traditional montage of newspaper headlines, and in a coda, Nora Shelley and Dilg travel to Washington to see Lightcap assume his seat on the Supreme Court Bench: the romantic ambiguity being resolved by Lightcap surrendering Nora to Dilg and dedicating his life to the Bench, and to the ministrations of Tilney, his faithful (black) manservant.

Adam's Rib pursues a parallel argument about the strained relationship between law and justice, but from a gendered perspective.[35] The film opens with the camera tracking a woman (Doris Attinger) as she follows a man that we soon assume to be her husband (Warren, played by Tom Ewell) to the apartment of his lover, and shoots him, wounding him seriously enough for him to be hospitalized (though we do not find out that he is alive until the next scene). There is a cut to the apartment of Amanda (Katherine Hepburn) and Adam (Spencer Tracy) Bonner, a married couple who are both lawyers, Adam working for the District Attorney's office and Amanda in what appears later to be a sole private practice. During the course of breakfast (brought to them in bed by their maid), Amanda notices the report of the story on the front page of the newspaper, and identifies the prosecution of the woman as an anomaly, since men in a similar situation successfully plead provocation. They pursue the discussion on the way to work, with Adam supporting the prosecution on the grounds that 'a crime should be punished not condoned', and Amanda identifying the issue in the case as being the way in which gendered attitudes to domestic violence permeate legal judgments:

> *Amanda:* Look! All I'm trying to say is that there are lots of things that a man can do and in society's eyes, it's all hunky-dory. A woman does the same thing – the same, mind you, and she's an outcast.
>
> *Adam:* Finished?
>
> *Amanda:* No. Not that I'm blaming you personally Adam, because this is so.
>
> *Adam:* Well that's awfully large of you.
>
> *Amanda:* No, no, it's not your fault. All I'm saying is, why let this deplorable system seep into our courts of law, where women are supposed to be equal?

When Adam arrives at work he discovers that he has been allocated the Attinger case, and after hearing this in the course of a telephone conversation, Amanda seeks out the defence role, but doesn't tell Adam before she announces it in front of a dinner party comprised of judges and the Bonner's next door neighbour, the ultra camp pianist and composer Kip. The middle passage of the film follows the preparation of the cases for each side, interwoven with the increasing domestic strain and competition in the Bonner household. Initially, the domestic scenes are intimate, with discussion of the case conducted during shared preparation of a meal, or a mutual massage, and elements of domestic intimacy are allowed to intrude into the courtroom, as Adam deliberately drops his pencil so that he can exchange blown kisses with Amanda under the table.

However, increasingly, the real tension in the case, which is between Amanda's view of it as a necessary piece of cause lawyering which merits dramatization along the lines of the Boston Tea Party ('they dramatized an injustice. That's all I'm trying to do'), and Adam's view of the case as primarily concerned with the Rule of Law, is heightened. Amanda introduces an attack on the gendered character of law and society from the first jury challenge, where she asks the male juror whether he believes in equality for women: asked to justify this challenge, she responds:

> I submit that my entire line of defence is based upon the proposition that persons of the female sex should be dealt with before the law, as the equal of persons of the male sex. I submit that I cannot hope to argue this line before minds hostile to and prejudiced against the female sex.

The tensions accentuate to generate alienation and estrangement in two key scenes: in the middle of the mutual massage, Adam responds to Amanda's earlier playful slap to the behind with a blow which communicates real violent intent, and in the following day's courtroom scene, Amanda achieves a *coup de theatre* with three witnesses designed to epitomize women's potential as equals of men in intelligence, organizational skills and strength. The final witness, a vaudeville performer named Olympia LaPere demonstrates her physical strength at Amanda's request by lifting Adam bodily over her head. The enmeshing of private and public conflict is encapsulated in the speech Adam makes as he leaves home that evening:

> . . . I see something in you I've never seen before and I don't like it. As a matter of fact I hate it . . . Contempt for the law, that's what you've got. It's a disease, a spreading dis. . . You think the law is something you can get over or under or get around or just plain flaunt. You start with that and you wind up in the . . . Well, look at us! The law is the law, whether it's good or bad. If it's bad the thing to do is to change it, not just to bust it wide open

The apparently irretrievable breakdown of the Bonners' marriage is exacerbated by Adam's discovery of Amanda with neighbour Kip in an apparently compromising situation, and his threatening behaviour with a gun which turns out to be made of licorice. Whilst she still believes in the threat, Amanda calls out 'Stop it Adam. Stop it! You've no right! You can't do what you're doing. You've no right!'. Adam believes he has proved his point, but Amanda sees this as a cheap trick, motivated by his envy of her success.

The legal dispute is never resolved: neither Amanda nor Adam ever recant on their public positions: the private impasse is resolved by means of Adam simulating tears at the office of their lawyers as they try to sort out their financial affairs prior to divorce. The ambivalent stance the film maintains in relation to gender difference in the law is thus finally transferred into the private sphere, as with their closing lines, Hepburn and Tracy confirm the coexistence of sameness/difference. In the public sphere the result is similarly ambiguous: Amanda's triumph is submerged in the media frenzy which is busy re-authoring the Attinger's story as one of reconciliation, and one can speculate that Amanda's argument will have made no new law, as it was likely to be seen as a perverse jury decision. Characteristically, the comedy provides no answers to the complex layers of the relationship between gender and the law, but leaves lingering questions and doubts.

Talk of the Town: from the citadel of law to the frontier of experience

We noted above the way in which the plot of *Talk of the Town* represents a combination, almost a clash, of genres, and we have argued that this simultaneously reflects the theme of legal ambiguity, whilst identifying this ambiguity as resting between the dichotomy of Kantian and Realist views of justice. These structural properties of the plot may be seen as reflected in the screenplay and *mise-en-scène*. Michael Lightcap may be seen as *descending* into Lochester, initially from the Ivory Tower of academe, but implicitly from the citadel of Kantian justice which is taken as being embodied in the Supreme Court, to membership of which he aspires. The distinction between the two worlds is reinforced by the low angle shots of the Supreme Court, which exaggerate the majestic heights of the architecture, and the lighting of Lightcap's ascension to the Bench, which produces a classical *chiaoscuro* effect. The contradictions inherent in Lightcap's detached view of the law are underscored by subtle references in the screenplay. The project on which Lightcap is engaged during his stay in Lochester includes an essay entitled, 'The Influence of Literature on Legislation in the Eighteenth Century in England', and the initial paragraph dictated to Miss Shelley appears as a paean to the view of the law as the product of the Enlightenment:

> The Law is the sum of the experience of civilized Man – the sign that Man has emerged from the Jungle. The eighteenth century represented perhaps the high point of Man's intellectual development. Reason, simple and pure, was the weight against which human problems were held in balance. Law became for the first time the instrument of pure logic with each man's rights and responsibilities considered from the

viewpoint of the possible and reasonable rather than the feudal conventions of divine and everlasting rights. It was the aim of the law makers and the law administrators to build the law firmly on principles which are above small emotions, greed and the . . . of everyday life.

The irony of this portrayal of the eighteenth century cannot be lost on a twenty-first century audience. As commentators such as Hay,[36] Thompson[37] and Hughes[38] have noted, the eighteenth century in England was characterized by an unparalleled explosion in capital offences, self-consciously designed to use terror as an instrument in the protection of property. As Hay notes, the Divine Will had indeed been succeeded, but not by the rule of reason, but of property.[39] Thompson argues that the eighteenth century:

> governed as it was by the forms of law, provides a text-book illustration of the employment of law, as instrument and as ideology, in serving the interests of the ruling class. The oligarchs and the great gentry were content to be subject to the rule of law only because this law was serviceable and afforded to their hegemony the rhetoric of legitimacy.[40]

The literature of the eighteenth century, moreover, through the work of novelists such as Fielding, depicted the Rule of Law as the brute exercise of power, in the pursuit of self-interest and profit.[41] Where mercy prevailed, it was, as Douglas Hay shows, not due to the influence of reason, but of patronage.[42]

The parallels between the justice of the eighteenth century and the justice of the Western frontier,[43] embedded in the living memory of those alive in the 1940s, are marked, and are exemplified in the persons of Holmes and Grundstadt: Holmes owns the town of Lochester much as Judge Roy Bean owns the fictional frontier town of *The Westerner*. Lochester is represented as a form of frontier between the civilized urban East Coast which houses the Supreme Court and the anarchy of small town personalism and patronage: disputes between Dilg's attorney and local supporters of Holmes are settled in fisticuffs, to the evident discomfort of the bystanding Lightcap, and the mob is aroused by Holmes' demagoguery and control of the press into a swirling mass which eventually engulfs the centre of Lochester and the courtroom where Dilg stands trial, in its attempts to enforce lynch justice.

Michael Lightcap is initially resistant to his contact with everyday life: his physical and intellectually fastidious nature is repelled both by the people of Lochester and their practices: his closest previous relationship has been with his black manservant Tilney, who acts, in line with one of the stereotypes of that screen age, as the guardian of the Professor's conventional conduct as well as his person. Lightcap's class is physically embodied in this fastidious and mannered deportment (and in the casting of the obstinately British Colman), and the class difference between Lightcap and Dilg is physically marked by Dilg's snoring, his failure to observe conventional niceties of personal space and his indifferent table manners. There are few attempts to erase this class difference, although the intimate trios involving Lightcap, Dilg and Nora Shelley (who occupies an intermediate space in terms of class) provide a bridge. Even when attempting by subterfuge to elicit the foreman Clyde Bracken's whereabouts from his girlfriend, Lightcap's only disguise is to remove his beard, and his barely concealed contempt for her culture, language and occupation (manicurist) emphasize the isolation of his character, and the image of the law he represents, from everyday life.

Lightcap's *haut bourgeois* class position and his attachment to a universalist vision of the law may therefore be seen as inextricably linked, and initially they act as an impermeable barrier between his identification with the law and his perception of the real world. Dilg initially criticizes Lightcap's view of the law as both lacking 'passion' and commonsense, an understanding of how America really works: over breakfast he declares, 'you don't live in this country Professor, you just take up space in it'. Initially, after his arrival at Sweetwater, Lightcap expects to become the centre of this small community and accepts service as of right, together with the fact that in a succession of noisy arrivals, the world comes to see him. His sentimental journey into Lochester and into his triangular relationship with Dilg and Nora Shelley blurs the boundaries he has erected between Law and Emotion.

Lightcap's 'solution' to the crime is brought about with the aid of, initially subterfuge, and finally physical coercion and the threat of lethal force. However, within the world of the film, this is never allowed to compromise his moral authority, nor ultimately his capacity to assume his Supreme Court seat. Even before his recapture, Dilg has retreated from his earlier criticism of Lightcap by recognizing that disorder and absence of law is as much a threat to him and those he represents as the prejudice and corruption of Grundstadt.

Initially Dilg's more critical view of the law, a form of legal realism's fact scepticism, is echoed in his response to Lightcap's idyllic view of law as the rule of reason: it is, he argues, 'a gun pointed at someone's head', and he later develops the idea of the law as a form of practical reason and action. The climax of the film, Lightcap's courtroom speech to the citizenry of Lochester, absorbs this view of law as practical reason, and the Rule of Law as contingent on the emotional allegiance of its subjects and their willingness to translate this into action. His words imply an endorsement of Dilg's activism and of the lawyering of Sam Yates, which encompasses defending his client's good name with his fists:

> The law must be engraved in our hearts and practised every minute to the letter and spirit. It can't even exist unless we're willing to go down into the dust and blood and fight a battle every day of our lives to preserve it, for our neighbours as well as for ourselves.

This alternative model of the universality of law, a universality embodied in daily practice rather than simply abstract principle, might be interpreted as arguing that the law is 'discursively negotiable',[44] but it might equally be seen as a call to citizens to fall in behind the Rule of Law, a call to extend its reach beyond the purview of the courts. Ultimately Dilg's case is an embodiment of fact scepticism: Dilg was evidently never guilty of the crime with which he was originally charged (though he does appear mysteriously to escape punishment for a violent assault on a prison guard) so his case challenges the practice of law in its local jurisdictions, not the essential principles in which Lightcap trades. Those principles are subjected to a far more rigorous challenge by *Adam's Rib*.

Adam's Rib and the problem of formal equality

The polarities of gender equality–difference debates represent the warp and woof of the texture of Adam's Rib. As in *Woman of the Year*, directed by George Stevens, every effort is made to ensure that Hepburn's character disrupts conventional stereotypes. Of the two lawyers in the marriage, Amanda is clearly represented as the more successful and the more independent (Adam is obliged to take on the Attinger case while Amanda chooses to); in the courtroom Amanda is fluent and charismatic while Adam is pedestrian and stumbling, prone to confusing his words under stress. It is Amanda who drives the two of them to work (even if the film represents her driving as stereotypically erratic and impulsive) while Adam is clearly dominant in the kitchen. In line with the limitations of vision of the time, this equality is only possible because the couple are childless:[45] an embarrassing home movie display of their country home focuses attention on their dogs as their surrogate children (and it is to the dogs that they happily return at the end of the film), children who apparently require no physical care. In addition to the homology of their first names (Adam/A-man-da), the two share a common nickname, distinguished only by the final syllable (Pinkie/Pinky). This equality is clearly the consequence of a settled relationship, which is made to appear even more hermetically sealed at the beginning of the film by the framing of the film in a theatrical proscenium arch form, with the two characters disappearing stage left and right whilst maintaining intimate conversation and discussion.

A narrative of difference is also embedded in the film from the start, however. Orit Kamir argues that the women in *Adam's Rib* 'do not share a unique, distinctive "feminine culture"', and emphasizes Amanda's difference from the other women in the film,[46] but of course this is one of the points about her success as a lawyer in that era – women 'pioneers' in the legal profession on both sides of the Atlantic tended to be the product of middle class, often legal backgrounds, and were dependent on personalist ties for their careers (a point emphasized in the film by the legal dinner party consisting of the Bonners and a group of judges and their (non-legal) wives).[47] Nevertheless even if Amanda cannot share this elusive common culture, she clearly shares a distinctive feminine viewpoint. Her first reaction to the newspaper report of the Attinger story is 'Serves him right the little two-timer', and the Bonners' maid, reading about Doris Attinger's shooting of her husband, in the course of clearing the breakfast things cries out 'Atta Girl!'. Grace, Amanda's secretary, also sympathizes with Doris's position and act, alongside Amanda, even though she appears initially to endorse a double standard in relation to judgements about transgressive sexual activity.

This standpoint reinforces Amanda's fundamentally different view of the law: it is clear from the telephone conversation between the couple which sparks her involvement in the case that she has a history as a cause lawyer, and that this is a cause of tension between them. In the course of their initial discussion of the Attinger case, she appears to adopt a legal realist stance, although in contrast to Leopold Dilg's essential fact scepticism in *Talk of the Town*, Amanda is a rule sceptic who sees gendered bias embedded in the application of the provocation defence to a previous case (the 'Lennehan' case mentioned in an early scene). Where does this lead her in terms of preparing a defence for Doris Attinger? It is clear that in the course of her initial interview with the defendant, Amanda is being offered several different options in terms of defences or mitigations. Doris was the victim of abuse ('he started battin' me around . . . eleven months ago') and she appeared to be not entirely aware of her actions ('I didn't decide nothin'. I was doing everything like in a dream. Like I was watchin' myself, but I couldn't help it – like in a dream'). During the interview, it becomes evident that Amanda is considering the question of intention when discouraging Doris from pleading guilty:

> *Doris:*   No accident. I wanted to shoot him.
> *Amanda:*   Suppose we decide later just what you wanted to do.
> *Doris:*   Silly.
> *Amanda:*   The difference between ten years in prison and freedom is
>   not silly Mrs Attinger.

However, Amanda eschews the more orthodox approaches to defence and mitigation in favour of a principled argument grounded in formal equality, expressed most neatly in the jury challenge described above. The right she ultimately claims for Doris Attinger on behalf of all women is the right to defence of hearth and home, not the right to defend herself against violence.

The drawback of the formal equality strategy is that the idea of equality is predicated on a male comparator, and 'the problem with relying in this way on a male norm is that the existing values in a male-dominated world are accepted without challenge, and women are required to compete on their terms.'[48] Amanda realizes the principle of the male comparator in a form of burlesque through her parade of three women 'each representing a particular branch of American womanhood, for not only one woman is on trial here but all women'. However, the audience, both in the courtroom and in the cinema, is positioned in such a way as to see Amanda's attempt to erase gender difference as simply reinforcing the otherness of successful women: even a twenty-first century critic sees the successful chemist, the woman factory supervisor and the powerful and athletic vaudeville entertainer as 'caricatures'.[49] Certainly, their effectiveness as witnesses rests on their particular status as exceptions: they therefore simultaneously make the claim of sameness whilst underlining the universal character of gendered difference in the labour markets that they represent. Similarly, the thought experiment in Amanda's closing address to the jury which transforms Tom Ewell's Attinger into a simpering blonde can be seen as suggesting the impossibility of transforming gender roles.

The question arises as to why, when the issue of physical abuse is so effectively highlighted in the script, Amanda chooses not to pursue this either as defence or mitigation. Her stance could either be taken as illustrating the powerlessness of battered women in terms of legal remedy at this time, but alternatively as a radical vindication of women's subjectivity. Battered Woman Syndrome has, as we noted above, been extensively criticized as pathologizing the woman, attributing to her a state of learned helplessness and thereby representing a further denial of her subjectivity. By contrast Amanda's strategy largely fits with her liberal feminist approach in its attribution of agency to Doris and her argument that the assault was rational. This is particularly interesting as Doris seems to exemplify the legal stereotype of the female offender as 'passive, irresponsible, irrational who commits the deed without conscious volition, without comprehension . . .'.[50]

The narrative within which Amanda situates Doris's agency is one which does not accord with the modern provocation defence, and this, it might be argued, is one of its strengths. Both the patriarchal and antique character of the defence is revealed in the fact that it originally allowed individuals whose honour had been impugned to discharge the state function of punishing wrongdoing. Loss of self-control was not essential for retributive retaliation, but rather violation of honour, thereby making it a justification rather than an excuse. Given the doctrine of 'femme coverte', such an honour killing could also be viewed as protection of property. In her portrayal of Doris as a wronged spouse acting in defence of her home, Amanda therefore seems to be drawing both on this older conception of provocation *and* the ideology of motherhood, whilst explicitly deploying the liberal feminist argument that women are equal to men.

However, just as Amanda is apparently realizing an affirmation of liberal legal formal equality, her position is partially undermined for the audience by her strategy. As we have argued above, her argument can be seen from the twenty-first century as almost the antithesis of a feminist perspective on domestic violence, in that if it is construed as giving women the right to participate in a culture of honour killing it is no form of freedom, and merely endorses patriarchal values.[51] Amanda appears to recognize this earlier in the film when engaging with Adam's positivist approach:

> Darling, please, please, this means a great deal to me and it is not a
> stunt. This poor woman – isn't she entitled to the same justice, I mean,
> that's usually reserved for men? The same unwritten law that got Lenna-
> han off . . . I know what you are going to say. That he should have been
> convicted too. But, he wasn't . . . And you're not going to put this poor
> soul away just because she had the misfortune to be born a female . . .
> not if I can help it.

In this passage, however, Amanda's reference to 'unwritten law', and her use
of the jury challenge, direct our attention to an important aspect of the film
which runs parallel to the legal argument which Kamir finds so wanting.

Amanda and Adam recognize from very early on that the way she conducts the trial is going to be subversive of the authority of law: Adam talks
of her 'turning a court of law into a Punch and Judy Show', and Amanda
describes her approach as dramatizing an injustice in the same way that the
Boston Tea Party did. The combination of legal argument and burlesque is
designed to appeal to the jury which she has selected by challenge, but also
to the audience in the court, principally of course the women. To this
extent, *pace* Kamir, her courtroom strategy is based on establishing an imagined community of women, which transcends class distinction, and the ideological cement for this community is the women's association with the
private sphere, the threatened home, and their universal experience of the
sexual double standard. So paradoxically, whilst much of her evidence is
based on demonstrating formal equality, and the exemplars are apparently
childless, Doris Attinger's defence as managed by Amanda, is dependent on
her response to the neglect, rejection and abuse of her and her children in
the private sphere, and represents an appeal for justice which is grounded in
emotional identification.

It is Amanda's courtroom practice, therefore, her clear intention to lawyer
differently, as much as her legal arguments, which marks her position as
feminist. The screenplay, however, makes it difficult for the viewer to
identify entirely with this project. Whilst Amanda does not appear to shift
her legal position in the course of the trial or afterwards, the entanglement
of her strategy with her own private relationship leads her to wonder
whether she had 'gone too far'. As is the case in one of Hepburn and Tracy's
other comedies, *Woman of the Year*,[52] the ruthless drive of Hepburn's character, and her willingness to sacrifice private relationships on the altar of
success, is seen as self-destructive, and the audience's sympathies are directed
towards the apparently more humble and apparently honest Tracy.[53] Similarly, the very success of Amanda's courtroom carnival, and her use of a dual
equality/difference and particular/universal argument has the potential to
damage the cause of women by validating the 'passionate lover' version of
honour killing.[54] This particular example however, of a general threat
offered to the Rule of Law by this strategy is underlined by Adam's general
assault on Amanda's emotionalism in the course of one of their private

arguments. From his standpoint it is manipulative and instrumental both in their private life and in the courtroom

> A few female tears ... stronger than any acid ... but this time they won't work ... You can cry from now until the time the jury comes in and it won't make you right and it won't win you that silly case.

By contrast, Adam is committed to working for a conviction, in spite of the evident personal distaste he feels during his initial interview with Attinger and his mistress. The binary opposition thus created is a subtle one: Adam fulfils the masculine stereotype of legal rationalism, but from a subordinated personal position, and evidently detached from ambition in the public world, whilst Amanda is seen (by Adam and those in the audience positioned alongside him) as a 'he-male competitor', but one who relies on and uses emotion in a way that Adam characterizes as typically feminine.

The message of *Adam's Rib*, as Kamir points out, is, in consequence of its character as a multivocal and multi-layered text, profoundly ambivalent: it has been interpreted as both a ground-breaking feminist film and alternatively a repudiation of the possibility of women's equal participation in the public sphere. Possibility is, however, one element in which the film is peculiarly rich. In spite of gruelling experience of the Attinger case, Amanda looks forward to the possibility of taking her struggles on to the political stage (as a Democrat in opposition to Adam's Republican). The possibility of reconciling equality and difference is suggested in the closing reel. But most significantly, Amanda's example provides for the possibility that women can practise as successful lawyers who can challenge convention in the male theatre of law in order to stake out a territory for women as autonomous subjects in a territory over which they have achieved proprietorial rights.

Conclusion

We have argued that screwball comedy represents a particularly apt genre for dealing with the complex and ambiguous conceptual terrain surrounding gender, power and law. This is partly because of the way in which the screwball framework allows for the stretching and blurring of categorical boundaries, such as the male/female boundary in *Adam's Rib*, and the law/emotion boundary in *Talk of the Town*. Also characteristic of the genre are the juxtapositions which are designed to destabilize the solid structures of the world: in the Howard Hawks comedy *Ball of Fire* the bizarre collision between Barbara Stanwyck's gangsters' moll and Gary Cooper's collection of hermit lexicographers undermines the certainties of prescriptive linguistics, whilst in *Bringing Up Baby*, also directed by Hawks, Cary Grant's paleontologist sees both the certainties of everyday life and the value of his science undermined by Hepburn's chaotic heiress. Such juxtapositions are also evident in the two films that we are discussing: in *Adam's Rib* the Bonners' secure middle-class marriage and the cohabitation of their divergent views of the role and practice of law are gradually undermined by their entanglement with the abject disorganized relationship of the working class Attingers, whilst in *Talk of the Town* the granite face of Michael Lightcap's black-letter law erodes in the face of the realities of small-town life. The resulting uncertainty about the nature of the Rule of Law and the possibility of its realization is the fulcrum around which each film revolves. Rosenberg identifies this uncertainty with the ferment in the legal field in the USA in the New Deal Era,[55] yet as we have sought to demonstrate, the issues dealt with in each film resonate equally in the early twenty-first century with our own uncertainties about law, particularly in relation to gender and power. By blurring the boundaries between public and private legal worlds, and by arguing for the possibility of practice in the legal field which reconciles an emotional response to particular injustices with attachment to universal principles, these films ultimately serve to reinforce the collective attachment of the audience to the law.

Notes

1 D. Byrge and R. Milton, *The Screwball Comedy Films: A History and Filmography 1934–1942* (Jefferson, N.C.: McFarland): W. Gehring, *Screwball Comedy: A Genre of Madcap Romance* New York: Greenwood Press (1986).
2 P. Bourdieu, *Language and Symbolic Power* Cambridge: Polity (1991), p. 42.
3 Ibid.
4 Ibid.
5 Norman Rosenberg, 'Professor Lightcap goes to Washington: Rereading Talk of the Town', *University of San Francisco Law Review*, 30: 1083–1095 (1996).
6 Rosenberg criticizes Robert Post's analysis of *Talk of the Town* on just the basis that the film is presented as a univocal legal text, 'Professor Lightcap goes to Washington', p. 1085.
7 Craig Brandist, 'The hero at the bar of eternity: the Bakhtin Circle's juridical theory of the novel', Economy and Society, 30, 2: 208–228 (2001), p. 216.
8 See J. Deigh, 'Emotion and the Authority of Law', in S. Bandes (ed.) *The Passions of Law*, New York: New York University Press (1999), p. 294.
9 See T.A.O. Endicott, 'The Impossibility of the Rule of Law', *Oxford Journal of Legal Studies*, 19, 1–18 (1999).
10 Ibid., p. 6.
11 See Deigh, 'Emotion and the Authority of Law', p. 286.
12 See particularly V. Kerruish, *Jurisprudence as Ideology*, London: Routledge (1991).
13 P. Williams *The Alchemy of Race and Rights*, Cambridge, Mass: Harvard UP (1991).
14 H. Charlesworth, 'What are women's international human rights' in R. Cook (ed.) *Human Rights of Women* Pennsylvania: University of Pennsylvania Press (1994) p. 58.
15 S. Noonan, 'Battered Woman Syndrome: Shifting the Parameters of Criminal Law Defences', in Anne Bottomley (ed.) *Feminist Perspectives on the Foundational Subjects of Law*, London: Cavendish (1996), pp. 191–221.
16 Ibid., p. 219.
17 J. Horder, *Provocation and Responsibility*, Oxford: Clarendon (1992).

18 Noonan, S. 'Battered Woman Syndrome . . .', p. 216.

19 N. Rimonte, 'A Question of Culture: cultural approval of violence against women in the Pacific-Asian community and the cultural defense', *Stanford Law Review*, 43 (1991), at p. 1311.

20 Ric Sheffield, 'On Film: a social history of women lawyers in popular culture 1930 to 1990', *Loyola of Los Angeles Entertainment Law Journal*, 17: 73–114 (1996).

21 Carol Shapiro, 'Women Lawyers in Celluloid: why Hollywood skirts the truth', *University of Toledo Law Review*, 25: 995–1011 (1995).

22 Sheffield, 'On Film', p. 94.

23 Sheffield, 'On Film, p. 77.

24 Shapiro, 'Women Lawyers in Celluloid', pp. 96–97.

25 See for example A. Norrie, *Crime Reason and History: a critical introduction to Criminal Law*, London: Butterworths (1993), and *Punishment, Responsibility and Justice – A Relational Critique*, Oxford: Oxford University Press (2000).

26 Norrie, *Crime Reason and History*, p. 107.

27 E.P. Thompson, *Whigs and Hunters*, Harmondsworth, Penguin (1975), p. 266.

28 G.R. Sullivan, 'Is Criminal Law Possible?', *Oxford Journal of Legal Studies*, 22, 4: 747–758 (2002).

29 Rosenberg, 'Professor Lightcap goes to Washington', 1091–1094

30 D. Sugarman, 'Legal Science, Liberalism and Imperialism', in Peter Fitzpatrick (ed.) *Dangerous Supplements: Resistance and Renewal in Jurisprudence*, London: Pluto (1991) pp. 60–61.

31 N. Rosenberg, 'Professor Lightcap goes to Washington'.

32 Orit Kamir, 'X-Raying Adam's Rib: Multiple Readings of a (Feminist) Law Film', *Studies in Law, Politics and Society*, 22: 103–129 (2001).

33 M.M. Bakhtin, *Rabelais and his World* (tr. H. Iswolsky), Cambridge, Mass: MIT Press (1968), p. 10.

34 Released in 1942, *Talk of the Town* was directed by George Stevens for Columbia Studios and scripted by Irwin Shaw and Sidney Buchman, who was subsequently blacklisted in the McCarthy era. The film received seven Oscar nominations but no award.

35 Released in 1949, Adam's Rib was directed by George Cukor, and forms part of a trio of works directed by Cukor and starring Katherine Hepburn and Spencer Tracy which explored 'modern' ideas about the changing role of women (the other films being *Woman of the Year* (1942) and *Pat and Mike* (1952)). The film was scripted by the husband and wife team of Ruth Gordon and Garson Kanin (stage actors who turned to writing in mid-career and who also scripted *Pat and Mike* – the influence of the stage is evident both in the script and the *mise en scène*). The film poster flagged the gender issue with the tag 'It's the hilarious answer to who wears the pants'.

36 Douglas Hay, 'Property, Authority and the Criminal Law', in D. Hay, P. Linebaugh, E.P. Thompson and C. Winslow (eds) *Albion's Fatal Tree* (Harmondsworth, Penguin, 1975), pp. 17–63.

37 See E.P. Thompson, *Whigs and Hunters*, Harmondsworth, Penguin (1975), as he draws attention to the widespread analogy between the 'statesman' and the criminal most tellingly represented in Fielding's *Jonathan Wild*.

38 R. Hughes, *The Fatal Shore* London, Collins Harvill (1987), pp. 26–42.

39 Hay, 'Property, Authority and the Criminal Law,' p. 1.

40 E.P. Thompson, *Whigs and Hunters*, p. 269.

41 For example, Fielding's description of Squire Western's performance of his duties as a magistrate in *Tom Jones* London: Macdonald (1953), p. 272; or the ironic contrast provided by Mrs Heartfree's description of the virtues of an African magistrate in *Jonathan Wild* (London: Hutchinson, p. 180).

42 D. Hay, 'Property Authority and the Criminal Law', p. 45.
43 See Craig B. Little and C. Sheffield, 'Frontiers and Criminal Justice: English Private Prosecution Societies and American Vigilantism in the Eighteenth and Nineteenth Centuries', *American Sociological Review*, 18: 796–808 (1983), and R. Abrahams 'Vigilantism' in Olivia Harris (ed.) *Inside and Outside of the Law: Anthropological Studies of Authority and Ambiguity*, London: Routledge (1996), pp. 42–55, for the idea that vigilantism exists on a fuzzy, ambiguous frontier of the state.
44 Ronen Shamir, *Managing Legal Uncertainty*, Durham: Duke University Press (1995), pp. 141–147, also cited in Rosenberg, 'Professor Lightcap goes to Washington', at p. 1092.
45 For discussions of the significance of childbearing for gender equality in the legal profession, see Hilary Sommerlad and Peter Sanderson, *Gender Choice and Commitment*, Aldershot: Dartmouth, pp. 199–203.
46 Kamir, 'X-raying Adam's Rib', p. 115.
47 See for example Virginia Drachman, *Sisters in Law: Women Lawyers in Modern American History*, Cambridge, Mass.: Harvard University Press (1998), who notes that the pioneers 'experienced first-hand what it meant to give up the comforts of female friendship and to interact in a community without women', p. 50.
48 Sandra Fredman, *Women and the Law*, Oxford: Oxford University Press (1997) p. 15.
49 Orit Kamir, 'X-Raying Adam's Rib', pp. 112–113. Of course the film was produced very shortly after the Second World War, during which women had been drawn into the labour market in large numbers to occupy traditionally male roles, as *Rosie the Riveter* so powerfully demonstrates.
50 H. Allen, 'Rendering them harmless: the professional portrayal of women charged with serious violent crimes' in P. Carlen and A. Worrall (eds) *Gender, Crime and Justice*, OUP (1988), p. 84.
51 Ibid.
52 1942, directed by George Stevens and written by Ring Lardner Jr. and Michael Kanin, Garson Kanin's brother. The dramatic fulcrum of *Woman of the Year* is Hepburn's adoption, and subsequent neglect, of a child. It is Tracy, of course, who ultimately expresses the more feminine anxiety about the child's emotional well-being, and who asserts the primacy of the private realm.
53 See Kamir, 'X-raying Adam's Rib', p. 120 for a full discussion of the contrast.
54 Kamir, 'X-raying Adam's Rib', p. 114.
55 Rosenberg, 'Professor Lightcap goes to Washington', p. 1095.

11 Five find treasure

Penny English

Introduction

Although a society apparently priding itself in the wealth of its cultural heritage, the law to protect archaeological remains is weaker in England and Wales than in almost any other part of Europe.[1] Attempts to reform the law have always met with opposition, from the earliest attempts to introduce legislation to protect ancient monuments in the late nineteenth century, which were seen to be an intrusion on private property rights,[2] to the late twentieth century reform of the prerogative of treasure trove which led to the Treasure Act 1996. Cultural property, and the allocation of ownership and control of it has always had the potential to be a site of contestation. Such material has more than a purely monetary worth: it is also valued as part of a national heritage, as an inheritance, and as part of a non-renewable resource. Where property has multiple meanings, the competing values may not always be reconcilable.

In this chapter, Enid Blyton's book *Five on Finniston Farm* is used to illustrate the competing claims to ownership of such property, and the extent to which the law in mediating between these claimants is doing more than simply providing a regime which will ensure the protection of the cultural heritage for the future. Although an adventure story for children, the attitudes of the various characters to the rightful ownership of archaeological and historical material express a range of conflicting views which illustrate vividly the arguments (and strong emotions) which lie at the heart of debate over how the law should regulate rights in such property. Moreover, the setting of the story is particularly apt as a setting for exploring these issues. Finniston Farm lies in what is nostalgically perceived as the quintessential English landscape: the post-enclosure landscape of fields and villages, a landscape which is inextricably bound up with ideas of English identity. It provides a snapshot of a place where social and cultural identity is reinforced by a strong sense of belonging to the land and of continuity between the past and the present, highlighting the importance of the tangible archaeological and historical remains which form part of that heritage.

Archaeological remains can be divided into two broad categories: sites and monuments, and portable antiquities. This reflects the distinction in law between chattels and land. 'Portable antiquities' covers a wide range of artefacts of archaeological or historical significance, from broken sherds of cooking pot to fine examples of jewellery or statuary. Such material has value which cannot be measured in purely monetary terms.[3] This has had the result that, to varying degrees, the law recognizes that they should be subject to regimes of ownership and control which are different from those applying to 'ordinary' property. Although some finds command high prices in the art market, for the majority of finds and archaeological sites their value is in the information they provide about the past and the societies that produced them. Some of this is derived from the object or monument itself, but much of the value depends on the context in which they are found, whether to help explain the use or date of a site, its relationship to its setting, or to indicate the location of an unknown site.

Portable antiquities

Countless thousands of objects lie hidden in the ground, but there is no system to ensure that finds of archaeological interest (other than those which fall within the limited category of precious metal) which come to light are reported at all.[4] Since the owner is free to do as he or she pleases with them (subject to certain limitations on export), objects can effectively disappear, and with them, the information which could have been provided by their context. Knowledge that they even exist need never reach the public domain.

From the middle of the nineteenth century until the Treasure Act 1996 came into force, the prerogative right of treasure trove (whose original purpose was to secure unowned bullion for the King) was used to assert public ownership of valuable antiquities. It took no account of the archaeological or historical significance of finds, as it applied only to objects of gold or silver. The inadequacies flowing from the use of a law for a purpose other than that for which it was designed are obvious: the material composition of an object does not necessarily bear any relationship to its archaeological or historical value. Moves towards even limited reform met with little success until the end of the twentieth century. Two Bills introduced into the House of Lords[5] failed to reach the statute book for want of government support. As Baroness Birk commented 'It comes into the category to which governments prefer to turn a blind eye'.[6] However, like the dragon in *Beowulf*, which rose up in anger when the treasure it was guarding was looted, the government eventually accepted the need for urgent action to ensure that irreplaceable knowledge of the nation's cultural heritage was not lost for ever. The action took two forms; reform of the existing law of treasure trove (resulting in the Treasure Act 1996) and a voluntary system for the effective recording of all archaeological finds, not just the small percentage which fall within the statutory definition of treasure. Even though the reforms did not represent a radical change in the law concerning the ownership of antiquities, opposition to it was vociferous in some quarters. To some, it was shifting the balance too far in favour of the state and the professional archaeologist at the expense of the individual. Not only are there different sets of value which can be ascribed to antiquities, there are competing interest groups claiming the right to own them.

Archaeological sites and monuments and historic buildings

A similar tension between different interests can be seen to underlie the law concerning monuments and buildings, which again seeks to balance a public interest in the preservation of such places against those of the individual, here the landowner's rights in his or her property. The first legislation to protect ancient monuments in England and Wales, the Ancient Monuments Protection Act of 1882, met with opposition on the basis that it was under-mining property rights.[7] This was despite the fact that it had very little practical effect. It did establish a schedule, or list, comprising a limited number of ancient monuments, all of which were prehistoric. This schedule remains the backbone of legislation to protect ancient monuments. Since the 1882 Act there has been a gradual shift in the balance between the indi-vidual rights of landowners and the public or state interest in monuments which are considered to be a part of the national heritage. A number of further Acts[8] strengthened the protection given to ancient monuments, extending the category of Scheduled Ancient Monument (SAM) to include medieval remains; unlike the original Act which had concerned itself only with prehistoric monuments, specifically excluding any of later date. Sched-uling now requires that before any works can take place on any site desig-nated as a SAM, consent must be sought.[9] The number of monuments included in the schedule has increased since the original 50 and a consider-able increase has taken place in recent years under the Monuments Protection Plan, which was introduced in order to ensure that a more representative selection of sites of national importance are protected.[10] However, scheduling could only ever cover a small percentage (perhaps around 10 per cent) of the total number of known archaeological sites.

It was not until half a century later that inhabited buildings received legal protection. This represented a further shift in the balance of interests away from that of the owner, since listing restricts their rights over not just an abandoned monument, but a building in contemporary use. The effect is similar to that of scheduling as an ancient monument, in that consent is required before alterations or demolition can take place. The Town and Country Planning Act 1932 first allowed local authorities to designate buildings of special architectural or historic interest and to submit them to a Preservation Order. The Town and Country Planning Act of 1944 empow-ered the Minister to prepare lists of such buildings, a measure which was carried over into the 1947 Town and Country Planning Act, which was the first comprehensive code for regulating development. The destruction of much of the architectural heritage of Britain in the Second World War heightened concern to prevent further destruction.

Listing of historic buildings is now covered by the Planning (Listed Buildings and Conservation Areas) Act 1990. In addition to the statutory framework, government Planning Policy Guidance (PPG) notes set out the policies in more detail. PPG 15 *Planning and the Historic Environment* encourages planning authorities to take account of the historic dimension of the environment:[11]

> it is fundamental ... that there should be effective protection for all aspects of the historic environment. The physical survivals of our past are to be valued and protected for their own sake, as a central part of our cultural heritage and our sense of national identity ... Their presence adds to the quality of our lives, by enhancing the familiar and cherished local scene and sustaining the sense of local distinctiveness which is so important an aspect of the character and appearance of our towns, villages and countryside.[12]

A listed building is one that is recognized by the government as being of special architectural or historic interest. It should retain an economic use, but tighter controls are imposed on alteration and development.

In June 2004, the government announced proposals for a radical overhaul of the heritage protection regime, following extensive public consultation.[13] The package will introduce a new unified 'Register of Historic Sites and Buildings of England', which will bring together the current scheduled monuments and listed buildings, as well as registered parks, gardens and battlefields and World Heritage Sites. When this is in place, a simplified integrated heritage consent will be administered by local authorities. A number of pilot projects have been launched, and it is intended that new legislation will be introduced in 2006–2007. In the short term, the criteria for listing buildings is being reviewed and English Heritage will take over responsibility for listed buildings from April 2005.[14]

Enid Blyton's *Five on Finniston Farm*

Although the *Famous Five* books are adventure stories for children, perhaps unexpectedly (given the intense criticism they have sometimes received for their lack of literary merit), they are capable of a deeper and more symbolic reading. The tradition to which the stories belong opens up this possibility, which is particularly appropriate in the context of considering cultural property, since it is itself heavily laden with symbolic significance. A particular characteristic of Blyton's writing identified by Rudd is that her writing is located in the oral, Homeric, rather than literary tradition.[15] It takes as its model the folk tale, where the telling is a performance and character is secondary to action with characters who are schematically drawn, often stock figures, archetypes or stereotypes.[16] Moreover, the narrative has a dreamlike quality and the action takes place in mythic time and place, isolated from the everyday. This distance from reality is accomplished by the action of the children's adventures, usually (as in this story) taking place in the summer holiday.[17]

One of the characteristics of the oral tradition is the idea of the story as a work in progress, a story which unfolds as it is told. The consequence can be that if it is analysed as a literary work, it appears deeply flawed. This is certainly the case with *Five on Finniston Farm*.

> This was the biggest mess I had to unravel. I think Blyton probably had 'flu when she wrote it. Characters drift in and out at random. Two characters called Bill and Jamie, never having any real place in the story, suddenly turn up on page 121 to resolve the crucial impasse of the children being trapped underground (where else?). There are two antique dealers, one good and the other a baddie, two offensively stereotypical Americans, a Great Grandad who could give Lear a run for his money in the railing against fate department and – probably inevitably – a dog called Snippet and a pet jackdaw called Nosey.[18]

Much of the criticism of Blyton's writing relates to its shortcomings as literature, which is perhaps unjust: '...the oral tradition seems a more apposite way of talking about Blyton's writing, moving away from the supercilious sneering of earlier criticism'.[19]

In *Five on Finniston Farm*, the characters are indeed stereotypes. They each play a symbolic role which embodies a competing interest in cultural property. Their dispute concerning the antiquities on the farm articulates these interests and claims to ownership. Viewed as part of the oral tradition, the stereotypes, rather than flawed and wooden, become vehicles to illuminate tensions, much in the same way as the stereotyped wicked stepmothers in Cinderella and Hansel and Gretel highlight the tensions and complexities in family relationships. This is aided by the setting for the story. The landscape in which it is set is 'iconically English'.[20] Throughout the series of adventures involving the *Famous Five* there is a powerful discursive thread of nationhood which is particularly evident in this story, and which provides the backdrop for this contest for rights over elements of the heritage. It is '...work which seems to promulgate, long past the Empire's sell-by date, a vision of a cosy, contented world, yet one where, beneath the surface, all is less tranquil'.[21] Symbolically as well as in reality, the *Five* 'draw attention to the holes in the homely fabric; literally "gaps", frequently leading to tunnels and passageways. The *Five* like to inhabit these interstices, the passageways between walls...'.[22] Not only does a vital part of the action involve an underground tunnel, the dispute exposes dormant emotions. The surface tranquillity of its English rural setting, apparently timeless and secure, is disrupted and the fractures hidden beneath the surface are revealed. In doing so, a range of competing arguments concerning the ownership and control of cultural property are voiced in a tale of a group of children and their summer holiday adventures.

Outline of the narrative

The Famous Five are paying guests at a farm in Dorset, at the start of another long summer holiday of ginger beer, ice-cream and adventure. Also staying at the farm is Mr Henning, an American who has been purchasing antiquities at bargain prices for his private collection. The farm has fallen on hard times and the family have reluctantly sold some items to Mr Henning. Shortly after arriving, the five children come to hear of a castle somewhere on the farm, whose location is now unknown. It had been razed to the ground as the result of a fire in 1192. The exact circumstances are unknown, but it is thought that the castle was stormed by enemies whilst a traitor within its walls set it alight. The story recounts that Lord Finniston was killed but that Lady Finniston and her children escaped, possibly by way of a secret underground passage. The walls of the castle collapsed, sealing off the cellars and dungeons and the castle site was eventually forgotten.

   The Famous Five succeed in locating the site after the dogs bring a number of oyster shells and bones out of a rabbit burrow, which Julian rightly surmises must indicate the site of a kitchen-midden. Nearby they find the castle itself. However, when Mr Henning hears about it, he enters into an agreement with the farmer giving him permission to excavate the site. Whilst excavations are proceeding, the *Five* decide to look for the underground passage leading to the castle. They find the passage and follow it to the castle where it leads to a large underground storeroom. In it are several suits of armour, an iron-bound wooden chest full of gold coins, another chest of jewellery (including some items of gold), and around the walls, racks of swords and knives. Despite a tense interlude when they are trapped in the underground passage, the children return to the farm with some of the treasures, and revived fortunes for the farm are predicted with the proceeds. Mr Henning returns, having successfully broken through the cellars of the castle, and unaware of the exploits of the intrepid *Five*. He has drawn up a new agreement which he hopes the farmer will sign, relating to a further payment for the contents of the cellar (representing it as worth considerably less than its true value). The farmer, now aware of the true worth of the treasure, refuses to do so. He then withdraws the permission to excavate, intending to complete the investigation of the cellars himself.

The scene is set

The opening scene is evocative. It is a hot summer's day. The boys, Julian and Dick, are sleeping by a hedge on a hill above a village in Dorset (reinforcing the dream-like quality of the narrative). The village at the bottom of the hill is still, 'old and peaceful and half asleep' in the hazy heat. When they wake, the boys cycle down to the village, where they find that the village shop provides ginger beer and ice-cream. The picture it conjures up immediately resonates with a mythical vision of rural England which still endures, almost half a century after the book was published. It is the 'landscape-as-heritage [which] lends itself to nostalgic myth-making: childhood memories 'of sunlit fields where we could play all day without fear, of picturesque villages unshaken by foreign juggernauts'.[23] The image is of an essential Englishness, which is founded on a certainty about the constitution of a national identity with reference to place, an identity which is a product of the countryside '. . . a peaceful, picturesque landscape in which an organic society had survived . . .'.[24] Martin Weiner influentially argued that the imagined essence of the nation had been rural since the late nineteenth century: 'a conception of Englishness that virtually excluded industrialism'.[25,26] Numerous books were published in the years before the Second World War which focused on the theme of English rural heritage, which laid the foundation for its value as a unifying force during the war, when the sense of national identity was both questioned and heightened. The rural image was deliberately used as a means to strengthen national cohesion. The image presented through the BBC was founded in the popular inter-war construction of a nation centred on 'a mythic rural vision of the 'traditional' English countryside'.[27] Similarly, film and poster propaganda drew on the same vision of romantic rural scenes.[28]

National myths play an important role in the formation of national identity. Without some strong attachment in the minds of the inhabitants, a nation can have no cohesion. It has existed in the minds of the inhabitant, to be an 'imagined community' capable of linking people across space and time.[29] These myths are reinforced by being associated with a distinctive history and culture, which in turn provides the basis for a national heritage. A scene is therefore set in this first chapter for the relationships between people and place and identity to be highlighted. Identification with a specific place, whether this is a nation, region or locality is a basis for claims to rights over its cultural heritage.[30]

Next, we see the farmhouse where the children are to be staying. It is, as might be expected, old with the 'rather small windows belonging to the age in which it was built', whitewashed and with roses growing over the porch. An old wooden door is wide open revealing a wooden chest and carved chair in the dim hall. A grandfather clock ticks slowly and loudly. The beams and floors are described as solid oak. The atmosphere is that of the hallowed stillness of a church. The almost sacred atmosphere is maintained when Julian looks around the farm yard and describes the barn: 'I *say!* I never saw such a fine barn in all my life! It's as old as the hills – look at those beams soaring up into the roof – it reminds me of a cathedral, somehow.' Tea is then served on a table which is 'a big, solid affair of old, old oak.' The reader is left in no doubt that this farm has a special aura of age, solidity and permanence which has elevated it beyond the mundane.

The central characters

The first character we meet is Mrs Philpot, the wife of the farmer. She is much preoccupied with the financial difficulties the farm is facing. She is realistic, practical and seeking pragmatic solutions to the problems. Great-Grandad, emerging from invisibility in his chair in the corner is 'a magnificent figure with his head of snow-white hair and his long beard' looking, as Anne observes 'like someone out of the Old Testament'. Through him, a theme of ancestral ties and family continuity is introduced.

At tea-time we are introduced to the other lodgers, an American, Mr Henning and his young son, 'Junior'. They are exceptionally unsympathetic characters (although later in the book Blyton is at pains to suggest that they are not typical of most Americans). Junior appears to have no redeeming features as well as no name, given to utterances such as 'Aw shucks, Pop, lemme come!'. It is essential for the development of the theme of English identity and heritage which underlies the story that Mr Henning is not English, but equally it is not by chance that Blyton has made him an American. The 1950s had seen a climate of concern about an invasion of American culture against which Blyton was seen to stand.[31] From their first introduction in the narrative they are portrayed as outsiders and very clearly culturally alien. They are excluded from the social discourse and unaware of the unspoken cultural norms and expectations which are shared by the five children and their hosts. When Junior expressly ignores the wishes of Mrs Philpot, the farmer's wife, even George (a person not normally noted for her respect of social niceties, often portrayed as rude and stubborn herself) is shocked: George scowled 'How dare he go out milking against the wishes of his hostess?' We hear that Mr Henning has spent the day buying a considerable number of old objects which were 'cheap as dirt'. It may be possible legally to trade in antiquities but it is clear (not least from the portrayal of him as an unattractive stereotype) that this may not always be morally acceptable. Money, commercial transactions and market value are introduced as themes. Mr Henning represents one class of claimant for the ownership of antiquities: the private collector. These objects are clearly capable of value as goods and the subject of straightforward economic transactions between willing buyer and willing seller (though perhaps reluctantly willing, driven by necessity).

One of the approaches to cultural property is the idea that it should be possible for it to circulate freely on the international market.[32] The argument is that cultural property should not (except perhaps in the case of exceptional 'national treasures') belong to one nation or social group, and that national laws which either prohibit all export of cultural goods or which deem all such material to be state property are unduly restrictive.

This is based on the view that there is a universal interest in all cultural property and that it forms part of the common heritage of mankind. Allowing such goods to be sold on the international market means that they are accessible to a wider public than if they remain in their country of origin. There is also a practical argument, that the preservation of individual objects is more likely to be secured in the context of the market. They also allow the economic value of the goods to be realized, providing a needed source of income, as in this case. Finally, restrictions on the legitimate trade in antiquities is likely simply to drive the practice underground. These conclusions are, however, disputed by many concerned with the problem of illicit trade in cultural property.[33] Much of the cultural material sold on the international market has been looted from archaeological sites, with a consequent loss of the information which they could have yielded. Objects divorced from their context have lost much of their value to archaeology. Moreover, this trade is largely one-way: from poorer countries to richer ones, thus doing little to promote universal cultural understanding for the exporting countries. The economic argument is also weak; although the value of the international trade in antiquities is large, very little of this benefits the local economies in the source countries.

The buildings

The children explore the farm buildings after tea. The buildings are not just placed on the land, they are shown as being a living part of it: 'The roofs had great Dorset tiles, made of stone, uneven and roughly shaped. They were a lovely grey, and were brilliant with lichen and moss'. They are all old and falling to pieces, integral to an organic cycle, and are now entering the process of decay. We are left in no doubt that they belong to this place. The children notice that part of one roof has been replaced with modern tiles which prompts a discussion about the sale of such tiles which are 'a bit of old England' for export. Similarly, when the children find a heap of castaway junk in a barn, including a cartwheel and old tools the same theme is picked up. Just as the buildings have an organic connection to place, so do these objects. Their origin was here, with strong ties to the people who made them. As Julian observes when they find the wheel: 'My word, they must have made all their own wheels here in the old days – in this very shed perhaps'. We are being invited to conclude that such things ought not to be removed from their place.

Mrs Philpot tells that they had indeed sold some of the tiles to an American, much to the dismay and anger of Great-Grandad, who 'shouted day and night ... and went about with a pitch-fork in his hand all the time, daring any stranger to even so much as walk over the fields!'. He is also vehemently opposed to any clearing-out of the junk in the sheds, having promised his own Grandad not to let the objects go to anyone. Great-Grandad personifies the idea of stewardship of an inheritance. He is holding on trust the property which has been passed down through the family, which he clearly feels very strongly about. This guardianship of the heritage cannot easily be cast aside. The idea that cultural property should belong to the people who created it forms the moral basis of much legal protection of antiquities, and of disputes over repatriation. It is the justification for nations imposing state ownership of cultural property, or of setting restrictions on the export of such material out of their territory; cultural property rightfully belongs to that nation because it was produced by the ancestors of its citizens. Similarly, claims by indigenous peoples or nations for the repatriation of cultural property from museums and collections are based on the strong ties between the material and the descendants of those who made it.

A wider context

The following day, the children are taken on a tour of the farm by a farm-hand, Bill. The context has thus broadened from the initial scenes in the farmhouse and the surrounding farm buildings to a wide sweep of country-side. The idyllic English rural setting is further reinforced, as is the idea that this is something organic. As Bill says:

> Ay. It's taken centuries to grow. All them names I told you – they'm centuries old too. Nobody knows now who was hanged down in Hangman's Copse – or what Tinkers came to Tinkers Wood. But they'm not forgot as long as they fields are there!

Anne recognizes exactly what he is saying: 'Why, that was almost poetry, she thought'. She and Bill are both insiders to this shared cultural sensitivity, 'You understand all right, miss, don't you. That Mr Henning, he raves about it all – but he don't unnerstand a thing'. Again, the outsider status of Mr Henning is demonstrated, reinforcing the shared socio-cultural identity of the *Five* with the inhabitants of the farm. It is Julian (who else) who makes an explicit reference to nationality as he voices the feelings of the others: 'That was good, very good. I somehow feel more English for having seen those Dorset fields, set about by hedges, basking in the sun.' The three elements of place, time and identity are linked. The perception of a shared cultural history rooted in a specific territory has given them a heightened sense of social cohesion in the present. Julian has no personal connection with this specific place, but articulates this identity at the level of the nation. Just such a connection between national identity and a common history underlay much of the nineteenth century legislation to protect antiquities in Europe, as it did for legislation put in place by new nations in the context of twentieth century decolonization. The social and political unit of the nation is given legitimacy by a shared cultural history. The monuments and artefacts of that past then become part of a national heritage, belonging to the nation.

In the public domain?

The children pay a visit to the village, where a new theme is introduced. Should knowledge of the existence and location of ancient monuments be in the public domain, or guarded by those who know their whereabouts? We meet Mr Finniston, owner of the antique shop in the village, and descendent of the Finnistons of the Finniston castle. He explains (slightly unconvincingly) why there are no visible remains of the castle site. He does say though that there are reused stones from the castle on the farm, but that only he and Great-Grandad know where they are. He is unwilling to say more: '...but no, I musn't tell you those secrets. You might tell them to the Americans who come here and buy up all our old treasures!'. From a practical point of view, this is about protecting any antiquities which might be concealed in the remains from potential sale. While still hidden and generally forgotten, they are held safe. This does, though, also raise the question of whether knowledge about the existence of sites should be in the public domain. If such a site is potentially of national interest, should its existence be concealed? If archaeological remains have a scientific, informational value which adds to the total sum of what is known about the past, then there is strength in the argument that whatever the legal rights of ownership to the property, knowledge about it should be public. The furtherance of knowledge does not appear to be at the forefront of Mr Finniston's thinking. He has a very emotional response to the things of the past. He reveals that the farmhouse door came from the castle, and his response to Anne's admission that she had not really looked at it properly is 'Couldn't you *feel* that that door was real – was as old as the centuries – and once hung on great hinges in a *castle*? Don't you know when things are grand with the weight of years?' He has immersed himself in the past to the extent that 'His mind had woven for him a living fantasy, a story that had no certain foundation, no real truth', which makes Anne feel sorry for him. For him, the myth may be more important than the reality.

The dispute heats up

Dinner that night sees a heated discussion, involving 'quite a bit of shouting' about the rights and wrongs of selling antiquities. Mr Henning views it in purely commercial terms: 'All I want is to buy things you want to sell. You want new tractors – I want old junk and I'm willing to pay for it. That's all there is to it – buying and selling'. What is 'junk' to Mr Henning, has a value which cannot be measured in monetary terms for Great-Grandad. 'OLD JUNK! Do you call that great old cartwheel you bought OLD JUNK? Why, that's more than two hundred years old! My Great-Grandad made it – he told me so, when I was a mite of a lad.' Though recognizing that there may be a strong financial imperative which makes selling some objects necessary, Great-Grandad is particularly concerned that they do not leave the country 'Why can't we sell 'em to our own folks then? . . . Taking them out of the country! Part of our history, they are! Selling our birthright, that's what we're doing – for a mess of pottage'

As her contribution to the debate, Mrs Philpot expresses a coolly rational point of view, 'Surely it's better to sell old things that we shall never use, in order to buy new tools, or wood to mend the barns?' As she tries to calm the agitated Great-Grandad, she indicates that she is well aware that the world is changing: 'You belong to old times, and you don't like the new times, and I don't blame you. But things change, you know.' The date the book was published, 1960, is significant here. Despite the strength of the image of England as timeless and rural, this was an era of rapid change. McDowell argues that this can be seen as a pivotal point of social transition.[34] From the perspective of the present, where postmodern society seems to be character-ized by the severing of links between identity and locality and the conse-quent restructuring of the association between people and place, the 1950s are viewed with nostalgia. This was 'the period in which it now seems that there was a set of clear relationships between people and place, a period when people knew their place, not only in the sense of deference but in a sense of belonging to a place'.[35] She argues that the view we now have of the 1950s, as a period of certainty which contrasts with the endless change of the present, is as misleading as the view that in the present the links between place and identity have been completely recast: 'Increasingly the 1950s are being seen by social and cultural theorists as a key period in understanding more recent shifts in the relationships between identity, meaning and place.'. . . 'The preconditions and origins of the contemporary set of socio-spatial changes lie in the 1950s', with the years between the mid 1950s and the end of the 1960s being a period of 'extraordinary trans-formation'.[36] *Five on Finniston Farm* is set in precisely this era, and it is this fracturing and disruption of the old order which allows the disputes over cultural property to come to the surface.

Fixtures and fittings and finders

Mr Henning, now with an advisor, Mr Durleston, is interested in removing some of the fixtures in the farmhouse, including the oak door which had purportedly come from the castle (quite how this had survived the devastat-ing fire is not explained). He is also interested in a fireplace, concerning which Mr Durleston suggests: 'Now that's worth buying. You could rip that out and use it in your own house – a beautiful thing.' He also looks at the old chapel, now in use as a grain store, and expresses a wish to dismantle it stone by stone for re-erection in America. This, however, is a suggestion too far for Mr Durleston, who draws back: 'Can't advise that. Not in good taste', to the relief of Anne: 'at least the other man stopped him from his mad idea of removing the chapel stone by stone. I couldn't *bear* that beautiful old place to be torn up by its roots and replanted somewhere else.' Anne, despite her reputation for a preoccupation with domestic chores, is given the most perceptive lines by Blyton, including at this point where she succinctly sums up the problem: 'He – he wants to buy history just as if it were chocolate or toffee!'. This makes the others laugh, but she has hit the root of the problem. Cultural property is *not* just like any other property, which is why the law treats it as, to some extent, outside the normal property regime.

The law begins to make itself felt at the conclusion of the tale. Fortunately, the agreement with Mr Henning had only been to give him permission to excavate, and that should he want to retain anything he found then this would be the subject of a further agreement. In discussing whether the treasures will belong to the family as landowners, the suggestion is made that the Crown may be able to claim some of it. This sends the Great-Grandad into another burst of indignation: 'THE CROWN! The CROWN! No, SIR! It's mine! Ours! Found on my land, put there by our ancestors.' Here, then, we have another claimant for ownership: the state.

How would the law determine the owner(s)?

The story has clearly established that there are a number of claimants to rights over cultural property, and that these different claims are not easily reconciled. The situation at the time the book was written would differ in some respects from the present, as since 1960 the law relating to the cultural heritage has undergone various revisions.

With regard to the treasures found in the cellar of the castle, their ownership would, in 1960 have been governed by the prerogative of treasure trove. The Treasure Act 1996 has tidied up the worst anomalies of the prerogative by creating a statutory definition of treasure. In either case, the finder of potential treasure should report the find to the coroner, either directly or through the police or a museum. No doubt Julian would have cycled to the village and informed the local constable, as prior to 1968 concealment of treasure was an offence.[37] The Treasure Act makes it a summary offence to fail to inform the coroner within 14 days of a find which might be treasure.

Before the Act, deciding whether goods were treasure would have been the task of a coroner's jury, who had to determine that the owner was unknown, that the objects were 'substantially'[38] composed of gold or silver and hidden in the ground or a building with intent to recover them (*animus revertendi*). The near impossibility of deciding what was in the minds of unknown persons hundreds or thousands of years ago was one of the problems that the Act sought to redress.[39] If objects were declared treasure trove, they would become the property of the Crown and the finder would be paid an *ex gratia* payment equivalent to the market value. If not, they would belong to the landowner. The contents of the cellar as a whole represent a very rare example of an undisturbed assemblage of material from the twelfth century. However, the state would have had no automatic right to the items which were not composed of precious metal. In the case of the finds in

Finniston Castle, once the coroner had been informed, he would have had to summon a jury to consider the case. It would have been likely that there would have been some bizarre consequences, for example in the case of the chest of gold coins, which we are told was in the cellar. If any of the coins had been base metal, or contained only a small proportion of gold or silver they would not have been treasure trove. They, together with the chest in which they were found, would have belonged to the landowner. Others, with substantial precious metal content, would have belonged to the Crown. Similarly, the contents of the chest of jewellery would be split between different owners: the gold belt may have been treasure trove whereas the gemstones could not.

Having decided that there were objects with a sufficient precious metal content, the jury would then have had to consider whether they had been deliberately hidden with intent to recover them. Given that the facts of the disaster which befell the castle are somewhat hazy, and Mr Finniston's account possibly unreliable, the task of deciding what was in the minds of the inhabitants of the castle on that fateful day will not be an easy one. Were the chests brought to the cellar in an act of hasty concealment when the enemy was at the door and Lord Finniston's intention to retrieve them thwarted by his untimely death? On the other hand, were they still lying in place where they were normally kept, abandoned when their owner fled?

The 1996 Act has made the position considerably clearer. There is now a statutory definition of what constitutes 'treasure' (section 1). It includes any object which is at least 300 years old and has metallic content which is at least 10 per cent by weight precious metal. Also covered are objects of materials other than gold or silver, where these are found in clear archaeological association with objects which are treasure. Virtually all coin hoards older than 300 years are included, regardless of their precious metal content (section 1(iii)). Single coins are excluded from the definition of treasure. The requirement of establishing *animus revertendi* is abolished. It would now therefore be unnecessary to establish the metallic composition of each of the coins in the chest in the cellar, nor make any attempt to determine the intentions of the owner.

The law does not make all objects of archaeological interest which are discovered the property of the Crown. To that extent it does not go very far towards ensuring that all items which might be of an archaeological value are even reported, let alone taken into public ownership. No one need be made aware of the existence of finds, no record need be made of them, nor can they be protected from destruction. The reform of the law of treasure did not substantially change the position. The balance does not shift substantially in favour of state rights, but does make some rational improvements to what was an extraordinarily inappropriate regime. However, the changes did rouse opposition from those who feared that this would amount to a substantial shift in the balance between the rights of the state against the rights of the finder (especially those using metal detectors).

Objects which do not fall within the definition of treasure, and which are buried in the ground will be the property of the landowner. In the absence of a claim from the original owner or his or her heirs, then the owner or occupier of the land or building has title if the object is buried in or attached to the land or building.[40] An item not attached to the land also belongs to the occupier if he had manifested the intention to exercise control over the land or building and the things found on it. Otherwise the finder will have better title than anyone, except the original owner or his or her heirs.[41] There is, however, a possibility not explored by Blyton. A requirement of the common law of treasure trove (retained by the Treasure Act) is that the owner or his heirs are unknown. Mr Finniston, the owner of the village antique shop is supposedly a descendant of the original owners of the castle. If he is able to establish his line of descent back to Lord Finniston, he will have better title that either the Crown or landowner. The Crown only has rights to treasure in the absence of the original owner or his successors in title.

The legal and moral conflict which *Five on Finniston Farm* illustrates is not confined to fiction. This was clear from the debate surrounding the passage of the Treasure Act. Even though the reforms amounted to little more than a tidying-up process, some of the opposition to it was vehement. Although fears were expressed concerning the erosion of property rights, the Country Landowners Association and the National Farmers' Union, after consultation and revision, supported the measure. The strongest opposition came largely from those who pursue metal detecting as a hobby, who saw reform as an unwarranted extension of state ownership, fearing the eventual nationalization of all archaeological finds and the banning of metal detecting. The government made it clear that the Act was not intended to be an attack on the rights of metal detectorists, and some modifications were made in the light of their concerns.[42] In fact relationships have since improved. The Treasure Act, since it covers such a limited range of material composition, clearly only secures ownership for the state for a small percentage of the total number of archaeological finds. It has resulted in a substantial increase in the number of items reported. Section 2(1) of the Treasure Act gives the Secretary of State the power to designate any class of object which he or she considers to be of outstanding historical, archaeological or cultural importance. Under this power, the classes of object designated as treasure have been extended to cover prehistoric hoards of base metal.[43] This is a further move towards recognizing a state interest in object with an archaeological value which does not equate with its precious metal content.

Echoes of the same opposition to change were heard again in 2000 when the UK announced that it would ratify the Council of Europe Convention on the Protection of the Archaeological Heritage 1992 (known as the Valletta Convention). Although in this case it appears to have been resolved in most quarters, the same issue of the balance between public and private rights over ownership of and access to the cultural heritage was evident. The fears expressed were similar: that this was a move to oust the amateur from active engagement in discovering the past by prioritizing the interests of the state-sponsored professional.[44] The Convention requires states that are party to it to undertake to maintain a legal system for the protection of the heritage of a high standard; in that respect it strengthens the commitment by the state to the protection of the archaeological heritage. It covers a number of areas, but the two points which raised concerns that it might limit the activities of amateur archaeologist and metal detectorist were Article 2 (which concerns the compulsory reporting of chance finds) and Article 3 (which seeks to promote high standards in archaeological investigation by ensuring that investigations are authorized and carried out by qualified persons). The lack of a mandatory reporting system appears on the face of it to be contrary to Article 2 of the Valletta Convention, which commits states party 'by means appropriate to the state in question' to 'mandatory reporting to the competent authorities by a finder of the chance discovery of elements of the archaeological heritage and making them available for examination.' However the accompanying advisory notes suggest that 'a state, however, may only require mandatory reporting of finds of precious metals or on already listed sites.' The UK was involved in the drafting of this provision.

It was recognized at the time of the Treasure Act, that there needs to be some mechanism to ensure that finds which are not 'treasure' are recorded in some way. These comprise the vast majority of finds (treasure amounts to only about 5 per cent of all finds which are made). Their archaeological value may be as great or greater than that of an object which happens to be made of precious metal. Even very mundane objects may have considerable archaeological value. The contents of the kitchen-midden at Finniston Farm were perceived of interest only because they indicated that the castle was in close proximity. In archeological terms, it would have had enormous potential informational value. A system for ensuring that all finds are reported in some way, so that their existence becomes public knowledge would clearly be desirable. The government sought views on whether there should be a voluntary code of practice for recording or legislation to make such reporting obligatory, perhaps on the lines of the system operating in Northern Ireland, whereby the finder of any archaeological object must report the find and the circumstances of finding within 14 days.[45] The responses strongly favoured a voluntary scheme. Therefore, such a scheme was introduced, which was intended to encourage all finds to be reported in order to allow them to be recorded, without any change in the legal ownership. The pilots for the Portable Antiquities Scheme set up in 1997 were a success, and it has been extended.[46] Its future remains somewhat precarious, as it has been dependent on short-term funding from the Heritage Lottery Fund. It has had the effect of bringing the knowledge of the existence of a great many finds into the public domain. Although only a voluntary scheme, and not in any way altering the property rights of the owner, it does represent a perceptible shift towards a recognition that there is a public interest in *all* archaeological finds. At present, basing the law concerning portable antiquities on the idea of 'treasure' does have the effect of suggesting that the state's interest is largely in objects which have a high monetary value, rather than those which have a high archaeological value.[47] The Portable Antiquities Scheme may eventually be successful in creating a culture where reporting of all archaeological objects becomes the norm. It has been judged a success so far. Not only have tens of thousands of objects been recorded, but archaeological sites have come to light through the reporting of finds.

Article 3 of the Valletta Convention also caused some concern. It requires that there are procedures 'for the authorization and supervision of excavation and other archaeological activities', both in order to prevent illicit excavation and removal of objects and to ensure that excavation is 'undertaken in a scientific manner'. It also requires that the use of metal detectors and other detection equipment for archaeological investigation should be subject to prior authorization (Article 3 (i)(f)). The problem was whether this would affect the status of amateur excavations and the hobby of metal detecting. It was feared that this would lead to the need for licensing of excavations and the prohibition of metal detecting.

Digging is a destructive activity. Even the most meticulous and scientific of excavations destroys the very evidence it is gathering. Mr Henning's use of drills to break his way into the castle would appear to fall short of the highest excavation standards, even of his day. His primary purpose was not to unravel and record the stratigraphy of the site, but to rob it of objects which might be of value to him. There is clearly an argument that there should be limitations placed on such destructive activities in order to ensure this fragile and irreplaceable evidence is recorded adequately. In Northern Ireland, in parallel with the law in the Republic of Ireland, all digging or excavating for the purposes of searching for archaeological objects has to be by licence (Historic Monuments and Archaeological Objects (NI) Order 1995). In the rest of the UK it is not necessary to have a licence to dig.

Inappropriate excavations are probably not a major threat to the archaeological heritage, and additional bureaucracy may prove counterproductive. The government has stated that it has no intention of introducing a licensing system for excavations. In a Written Answer it stated that the government does not believe that there is a need for any further legislation in order to comply with the requirements of the Convention as the vast majority of intrusive work is already 'authorized' in some way, whether through Scheduled Monument Consent, planning permission or through peer review of grant applications.[48] It also considers that the strict interpretation of the wording the Convention allows it to limit its application to metal detectors to their use in archaeological investigations. It is therefore not necessary to control the general use of them.[49]

The site of the castle would almost certainly, once it was known about, have been subject to scheduling as an ancient monument. This covers any monument deemed by the Secretary of State to be of national significance. Such a site from this date would certainly be an obvious candidate for being considered of national importance. This is covered now by the Ancient Monuments and Archaeological Areas Act 1979 (AMAA 1979). Section 1 of the Act gives the Secretary of State the power to include in the Schedule any monument she deems to be of national importance. Scheduling would not necessarily mean any change in the ownership of the site. What it does is to recognize that there is a legitimate public interest in curtailing the owner's rights to alter or destroy a monument on her or his land. Any works taking place on the site would then require Scheduled Monument Consent. Section 2(1). It would not affect ownership of any finds from the site (other than treasure), although the Act does allow for some investigation to be made of finds from such sites (section 54), but they can only be retained for a reasonable period. The owner is subsequently free to sell or dispose of them.

The farmhouse and its outbuildings would almost certainly be listed. This has a similar effect to scheduling as an ancient monument, but applies to inhabited buildings. Under section 1(1) of the Planning (Listed Buildings and Conservation Areas) Act 1990 the Secretary of State has discretion to list any building of 'special architectural or historic interest'. All buildings dating from before 1700 which survive in anything like their original condition are listed, as are most dating before 1840. Although the date of Finniston Farm is not expressly revealed, it is implied that it is several hundred years old, and contains a wealth of original features. Listed Building Consent would be required for interior works which affect the character of the building. This would undoubtedly include such activities as Mr Henning had in mind, like removing fireplaces.

The objects Mr Henning bought would have been subject to a requirement to obtain permission to remove them from the country.[50] This was originally under the Import, Export and Customs Powers (Defence) Act 1939. The Export Control Act 2002 now establishes a new legislative framework for export controls on both strategic goods and objects of cultural interest. The purpose of the export controls is to give an opportunity for retention in this country of goods which are considered to have outstanding national importance. Again there is a balance to be made between the protection of the national heritage against the property rights of owners to dispose of the goods as they wish, and of exporters and purchasers. The principles followed when exercising the licencing powers are based on the 'Waverley Criteria' (named after the Waverley Report 1952). The first is whether the object is so closely connected with our history and national life that its departure would be a misfortune. The other two cover objects of outstanding aesthetic importance, or objects of outstanding significance for the study of some particular branch of art, learning or history. This system was designed as much to facilitate the free trade in cultural material as to protect the national heritage. It covers individual objects, largely of artistic significance, and takes little account of the specific problems of archaeological material where context is pre-eminent.[51] A non-statutory, independent body, the Reviewing Committee, advises whether an object falls within the

Waverley criteria. Of the 8–10,000 objects for which applications are made each year, only 25–50 are refused licences.[52] This clearly does little to prevent the export of more mundane objects, such as many of the antiquities Mr Henning was seeking to export.

Since the date of *Five on Finniston Farm* this area has become, in addition to domestic law, also the subject of EC law. An export licence is required for the export of archaeological objects outside the EC (Regulation 3911/92 on the export of cultural goods, which acts in conjunction with Directive 93/7 on the Return of Cultural Objects Unlawfully Removed from the Territory of a Member State). In addition, international law has begun to concern itself with the problems associated with the illegal trade.[53]

Conclusions

Cultural property rights have evolved, and are still doing so. The boundary between the public and private rights to own and control this property is not a static one. The legislation in this area involves various limitations on property rights which recognize that there is a public interest in such property which justifies restrictions on private ownership. These restrictions take a number of forms. The scheduling of ancient monuments and listing of historic buildings limit owners' rights to alter or demolish their property. Export licences restrict the freedom to sell antiquities out of the country, thus overriding the owner's right to freely transfer property. The portable antiquities recording scheme establishes the idea of a general right of access to objects (albeit on a temporary basis for recording). This ensures that the knowledge of and about the object is available to others. The extension of the category of treasure (even though very limited) is part of the same general trend. The divisions between public and private rights over cultural material are clearly fluid.

As a vehicle for highlighting the issues, the fictional setting and characters of *Five on Finniston Farm* help to illustrate the emotions which are attached to such property. Julian and Anne express the relationships (difficult to quantify) between locality, the nation and the past. The intensity of the violent outbursts of Great-Grandad, and the emotional relationship Mr Finniston has with the past illustrate, more powerfully than any dispassionate balancing of the relative importance of the values attached to such property, not only that the views between the individuals involved are strongly held, but also that where the cultural heritage is involved emotion and myth cannot be ignored. The arguments expressed in *Five on Finniston Farm* concerning the rights to own and control archaeological and historical material are as topical as they were in the middle of the last century. The conflict is between the purely commercial and the symbolic value (as a part of national, social or family identity) of cultural property. Although there have been some changes in the law which have shifted the balance between competing rights, it remains a disputed area.

Notes

1 One need not travel far to find substantial differences in the law which contrast with the limited protected afforded to such remains in England and Wales. In Northern Ireland and Scotland the law is different in significant respects. For example, in Scotland, *bona vacantia* applies, stemming from the civil law concept *quod nullius est fit domini regi*, whereby all unowned objects are vested in the Crown. Further afield, the Cultural Heritage Act 1979 in Norway provides that all material dating from before the Reformation belongs to the state.

2 See Carman, J. *Valuing Ancient Things; Archaeology and Law* (Leicester, Leicester University Press 1996), pp. 67–91, Chippindale, C. 'The Making of the First Ancient Monuments Act, 1882 and its Administration under General Pitt-Rivers' *Journal of the British Archaeological Association*, 136 (1983) pp. 1–55; Murray, T. 'The history, philosophy and sociology of archaeology: the case of the Ancient Monuments Protection Act (1882)' in V. Pinsky and A. Wylie (eds) *Critical Traditions in Contemporary Archaeology* (Cambridge: Cambridge University Press, 1989) pp. 55–67 for accounts of the passage of the 1882 *Ancient Monuments Protection Act*.

3 There are a range of different values which can be applied when ascribing significance to such material. See Warren, K. (1989) 'A Philosophical Perspective on the Ethics and Resolution of Cultural Properties Issues' in P.M. Messenger (ed.) *The Ethics of Collecting: Whose Culture? Whose Property?* (Albuquerque: University of New Mexico Press, 1989), pp. 1–25; Carver, M. 'On Archaeological Value' *Antiquity* 70 (1996), pp. 45–56; Lipe, W.D. 'Value and Meaning in Cultural Resources' in H. Cleere (ed.) *Approaches to the Archaeological Heritage* (Cambridge: Cambridge University Press, 1984), pp. 1–11; Bruier, F.L. and Mathers, W. *Trends and Patterns in Cultural Resource Significance: An Historical Perspective and Annotated Bibliography* (Alexandria, Virginia: US Army Corps of Engineers, 1996).

4 A study has estimated some 400,000 finds are made by metal detectorists each year (Dobinson, C. and Denison, S. *Metal Detecting and Archaeology in England* (London: English Heritage and Council for British Archaeology, 1995).

5 By Lord Abinger in 1982 and Lord Perth in 1994.

6 Hansard *House of Lords Debates* 8.2.82 col. 20.

7 Baldwin Brown, G., *The Care of Ancient Monuments* (Cambridge: Cambridge University Press, 1905) p. 153; Chippindale, C. 'The Making of the First Ancient Monuments Act, 1882 and its Administration under General Pitt-Rivers' *Journal of the British Archaeological Association*, 136 (1983) pp. 1–55 at 13; Murray, T. 'The history, philosophy and sociology of archaeology: the case of the Ancient Monuments Protection Act (1882)' in V. Pinsky, and A. Wylie (eds) *Critical Traditions in Contemporary Archaeology* (Cambridge: Cambridge University Press, 1989) pp. 55–67 at 62–63.

8 Ancient Monuments Protection Act 1900, Ancient Monuments Consolidation and Amendment Act 1913, Ancient Monuments Act 1931, Ancient Monuments and Archaeological Areas Act 1979 (as amended by the National Heritage Act 1983).

9 Ancient Monuments and Archaeological Areas Act 1979 s 2.

10 Darvill, T. and Wainwright, G. 'The Monuments at Risk Survey: an Introduction' *Antiquity* 64 (1994) pp. 820–824.

11 Secretary of State for National Heritage and the Secretary of State for the Environment *Planning and the Historic Environment* (London, 1994).

12 Ibid., para 1.1.

13 Department of Culture, Media and Sport *Protecting our historic environment: Making the system work better* (London, 2003) www.culture.gov.uk/global/consultations/2003+closed/HPR_Consultation.htm (site accessed 04-08-04).

14 Department of Culture, Media and Sport *Review of Heritage Protection: the way forward* (London, 2004) www.culture.gov.uk/global/publications/archive_2004/review_heritage_protection.htm (site accessed 04–08–04).

15 Rudd, D. 'Enid Blyton and the Paradox of Children's Literature' in N. Tucker and K. Reynolds (eds) *Enid Blyton: A Celebration and Reappraisal* NCRCL Papers 2 (London: NCRCL, 1997) pp. 17–29; and (in the same volume) 'Why the Emphemeral Blyton Won't Go Away' pp. 36–40 and Rudd, D. *Enid Blyton and the Mystery of Children's Literature* (Basingstoke: Macmillan Press, 2000) pp. 155–169.

16 Rudd, D. 'Why the Emphemeral Blyton Won't Go Away' p. 47.

17 Rudd, D. 'Enid Blyton and the Paradox of Children's Literature' p. 23.

18 Cresswell, H. 'Adapting the Famous Five for Television' in N. Tucker and K. Reynolds (eds) *Enid Blyton: A Celebration and Reappraisal* NCRCL Papers 2 (London: NCRCL, 1997) pp. 96–104.

19 Rudd, D. *Enid Blyton and the Mystery of Children's Literature* (Basingstoke: Macmillan Press, 2000) p. 169.

20 Ibid, p. 91.

21 Ibid, p. 1.

22 Rudd, D. 'Enid Blyton and the Paradox of Children's Literature' p. 19.

23 David Lowenthal 'British National Identity and the English landscape' *Rural History* 2, 2, 1991, pp. 205–230 at 217.

24 Weight, R. and Beach, A. 'Introduction' in R. Weight and A. Beach (eds) *The Right to Belong: Citizenship and National Identity in Britain 1930–1960* (London and New York: I.B. Taurus, 1998) p. 3.

25 Weiner, M. *English Culture and the Decline of the Industrial Spirit* (Cambridge, Cambridge University Press. 1981).

26 Ibid., p. 5.

27 Nicholas, S. 'From John Bull to John Citizen: images of national identity and citizenship on the wartime BBC' in R.Weight and A. Beach (eds) *The Right to Belong: Citizenship and National Identity in Britain 1930–1960* (London and New York: I.B. Taurus, 1998) pp. 36–58 at 37.

28 Hogarth, T. 'Citizenship, Nationhood and Empire in British Official Film Propaganda, 1939–45, in R.Weight and A. Beach (eds) *The Right to Belong: Citizenship and National Identity in Britain 1930–1960* (London and New York: I.B. Taurus, 1998) pp. 60–88; Bunce, M. *The Countryside Ideal: Anglo-American images of landscape* (London and New York: Routledge, 1994).

29 Anderson, B. *Imagined Communities* (London: Verso, 1991).

30 There is a considerable literature on the link between archaeology and national identity. See, for example Kohl, P.L. and Fawcett, C. *Nationalism, Politics and the Practice of Archaeology* (Cambridge, Cambridge University Press, 1995); Díaz, Andreu M. and Champion, T. (eds) *Nationalism and Archaeology in Europe* (London UCL Press, 1996); Graves-Brown, P. Jones, S. and Gamble, C. (eds) *Cultural Identity and Archaeology: the Construction of European Communities* (London: Routledge 1996); Jones, S. *The Archaeology of Ethnicity: Constructing Identities in the Past and Present* (London: Routledge, 1997).

31 Rudd, D. *Enid Blyton and the Mystery of Children's Literature*, p. 33; see also Weight, R. *Patriots* (Basingstoke: Macmillan, 2002) pp. 175–186.

32 Merryman, J.H. 'Two ways of thinking about cultural property' *The American Journal of International Law* 80 (1986) pp. 831–855; 'The Public Interest in Cultural property' *California Law Review* 77 (1989) 339–364; 'The Nation and the Object' *International Journal of Cultural Property* 3, 1 (1994) 61–76. A number of articles in *International Journal of Cultural Property* 1, 4 (1995) discuss the theme of licit traffic in cultural property.

33 Brodie, N., Doole, J. and Watson, P. *Stealing History* (Cambridge: McDonald Institute for Archaeological Research, 2000).
34 McDowell, L. 'Introduction: Rethinking Place' in L. McDowell (ed.) *Undoing Place? A Geographical Reader* (London: Arnold, 1997) pp. 1–12 at 1.
35 Ibid., p. 3.
36 Ibid., p. 5.
37 This was abolished by the Theft Act 1968 s (1)(1).
38 *Attorney-General of the Duchy of Lancaster* v. *G.E. Overton (Farms) Ltd.* [1982] 1 ch 277 [1982] 1 All ER 524 involved a hoard of debased Roman coinage, where the actual silver content was found to be too low for them to qualify as treasure trove.
39 *Attorney-General* v. *Trustees of the British Museum* [1903] ch 598. Farwell, J. likened the arguments of the expert witness to 'fanciful suggestions more suited to the poem of a Celtic bard', (at 610).
40 *Elwes* v. *Brigg Gas Company* [1886] 33 ch 562.
41 *Amory* v. *Delamirie* [1721]; 1 Stra 505; *Parker* v. *British Airways Board* [1982] QB 1004, restated in *Waverley Borough Council* v. *Fletcher* [1995] 4 All ER 756.
42 Sir Anthony Grant, Hansard *House of Commons Debates* 8 March 1996, col. 555.
43 Treasure (Designation) Order 2002.
44 See the Council for Independent Archaeology website www.independents.org.uk (site accessed 30.05.03) and the National Council for Metal Detecting www.ncmd.co.uk/valetta.htm (site accessed 30.05.03).
45 Historic Monuments and Archaeological Objects (Northern Ireland) Order 1995.
46 Portable Antiquities Scheme Annual Reports are available on its website www.finds.org.uk.
47 See the Council for British Archaeology's Portable Antiquities Group response to the Consultation on the Treasure Act Review 2001, which discusses the problem of the idea of 'treasure' as a source of personal financial gain. www.britarch.ac.uk/cba/ta2001.html (site accessed 30.05.03).
48 13 July 2001 Hansard *House of Commons Debates* col. 696W.
49 For a comment on the Convention see the Council for British Archaeology response www.britarch.ac.uk/valletta/valletta_final_cba_full.html.
50 DCMS website www.culture.gov.uk.
51 Comments from the Portable Antiquities Working Group of the Council for British Archaeology to the Department of Culture, Media and Sport for the Review of the Reviewing Committee on the Export of Works of Art. www.britarch.ac.uk/cba/rrcewa.html.
52 DCMS website www.culture.gov.uk.
53 The 1970 UNESCO Convention on the Means of Prohibiting and Preventing the Illicit Import, Export and Transfer of Ownership of Cultural Property attempts to restrict this illicit trade. It is supplemented by the 1995 Unidroit Convention on Stolen or Illegally Exported Cultural Objects. The UK is a signatory to the former but not the latter.

Bibliography

1 Cookson, N. *Archaeological Heritage Law* (Chichester: Barry Rose, 2000).
2 Hunter, J. and Ralston, I. (eds) *Archaeological Resource Management in the UK: an introduction* (Stroud: Sutton, 1993).
3 Pugh-Smith, J. and Samuels, J. *Archaeology in Law* (London: Sweet and Maxwell, 1996).
4 Renfrew, C. *Loot, Legitimacy and Ownership* (London: Duckworth, 2000).

5 Skeates, R. *Debating the Archaeological Heritage* (London, Duckworth, 2000).
6 Walker Tubb, K. (ed.) *Antiquities, Trade or Betrayed: Legal, Ethical and Conservation Issues* (London: Archetype 1995).

Websites.

Council for British Archaeology www.britarch.ac.uk.

Department for Culture, Media and Sport www.culture.gov.uk.

English Heritage www.english-heritage.org.uk.

Portable Antiquities Scheme www.finds.org.uk.

Reviewing Committee on the Export of Works of Art. www.britarch.ac.uk/cba/rrcewa.html.

12 Contesting the ideology of hyphens

Intellectual property, legal imperialism and the global music industry

Kwela Sabine Hermanns

This chapter takes a critical view of the Intellectual Property Rights (IPR) in relation to the global music industry. It argues that historical perspectives are invaluable for the analysis of the contemporary IPR system and music copyright. The intent is to expose the reductionist ideology behind the 'justificatory schemata of IPR'.[1] An examination of past and contemporary music industry rhetoric is to reveal its ideology as a continuing process of discourse formation(s), particularly around notions of so-called *piracy*, in an increasingly global context.[2] By contrast, non-Western conceptions of cultural and intellectual production are presented with a view to opening up the excluded spaces within IPR ideology.

By discussing the 'exclusion of the middle' in IPR history, rhetoric and enforcement, the chapter takes recourse to cultural theory, specifically applying contributions to the field from post-structuralism and deconstructivist theory in their respective attempts to expose and more fully understand the effects of various binary, juxta-positioned analytical traditions largely inherited from Enlightenment thought, as well as differing accounts of modernity. The chapter's approaches thus follow Foucauldian perspectives for analysing power relations, and Derrida's tacit thesis that 'the violent denial of difference is the secret to the history of the West'.[3] Given that this Western history has produced uneven power relations and economic dominance, the notion of difference – or indeed its denial – is central to providing a critical account of a globally expanding IPR system.

For example, the exclusion of difference can be brought to bear upon movements of intellectual artefacts through space; a movement that is often central to piracy claims and to actions taken in the name of fighting it and other forms of copyright infringement. Whilst the analysis may develop different foci depending on whether such transitions occur in the physical realm (CDs or DVDs travelling and appearing across 'porous' copyright borders) or in the digital environment (music moving as zero's and one's over the Internet), the question of whether travelling copyrights remain stable and pure categories in changing environments remains valid. In the endeavour to posit a thought-provoking problem at the centre of such a debate, the concept of *legal imperialism*[4] is suggested, and Actor-Network-Theory (ANT) is introduced into the socio-legal and political analysis of copyright.

Digital home and developing other

Several key challenges face the globalizing music industry. One is the fight against digital copyright infringement 'at home' in the mature music markets typically characterized by low physical sound-carrier piracy. Here, personal litigation against end users, illegal downloading, newly legal online music sales models, and case law emerging from recent legislation provide a rich field for analysis.[5] Another challenge is the exploitation of developing music territories often situated in what became known as the 'Third World' in the process of decolonization.[6] These non-Western markets possess higher piracy rates of between 25 and 50 per cent. There is also the group of so-called emerging music territories, chiefly in the former Eastern Bloc, whose transitions into capitalist market economies has opened up new opportunities for the music industry, despite obstacles to effective copyright infrastructures.[7] The chapter somewhat focuses on this particular challenge for the maintenance and expansion of the copyright system, which on a conceptual and practical level has produced highly institutionalized counter-structures.[8]

Much has in recent years been made of the increasing commodification of common property resources through the rapid growth of the global intellectual property rights system (IPR hereafter), of which copyright is one of three principal pillars.[9] IPR is arguably one of the most pressing issues within development debates in the twenty-first century.[10]

There are different types of piracy driven by different norms and values, which in turn create different effects. Domestic copying, for instance, which music copyright law has traditionally treated as 'acceptable' personal use and which some legislatures address via blank levies, needs to be distinguished from commercial reproductive piracy, which is seen as a legitimate target by the anti-piracy lobby. Such 'entrepreneurial piracy' aimed at replacing the 'real' artefact with a 'lesser' copy, it is argued, may lead to the collapse of indigenous markets.

Whilst the chapter deals mainly with forms of physical piracy, this is here examined at its core conceptual level in relation to ownership claims and concepts such as 'theft', 'legal' and 'illegal', and treated as a series of effects. The relationship of developing music territories with their Western counterparts, in terms of IP protection and enforcement, is at the heart of the inquiry, as is the possibility that informal economies may constitute responses to uneven development and power relations.

At home with what we own

Visitors to the World Intellectual Property Organization (WIPO) website in 2001 were greeted by this message:

> *To go home is to enter a place built and filled with human creativity and invention. {F}rom the objects and appliances we use for everyday life; the can opener, the refrigerator, the telephone, to the music, the books, the paintings, and family photographs that make us smile; everything with which we live is the product of human creativity. These things are creations of the human mind –* **intellectual property.** *They are with us every day of our lives, from dawn to dusk, even as we sleep. They may, like a soft mattress, put us at ease; they may, like an alarm clock, annoy us. They may make us dream, a novel, a symphony, a film, and make us think. Or they may do the thinking for us, a software program, a calculator, a computer. If we at times take them for granted, we are often times amazed. We are always enriched.*[11]

Besides a somewhat romantic, soft-focus vision of twenty-first century human-machine cohabitation, what is striking about this representation of people's relationships with everyday objects and artefacts is the swiftness with which the text equates the creativity that inhabits them (or which they inhabit?) with the notion of 'property'.[12] Adorno and Horkheimer's famous creation of the term 'culture industry' critically combined two previously separate spheres of human activity. The ideology of intellectual property brings into close eulogistic relation two similarly distinct concepts from the socio-material world: creativity and property.[13] Note how the WIPO text uses the hyphen to translate *creations of the human mind* in one fell swoop into – (hyphen) *intellectual property.* Full stop. The hyphen is the only mediation offered, and indeed, it is the only mediation required to get the message across.

Intellectual property has become a naturalized concept, the black-boxed bedfellow of creative endeavour. This historical and rhetorical naturalization found its most recent logical conclusion in the watershed Agreement on Trade Related Aspects of Intellectual Property Rights (TRIPs), under which all creativity or knowledge is rendered into property and 'someone must own it'.[14]

That said, the universalized black-box of copyright has in recent years come under intense scrutiny through the proliferation of file-sharing services in the digital domain. Napster reawakened the music industry to its home-taping nightmares from the 1970s, with users apparently conspiring in acts of civil disobedience.[15] Many saw in it the embrace of a gift economy versus the electronic marketplace on the Internet. It was even suggested that Napster and its various (re)incarnations might spell the sacrifice of the music industry on the altar of global capitalism, and that copyright would either organically disappear as an outmoded, unsustainable regime, or radically be abolished.[16]

Two critical observations are appropriate. One is that, according to the Actor-Network-Theorist John Law, we do 'occasionally [. . .] find ourselves watching [. . .] as an order comes crashing down. Organizations or systems which we had always taken for granted [. . .] are swallowed up [and] disappear from view. These dangerous moments offer more than political promise.'[17] In other words, revolutionary potential does seem to be there, somewhere; and the breakdown of the system is a real danger to the established music industry.[18] The second observation is that, despite the celebrated political promise of the Internet and Napster, the revolution has not actually happened. On the contrary, the music industry has fought a number of successful court cases, resulting in Napster's closure and consequent courting by a major record company. File-sharing has since continued in alternative sites,[19] although the music industry is gradually experimenting with legitimate online music selling models.[20] The utopia of the gift economy, it appears, is set to reach its inevitable destination, the marketplace.[21] Some challenging developments include Technological Protection Measures (TPMs) and 'online contracts', which may force legitimate users to first break the law in order to access or 'play' material, and which have also led to the place-shifting versus space-shifting debates.[22] The recent US Digital Millennium Copyright Act seeks to address intermediate liability in relation to Internet Service Providers (ISPs), examples of which are the Verizon, Napster, Aimster and Grokster rulings.[23]

Why is the music industry relatively successful in overcoming and colonizing sites of resistance? To address this question, we turn to the history of IPR development, the philosophy of copyright law, and to the enduring justifications for their ideological and practical enforcement.

Discourses of rights and wrongs

There can be little doubt that the ideology around ownership and commodification of cultural and intellectual production has been universalized in the form of various discourses, as the WIPO quote illustrates. Following Foucault, a discourse consists of a series of events whose basic unit is the statement, which in turn forms relationships with other statements. In the field of law these 'establish the conditions for the truth upon which [the law] arbitrates and makes judgements'; however, formations of discourse, like Althusser's manifest and latent texts, 'are defined as much by what lies outside of them as what lies within'.[24] Such discernment renders discursive 'blackboxing' interceptable and contestable; it can be ruptured open, as the impact of file-sharing has shown. The question of whether such ruptures are conscious acts of resistance or, rather, symptoms of indifference by a generation of computer literates who simply do not respect copyright logic is interesting. An effect is nevertheless the actualization of a breakdown in an otherwise and hitherto naturalized system. Blackboxing or *punctualization*, to use an Actor-Network-Theory term, 'works' by making heterogeneous networks of interacting socio-technical materials come to appear as single and stable blocks until their complexities virtually disappear from view.[25] It is the (temporary) effect of a series of *translations*. In the punctualization of 'copyright', 'copyright' may be taken as a straightforward concept until something interferes with it; and 'the music industry' may simply be this until copyright infringements present 'the music industry' as the complex network of actants and actors that it actually is, consisting of many points and parts with differing agenda, interests, messages – in short – *programs* to be translated via *ordering strategies*.

How, then, do punctualizations come about, despite the fact they are forever contested? Put differently, how can power relations be explained and are they causes or effects?[26]

In the case of the music industry, ordering strategies come to light within the ideology of rights discourses. Copyright prevents the reproduction of literary and artistic works without the permission of the creator or owner of the copyright, which may have been licensed to another party.[27] It is the expression of the idea that is legally protected in the form of a recording, for example, rather than the idea itself.

Yet a critical analysis of the histories of these discourses destabilizes the very categories upon which they rely, operate, and continue to survive and thrive. Copyright and authors rights, or IPR generally, have not always existed, but are historically, socio-politically, and philosophically constructed.[28] What is more, these contingent constructions, or indeed their absence, did vary from one 'copyright geography' to another.[29]

In ancient times, cultural production unfolded in the context of collaboration and, at best, attribution. Although in Greece and Rome notions of authorship did exist, oral cultures did not lend themselves to exact fixation of texts, and Greek poets, for instance, worked towards collective achievement as part of a school, guild or group.[30] In India, where no copyright developed, the message was considered more important than the messenger; while the oral culture of Bali saw art as collective endeavour.[31] During the Middle Ages, Christian paternalism forbade the very notions of unique individual achievement. Concepts of individual cultural ownership and authorship distinctly developed within the historical context of Western countries, and this is routinely explained by the combined effects of the printing press, the rise of Neo-classicism, Romanticism, and capitalism.[32]

In Anglo-American law tradition John Locke's labour theory of property lay the foundations for the modern conceptions of creative ownership.[33] The rationale of his 1690 labour theory of property can today be traced directly to the principles of the World Trade Organization's patents practices. Conversely, Friedrich Hegel's self-developmental theory paved the way for continental legal tradition in which the work of art is seen as inalienable from the author-as-genius.[34] With the Enlightenment project, industrialization and the capitalist organization of Western socio-economic relations, these philosophical perspectives gained systematic expression in national and international law. From the first authors' society, French SACEM in 1850,[35] to the 1886 Berne Convention and its numerous extensions covering new technological platforms, and finally to TRIPs, the international music industry has a strong track record of protecting the interests of rights owners and authors. However, legal-philosophic differences remain even in the developed world. The US Constitutional Convention of 1787 grants copyright with the welfare of the public in mind; this public is presumed to benefit from 'promoting the progress of science and useful art'.[36] Continental law privileges authors' rights by protecting the intrinsic human right of individual creators in their own works.[37] These respective emphases reflect the legal variations between Common Law countries led by the US and the Civil Law tradition of Continental Europe with its focus on the 'moral right'.[38]

In the face of challenges to these legal philosophies and their interpretations, the IPR regime draws upon historical 'origins' and renders the discourses and ideologies which it helped to shape as explicitly universal and unquestionable, seeking to stabilize them time and again. Smiers' argument against the naturalization of intellectual ownership draws on intertextuality debates: '[O]riginality is a misleading and romantic concept', not least because the author's sources which include language, images, tonality, rhythms, colours, movements, meanings, humour and so on – [. . .] belong to our common cultural and intellectual domain.'[39] This is supported by May's analysis that only ever the latest contribution to intellectual production is legally protected and commercially rewarded, increasing private commodification to the detriment of the public domain.[40] James Boyle asks: 'How does one break the grip of a rhetoric of entitlement that systematically obscures and undervalues the contributions of one part of the population and magnifies those of another [. . .]?'[41]

In music, this is particularly problematic with regards to the appropriational techniques in the creation of 'world music', where '[s]ources become a "commons" whose exploitation is justified or obscured by an author theory'[42] and where the first person to fixate a folk song becomes its author.[43] When taking a wider perspective on IPR by including patents and trademarks, there are other alarming examples of the private ownership of knowledge and common property resources. These include the patenting of seeds by transnational corporations and increasing attempts by employers to own employees' innovations. Smiers argues that 'commercial enterprises [should] pay the public domain because they are using elements of the common cultural heritage!'[44] MacDonalds have registered 131 trademarks on phrases ranging from 'You deserve a break today' to 'We love to see you smile',[45] and in the US there were attempts to prevent girls scouts from campsite 'public performances' of copyrighted songs.[46] The IPR system and its rhetoric of 'theft' and 'illegal use' has become a blackbox. It has become so punctualized that its complexities and weaknesses are only made visible when parts of it break down or are (un)consciously contested, through various forms of piracy, for instance.

Excluding the middle/denying hybridity

The critiques made of IPR ideology and music copyright rhetoric range from the practical-realist to arguments around creativity, and from the deconstruction of 'authorship' to philosophical inquiry.[47] Porter undertakes an elegant examination of the 'uncritical adoption of old-fashioned legal concepts for [new technologies in the 20th century]'.[48] He analyses the foundations of copyright in relation to semiotic language systems' representational interplay of langue, parole, referent, signifier and signified.[49] Porter argues that the new sign systems brought about by technological advance are, in semiotic terms, 'speech acts without a language system, a series of *paroles* without a *langue*' and that, in the attempt to extend the reach of copyright to cover these innovations, 'the legislators have ducked the intellectual challenges which faced them'.[50] This, in turn, blurs the division between idea and expression and fails to provide 'any rationale which would not equally justify copyright protection for the tangible expression of any and all original ideas'. As a result, copyright developments benefit investors rather than authors or the public.[51] Practical-realist approaches to IPR criticism point to the internal contradictions implicit in copyright ideology. They frequently address the economic-cultural axis and include direct attacks on record companies by artists.[52] Other voices evoke the industry's flawed argument that economies of scale and global exploitation of rights are necessary to ensure the continuous re-investment of profits into newly emerging talent.[53] Given that most musicians operate variously in community, voluntary or amateur settings, and that about 10 per cent of royalty collection society members receive 90 per cent of revenues,[54] the question arises of just who benefits from the growing significance that music industries play as part of the cultural and creative industries in mature territories.

A key argument in justifying IPR is the popular belief that without potential economic and personal rewards, artists will cease, either to make art, or to strive for excellence. Competition is healthy, the argument goes, and in its report, *Competition Policy and Intellectual Property Rights* the Organization for Economic Cooperation and Development states:

> *Intellectual property rights are designed to promote the creation of innovations and thus to promote economic advance and consumer welfare. This occurs by giving the innovator an exclusive legal right to the economic exploitation of his innovation for a period of time; the reaping of profits serves both to reward the innovator for his investment and to induce others to strive to innovate [. . .] property rights, of course, are the cornerstone of any efficient market economy.*[55]

Not only do cultural producers overwhelmingly pursue their artistic endeavours outside the commercial marketplace, in part because the marketplace tends to embrace and buy formulaic products seen to possess calculable commercial potential, thus functioning as a hegemonic gate-keeper.[56] Also, IPR justifications in the name of 'excellence' entirely neglect the possibility that copyright actually reduces the availability of resources for artistic creations and, therefore, limits the freedom and scope to create what may be considered 'innovative' or 'authentic' cultural products.[57] Kretschmer points to the 'thriving commerce in markets presently beyond the effective reach of IPR', such as India's music and film industries.[58]

May further illuminates these themes by identifying the key perspectives mobilized to make durable the institution of intellectual property.[59] These include the 'instrumental' and 'self-developmental' justifications of property. The first follows Lockean assertions of the value-adding effect of mixing labour and nature, where individuals possess property in their own endeavours and thus 'the reward for utilizing this exertion to add value is ownership of the result'.[60] In turn, these endeavours are only encouraged by the ownership of the product. At the centre of Lockean thought is both the ownership of effort and the alienability of their product.[61] In relation to Locke's fundamental assumption that labour is expended for economic rewards, Bettig writes: '[F]rom our historical analysis we see that throughout most of human history there existed no concept of intellectual property rights. Nevertheless, humans still produced technological and cultural artefacts'.[62]

The second perspective follows the work of Hegel, for whom an individual's personality is expressed in the fruits of his mastery over nature and his freedom, and 'ownership protects the individual from the "unreasonable" rights or interests of others in society, and from state intervention'.[63] In contrast to Lockean theory of property, Hegel's perspective privileges possession over labour and emphasizes the self and spirit as the main motivators for human expression.[64] Both these influential theories of property have had lasting effects on the development of Western IPR ideology, but both possess flaws which render them, at best, *lacking*.

The IPR regime's ideology both masks and exposes such absences. Its insistence on distinctions between private and public ownership, its oppositional positioning of 'legal' and 'illegal' use, its naturalized delineation of 'property' against other claimants, and the resulting rationale of various versions of 'them' versus 'us', all reveal a fundamental reliance on classical Western philosophical thought around Aristotlean logic of identity.

The three constituent parts in the logic of identity posit that:

1   whatever is, is;
2   nothing can both be and not be;
3   everything must either be or not be.

They express the laws of identity, contradiction, and excluded middle.[65] The logic of identity produces thought systems in the tradition of diacronicity, in which apparently stable, pure, and opposing categories are used and applied as mutually exclusive. These categories are reductionist. In the work of Derrida and other theorists, the space of the excluded middle has been explored and (the validity of) its existence argued. Actor-Network-Theory sometimes refers to this space as *hybridity*.

For the critic or theorist of IPR and music copyright, and of the ownership of culture generally, the implications of opening up the logic of identity to the middle, hybridity, and syncronicity it denies are significant. The ideology and rhetoric of the globalizing music industry prescribes that a piece of music, or intellectual artefact, in its expression in physical or digital formats must always be either subject to copyright protection, or part of the public domain. However, this is a deterministic treatment of the fruits of cultural labour and excludes from vision and practice many historical, philosophical, socio-cultural *differences*. Nevertheless, these differences both did and continue to exist, albeit that their existence is increasingly threatened within contemporary legal structures. Jamaica only formally introduced copyright in 1991, while in China, the birthplace of printing, copyright did not exist until the late twentieth century (Jackson 2002: 417).[66] Islamic intellectual production historically treated information as moral and ethical imperative, rather than commodities, and in Asia the copying of works was considered an *honour* by authors and artists.[67,68] Western IPR concepts are 'a foreign notion in many parts of the world',[69] and Kretschmer's profound observation is: 'If a country has no copyright protection there is nothing illegal in disseminating information wherever it comes from'.[70] In (post?)modernity or late capitalism, however, the notion of (legislative) *difference* is disappearing fast, or is being rendered into the blackbox of *piracy*. As such, IPR ideology forms part of the coercive agenda of neo-liberal policies and their accompanying program of globalism.

Legal imperialism and the globalizing music industry

IPR is part of the 'gospel of modern economic growth'[71],and so is the music industry in relation to free-trade ideology and neo-liberal economic policies, complete with deregulation, global concentration, corporate integration, and technological change.[72] Popular music debates reflect various schools of thought around globalization, particularly within the ongoing tussles over cultural exemptionalism, government intervention, and subsidies of local industries and cultures.[73] In his analysis of the entertainment industries, Jameson views globalization as a communicational concept which both obscures and transmits cultural and economic meaning.[74] He is concerned about the rhetoric of free market and the worldwide US-led standardization of culture which, aided by agreements like TRIPs and the North American Free Trade Agreement (NAFTA) and the drive for economic expansion, undermine politics of cultural subsidy and quota in non-Western parts of the world:

> [The] freedom of ideas is important because the ideas are private property and designed to be sold in great and profitable quantities [. . .] my

freedom results in the destruction of other people's national culture industries [. . .] the new freer market emphatically does not result in an increase in your competitor's business as well.[75]

Negus points out that since the mid-1980s music companies have engaged in consolidation and globalization strategies through geographical expansion 'in search of markets outside of their North American and European national bases [. . .]. Hence, the world markets for popular music have been constructed to provide a series of opportunities for British and American artists across the globe'.[76] The implication is that 'not everyone is invited to the party'.[77] Is attendance at the party desirable? Territories coerced into opening up their borders to Western products and investment frequently find that the resulting economic and cultural effects are problematic and ambiguous.[78] The argument is that WTO has removed countries' ability to treat IPR protection and enforcement as a domestic issue; instead, they have to align themselves with Western laws 'without much sign of the benefits claimed for it',[79] and 'TRIPs [. . .] enhances the enforcement of rights of transnational corporations [and] reduces or eliminates the capacity of the nation-state to regulate or attack such monopolies.'[80] Rights issues express political and economic interests rather than moral considerations.[81] Similarly, Lovering argues that Western companies' targeting of markets overseas result in legal structures becoming sensitive issues, and the primary concern is with 'putting in place regulatory systems so that [they] can be sure they will get their dues', despite different economic contexts: 'The world's poor do not even buy cheap CDs.'[82] This perspective evokes Wallerstein's World Systems Theory in suggesting that the reorganization of the leading music companies concentrates resources 'in a select group of strategically placed world centres'.[83] Doubts therefore persist over the so-called level-playing field: 'One challenge will be to maintain the balance between interests of countries exporting copyright and those of countries that import it, especially in the developing world'.[84]

Tensions over who benefits from increased (global) trade revealed themselves as early as 1883 when music trade magazines reported on the difficult negotiations over international IPR interest, leading up to the BERNE Convention three years later:[85]

> [A] book published in England can be re-published by someone in America (and vice versa) without authors receiving a farthing. England would agree to a copyright treaty to solve this tomorrow if America were willing, but America is not [. . .]. The balance of exchange is all in her favour. Meanness, we think, can hardly go farther, or sink deeper.[86]

Back catalogue in the form of rights to the exploitation of intellectual property remains the principal economic asset of the music industry,[87] and power relations reveal(ed) themselves within the differing degrees of intellectual commodities a given territory controls, and their perceived commercial potential: 'United States publishing interests were antagonistic to attempts to enforce payment to foreign authors when the US itself had little copyright material for export'.[88] Only from the 1890s, when US catalogue gained popularity abroad, did the US begin to veer from its previous position that 'royalty payments would be a "tax on knowledge" and would cause a balance of payments deficit in the cultural field'.[89] Laing rightly goes on to assert that 'such arguments have been deployed in more recent times by governments of Asian and African countries against the demands of US copyright interests for extended protection for US works'.[90] Debates over the (il)legitimacy of enforcing universalized normative conceptions and infrastructures for global IPR management are further advanced through the illumination of discourses on piracy. Smiers points out ironically: '[W]hereas the origins of industrial development are intrinsically related to the act of widespread copying, the Western world now seems to be saying to the developing world that they cannot do the same'.[91] It produces the question of whether the globalizing music industry is engaging, by means of IPR, in neo-imperialist strategies fundamentally driven by the exportation of laws, and whether it is therefore legitimate to posit the notion of *legal* imperialism, a legislature led *recolonization?*

The somewhat 'old-fashioned or eccentric notion of cultural imperialism'[92] has historically been theorized through a set of proposed characteristics and effects which are useful to illuminate the proposed notion of *legal* imperialism. *Legal* is here chosen over its associated adjective, *legislative*, to allow a closer positioning with related theorizations of imperialism.[93] Cultural imperialism denotes the domination and invasion of local cultures through the political and economic subjugation of non-Western parts of the world,[94] territorial annexation and its resulting dependency,[95] and the loss to varying degrees of national sovereignty for regulating business activities.[96] While prone to conspiracy theories, cultural imperialism has been seen by some commentators to be all pervasive, the backbone of modern industrial forces in which cultural dominance is increased and achieved through the monetary or resource transfer from dominated to dominating groups.[97] In short, it has replaced former versions of territorial imperialism by the old colonial powers. Vandana Shiva, in *The Second Coming of Columbus*, both supports this reading and provides an analytical link to twenty-first century imperialist strategies based on legal discourse and enforcement. Describing colonial acts of piracy as rendered into divine will by charters and patents, she argues that

> [F]ive hundred years after Columbus, a more secular version of [. . .] colonization continues [. . .] The Papal Bull has been replaced by the GATT treaty [. . .] The duty to incorporate savages into Christianity has been replaced by the duty to incorporate local and national economies into the global marketplace, and to incorporate non-Western systems of

knowledge into the reductionism of commercialized Western science and technology [. . .] The creation of property through piracy of others' wealth remains the same.[98]

Legal imperialist IPR harmonization and enforcement strategies rely on reductionist rhetoric and ideology, on coercive integration of those with diminished *actual* bargaining power into a Western-led and defined global regime, and on commodification and exploitation of the former's cultural and economic resources. *Legal* imperialism would thus correlate to a definition of imperialism as 'seeking to subordinate or delegitimate other approaches'.[99] In the process, local, national, and historical differences and needs are increasingly denied existence through legal expression within this regime. Through legal discourses, the continuing effects of these differences are then punctualized as piratical acts committed by the 'developing other', whose development is in effect encouraged only in narrow and prescriptive terms. And whilst the adverse effects of so-called cultural imperialism can at least in part be rescued through (sub)cultural readings of loci of agency, resistances to legal imperialism are reduced to, albeit not deactivated by, deterministic narratives of 'piracy'.

Punctualized piracy

In the decade from 1991 to 2000 the value of the global recording industry rose by nearly 20 per cent. The global retail value of sound recordings was $33.6 billion in 2001, and North America's share in this was at 40 per cent.[100] During the same period the sale of local music repertoire saw a significant increase in most territories, rising from 58 per cent in 1991 to 68 per cent in 2000.[101] Simultaneous with the success of domestic and international music sales, however, is the acceleration of (CD) piracy. According to the International Federation of Phonographic Industries, in 2000 over one in three music recordings sold worldwide was pirate product. IFPI's claims are strikingly similar in tone to WIPO rhetoric:

> *Music [. . .] has become a part of the fabric of our lives. We listen to recorded music at home, in our cars, at work [. . .] Piracy stunts the growth of the information-based economy, erodes innovation and cultural creativity and has increasingly impacted on the reputations of countries that have failed to protect intellectual property rights.*[102]

Smiers notes how Western advocates for stronger copyright laws 'always present the argument that it is in the self-interest of non-Western countries to fight piracy', despite many an indication that piracy can have desired effects on economies,[103] and a salient point here is whether said piracy is of indigenous or imperial product.

Any statistics which underpin these claims must generally be viewed with care, of course,[104] and Actor-Network-Theory treats such data as agency possessing actors and effects. Negus observes the limitations in official recording industry sales figures due to the fact that they 'prioritize individual purchases of legally manufactured products', failing to account for 'the way in which recordings are produced and distributed through unofficial channels such as [...] unauthorized manufacture'.[105] Drawing on Fabbri's analysis of the Italian music industry, Negus addresses what this text posits as the music industry's reductionist view of these activities as *purely* piracy, by developing the argument that 'illegal' dissemination of music may also be seen as contributing to the musical economy in a given market.[106] Discussing the music industry also, May argues 'the representation of piracy as theft is an attempt to establish a particular reading of intellectual property',[107] and Godwin says copyright industries seek to 'build a consensus that copyright infringement is morally identical to theft'.[108] In the light of an industry's global fight against a myriad of local, sociocultural, and economic activities punctualized into 'piracy', Chanan observed that this same industry 'placed on the market devices that invite people to transgress the laws on which the market operates'.[109]

TRIPs into 'other' territories

Piracy acts may variably express 'active' acts of resistance in the contemporary IPR regime, or as embedded responses and effects which arise in differing legal-geographic and economic-cultural contexts and conditions; and there is much opportunity for research into the attitudes to piracy by the pirates and the consumers of pirated material themselves. A recent study into music on the Internet examined illegal downloading and the attitudes to 'theft' by the perpetrators of these copyright infringements; thus highlighting the potential for fuelling debates over what the music industry is excluding from discussion, namely, why piracy exists and what it means or represents to its perpetrators.[110] In the digital piracy domain, some voices are beginning to shift the focus from authors' and rights owners' interests towards consumer attitudes – a reorientation that may create potentially useful insights for the music industry in persuading consumers to pay for music on the Internet.[111] A similar approach is needed for understanding and appropriately addressing piracy in under-developed territories where Internet penetration remains low, but will inevitably become an issue in the future.

Whether the ideology and enforcement of IPR comes under scrutiny and attack from intertextuality and post-structuralist schools of thought,[112] or from perspectives along the cultural-economic axes,[113] the IPR critic faces tough choices and obstacles in imagining possible alternatives to the current regime, such as May's call for an 'Environmentalism of the Net',[114] and Smiers' notion of an 'IPR-NGO' or 'abolition of copyright'.[115] In their analysis of music royalty collecting societies, they also conclude that 'the present structure of music copyright is likely to collapse'.[116] Kretschmer asserts that '[c]opyright cannot be reformed from within' and calls for a three-tier copyright system.[117] Overwhelmingly, this criticism is received with a sense of pitying disbelief by the inhabitants of an age characterized by the loss of utopia and an overwhelming focus on the pragmatism of Third Way politics.[118]

Although Kretschmer's earlier argument regarding the autonomy of non-Western legal copyright geographies is valid in theory, increasingly it does not hold in practice. As part of the wider global agenda for the strengthening of free trade and neo-liberal economic policies, the 1993 Uruguay round of the GATT negotiations included IPR in the international trade regime for the first time.[119] TRIPs was signed by more than one hundred states in 1994 and had two key objectives: the global harmonization of IPR across all territories, whose legislative accordance with TRIPs requirements varied depending on development status, and the provision of effective enforcement mechanisms.[120,121] Under TRIPs, which is administered by WTO, members are required to comply with the Berne Convention. The logic behind TRIPs was to eradicate international piracy and to do so with a common set of minimum protection 'at source', rather than applying hindsight to circulation.[122] But it can also be read as a global auction, the 'rather unrestricted possibility to buy rights on knowledge and creativity everywhere in the world in order to exploit those rights', the result of which concentrates the world's sum total of creativity in less than a dozen multinationals.[123] Bettig argues that TRIPs 'ultimately prohibits less industrialized nations from applying intellectual property laws so as to foster technological and economic development'.[124] Developing states showed resistance during the negotiations, arguing TRIPs forced them into a universalized discourse of knowledge as property, effectively prohibiting alternative conceptions of valuing knowledge.[125] According to WTO rhetoric, these negotiations unfold on a level-playing field, and while it is true that WTO operates on a one-country-one-vote basis, the agenda to be voted upon tend to be set by the industrially advanced countries (IACs). In 1997, the attempt to put copyright protection of folklore on the WTO agenda in Geneva failed. American and British delegates disagreed since 'the world's biggest entertainment industries are found in their countries'.[126] The settlement of IPR is effectively based on (unequal) bargaining power (Kretschmer *et al.* 1999: 180).[127] Chang (2000) has publicly called for the abolition of TRIPs, or for radical changes to it.[128] One problematic is the fact that TRIPs works against non-Western countries' interests by weakening control over their domestic markets; however, non-participation in the global IPR system can lead to significant trade and other sanctions.

The North American Free Trade Agreement (NAFTA) also reflects the restrictions placed on developing markets in taking measures to protect and account for local or national interests along the very lines of US interests some 130 years ago. NAFTA was arguably a blueprint, or testing ground, for TRIPs, and in resolving IPR disputes between the US and México, raised the profile of international intellectual property protection.[129] Like TRIPs would do shortly afterwards and on a global scale, NAFTA introduced effective enforcement mechanisms in the realm of IPR, allowing violations to be punished by retaliation in areas other than where the trade dispute occurs.[130]

Incidentally, the Méxican music market, along with China, lends itself to IPR research on account of its unique characteristics.[131] It is the only non-Western music market in the ten most successful industries for the sale of recorded music.[132] Simultaneously, it has an estimated piracy rate of over 50 per cent. At the time of writing, México's particular constellation as a highly piratical yet highly successful market and member of NAFTA singles it out as a 'copyright geography' for study in relation to the themes developed here. What is more, its accession to NAFTA impacted on other territories, such as the Caribbeans.[133] But even before NAFTA, the Recording Industry Association of America (RIAA) lobbied for the revision of copyright law in México, with a view to earning record companies some $75 million a year.[134] At the same time, local Méxican musicians are said to be facing difficulty signing contracts with international record companies due to piracy.[135] In 2001, three Méxican independent record companies submitted data to the IFPI, by whom they are described 'big players'. Jones elaborates that under NAFTA generally, 'record companies are quite the winners' and the perceived threat from piracy explains the music industry's focus on México during the negotiations since it 'represents both an untapped market and a site of piracy, and consequently NAFTA would appear to the RIAA as the stone that will kill [the two] birds' of protection and exploitation and 'its current strategy seems to be one of establishing similar legal structures in other areas of the world it wishes to exploit'.[136] More importantly, both TRIPs and NAFTA provide the dominant IPR regime with effective dispute-settlement procedures via trading sanctions.

Against the backdrop of Latin America's overall trend of falling domestic repertoire *and* slightly falling major record companies market share,[137,138] Jameson's discussion of the work by Canclini and Yudice on 'the liberating effects of commercial mass culture [. . .] with special emphasis in the Latin American areas' reveals the tensions within globalization theories. He views the claim that local music performs more strongly than imported North American product and is invested into by transnationals as the exception to the rule.[139] Whether economic and cultural evaluations of agreements like NAFTA and TRIPs take celebratory or critical views, it does seem to be the case that the contemporary settlement of IPR fails to take into account effectively, or reflect fully, the myriad historical, political, and socio-economic differences and contexts within different 'copyright-geographies'. The argument holds that the 'efforts towards the establishment of an effective regime for the protection of IPRs was aimed at furthering the interest of the western industries and not those of the developing countries'.[140] And as in conception, so in practice: A 2000 study into musical trade between developed market economies (DMEC) and the developing world showed a six-fold rise in exports of recorded music by DMEC into developing territories, compared with only a five-fold increase of imports from developing countries into DMEC.[141]

Travelling copyrights

The claims I have made over intellectual property in relation to the music industry in this chapter are as follows.

1   The music industry's core assets are intellectual property rights whose tenacity and purity it promotes through the use of ideology on an increasingly global scale.
2   The rhetoric and rationale underpinning this ideology are historically constructed and reductionist, denying hybrid spaces and excluding alternatives via specific rights discourses.
3   The expansion of IPR ideology into non-Western or developing 'copyright geographies' unfolds within wider globalization processes and is aided by legal texts such as TRIPs.
4   This expansionist export of legal conceptions and infrastructures from the 'home' to the 'other' constitutes a form of *legal imperialism* as part of wider neo-liberal agenda and policies; it is coercive and excludes difference.
5   The exclusion of difference is partly pursued through the global fight against punctualized piracy.
6   There exist resistances to the ideology and global enforcement of IPR, and these sites may be both actively construed *and* effects of the exclusion of difference.
7   All of these processes must be seen in the context of power relations which the former reflect, help construct, make durable, and contest.

The core argument, then, is that different actors in the music industry have different interests depending on where and how they are situated. These varying interests produce programs in need of translation. For example, the author's or rights owner's program is the protection of an 'original' idea via its expression in physical or informational form by preventing others from copying it and securing exclusive access to the rights over its licensing and use. Specific loci of interest may vary here from concerns with moral rights to maximum economic exploitation. In every case, the program quite simply is, 'Do not copy, do not steal, do not use without authorization'.

The statement might be reinforced with a myriad of innovations, ranging from printed copyright statements on sound-carriers to Anti-Piracy-Unit publications, and messages disseminated via media channels as discourses. But people do infringe copyrights. They engage in home taping; they copy a

CD for a friend; they make boot-leggings and counterfeits; and they download music from the Internet without paying for it. With the program's failure to translate successfully, or in the presence of anti-programs, anti-anti-programs may be presented through the use of encryption and water-marking techniques, the introduction of tape levy, and via raids and court cases. As we have seen, controversial new technological measures such as TPMs threaten to translate the message in such a way that legal access may have to be obtained by illegally circumventing such protection devices. This, again, is a process of translation along a network of heterogeneous interacting actors and actants, both social and technical. At all the various parts of this socio-technical network different actors must keep doing their respective jobs, seeking to stabilize the network time and again in the face of interceptions, contestations, and anti-programs. In this network, every part is an actor-as-effect, making both durable and contested the interplay of human and non-human elements. In its analysis of power relations ANT unites the social and the technical into *the-social-and-the-technical*[142] and this activates the hybrid spaces between ostensibly stable and pure categories. 'The social' versus 'the technical', 'object' versus 'subject', 'legal' versus 'illegal' are opened up to their impurities, their 'lacking', their being hybrid.

Marianne de Laet's study of travelling patents, which in part draws on ANT, illuminates this problematic. In the following I will suggest that its method of inquiry allows for a useful application to copyright also, illuminating the various strands of arguments made in this chapter so far.

Like patents, copyrights *do* various things. They *protect* creative effort, they *describe* this creativity and its boundaries and specificities, they *contain* exact information about what is being protected, and they *confer* a property right. Like patents, copyrights *hold* the creativity to which this right corresponds.

De Laet argues that patent rights are a series of representations. They represent subjects (the patentee), objects (the patent), and knowledge (the technical innovation, the invention 'held' by the patent). Similarly, but not identically, copyrights *represent* authors and rights owners (subjects), the fixated expression of an idea (objects), and creativity (the encoded creative effort).[143] At basic level, both knowledge (in patents) and creativity (in copyrights) are *information*. Where their similarities slightly diverge is at the point where one might become discerning about the type of information, or even the information's idiosyncratic properties or *potentialities* which this third component in each series of representation encodes, and determining this is also linked somewhat to the notion of purpose. In the case of patents, the knowledge represented is transferable and exploitable and is crucially seen to possess novelty, non-obviousness, and usefulness as the three criteria for the granting of a patent. Although copyrights arguably also embody degrees of knowledges (of compositional technique, of software programs, of knowing how to operate a tape recorder, of being literate), it is here the notion of creativity that is central to the object. This difference is also reflected in the fact that one has to apply to register a patent. By contrast, copyright in an 'original' piece of intellectual work simply exists, and one only has to prove authorship through the expression of the idea in fixated form.[144] Where patents and copyrights as pure information further diverge is in the notion of 'usefulness'. Copyrights do not have to be useful, although we know that they are. Where industrial innovations as patents have an instant economic application and purpose, copyrights do not. However, as the discussion of the globalizing music industry has shown, there can be no doubt about copyright's commercial value, transferability, and exploitability. In the era of economic rights and TRIPs, both patents and copyrights, as series of representations of subjects, objects, and knowledge/creativity, can be equated in the context of their ownership and control value for commercial exploitation. It is on these grounds that I propose the application of Laet's analytical approach to the analysis of travelling patents to copyrights.

Like the way in which patents are used and viewed can differ, even within a 'harmonized patents order and standard definition of the patent',[145] so conceptions and organizations of copyrights diverge in what was previously posited as different 'copyright geographies'. We have seen this from a historical perspective, and we continue to observe it in the contemporary context of copyright. Collins refers to the harmonized copyright order as resting on 'assumptions that a specific art-work or intellectual idea is created by a single or restricted number of individuals who are therefore easily identifiable and that older forms rooted in pre-industrial peasant society (i.e. folklore) can be regarded as public property as their authors are unidentifiable and anonymous'.[146] Collins here points to the problems of 'folkloric-copyright' in Ghanaian folk culture, which he posits as relevant to other Third World countries, too.[147] In the case of Japan, which had no concept of 'rights' before Westernization, difference also continues to persist despite the idea of 'rights' being transplanted to Japan. Mitsui argues that '[n]o matter how convincing the Western conception of individualism is [. . .], traditional collectivism has maintained a resolute persistence in Japan' and that 'not only the people in the East but also those in the West should be aware that the peculiar circumstance of Japan is to be shared in the course of time'.[148] The 'Iron Cage'[149] of the globalizing IPR system continues to grapple with attitudes, perceptions, traditions, conceptions and practices that are not automatically absorbed by and changed through the signing of an international convention and by the introduction of its directives into national laws.

In her analysis of travelling patents, Laet de illuminates this difficulty further by pointing to the tensions between promoting the patent as *protector of rights* compared to *source of information*. Depending on differing interests and emphases, patents can therefore mean different things in different places. Their nature and performance can shift and they are complex representations.[150] For intellectual artifacts to move through space and remain one and the same thing always, they have to be stable and possess tenacity. Upon closer inspection this is clearly not the case. Travelling patents and copyrights are met with different conditions for their existence, for their performativity and for the role they play in different places. The IPR system can be understood as a complex series of network effects brought about by, and continuing to bring about, processes that seek to make durable tenacities that are, in turn, forever contested and intercepted.

Let us consider this network more closely. Depending on who, where and what an actor is within the network, interests and agencies will differ. For the author of a copyright, the creativity represented by it is likely to remain stable. From my point of view, my composition is always my composition, no matter where it travels. The owner of my copyright, to whom I have assigned the rights to commercial exploitation of my creative labour, in turn attaches a particular value to that same composition, and this value, again, will ideally not change during transportation. By the time the composition reaches potential consumers, they will all consume the same thing, the same bits of information which encode and represent my composition. Transport does not compromise copyrights 'for their words [or sounds] do remain the same no matter who reads [or hears] them, or where, or when' and 'it should not matter what their vehicle [. . .] it should not make a difference whether they travel on paper, on CD-ROM, or through the Internet'.[151]

The normative assumptions on which my Western reading of the author's, rights owner's, and consumer's interests and situatedness within the network rests, are reductionist and reflect the IPR system's design of-and-for tenacity. For my composition and its vehicle, the sound-carrier, can indeed be different things in different places. Post-structuralist theory has convincingly argued that to create is 'to give to do',[152] and in the digital domain it is increasingly possible for my composition to be altered by others. Actants in the network *do* different things to and with a sound-carrier, and they do it in different places. What actors and actants do with a sound-carrier, and how they do it, is affected by translations, transportation and translocation. The travelling soundcarrier is changed by contexts of socio-political, cultural and economic receptions; it both receives and is being received. The values attached to it via copyrights, both commercially and in terms of programs such as 'Do not copy me without permission', are variable values. Copyrights change, and are translated by politics, by economics, by cultures and legislations; their 'tenacity' is made. For Laet de,

> it does not take much for [patents] to be unmade. It takes only a slight displacement [. . .] in order for the patent to protect it has to be a tenacious representation, the intricacy of the order of rules, legislation, jurisprudence, and enforcement that enables representation and protection [. . .].

As we have seen, this order can sometimes break down, and its underlying rationale 'is viable under a certain rationale but not necessarily under others'.

The rationale 'only upholds as long as it remains uncontested. [. . .] It may be counteracted by other rationales [. . .] It may be disregarded or it may simply be unknown [. . .]'.[153] As is the case with travelling copyrights, Laet de points to the possibility of absence; the absences of laws, of enforcement infrastructures, of knowledges, of protection. It should be considered whether the absence of adherence to normative regulations may play a role here, too. After all, the fundamental theory of property does incur the notion of consent; and when faced with only sketchy or incomplete presences of consent, property relations are called into question and crisis.

To put it differently, for copyrights to work effectively as representations of universal rights, and as vehicles for 'creativity transfer' exported to different places, 'some kind of order to enable their work must be integrally present in these places as well',[154] and '[e]xternal conditions are required to make the [copyright] work'.[155] It is local culture that determines how well laws work,[156] and the international IPR regime assumes 'the existence of functioning registers of works and copyright holders [which is] a major problem in any country [. . .] where copyright is not institutionalized'.[157] Yet the logic behind TRIPs clearly is to 'oblige developing countries to restructure their national laws so as to accommodate the needs and interests of the North'.[158]

If Laet de's analysis is correct, and if my attempt to apply its method to copyright is 'legitimate', then the implications for the music industry are threefold:

1 Copyrights travel, and although they may travel successfully, their tenacity is not ensured.
2 Travelling copyrights may 'hesitate to make the voyage', and even if they do reach their destination, they may not meet with the conditions necessary for them to operate; their representational system breaking down as they fail to represent owners and their rights.
3 For copyrights to be(come) tenacious, the entire series of representations has to make the journey intact, and encounter at destination its correspondent 'persecution and jurisprudence' structures.

The music industry's ordering strategies towards universal tenacity for copyrights reflect its latent awareness that this tenacity is subject to external conditions. Its three-stage global strategy to fight piracy includes 'throwing a cordon sanitaire around 90 per cent of the world's production' and 'clearing the countries' that are largely piratical and mainly located in the Third World.[159] Its rhetoric and ideology actually amount to an acknowledgement of difference; difference which is then denied existence within the hybrid spaces it reveals. Foucault has shown how the creation of universalizing discourses through blackboxed concepts produce reality, a reality which is in turn utilized to explain and legitimize the very interests and power relations which brought it about in the first place. The global music industry is engaging in similar ordering strategies, increasingly so through legal-imperialist discourses and practices. However, Latour reminds us that 'the *force* with which a speaker makes a statement is never enough [. . .] to predict the path that the statement will follow. This path depends on what successive listeners do with the statement'.[160] Herein lies Law's earlier notion of political promise. 'The question is not so much how we define power relations, but how domination is achieved' and 'the fate of a statement is in the hands of others'.[161,162] If others do not speak the same language, the statement is reduced; or, put differently, if a series of representations do not travel successfully, then copyright as a statement lacks tenacity. Only 'when actors and points of view are aligned [do] we enter a stable definition of society that looks like domination. When actors are unstable and the observers' points of view shift endlessly we are entering a highly unstable and negotiated situation in which domination is not yet exerted'.[163]

The global IPR system, and music copyright within it, operates as a blunt instrument which at present fails to successfully address a whole range of cultural-economic interests, conceptual categories, technological platforms, multiplicities and differences. This is a serious shortcoming in the twenty-first century in which, as Anthony Giddens persuasively argues, a multitude of socio-economic changes have produced human subjects called upon to actively and self-reflexively construct their multiple identities.[164] Should not their laws reflect these changes and this heterogeneity? Are we yielding agency to subject-ified actants, concepts and processes (technologies, capitalist economic organization, reductionist rhetoric and impoverished ideologies) in managing the relationship between private protection of property and public access to culture and resources? There are warnings against the social dangers of limiting democratic discourse and spoiling its quality by ring-fencing discourses within private property relations. We must take such warnings very seriously indeed. The development in the twenty-first century of the IPR regime generally, and of music copyright more specifically, ought to be as open and as closed as we make it. Its future ought to be up for negotiation. But any optimism about resolving the tension between that which ought to change in the IPR system, and that which actually happens, may well be misplaced. Too much, and then again, too little appears to depend on our willingness and capacity to critically engage with hyphens and the myriad effects and meanings they mask –

Notes

1 C. May, *A Global Political Economy of Intellectual Property Rights* (London: Routledge, 2000).

2 I am grateful to Professor Pamela Samuelson, Co-Director at Berkely Centre for Law and Technology, for alerting me towards a more sensitive use of the term 'piracy', a concept she deems more appropriately expressed via 'mass infringement'. I herewith acknowledge her views, but will use the more widely known term for the purpose of this chapter.

3 A. Elliot, L. Ray, *Key Contemporary Social Theorists* (Blackwell, 2003).

4 I have also suggested this concept elsewhere as a way of better apprehending current transnational expansive strategies and economic-political changes. The term is designed to illuminate a novel form of conglomerate behaviour instrumented via the logics of law-making and exporting. See K.S. Hermanns, 'The Hand That Sets The Table: The Political Economy and Self-Reflexive Project of Intellectual Property Law in relation to Traditional Knowledge', in *International Journal of Media and Cultural Politics*, 1, 1 (Bristol and Portland Oregon: Intellect Books, 2004).

5 See, for example, case law ranging from *Religious Technology Center* v. *Netcom Online Communications Services, Inc.* (1995), *ALS Scan, Inc.* v. *ReMarq Communities, Inc.* (2001), *A&M Records, Inc.* v. *Napster, Inc.* (2001), *RIAA* v. *Verizon Internet Services, Inc.* (2003),and *Metro-Goldwin-Mayer Studios, Inc.* v. *Grokster, Ltd.* (2003).

6 J. Quiggin, *Interpreting Globalization: Neoliberal And Internationalist Views Of Changing Patterns Of The Global Trade And Financial System*, Draft paper prepared under the UNRISD project, Australian National University (2002). In their analysis of IPR in the music industry, Kretschmer *et al.* posit, 'In the developed economies, a state of maximum horizontal consolidation may have been reached during the last decade. Scope for multinational expansion appears to remain only in underdeveloped markets (such as India, Korea or Brazil) and in the vertical integration of music businesses into media conglomerates': M. Kretschmer, G.M. Klimis, R. Wallis 'The Changing Location of Intellectual Property Rights in Music: A Study of Music Publishers, Collecting Societies, and Media Conglomerates' in *Prometheus*, 17, 2 (1999) pp. 163–186 at p. 168. Lovering also predicts that, '[m]ature markets in Europe and the United States are unlikely to generate a significant growth in sales': J. Lovering 'The Global Music Industry: Contradictions in the Commodification of the Sublime' in Leyshon, Matless, Revill (eds) *The Space of Music* (Guildford, 1998) at p. 41.

7 'Legislative fatigue' is one of these obstacles: 'The pressures on poorer countries to fight piracy brings them into a situation in which they have to spend many resources for the enforcement of intellectual property rights instead of the enforcement of other laws which are perhaps more important for the development of their economic, social and cultural life': J. Smiers 'The Abolition of Copyright' in *Gazette*, 62, 5 (2000) at p. 395. *The Economist* estimates it will cost a poor country up to $2m to implement TRIPs, and in doing so they are no longer allowed to move at their own speed: *The Economist* 'The right to good ideas' (2001a) pp. 27–29 at p. 28.

8 These include, for example, the IFPI's Anti-Piracy Unit (APU), the Priority Watch List and US Trade Representative (USTR), the International Intellectual Property Alliance (IIPA) and the World Intellectual Property Organization (WIPO).

9 The IPR system also governs trademarks and patents. Where the entertainment industries are concerned, the delineation between copyrights and patents is not always clear: V. Porter 'Copyright: The New Protectionism' in *Intermedia* 17, 1 (1989) pp. 10–17.

10 J. Boyle, *Shamans, software, and spleens: Law and the construction of the information society* (Cambridge: Harvard University Press, 1996).

11 (www.wipo.org; accessed April 2001, original emphasis).

12 Roth described concepts of Western copyright as defining a particular way of 'reconciling mind with money': quoted in M. Kretschmer 'Intellectual Property in Music: A Historical Analysis of Rhetoric and Institutional Practice',

forthcoming in *Studies in Cultures, Organizations and Societies* (1999) pp. 1–22 at p. 15.

13 Unlike IPR ideologists, Adorno and Horkheimer were, of course, highly critical of the paradigm shift their neologism represented.

14 W.K. Tabb 'The World Trade Organization? Stop World Take Over', in *Monthly Review*, 51, 8 (2000) at p. 1. The roots of this rationale date back to the seventeenth century. May (2000: 23) writes, quoting Macpherson 1978: 9): '[T]here had previously been a recognition of both private *and* common property. However [. . .] while private property remained, common property 'drops virtually out of sight' being treated 'as a contradiction in terms'. After this period everything had to *belong* to *someone* [. . .]', original emphasis.

15 R. Barbrook 'The Napsterisation of Everything' in *Science as Culture*, 2, 11 (2002), pp. 277–285.

16 The economist, Jaques Attali, is perhaps the most notable prophet of the music industry's pending demise. At a Cybercafe event at London's ICA in April 2000, he summarized the then ongoing work on updating his seminal book, *Noise*, by saying that copyright in the digital age would be non-enforceable; its enforcement would otherwise spell a 'totalitarian society'. See J. Attali, *Noise: The Political Economy of Music* (University of Minnesota Press, 1985).

17 J. Law 'Notes on the Theory of the Actor-Network: Ordering, Strategy, and Heterogeneity' in *Systems Practice*, 5 (1992), pp. 379–393 at p. 379.

18 M. Kretschmer, G.M. Klimis, R. Wallis, Ibid.

19 Barbrook op. cit. n 15, p. 9. IFPI estimates that in June 2002 three million people simultaneously used peer-to-peer file sharing services like Kazaa, iMesh and Gnutella, with 500 million music files being available. In comparison, during Napster's peak in February 2001, there were 1.6 million users sharing 345 million files: IFPI, *The Recording Industries in Numbers* (London: IFPI, 2002) at p. 9.

20 At the time of writing, these include Listen.com (Rhapsody), MusicNet, Pressplay, FullAudio, Emusic, OD2, Wippit, and Tornado Virtue. Record labels have also announced the introduction of legitimate CD burning and permanent ownership of digital tracks: IFPI 'The Recording Industry in Numbers' (London: 2002) at p. 9. Over the past few years, the industry has been experimenting with online business models ranging from pay-per-track downloading to locker and subscription services: Music and Copyright (2001) pp. 11–14.

21 A very engaging discussion of gift communities is provided by L. Hyde, *The Gift: Imagination and the Erotic Life of Property* (Vintage, 1999). For a comprehensive overview of issues surrounding Napster, filesharing, and the music industry, see J. Alderman, *Sonic Boom: Napster, P2P and the battle for the future of music* (London: Fourth Estate, 2001). In his electronic mail review of this work, Barbrook op. cit. n 19, pp. 4–5 warns that '[t]he music industry has no veto over the future [. . .] Big mainframes serving encrypted tunes to passive consumers is a science-fiction fantasy from the Fordist past [. . .] Above all, the music industry must move from selling tunes to servicing fans [. . .] A more evolved form of capitalism will emerge from the advent of ubiquitous filesharing'.

22 This refers to the 1984 SONY Betamax case which ruled that it was not contributory infringement to make or sell technology with substantial non-infringing uses (SNIU) and that making private, non-commercial copies for time-shifting purposes was fair use. The burning of a CD onto a player shifts this question to 'spaces' and 'places'. Incidentally, Napster used SONY's defence in its court case in 2001.

23 The DMCA's European counterpart is the E-Commerce Directive. On online

intermediary liability, also see R. Julia-Barcelo, 'On-line Intermediary Liability Issues: Comparing E.U. and U.S. Legal Frameworks' in *European Intellectual Property Review*, 105 (2000).

24 G. Danaher, T. Schirato and J. Webb, *Understanding Foucault* (Sage, 2000) p. 35.

25 J. Law, 'Notes on the Theory of the Actor-Network: Ordering, Strategy, and Heterogeneity' in *Systems Practice*, 5 (1992), pp. 379–393.

26 C. May discusses power and models of change in the global political economy: C. May, *A Global Political Economy of Intellectual Property Rights*, pp. 39–42.

27 Copyright covers fiction and non-fiction, musical works including recordings, artistic works including amateur drawings and children's doodles, maps, technical drawings, photography, and CD-ROMs: C. May op. cit. n 26, pp. 8–9.

28 Kretschmer op. cit. n 12, pp. 1–22. Also see M. Foucault, 'What is an author?', in P. Rabinow (ed.) *The Foucault Reader* (Penguin, 1984).

29 I consciously avoid the term 'legislatures' here to allow for the historical absence of copyright provisions in numerous music territories.

30 M. Jackson, 'From Private to Public: Reexamining the Technological Basis for Copyright' in *Journal of Communication*, 52, 2 (2002) pp. 416–424 at p. 424.

31 R.V. Bettig, *Copyrighting Culture* (Oxford: Westview Press, 1996) pp. 11–13.

32 Jackson op. cit. n 30, p. 417, argues against what he calls a technological determinist reading of copyright development: '[C]opyright owes as much to the development of capitalism and changing social conditions as it does to the technology of the printing press. Similarly, current attempts to "adapt" copyright law to the internet have as much to do with the economic power of the copyright industries as with the new technologies of digital communication'.

33 R.V. Bettig op. cit. n 31, pp. 19–22.

34 C. May op. cit. n 26, pp. 26–28.

35 J. Attali, *Noise: The Political Economy of Music* (University Minnesota Press, 1985).

36 M. Kretschmer op. cit. n 28, p. 3.

37 V. Porter op. cit. n 9, pp. 10–17.

38 Civil Law emphasizes the moral right (droît moral) inherent in the 'peculiar relationship of the creator to his work', while Common Law stresses the 'stimulation of creativity to the *public good*, rather than a natural entitlement by the author to her work': M. Kretschmer, op. cit. n 36 at p. 17. Under the latter, everything is transferable and assignable; the former legislature ensures 'the publisher or producer does not get everything': M. Kretschmer *et al.*, Ibid., at p. 172. These differences continue to be played out.

39 J. Smiers, 'The Abolition of Copyright' in *Gazette*, 62, 5 (2000), pp. 379–406, at p. 380.

40 C. May, Ibid.

41 J. Smiers, Ibid.

42 J. Smiers, Ibid.

43 S. Frith, 'Copyright and the music business' in *Popular Music*, 7, 1 (1987), pp. 57–75, at p. 63. Also refer to K. McLeod (2001) who explains how the ubiquitous song *Happy Birthday* became to be commodified into private ownership: K. McLeod, *Owning Culture: authorship, ownership & intellectual property law* (Peter Lang, 2001). Incredibly, McLeod himself was granted a trademark on *freedom of expression*™ and is currently threatening to sue At&T for violating it.

44 J. Smiers, Ibid., at p. 384.

45 E. Brockes, 'Whose line is it anyway?' in the *Guardian*, G2, 03.07 (2001).

46 K. McLeod op. cit. n 43.

47 They also include investigations into the problems associated with 'cultural

ownership' in general, such as (1998) thought-provoking contribution to debates within social anthropology: M.F. Brown, 'Can culture be copyrighted?' in *Current Anthropology*, 39, 2 (1998), pp. 193–222.

48 V. Porter, 'Copyright: The New Protectionism', *Intermedia*, 17, 1 (1989), pp. 10–17, at p. 10.

49 For an overview, see Saussure's theory of language as a system of signs: J. Lechte, *Fifty contemporary thinkers* (London: Routledge, 1994), pp. 148–153.

50 V. Porter op. cit. n 48.

51 V. Porter op. cit. n 50, p. 12 and M. Kretschmer op. cit. n 38, p. 20.

52 S. Albini, *'The Problem with Music'*, www.negativland.com/albini.html [accessed 23.06.03] and C. Love, 'Courtney Love does the math', http://dir.salon.com/tech/feature/2000/06/14/Love/index.html, [accessed 23.06.03] (2000).

53 S. Frith op. cit. n 43, p. 60.

54 R. Wallis, C. Baden-Fuller, M. Kretschmer, G.M. Klimis, 'Contested Collective Administration of Intellectual Property Rights in Music', *European Journal of Communication*, 14, 1 (1999), pp. 5–35, at p. 18 and 19; and M. Kretschmer op. cit. n 51, p. 19.

55 OECD, 'Shaping the 21st Century: The Contribution of Development Co-operation', [www.oecd.org; accessed April 2001]OECD (1989), at p. 10.

56 T. Adorno, M. Horkheimer, *The Culture Industry* (London: Routledge, 1991). In suggesting this I do not intend to discount the insights generated by cultural studies, especially in the tradition of the Birmingham School, regarding consumer agencies.

57 K. McLeod op. cit. n 43, for instance, points out that the early Hip-Hop albums, commonly considered a truly fresh and cutting-edge contribution to popular music, could not possibly be made today. Since their creators engaged in intertextual appropriation of existing musical material in the folk tradition, as such actually reviving earlier influences, they temporarily managed to eschew the constrictions of the copyright system. As soon as the music industry began to counteract what it considered 'infringements', the ensuing pricing of the use of musical samples made it increasingly difficult for (emerging) artists to express themselves freely. Those who would today consider these pioneering works to possess 'excellence' may readily agree that copyright enforcement can indeed act as a barrier to artistic 'excellence'. It suggests that intellectual property is becoming too expensive for creators to create freely: J. Boyle op. cit. n 10. The criterion for using existing works becomes 'the ability to pay, thus favouring the values of the economic realm over those of the political and cultural realms': Porter op. cit. n 51, p. 16.

58 Kretschmer also mentions investment into markets like Italy, Spain, and México 'where there was no effective patent system for drugs': M. Kretschmer op. cit. n 54, p. 5. Another example is Switzerland whose patent laws lagged behind international law for most of the twentieth century, without damaging the country: H-J. Chang, *Historical Lessons and Emerging Issues*, paper for UNDP's Human Development Report 2001; presented at University College London on 17/11/00. Research furthermore suggests that companies do not necessarily become more innovative when patent rights are strengthened: *The Economist*, 'Patently absurd?', 23 June (2001), pp. 46–48, at p. 47.

59 C. May op. cit. n 40, pp. 22–29.

60 C. May, Ibid., p. 25.

61 C. May, Ibid., p. 26. In contemporary copyright law, Lockean theory continues to be reflected through compulsory licensing rationales, the general granting or licensing of rights to external parties, and the common law tradition more broadly.

62 Bettig op. cit. n 33, p. 25.
63 C. May op. cit. n 61.
64 C. May, Ibid., pp. 27–29.
65 J. Lechte, *Fifty contemporary thinkers* (London: Routledge, 1994).
66 May reminds us that '[u]nder communism there might be, and perhaps in pre-modernity there was, some form of possession that could be conceived of as property, and could be held socially by a group without rights being explicitly accorded to an owner': C. May, op. cit. n 61, p. 22.
67 J. Smiers op. cit. n 44, p. 386.
68 R.V. Bettig op. cit. n 62.
69 J. Smiers op. cit. n 67, p. 394.
70 M. Kretschmer op. cit. n 58, p. 7.
71 *The Economist* op. cit. n 7, p. 27.
72 R. Wallis op. cit. n 54, p. 5.
73 See S. Jones, 'Mass Communication, Intellectual Property Rights, International Trade, and the Popular Music Industry' in E.G. McAnany, and K.T. Wilkinson (eds) *Mass media and free trade: NAFTA and the cultural industries* (Austin: University of Texas Press, 1996), pp. 331–350 and L. Grenier, 'Cultural Exemptionalism Revisited: Québec Music Industries in the Face of Free Trade' Industry' in Ibid., pp. 307–328 For an overview of wider globalization debates, see J.A. Scholte, *The Sources of Globalisation*, Draft paper prepared under the UNRISD project, Centre for the Study of Globalization and Regionalization, University of Warwick (2002) and J. Quiggin op. cit. n 6.
74 F. Jameson, 'Notes on Globalization as a Philosophical Issue', in F. Jameson and M. Miyoshi (eds) *The Cultures of Globalization* (Durham and London: Duke University Press, 1998).
75 F. Jameson, Ibid., p. 68.
76 K. Negus, 'Feeding The World: Popular Music and the Global Entertainment Industry' in *Producing POP: Culture and Conflict in the popular music industry* (Arnold, 1992), pp. 3, 11.
77 J. Lovering op. cit. n 6, p. 35.
78 B. Andersen, Z. Kozul-Wright and R. Kozul-Wright, 'Copyrights, Competition and Development: The Case of the Music Industry', United Nations Conference on Trade and Development, 145, January (2000). Also F. Jameson, op. cit. n 75.
79 *The Economist*, op. cit. n 71, p. 27.
80 Raghavan: quoted in J. Smiers op. cit. n 69, p. 384.
81 S. Frith op. cit. n 53, p. 73.
82 J. Lovering op. cit. n 77, pp. 34–44.
83 J. Lovering, Ibid.
84 De Cuéllar: quoted in Smiers op. cit. n 69, p. 396.
85 The US were not amongst the first six signatories to the Berne Convention for the Protection of Literary and Artistic Works.
86 J. Coover, *Music Publishing: Copyright And Piracy In Victorian England* (Mansell Publishing Limited, 1985), at p. 13.
87 Interestingly, J. Lovering says, 'Marx argued that capitalism would tend to favour dead labor over living workers. The music industry shows that he was dead right': J. Lovering, op. cit. n 83, p. 44.
88 D. Laing, 'Copyright and the International Music Industry' in S. Frith (ed.) *Music and Copyright* (Edinburgh University Press, 1993), at p. 23 and M. Kretschmer op. cit. n 70, p. 17.
89 D. Laing, Ibid.
90 D. Laing, Ibid.

91 J. Smiers op. cit. n 84, p. 386.

92 F. Jameson op. cit. n 78 p. 60.

93 The proposed neologism of *legal* imperialism in this adjective form is more readily associable with 'colonial' and 'cultural' interpretations of imperialism and should be seen as both relational to and progressing these. In some ways, however, *legislative* imperialism would express more instantaneously the imposing nature of the proposed neologism, i.e. in German: *gesetzgebend*, meaning *law-giving*.

94 R. Shuker (ed.) 'We are the world: State music policy, cultural imperialism, and globalisation' in *Understanding Popular Music* (1994), 2nd edn, pp. 67–72.

95 Boyd Barret: quoted in K. Malm and R. Wallis, *Media policy and Music activity* (London: Routledge, 1992), at p. 210.

96 K. Malm and R. Wallis, Ibid., p. 211.

97 K. Malm and R. Wallis, Ibid.

98 V. Shiva Shiva, 'The Second Coming of Columbus', *Resurgence*, May/June (1997), at p. 2.

99 K.B. Jensen, *A Handbook of Media and Communication Research* (London: Routledge, 2002), at p. 254.

100 IFPI op. cit. n 20, p. 20.

101 IFPI, *The Recording Industries in Numbers* (London: IFPI, 2000), at p. 6, and IFPI, *The Recording Industries in Numbers* (London: IFPI, 2001), pp. 4–9. This global strengthening of sales of domestic product has been used to destabilize fears over cultural imperialism or Americanization of (musical) culture. While claims such as these are relevant in the wider discussion of globalization, they must take into account questions about the actual 'origin' of domestic musics and of economic flows that may yet reveal that the 'host' territory does not necessarily benefit from this phenomenon economically in straightforward lines.

102 IFPI, *The Recording Industries in Numbers* (London: IFPI, 2001), at p. 8.

103 J. Smiers op. cit. n 91, p. 395.

104 J. Quiggin, in a wider analyses of data gathering exercises on poverty, purchasing parity, and the technology gap shows that their underlying models tend to privilege certain determining factors over others: J. Quiggin op. cit. n 73.

105 K. Negus op. cit. n 76, p. 12.

106 F. Fabbri, 'Copyright: The Dark Side of the Music Business' in S. Frith (ed.) *Music and Copyright* (Edinburgh University Press, 1993). Others have argued that organized piracy has had adverse effects on (underdeveloped) countries (Manuel in Chanan 1995). These can include major record companies' abandonment of markets due to high levels of piracy. Also see Frith (1987: 61).

107 C. May op. cit. n 66, p. 139.

108 M. Godwin, 'Fear of Infringement', *Media Studies Journal*, Fall (2000), pp. 30–35, at p. 32.

109 M. Chanan op. cit. n 106, p. 163.

110 A. Lenhart and S. Jones, 'Music Downloading and Listening: Findings from the Pew Internet and American Life Project', forthcoming in *Popular Music* (2003).

111 For example, it is argued that the music industry's potential strength in the fight against digital piracy might be the ability to brand and deliver music product through new business models which include enhanced quality and ease of use.

112 See J. Gaines, *Contested Culture* (North Carolina Press, 1991) and L. Bently, 'Copyright and the Death of the Author in Literature and Law', Review Article in *The Modern Law Review*, 57, 6 (Blackwell, 1994).

113 F. Jameson op. cit. n 92.

114 C. May op. cit. n 107.

115 J. Smier op. cit. n 103.

116 R. Wallis op. cit. n 72, p. 5.

117 M. Kretschmer op. cit. n 88, p. 21. This should consist of 'long term author rights to recognition and compensation, limited financial incentives for investors, and direct public support for desirable creative activity': M. Kretschmer op. cit. n 117, p. 2.

118 S. Žižek, *An Introduction to the 150th Anniversary Edition of The Communist Manifesto* (Zagreb, 1998) and V. Forrester, *The Economic Horror* (Polity, 1999). In a footnote to *CYBERMARX*, N. Dyer-Witheford addresses calls for IPR reform, 'Within the current, capitalist context, legal protection [. . .] is appropriate and necessary. The dismantling of intellectual property rights should start from an assault on the legal fortifications of the corporations who are the beneficiaries of the current system, not those of individuals and small organizations': Dyer-Witheford, N. *CYBER-MARX: Cycles and Circuits of Struggle in High-Technology Capitalism* (University of Illinois, 1999), at p. 293.

119 A.O. Adede, 'The Political Economy of the TRIPs Agreement: Origins and History of Negotiations', paper presented at the Aberdare Country Club in Kenya, 30–31 July 2001.

120 M. Kretschmer, G.M. Klimis, R. Wallis op. cit. n 38, p. 163.

121 *The Economist* op. cit. n 7, p. 28.

122 J. Holyoak and P. Torremans, *Intellectual Property Law*, 2nd edn (Butterworths, 1998), at p. 4.

123 J. Smiers op. cit. n 115, p. 383.

124 R.V. Bettig op. cit. n 68, p. 225.

125 C. May op. cit. n 114, p. 85.

126 J. Smiers op. cit. n 123, p. 397.

127 An area of future research might be the notion of dialogics. Caution, however, must be applied to the dialogical principles, because the question of who is allowed to speak under which conditions of power and violence remains crucial. See also Gaines' response to Brown, '[I]f we are to encourage democratic dialogue, we must open these questions up to an 'urgently needed public discussion about mutual respect and the fragility of native cultures in mass society' ': C. Brown op. cit. n 47, p. 208.

128 Seminar at University College London, 17/11/2001.

129 R.V. Bettig op. cit. n 124, p. 208.

130 Prior to this, GATT dealt with IPR issues 'only in recognizing an exception that permits measures 'necessary to secure compliance with laws or regulations'[. . .]. NAFTA [. . .] requires each party to the treaty to ensure that its domestic law makes available enforcement procedures that permit 'effective action' to be taken against any act of infringement of intellectual property rights': P.E. Chaudhry and M.G. Walsh, 'Intellectual Property Rights: Changing Levels of Protection under GATT, NAFTA, and the EU' in *The Columbia Journal of World Business*, Summer (1995), pp. 80–92.

131 China's recent accession to the World Trade Organization (WTO) will make it an increasingly interesting territory for study in relation to IPR and the entertainment industries.

132 FPI op. cit. n 19, p. 16.

133 I am grateful to Kate McBain at Paisley University for pointing this out.

134 S. Jones op. cit. n 73, p. 338.

135 *The Economist* op. cit. n 7, p. 27.

136 S. Jones op. cit. n 134, pp. 341–344.

137 IFPI op. cit. n 19, p. 14.
138 Based on IFPI statistics, Latin American market share by the five majors (BMG, EMI, Sony, Universal, and Warner) was 72.6 per cent in 2001, compared with 73.2 per cent the previous year: IFPI, Ibid., p. 5.
139 F. Jameson op. cit. n 113, p. 69.
140 A.O. Adede op. cit. n 119, p. 4.
141 B. Andersen, Z. Kozul-Wright and R. Kozul-Wright op. cit. n 78, p. 10. Between 1988 and 1997 the value of DMEC musical trade exports into developing territories rose by around $1.5m. By contrast, DMEC imports of recorded music from developing countries rose by just $550m. Some of the reasons suggested for these asymmetries are weak institutional and political support, low levels of entrepreneurial capability, low value-added, overdependence on foreign manufacturing and distribution, and massive copyright infringement; rather than lack of available talent: Ibid., pp. 10–11.
142 J. Law op. cit. n 25.
143 Smiers reminds us that the neo-liberal, capitalist, and oligopolistic privatization of culture and science, not only deepens the North-South divide, but also takes place in 'fields which are decisive for social, cultural and economic development in the 21st century: *knowledge and creativity*': J. Smiers op. cit. n 126, p. 398, emphasis added. Knowledge is represented within the copyright as information or creativity. Unlike the industrial knowledge protected through the granting of patents, copyright does not have an inherent usefulness or applicability. Nevertheless, the commercial potential and exploitability of that which is protected under copyright is irrefutable in the global entertainment industries. Therefore, while copyright may not be as *specifically* linked to industrialization as patents are it is nonetheless linked to (the effects of) industrialization along with patents: M. Laet de, 'Patents, travel, space: ethnographic encounters with objects in transit', in *Environment and Planning D: Society and Space*, 18 (2000), pp. 149–168, at p. 152. Where the technology transfer of patents is concerned, Laet de argues that some development strategists mistakenly assume that in transporting one half of this connection – the patent – the other half – industrialization – will follow: M. Laet de, Ibid. As some of the rhetoric presented in this chapter indicates, a similar line of thought is applied to the transportation of copyrights, when IFPI, for instance, reasons that 'in countries where piracy proliferates the entire development of legitimate markets is impeded and [. . .] the growth of local musical talent and culture is severely hampered': IFPI, Ibid., p. 8.
144 For a discerning definition of 'originality' in relation to copyrights, see J. Holyoak and P. Torremans, 'Originality should not be taken in the normal sense here. Novelty or innovation are not required, the starting point is that the work is not copied and originates from the author [. . .] It is not required that the idea is new, because the idea is not covered by copyright at all [. . .] The author must only have expended 'skill, judgment and labour' or 'selection, judgment and experience' or 'labour, skill and capital' in creating the work': J. Holyoak and P. Torremans op. cit. n 122, p. 168.
145 M. Laet de op. cit. n 143, p. 154.
146 J. Collins, 'The Problem of Oral Copyright: The Case of Ghana', in S. Frith (ed.) *Music and Copyright* (Edinburgh University Press, 1993), at p. 146.
147 Also see the 1996 UNESCO and UN World Commission on Culture and Development report, *Our Creative Diversity*, '[T]raditional cultural groups possess intellectual property *as groups* [. . .] A case can be made for a new concept based on ideas inherent in traditional social rules. This might be more constructive than trying to make the forms of protection fit within a frame-

work which was never designed for them [. . .]': quoted in Smiers op. cit. n 143, p. 396.

148 T. Mitsui, 'Copyright and Music in Japan: A Forced Grafting and its Consequences' in S. Frith (ed.) *Music and Copyright* (Edinburgh University Press, 1993), at p. 142.

149 M.F. Brown refers to this also: 'Weber's iron cage has steadily expanded to include ideas and images, which have become tokens in economic exchanges facilitated by the new information technologies': M.F. Brown op. cit. n 47, p. 206.

150 M. Laet, de op. cit. n 145, p. 154.

151 M. Laet de, Ibid., p. 156.

152 See R. Barthes, 'Musica Practica' in *Image, Music, Text* Barthes, R. (London: Fontana Press, 1977) and P. Jaszi and M. Woodmansee, 'The Ethical Reaches of Authorship', in *The South Atlantic Quarterly*, 95, 4 (Duke University Press, 1996).

153 M. Laet de op. cit. n 151, p. 160.

154 M. Laet de, Ibid.

155 M. Laet de, Ibid., p. 161.

156 Barnet and Cavanagh: quoted in Smiers op. cit. n 147, p. 394.

157 Malm and Wallis: quoted in Ibid.

158 Nyerere: quoted in Ibid., p. 396.

159 D. Laing op. cit. n 88, p. 31.

160 B. Latour, 'Technology is society made durable' in J. Law (ed.) *A Sociology of Monsters* (Routledge 1991), at p. 104.

161 B. Latour, Ibid.

162 B. Latour, Ibid.

163 B. Latour, Ibid., p. 129.

164 A. Giddens, *Modernity and Self-Identity: Self and Society in the late modern age* (Polity, 1991).

13 The legal implications surrounding the practice of video sampling in the digital age

Yvonne Sarah Morris

Introduction

Copyright today, in relation to audio-visual works, is a hotly debated area. The practices of contemporary and unconventional digital art forms are challenging the dominance of traditional forms. Video sampling *(v.sampling)* has become incontestably the most controversial and, perhaps, the most maligned aspect of visual creation. It is a phenomenon that challenges existing copyright laws enshrined in the UK Copyright Designs and Patents Act 1988 (CDPA) and various other sources of law. This chapter considers whether the copyright provisions of the CDPA, and those of other relevant jurisdictions, adequately deal with the issues that pertain to *v.sampling*.

V.sampling is an appropriative practice, whereby clips *(samples)* of films, TV programmes or other audio-visual material, are digitally captured (i.e. *sampled*) for use in new works. The term 'sampling' became popular during the 1980s when the music industry began to use digital technology to record and manipulate 'clips' (or *'samples'*) from pre-existing sound recordings in new work.[1] *V.sampling* is a technique used in several seemingly quite disparate industries. From televised movie review shows and the film *Sleepless in Seattle*,[2] (both of which use *v.samples* of pre-existing movies) to Glastonbury music festival, at which video samples from numerous sources are often projected on to large screens to accompany the music on stage. This range of industries has one thing in common: video. Our society is currently in the midst of an explosion in video culture where we are constantly viewing, manipulating or appearing in, moving images throughout our daily lives. Within this myriad of applications, this chapter looks at *v.sampling* in three areas that represent the widest scope and relevance to copyright law. First, the rise of the Video-Jockey (VJ) and the subject of live video performance; second, the latest development in the Internet *fan fiction* phenomenon: *fan edits*; and last, film and television makers who use *filmic quotation* (excerpts from other films or programmes) in their work. These three areas are ideal subjects because they:

1   represent a wide range of commercial and non-commercial applications of *v.sampling*: fan edits are a largely not-for-profit activity whereas VJing and filmic quotation largely occur in *commercial* sectors;

2   exist within a diverse range of industries and endeavours: fan edits are mainly an Internet phenomenon; VJs present their work in a live performance context, i.e. in the *live events industry*; and filmic quotation happens solely in the *film and television industries*;

3   span different time frames: fan edits are an extremely new development; VJing, although relatively new, has some history attached to it; and filmic quotation, which is established and has been practiced for a relatively long time.

4   fall on both sides of copyright law: fan-editors and some VJs use *unauthorized* sections of video material; whereas filmic quotation is, with a few notable exceptions, an *authorized* activity.

Quantitative and qualitative methods of data collection were employed in order to carry out research on the three areas. Two questionnaires were used. The first, a web-based questionnaire, was posted as a hyperlink on a number of fan sites. The second, a printed questionnaire, was collectively administered at a VJ festival held in Milan.[3] The first (herein fan questionnaire) took a *cross-sectional* look at the knowledge and attitudes of fans towards fan edits and copyright law. Due to the nature of the World Wide Web, potential respondents were spread across the globe, albeit with, like the Web itself, an overwhelming North American bias (64 per cent of respondents lived in the US, the rest were spread globally).[4] The second questionnaire (herein VJ questionnaire) quantitatively and qualitatively tested the knowledge, views, and attitudes of VJs, and other attendees, on the subjects of *v.sampling* and copyright law.

Two interviews were also conducted to gain qualitative data. Both were conducted with VJs, in central London. The interviews were *semi-structured* and designed to gain insight into the current views and practices of VJs with regards to the use of copyrighted material and to gain suggestions as to possible courses of action to create a more balanced system of law. Several attempts to talk with a representative of Twentieth Century Fox were also made.[5] Much telephone and subsequent electronic correspondences were also engaged in, including questions put to representatives in the licensing, or clearance departments of Channel 4, the BBC and Viasat Broadcasting UK Ltd and others.

In addition to the above, a thorough review of all available secondary sources was carried out on the World Wide Web, in books, articles and journals. The lack of availability of any literature written on *v.sampling* and the law highlighted the need to clarify the issues surrounding this subject. Further research was carried out through attending conferences, festivals and seminars.

After a short definition of terms, this chapter briefly describes the historical and cultural factors surrounding each area, in the form of histories, which usefully illustrate how long these existing practices have been going on and how dated the current legal frameworks actually are. Theorists Gillette and Mauer describe the difficult, multi-threaded nature of the history of today's digital media: 'The digital realm . . . has become a point of convergence, a vortex . . . where so many histories and talents interact and recombine . . .'[6]

The first area is the newly forming art of the VJ. Like DJs mix records or CDs, VJs mix video content for live events. This video content can be either 'found footage' or created from scratch. Although there *is* a large original component to the work of many VJs, with respect to this chapter, the 'found footage' aspect is the most interesting because of the possibilities it presents for infringing copyright. The terms VJ and video artist are distinct but overlapping. 'VJing' is a live performance art where pre-recorded sequences are mixed together and manipulated to create a live work of video, often accompanying the live audio mix of a DJ. 'Video artists', create original work that is played back via some form of video.[7] One and the same person often performs these two distinct roles. Put simply, VJs are to video artists what DJs are to musicians. The point is not quite as simple as it seems, however, as DJs are increasingly seen as 'musicians' or 'creative artists' themselves and in the same way, the work of VJs can now be seen as art in its own right. The second area looks at Internet communities of fans of popular fictional books, TV programmes, movies etc. called *fan sites*, which have led to the growth in the phenomenon of *fan fiction. Fan edits* use, as their raw material, the actual footage of the original film or TV programme and rework it to create variations, e.g. by changing endings, relationships between characters or even cutting out entire scenes. VJs and fan-editors have been chosen primarily as a means of looking at the new media, which use *unauthorized v.samples*, in an attempt to consider the effectiveness of the relevant law. The third area has been included as a way to understand current *authorized* commercial use, and clearance of, *v.samples* in film and TV where the law is not so much in question and to consider how they might apply to the first two areas. For many years, film and TV programme makers have incorporated existing dramatic and historical footage or music video and film clips into their output.

Second, the chapter looks at the challenges posed to copyright law by the practice of *v.sampling*. It considers possible primary and secondary infringements, the problems associated with categorizing works in the CDPA,[8] focuses on how traditional notions such as authorship, substantiality and fixation are interpreted in the current law and asks how usefully these and legal principles, such as fair dealing and moral rights, can be applied to the phenomenon of *v.sampling*. With a distinct lack of legal precedent on *v.sampling*, this chapter provides some interesting parallels with digital *sound sampling*, commonly used in the music industry. It then speculates upon whether 'secondary creations' are new works and whether appropriative practices are 'new forms of art' in their own right. Also highlighted are practical and economic problems of sample clearance and the absence of legitimate avenues for *v.samplers* to access content through clearance procedures and licensing agreements, in a market geared towards corporate to corporate trade.

Third, the chapter concentrates on the postmodern paradigm and asks who benefits from the current state of copyright law. It has become clear that discussion in this area is not merely the history of a handful of media techniques but, in fact, a vital and integral part of the academic struggle to set the agenda for our emerging postmodern life and culture. Many writers believe that we are in a transitional state where the discrepancies between the Modern and postmodern paradigms are causing quiet revolutions of thought throughout our society. This calls for reflection on the legal strategies adopted by companies or corporations and their effects on our lives as individuals, to discern whether the resulting legal interactions between them and 'secondary creators' are 'fair and balanced' and to determine whether the copyright law is an *appropriate* mechanism for ensuring this.

Finally, in light of the current acceptance of, and potential for, *v.sampling* techniques as art, this chapter concludes that present copyright law fails to provide an effective legal framework for *v.sampling* and that it is necessary for clear guidelines and legal boundaries to be set, which are fair and balanced. Questions raised for future debate are a necessary condition for moving the subject forward. How do we measure what is creative or original and how do we differentiate between plagiarism and inspiration? What merits legal protection and what doesn't? How much, if any, can be appropriated? Who owns what, and for how long? What is mine, yours or theirs and who should be the arbiter? How do we balance intellectual ownership with the rights of artistic freedom and free expression? Is it possible to reconcile the concerns of the commercial content industry, paranoid about piracy and an emerging postmodern mode of artistic expression obsessed with digital appropriation, using a legal framework which fails to recognize the existence of widely accepted appropriative art forms? It would seem not. The technology has precipitated a crisis; law can no longer ignore it. A flock of potential disputes is lurking just around the corner and it is unlikely that the courts are ideally placed to deal with them. Nevertheless the 'here and now' demands that sense be made of this strikingly grey area before the battles commence.

Video and the cultural history of video sampling

The term *sampling*, although used in many different contexts, means essentially the same thing in most cases.[9] In their legal article on sampling film images, Waters and Eade refer to sampling simply as 'taking a small part of a larger work'.[10] Dr R.L. Cutler, in *Pilfering the Datapool*, defines sampling in a manner evocative of the language of the new digital media:

> To sample is to cut up: mine the archive; steal to subvert; recycle footage; assist a readymade; appropriate invention; elevate the fragment; drift through sequences of signs ... question the act of watching ... raise the dead ... become a curator; open up the cultural database ... eviscerate the author; materialize associative actions.[11]

In the CDPA, all moving image material is categorized as 'Film'. However, the overwhelming majority of 'moving image' material today is recorded and stored as *video*. 'Film' (i.e. celluloid) is used solely for the shooting and projection of movies for cinema release, although, high-resolution video projectors have recently technologically superseded this projection aspect.[12] Certainly the vast majority of sampling of 'films' must, for technical reasons, be done via video copies, rather than the original celluloid. Film, therefore, is an unsuitable label for a market dominated by the group of recording formats known as *video*. For all of these reasons the term *video* is a more appropriate umbrella term for this area than film, based on the extent of its usage in the creation of moving images today. Therefore the term *v.sampling* will herein be used to describe the sampling of *any* moving image, whatever its origin.

There are two principal types of video, *analogue* and *digital*. Unlike digital video (DV), analogue video encodes the data used by a television screen by representing it as a continuous waveform. DV is video whose signal is 'captured', or recorded, in a format recognized by a computer.[13] While this has distinct advantages for video production, it also introduces the possibility of 'cloning' (making perfect copies of video products) and therefore *v.sampling* and also piracy. Confusingly, with the release of DVDs,[14] the term 'video' has also come to apply to the VHS[15] format in order to distinguish the two. We now hear of movies being released 'on Video and DVD'. This is, of course, inaccurate, as DVDs are essentially discs that contain digital *video*. Therefore the term 'video' will be used in its widest possible interpretation.

The history of video, video art and VJing

On 2nd November, 1936, the BBC began to transmit a TV signal for half an hour a day.[16] People could, for the first time, watch a moving image, which had been broadcast live. Through the invention of the video camera,[17] the TV set was destined to become a staple electronic device for most of the industrialized world. As TV became accepted as part of mainstream culture its influence on the political and social agendas of its time did not go unnoticed by governments, many of whom, like Britain, set up their own broadcasting operations.

At this point, the technology needed to create TV was owned, almost exclusively, by large media broadcasting organizations, such as the BBC and NBC.[18] This changed when the Sony Corporation introduced the *portapack*[19] in 1965, the first consumer version of what would now be called the 'camcorder'. Connected to a television set, it could record (*sample*) broadcast television. Video production technology was no longer solely under the control of the TV Networks. While the Networks continued with conventional broadcasting and its traditions, the *portapak* had opened up a whole new palette of possibilities for video experimentation. Artists, such as the acclaimed Nam June Piak could now record video images. Paik is celebrated as the first artist to use video as an artistic medium in its own right. George Fifield comments:

> Until Nam June Paik, the medium of worldwide broadcast television was the engineers' temple. Artists were not invited. Yet by 1970, this 'vast wasteland', ... had transformed our culture, becoming the most powerful form of communication in the world.[20]

Referring to his new *portapak*,[21] Piak remarked, 'Television has been attacking us all our lives, now we can attack it back'.[22]

Many of Paik's early works used video equipment as part of sculpture, rather than creating the images themselves. These pieces modulated and distorted existing broadcast signals, as in *Exposition of Music – Electronic Television*,[23] in which 13 TV sets were placed on the floor on their sides and backs, their receptions altered in different ways. On one of the TV sets, *Participation TV*, when a viewer depressed a footswitch and spoke into a microphone, the voice translated an existing broadcast signal into an explosive pattern of points of light on a screen.[24] Through distortions of the received broadcast image, Piak had brought video outside of the realm of the standardized moving image. Although no copying was involved, Piak, in distorting existing signals for use in new work, had become the first person to *v.sample*.

Piak went on to experiment widely with video technology. He co-invented a machine called the Piak/Abe Synthesizer, which was to be an inspirational device in video history.[25] Fifield enthusiastically states:

> There are a few moments in history where a major advance in the arts is also an advance in engineering and directly responsible for a major acceleration of popular culture. The invention of the Paik/Abe Synthesizer is one of those perfect moments.[26]

Alongside Piak's work, many other artists such as Bruce Nauman and Bill Viola had also seen the importance of this new medium and had begun to experiment with it. 'Video became a canvas that the artist could literally paint on. The freedom of creative thought that Paik's creation spawned spread like wildfire'.[27]

Parallel with the emergence of video as an art form during the 1960s, Pop Art, Installation Art, Performance Art, and others, also pushed the boundaries of what was traditionally recognized as art. These forms spawned many hybrids, such as 'happenings' and 'video installations', which often combined performance, poetry, painting, sculpture, music, lighting effects and film projection, into environments in which audiences would participate interactively. Events, such as *Ken Kesey*[28] *& the Pranksters' 'Acid Tests'* in 1965 were 'unscripted spontaneous multimedia happenings', party-style gatherings bringing together artists from many disciplines to collectively contribute to the event, rather like some of the AV[29] acts becoming popular today. With the *Grateful Dead* supplying the music and Kesey & the Pranksters' psychedelic exploits projected around a decorated space full of dancers, these events were among the first to be viewed, audience and all, as a single, multimedia art form. In 1966, Pop Art veteran Andy Warhol and the band *Velvet Underground* staged their *Exploding Plastic Inevitable* 'happenings'. These new, highly conceptual, often appropriative, forms of art represented the avant-garde of the art world in the 1960s and 70s.

When, in the late 1960s, practices borrowed from Jamaican 'dub' reggae[30] came into widespread use in New York's clubs,[31] a new breed of live performer was born: the DJ. Unlike the old radio-style Disc Jockey, more of a presenter than a performer, this new style of club DJ,[32] or 'turntablist', created seamless mixes of others' songs, often not playing each in its entirety, playing two at once, or taking small, recognizable sections (or *audio samples*) of one song and using them to punctuate another. In the late 1970s, *Hip Hop* was born, finally using the new 'two decks and a mixer' technology to its full potential by introducing *scratching*[33] which gave the DJ even more creative input into the final sound.

In 1979 Stefan G was reportedly the first person to coin the term 'VJ'.[34] Although no definitive history of VJing has yet been written, some trace its roots to the party scene described above. The interactive and experiential nature of this scene contributed to a growing interest among video artists in recording real life scenes. This melded with Pop Art's concept of 'subversion through appropriation' in the approach of Michael Shamberg and the Raindance Corporation, in their 1971 book *Guerrilla Television.*[35] This influential publication, whilst recommending the recording of everyday life, also espoused the recording and collage of excerpts of broadcast television, i.e. *v.sampling*. It encouraged subversive political subject matters, interpreting the creation of video collage as a political act, freeing people to express their own worlds on video, as opposed to those of conventional broadcasting and cinema.

In 1972, Phillips released the first consumer Video Cassette Recorder (VCR). Cheaper than the *portapak*, it encouraged the public to 'time shift' their TV viewing.[36] Broadcasters and the film industry, as seems to be a subsequent trend, initially viewed the VCR with suspicion; as merely a pirating tool. The growing competition amongst TV channels during this period, alongside the popularization of the remote control,[37] changed the way people watched TV. People could 'channel surf' or switch between broadcast and recorded content. This, in Hart Snider's[38] opinion, laid the foundations for the 'discontinuous' way in which we watch video/TV today, and anticipated the viewing habits of the 'MTV[39] generation' of the 1980s.

The release of the personal computer (PC) in the 1980s, further increased the possibilities for graphic representation and manipulation of imagery. The 'Appropriation Art' movement brought much greater theoretical legitimacy for appropriative practices in the art world. The 'Scratch Video' movement, pioneered by the Emergency Broadcast Network (EBN)[40] in the US, began to use *v.sampling* together with new fast editing and video processing techniques to create video mixes which looked scathingly at the political and media establishment's portrayal of reality through TV. *Max Headroom*, which took a comic look at TV news-footage, was among the first programmes to use these techniques on mainstream TV. VJ Michael Heap commented:

> Most of the techniques used like rapid cut, editing and montage, most people claim, are directly from the MTV style ... editing for music videos but that has directly sprung from the Scratch video movement of the 1980s.[41]

Competing TV Channels, such as MTV, began to use brighter graphics and, like EBN, faster editing techniques to capture the dwindling attention spans of their young viewers. MTV began to use the term VJ to describe the person who presents and comments on music videos for TV programmes, rather like a radio DJ.

Music producer, Steinski,[42] working with John Kane and Glen Lazzaro, used the first PCs powerful enough to *v.sample*[43] to make political statements. He created *And The Motorcade Sped On*,[44] which sampled footage of the JFK assassination.[45] The 1990s saw the emergence of 3D Motion Graphics.[46] PCs' new-found power allowed filmmakers to create 'digitally composited' images in which it was not always possible to distinguish a 'real' image from a computer generated one. As opposed to the earlier video collage and montage techniques, which juxtaposed different images to create questions in the mind of the viewer about their validity and effect, the aim of 'digital compositing' was to create almost 'photo-real' fake realities. Lev Manovitch, states: Montage aims to create visual, stylistic, semantic and emotional dissonance between different elements. In contrast, compositing aims to blend them into a seamless whole, a single gestalt.[47]

Influenced by the likes of EBN and Steinski, bands such as *Coldcut* and *Hexstatic*, during the 1990s, in their performances, music videos and DVDs, brought the mixing of *v.samples* into its contemporary incarnations. Companies such as Addictive TV have brought the world of VJing to a wider audience by making programmes for broadcast TV showcasing VJs. Their TV productions are, of necessity, minus the *unauthorized v.samples*. As VJ Anyone commented:

> I have two sets ... a set where I play live and I play whatever I want and, when it comes to broadcasting or archiving, then I do exclusively my own stuff because I want to get rid of all these issues.[48]

Considering that 95 per cent of the VJs who responded to a questionnaire administered at the 2003 Contact Europe VJ Festival said that they used 'found footage' i.e. *v.samples*, in their work (and all of them had seen other VJs use them),[49] the above TV work cannot really be said to be representative of VJing as a whole.

Today, video production has been further democratized by a massive drop in prices.[50] Laptop PCs, running new editing software[51] have allowed video artists to bring their work virtually anywhere. Contemporary video art by the likes of Bill Viola and Gary Hill is now, for all intents and purposes, part of the artistic establishment. Events showcasing appropriative works, such as the 'Illegal Art Video Mash-Up Festival'[52] have become popular. Some even go as far as to say that appropriative video works now dominate twentieth century art exhibitions. A fairly recent ICA[53] exhibition, *Video Acts*, was a major collection of 'over 80 landmarks in the development of video art'[54] and Bill Viola's *The Passions*, was the major exhibition at the National Gallery.[55] There are also a number of international VJ web communities who meet at sites such as www.vjcentral.com to discuss VJing, exchange techniques and organize events. Recent discussions have included the potential of multicasting over the web (web TV) and the possibility of real-time, 'micro TV' channels.

Fandom and the Internet

Since time immemorial, societies have used storytelling as a method of cultural communication. Societies' myths and legends have never been static ideas, rather fluid concepts that change and adapt with the varying needs of communities. This phenomenon has begun to manifest in postmodern culture as Internet communities of fans of particular movies, TV programmes, novels, or even whole genres. Fandom proper began with the 'Fanzines'[56] dedicated to the first series of *Star Trek*[57] during the 1960s, when fans began using their favourite characters in stories of their own making. Beginning as a small-time endeavour,[58] this Fan-Fiction (or *fanfic*) and Fan-Art, quickly sprouted specialist sub-genres such as 'slash'.[59] Celluloid fans began to use 16 mm prints to re-edit their favourite movies and in the 1970s, VCR[60] revelations allowed many more people to watch movies at home. This, as well as the first generation of children growing up watching both TV and cinema, created a new-found sense of 'ownership' in fans over their favourite films and TV programmes.

> What Disney does not always seem to see is that there is a generation of film-goers who have an entirely proprietary feeling about popular culture ... The moment the corporation declares its exclusive rights of use it punctures this proprietary feeling, alienates the film-goer, and undermines the very engagement that Disney has done so much (and succeeded so well) in creating. The proprietary sense may have no foundation in legal fact, but pity the corporation that decides to ignore it.[61]

This statement evokes a concept similar to that of 'Cultural Property', often used in International Law and Politics, when dealing with the post-colonial repatriation and protection of traditional art. Some writers lament that the 'cultural property' of the people of Western nations has not been given similar protection. Jenkins comments:

> If we are going to tell stories that reflect our cultural experiences they will borrow heavily from the material the media has so aggressively marketed to us . . . media culture is our culture and, as such, has become an important public resource, the reservoir out of which all future creativity will arise. Given this situation, shouldn't we be concerned about the corporations that keep 'infringing' on our cultural wellspring?[62]

Fandom's greatest turning point came via the World Wide Web, which provided a forum for the collection and distribution of the products of what were, until then, diffuse and separate communities. Websites, such as www.fanfiction.net, have collected together this diverse bunch of writers, artists and editors, all of whom have two things in common: their love of media products and their desire to use the worlds and characters within them to tell their own stories. In *Jamming the Media*, Gareth Branwyn describes this phenomenon, 'A new form of media is growing up in cyberspace, a global do-it-yourself newsroom and cultural salon where individuals simultaneously create and consume news and information, blurring the distinction between publisher, reporter and reader'.[63] These communities mostly operate on a not-for-profit basis. Of the respondents to the web-based questionnaire to fans, 87 per cent said that they would not wish to gain financially from any edits they had made.[64]

Recently there has been a slew of high profile instances of fan-editing including *Star Wars Episode 1.1: The Phantom Edit*, in which an anonymous fan removed 20 minutes of footage from Lucas' original.[65] Lucas, while showing initial interest, said, after the edit became widely available on the Internet and on 'bootleg' videos, that he would never watch a *fan edit* again.[66] This may safeguard Lucas against possible court actions.[67] As Rogers[68] points out, Lucas, in a previous interview, made the highly ironic statement that the 'next big thing to shock the film world would be a low budget film created by some kid in his garage'. In the same article, discussing the release of his 'special edition' re-edits of the first *Star Wars Trilogy*, he went on to say: 'It's my artistic vision. If I want to go back and change it, it's my business, not somebody else's . . . so nobody can screw around with my stuff'.[69]

Lucasfilm has been at the forefront of the practice of shutting down fan sites for containing infringing material. Jenkins[70] reminds us that Lucasfilm's official rationale for this was that they could lose commercial control over their copyrighted material.[71] Only 15 per cent of respondents surveyed said that they would not comply with a request from a copyright holder to cease re-editing their films.[72] Hudson comments: 'Most people being caught in these battles lack the financial resources to take on a major corporation in court'.[73] This also applies to the fees that fans and VJs have to pay if they attempt to gain authorization for the use of these materials. Lucasfilm could be said to have acknowledged that fan edits contain *original* content in the terms of service of their offer of free web space to fans,[74] which states that authors posting materials voluntarily give up rights to their work, implying that they *have* rights to give up.

Another fan edit to hit the headlines is Russian fan-editor Goblin's[75] irreverent version of *Lord the Rings: The Fellowship of the Ring*.[76] This has gained popularity on the Russian pirate video black market, an unusual (and worrying, from New Line Cinema's point of view) crossover into the commercial sector for fan-editing. Golbin's version was the subject of an article in *The Observer* newspaper:

> In a move that has taken the Russian pirate disk world by storm and infuriated traditionalists and copyright lawyers, Puchkov has completely changed the script, turning the 'good' characters, like Frodo, into bumbling Russian cops, and the 'bad' Orcs into Russian Gangsters.[77]

Many of the fan edits available on the web are short, music-video/movie trailer style compilations of clips from movies or TV series', set to music. Thousands are available at www.fanmadetrailers.com.[78] Unlike fan edits such as the 'Kubrick Edit' of Steven Spielberg's *A.I.: Artificial Intelligence*,[79] which appropriate large portions of movies in order to change their storylines, these music-video style edits, or 'doujinshi', as one Japanese anime fan referred to them,[80] take much less of the original. They can be seen, rather than detracting from a video's market, as being free advertising, or even adding value to the original.

The main thrust of the argument to permit fan-editing is based on its non-commerciality; however, some commercial organizations are also beginning to re-edit movies. In the US, 'Clean Flicks', a video rental chain, are seeking a court declaration that their practice of editing out sexual or violent content from the movies that they lend, is legal. The DGA,[81] who are considering a countersuit, have declared that Clean Flicks' case is an effort to: 'legitimize the unauthorized editing and alteration of movies'.[82] This case highlights the very real prospect of future legal wranglings and the need for parameters to be secured and boundaries set. One journalist comments:

> We are headed towards a new conceptualisation of film as a permanent work-in-progress, which exists in multiple permutations, and can always be tinkered with in the future, whether by the Director or by anyone else. As editing tools improve, fans won't be limited to cutting, either. They'll be able to manipulate the scenes themselves, and create new ones.[83]

Cinema and filmic quotation

American Director D.W. Griffith[84] pioneered many now 'established' film-making techniques.[85] His most famous work (and most controversial due to its sympathetic stance on the Klu Klux Klan) was *The Birth of a Nation*, which portrayed two families' lives during the American Civil War.[86] New York based artist and cultural commentator Paul Miller (aka DJ Spooky), in a piece about his recent video 'remix' of Griffith's film entitled *Rebirth of a Nation*, comments:[87]

> *Birth of a Nation* ... floats out in the world of cinema as an enduring albeit totally racist – epic tale of an America that, in essence, never existed ... it's considered to be an American 'cinema classic' despite the racist content. By remixing the film ... I hoped to create a counter-narrative, one where the story implodes on itself, one where new stories arise out the ashes of that explosion.[88]

European directors, such as Soviet Sergei Eisenstein, created films like *The Battleship Potemkin*, developing theories of how the arrangement of shots could create associations in the minds of the audience.[89] By the mid-1920s technology had been developed to add synchronous sound to movies.[90] Even before the introduction of 'talkies',[91] movies had become a powerful common cultural reference point for Western society. The notion of Hollywood as 'The Dream Factory' and the glamorous exploits of stars, on and off screen, took on Herculean status in the minds of audiences. This contributed to a later trend for films about the influence of cinema/TV on people's lives or the way people view cinema/TV, often requiring the use of actual footage from earlier works i.e. filmic quotation.

> By the middle of the Twentieth Century, the direct incorporation of source material from pre-existing texts and popular culture became commonplace. Many of the most influential artists in their fields made collage-like appropriation a central part of their work[92] with the result that today this practice ... is no longer the preserve of the avant-garde.[93]

Bruce Conner's avant-garde short, *A Movie*[94] juxtaposes violent and erotic images with 'The End' titles to emphasize how many films play on human tendencies toward sexual and violent voyeurism. The 'as long as it's naked or explodes, we're entertained' mentality.[95] Godfrey Reggio's film *Koyaanisqatsi*, and its 1988 sequel *Powaqqatsi*, are often cited as classics of this technique of using found footage to create filmic collage.[96,97] They created an epic picture of the history of the development of humanity out of hundreds of pieces of archive footage. Without the use of this footage it would have been impossible for Reggio to create a film encompassing such a swathe of history. As Heap points out:

It is quite hard . . . to recreate the 1969 riots in Brixton or the cold war footage of all the missile carriers going through Red Square . . . I go back and use archive material . . . because there is no way I can replicate it. It is in an entirely different context.[98]

Woody Allen's *Zelig*, superimposes the main character onto footage of famous historical scenes.[99] Allen's technique influenced the 1994 Oscar-winning film *Forrest Gump*.[100] This is about to be continued in a project by Steven Spielberg's DreamWorks studio and Mike Myers,[101] a Hollywood version of BBC2's series *Staggering Stories of Ferdinand De Bargos*,[102] in which Myers will be digitally inserted into a series of classic movies to create new stories.

Film sampling is an exciting way to put an original spin on existing films and allow audiences to see old movies in a new light. Rap artists have been doing this for years with music, and now we are able to take that same concept and apply it to film.[103]

Artist and Filmmaker Douglas Gordon, in his piece *24 Hour Psycho*, used Hitchcock's classic *Psycho* slowed down over 24 hours.[104,105] Gordon refers to Hitchcock's obsession for being self-referential and for reworking older films. Horror, like other cinematic genres, is very self-referential. Wes Craven's 1996 film *Scream*, quoted John Carpenter's *Halloween*, and was, in turn quoted in its 1998 sequel: *Halloween H20: 20 Years Later*.[106–108] Much of the appeal of watching films like *Scream* is recognizing the references to other horror films within them.

The Romantic Comedy genre also has quite a tradition of self-reference. *Sleepless in Seattle* featured clips from the 1957 classic *An Affair to remember*, and in turn was quoted in *The Cable Guy* in 1996, and *How to Lose a Guy in 10 Days*, in 2003.[109–111] In quoting (*sampling*) other movies, a movie taps into its audience's memories and emotions about that film. These emotional responses to shared cultural material are exactly what gave rise to the phenomenon of Fandom, and are also a reason VJs use samples in the first place. It seems that the film establishment are happy to use these associations for their own commercial purposes, but are less than enthusiastic when they are unable to control or profit from the new meanings and associations being given to their 'property'.

One can see a developmental process here similar to that affecting 'scratch video' whereby an artistic 'movement' begins by inventing new techniques, using them to promote particular political ideas. If popular, these techniques are then appropriated by the mainstream media for commercial purposes, while their original polemical content is abandoned. The dance music movement of the late 1980s is a case in point. Originally, dance music and 'rave culture' was seen as a form of political rebellion. Thousands of people converging in a field and dancing to 'rave' music was seen as a political affront to the dominant Thatcherite politics of the time. Then came the Criminal Justice and Public Order Act 1994, which suppressed these gatherings, leaving 'rave' music without it's natural home. A very different picture is evident today. People pay to go in to clubs to listen to dance music *en mass* and its techniques are used widely in commercial music, cinema and television minus its original political connotations. Some also see this as a likely future for the VJing movement.

Copyright law and video sampling

The UK Copyright Act does not specifically accommodate or identify with many contemporary or unconventional art practices, *v.sampling* being just one. Like most areas that have yet to be fully explored by the courts, never mind the legislature, this area lacks hard and fast rules. The unauthorized use of *v.samples* challenges not only the existing principles upon which 'film' copyright law is based, but also the principles upon which artistic works are judged by the legal community. To put it simply, in order to avoid infringing, the secondary creator has to obtain permission or a licence from the copyright owners to cover the intended use. To see how this can or cannot be achieved, applying existing copyright law as it stands today, to the issues raised by *v.sampling*, although inadequate, is the only option. To tackle some of the legal issues surrounding *v.sampling*, my approach is to first consider, the legal position of the 'secondary creator' in the event of an alleged infringement, and second, the legal status of the 'secondary creation'.

The VJ or fan-editor and copyright infringement under the UK CDPA 1988

In the CDPA, under section 5B(1), a 'film' includes 'a recording on any medium from which a moving image may by any means be produced'. As we know, VJs sample from any visual material that contains a moving image. This audio-visual source material may not be a 'film' as it is generally understood; however, in order to adhere to the present law, infringement issues must be examined under this head.

Under the CDPA the principal director and producer of a film are joint authors and first owners of copyright.[112,113] Copyright protection for films expires 70 years after the death of the last of certain designated persons prescribed for in the Act, whether or not these persons are designated as co-authors.[114] It is important to establish whether the film being sampled is still in copyright or whether it has become public domain material but 'the mere fact that something is generally considered to be "in the public domain" does not obviate the need to determine whether it is protected by copyright'.[115] Furthermore, an appropriative, multimedia artist must establish whether each individual work is in the public domain and can be used without a licence. Of the respondents to the VJ questionnaire, 90 per cent claimed to understand the meaning of 'public domain' and yet some described it as 'anything filmed in a public space' or 'cultural events'.[116] This highlights the misconceived notions surrounding copyright terms and thus the need for clearer guidelines.

Copyright infringement can be divided in to two categories, namely, primary and secondary. Primary infringements relate to certain *exclusive rights* that copyright gives authors of certain types of works.[117] These rights relate to the acts that only the owner of the copyright can perform or authorize and are known as the 'restricted acts'.[118] The infringement is of the underlying source material. Secondary infringements generally relate to commercial use of a copyrighted work that has been the subject of a primary infringement, such as multiple copying, dealing, importing and facilitating.

Copyright infringements

With regards to *v.sampling*, the most significant of these exclusive rights are the prevention of unauthorized persons from copying, making adaptations of and performing the work in public.[119] An act restricted by copyright can be performed in relation to the whole work or any substantial part of it. The claimant must have also established an objective similarity between the works and must show a causal connection. If no permission has been obtained, it would seem that a VJ who samples the whole or substantial part of a work, adapts it, integrates it with other work and then performs a new work by showing it in public, is infringing the rights in the source on at least three counts. Copying in relation to a film, television broadcast or cable programme includes making a photograph of the whole or any substantial part of any image forming part of the film, broadcast or cable programme.[120]

Copying has taken place if a secondary creator simply records samples from a video onto a disc or HDD. Adaptation has occurred if the secondary creator makes changes to the samples or arranges them in some way. VJs, by performing these samples in clubs, show the material 'in public'. In the fan questionnaire, over one-fifth of the study population who had re-edited a film or television programme themselves, had further distributed it over the World Wide Web.[121] It must be noted that a VJ doesn't necessarily copy if the mixing of a number of films is a 'live' creation using the original source recordings (i.e. mixing using original 'off the shelf' DVDs or VHS cassettes).

Copyright is infringed when an unauthorized person performs a restricted act in relation to the whole or substantial part of the film.[122] The substantial part, as highlighted in one music sampling case, must be of the plaintiff's work, not of the defendants[123] and what exactly constitutes a substantial part has proven problematic. There is no authority in UK law dealing with *v.sampling* specifically but there have been some cases regarding music sampling. Measuring substantiality, it seems, is 'a matter of impression'.[124] Although there was no final decision, the judge, in the *Produce Records case*, confirmed that 'substantial' depended on not only quantity and quality, but that it was also a question of fact and degree.[125] In relation to artistic works, a House of Lords case emphasized that the first step is to identify the part that has been copied and then to ask whether this part is a substantial part of the copyrighted work.[126] Clearly, the less one takes the better, but sampling the 'heart' or 'essence' of a creation, no matter how short, is more likely to suggest infringement. The test of 'substantial taking' remains vague, perhaps inevitably, when the issue is widely agreed to be one of quantity and/or quality, fact or degree. This problem, combined with the lack of legal precedent, has led to a situation where neither the courts nor those to whom the law applies are sufficiently sure of their positions.

The only UK case with any relevance to *v.sampling*, viewed the practice in a harsh light and condemned virtually all duplication as infringement.[127] The Judges held (under the 1956 Copyright Act) that the copy only must be proven to be a copy of a substantial part only of the frame from which it was taken. The legal conception of film, as a disjointed series of separate 'photograph' frames meant that essentially any copying, no matter how insubstantial in quantitative or qualitative terms, resulted in an infringement. The 1988 Act, however, regarded film as a single whole work, thereby providing flexibility at the expense of certainty, over what constitutes a substantial part.

Protection also only extends to the expression of ideas, not the ideas themselves.[128] This dichotomy is not an express statutory rule but continues to frequently infiltrate copyright cases. Many authors and some of the judiciary infer that this dichotomy can be misleading.[129] The courts are usually loathe to give protection to an idea. This was exemplified in the notorious case featuring Guinness and commercials director Mehdi Norowzian. Here Norowzian lost his claim that Guinness had breached his copyright. Although Mr Justice Rattie accepted on the facts that the plaintiff's work had been referenced, that is, it was merely referred to in a general way as opposed to copied wholesale, there was held to be no copyright in a mere style or technique. The sentiment that the law protects specific ideas and not general ideas i.e. a style or a process, was reiterated by Lord Hoffmann in the *Designer's Guild* case when he said, rather cryptically, 'The law protects foxes better than hedgehogs'.[130]

It is important to note that a 'film' for the purposes of the CDPA, is the actual material recording, not the subject matter of the recording, that is to say, what is recorded on the actual celluloid or videotape. The first time Norowzian came before the High Court in 1988, it was held therefore that the film could only be infringed by a copying of the whole or a substantial part of the particular recording of the film. The problem accepted by the court was that the CDPA appeared to afford no protection to an original work of art, which was a film, as long as the film itself was not copied, although it would protect an original work which was recorded by the film. An important question decided by the Court of Appeal, which took a different view in this case was whether a film could constitute a dramatic work. It was held that copyright could subsist in a film itself, as a dramatic work in itself (and a recording of a dramatic work) since it was capable of being performed to an audience, even if it is not the recording of an underlying dramatic work. It must be noted that this revelation may be an advantage to the owner of the copyright in the film since there are some differences between dramatic works and films in terms of infringement. Nonetheless, in this case there was no copyright infringement because the test of substantiality had not been satisfied.

Many artists find ideas more important than their expression and lay claims to ideas as 'works' in their own right. For them, it is the idea that constitutes the work, rather than its execution. Professor A, and H.J. Lucas noted that 'the distinction between the idea and the form tends to be blurred with the development of conceptual art' whose followers share Sol Le Witt's view that, 'ideas can be works of art'.[131] The lack of a healthy relationship between law and art leaves many contemporary art forms stranded at sea. The law, in disregarding copyrights in 'ideas', is not therefore, of much avail to the contemporary artist seeking its protection. This highlights the problem with treating many, very different art forms in the same way, with regards to both infringement criteria and in determining whether a work attracts the protection of the law.

Secondary infringements

It is important to mention that there also exist various secondary infringements to which a VJ (or other relevant person) may fall foul. In contrast to primary infringers, secondary infringers must know or have reason to believe that they are dealing with infringing copies of a work.[132] Assuming the person is found to have this knowledge in accordance with the objective 'reasonable man' test,[133] copyright is infringed where this person:

1   imports infringing copy;[134]
2   possesses or deals with infringing copies;[135]
3   provides the means for making infringing copies;[136]
4   permits the use of premises for infringing performance;[137] and/or
5   provides the apparatus for infringing performance.[138]

Moral rights

Film is a multimedia work and therefore is made up of an enormous complexity and quantity of rights, besides those in the film itself. Although the producer usually has a licence or an assignment of the copyright, if not outright ownership, the authors' moral rights may not have been irrevocably and unconditionally waived. Those with any relevance to *v.sampling* are:

1   the right to be identified as author or director;
2   The right to object to derogatory treatment of a work;

3 the right to object to false attribution; and
4 the right to privacy of certain photographs and films.[139]

The right to be identified as the director must be asserted in one of the ways provided for in the Act.[140] Assuming the right has been asserted, the identification of the director must be clear, reasonably prominent and made in relation to each copy of the work or any substantial part of it which is commercially published, performed, exhibited or otherwise exploited.[141] In practice, the film producer is more likely to insist on the writer's waiver of moral rights in exchange for an agreed screen credit for the author in the film and subsequent derivatives.

The right to object to derogatory treatment of a work has two limbs. First, one must show 'treatment' has taken place and second, that that 'treatment' was 'derogatory'. 'Treatment' is defined as 'any addition to, deletion from, or alteration to or adaptation of the work'.[142] It is undoubtedly the case that both VJs and fan-editors treat the work, merely by taking samples. This is 'derogatory' if it amounts to 'distortion or mutilation of the work or is otherwise prejudicial to the honour or reputation of the author or director'.[143] Peter Wienand has pointed out that for VJs, it is unclear whether 'merely juxtaposing samples from one film against samples from another is a derogatory treatment'.[144]

One rare case to have looked into these rights involved the Monty Python team, who successfully claimed that the US television broadcaster ABC had infringed their copyright in the script by drastically re-cutting and re-assembling episodes of Monty Python's Flying Circus in circumstances where the writers had only granted the BBC (original licensee), the right to make minor changes.[145] The French courts hold moral rights as fundamental and vehemently upheld a director's right to object to derogatory treatment by ordering a ban on the colourization of a black and white film, *Asphalt Jungle*.[146]

The right not to have a work falsely attributed to you as author or director applies to the whole work or any part of it and it extends to adaptations or copies of the work.[147] The fourth moral right gives a person who, for private and domestic purposes, commissions the taking of a photograph or the making of a film, certain rights over its exploitation.

Most European legal traditions acknowledge the non-economic value of artistic works, and embrace moral rights as essential parts of their systems. However, the United States bases its intellectual property laws upon the economic value of creative expression.[148] The only expression of moral rights in the US legislation is contained in the Visual Artists Rights Act 1990. Otherwise, the courts rely on the laws such as defamation, competition and privacy. Despite its name, it provides only limited protection to a very narrow class of artistic works – those considered to be works of fine art. Many of the works most susceptible to digital alteration fall outside its definition of works of fine art, and therefore remain unprotected.[149]

In addition to the above, rights in performances, personality rights, trademarks (e.g. product placement) and the torts of libel and passing off, are but a few legal principles which must also be kept in check but which are beyond the scope of this chapter.

Defences

The CDPA attempts to balance the owner's rights with the public interest by providing an exhaustive list of 'permitted acts'. These are confined to using a copyright work in a fair manner solely for the purposes of research, private study, criticism, review, and reporting current events. These are termed the 'fair dealing' provisions.[150] Not many VJs or fan-editors could be said to sample for these specific purposes and so are unlikely to benefit from these fixed and inflexible provisions. The American 'fair use' provisions however are non-exhaustive and may provide a safe haven for a *v.sampler*, in certain circumstances.[151]

Through a series of cases, the US courts have admitted, albeit indirectly, that sampling is not always theft, in allowing parody to fall within the ambit of the 'fair use' defence.[152] For a parody to work, it often means a substantial reproduction of the work to be parodied and this is a problem if it is to be treated like any other alleged copyright infringement.[153] The UK CDPA however, contains no express parody defence and there is no intention to implement one. The Information Society Directive provides an exhaustive list of situations in which a Member State may provide for exceptions or limitations to copyright protection and actually introduces parody, but doesn't make it mandatory.[154] The UK's version of the Directive is called The Copyright and Related Rights Regulations 2003 and does not include parody.[155] People have become acclimatized to parodic tendencies, there being a long and distinguished tradition of parody, spoof and burlesque. Whatever the merits of such a copyright infringement claim, in reality a copyright owner will often be flattered and take it as a compliment. Not many people would want to expose themselves to the potential ridicule, which is likely to result from making a complaint.

Although there is a trend of using obscure *v.samples* and recontextualizing them, Bently points out that samples are often chosen because they are 'memorable clips', supposed to be recognized.[156] VJs often select samples precisely because of their popularity and familiarity, so people can relate to them or comment upon them. How can a VJ criticize, for example, Disney, in a VJ set without using Disney's copyrighted images, or comment upon war, without showing the footage? Arguably, present copyright laws are stifling VJing and other contemporary art forms' ability to mature by cutting off their access to corporate and newsreel/political mass imagery. Surely it is an infringement of one's freedom of expression to preclude these forms of comment. Should the 'fair dealing' defence perhaps be redrafted and made more flexible?[157] As it stands, the courts have failed to clarify the law on fair dealing. The interesting question lies between the clearly legal and illegal ends of the spectrum. It has been suspected that:

> ... in issues which require judges to measure a vague concept such as *fairness* rather than a more precise concept ... judges in the past have subconsciously worked back from the result they prefer and then massaged that result into the phraseology which empowers them to exercise that choice, rather than start from clear guidelines and definitions which are then projected into the facts before the court.[158]

The status of the secondary creation. Does the UK CDPA 1988 provide protection?

The second issue is whether the VJ set/event, or the fan edit itself, qualifies for copyright protection as a new work in its own right. To qualify as an 'artistic work', it must fall within a class of 'work' defined by the CDPA and be 'original'.[159] If copying from another artistic work, it must be visually different. There needs to be 'some element of material alteration or embellishment which suffices to make the totality of the work an original work'.[160] Using existing material for the basis of a new work will not necessarily prevent the new work form benefiting from copyright protection, in that, original thought is not required for originality, although the law will guard against plagiarism.[161] However, it is not necessary that a film be original, just that it is not copied from a previous film.[162]

Clearly, the law regulates different forms of creation separately and individually. Such outmoded distinctions between artistic disciplines such as film, painting and sculpture do not sit comfortably with the reality of creative forms today. 'Live video mixing' and 'installations' (which often incorporate elements of TV, animation, computer graphics, still photography) are hybrid art forms which cross artistic disciplines, lie between legal categories and are often marked by temporality.[163] To slot what a VJ does into the category of 'film' or into the existing taxonomy of 'artistic works' under the Act seems an unjustifiable and unworkable forced construction of this digital art form.

This lack of legal recognition has lead to arguments that it places limits on the legal protection of contemporary art forms and also imposes legal restrictions on artistic practices. As these practices continue to convolute and crossover, problems will only get worse. Copyright law must identify with multimedia productions and regulate the categories in the CDPA in a way that brings together many individual works into a single production.

Mr Justice Laddie, in one case exclaimed that the law has been 'bedevilled' by attempts to extend the scope of these categories.[164] This case suggests that the courts are more willing to consider the intention and status of the creator when deciding to classify a work. It was pointed out that if the creators didn't see themselves as artists this would be an indicator that it should not be classified as an 'artistic work'. In the same vein, if VJs (or video artists) do not consider their work to be a 'film' then why should the law classify it so, just because 'film' in the Act deals with the moving image?

However, even with artistic intentions, the issue of 'fixation' is problematic, despite there being no such express statutory requirement for 'artistic works'. Just as 'film' and the very categories of 'artistic works' would seem to involve fixation, it is submitted that some form of fixation is a necessary prerequisite.[165] Therefore, one basic problem of trying to copyright a multimedia work of art is that it is often temporal or time-based, such as the aforementioned installations and VJ sets, which may have a live, interactive and participatory element. Because these 'products' are non-tangible, 'one-off' experiences, under the present law, they are unlikely to qualify for copyright protection. In one case, an assembly of *'objets trouves'* was held not to be a collage as it was intrinsically ephemeral, existing only for a few hours. Laddie J rejected the general proposition that something, which has a mere transient existence, cannot be a 'work of art'.[166]

The VJ's 'live' performance, i.e. the mix of different media products and the people themselves, taken as a composite whole, is often argued to be a piece of installation art in itself, an 'interactive space' that has been 'atmospherically engineered'. Like postmodernism itself, trying to define what comprises an installation is a tricky question. The Thames and Hudson Dictionary of Art and Artists says installations 'only exist as long as they are installed' and elaborates a bit more by saying they are, 'multimedia, multidimensional and multi-form works which are created temporarily for a particular space or site either outdoors or indoors, in a museum or gallery'.[167] This scope is wide and examples illustrate that installations do not share any particular characteristics, in that, some will be site-specific[168] and some will demand audience participation.[169]

Filmic quotation, licensing and clearance

Any risk attached to copying can be minimized by applying principles such as substantiality and fair dealing or by gaining clearance or entering into a licence agreement. It is not surprising therefore that following on from the plethora of copyright issues that are raised by *v.sampling* there are a medley of clearance and licensing issues. A huge panoply of rights can attach to a multimedia work and thus a potentially huge number of clearances may have to be obtained in order to sample a video clip and to show it in public, integrated within a new work. In the absence of any legal and equitable avenues to obtain the appropriate clearances, for a VJ, the task would be painstakingly expensive and time-consuming. For other types of copyright works such as musical works and the visual arts, there exist 'collecting societies' to represent the artist and/or copyright owner such as the MCPS[170] and the DACS[171] respectively. With the exception of VPL,[172] which deals with the licensing of music videos and DPRS,[173] which only represents British, freelance film and TV directors, there are no such societies for film and television. Furthermore, a VJ's clearance requirements would stretch well beyond their scope. Put simply, none of the above serves the artist who wishes to *v.sample*.

Instead, image banks and footage archives are emerging.[174] Thus, a *v.sampler's* only option, is to enter into a direct negotiation with the copyright owner/s or to adopt the 'wait and see' approach. The latter may refuse to deal or charge an extortionate fee and/or impose powerful conditions upon the use. These traditional *rights protected licences* involve licensing images for 'specific uses' for a fee, ordinarily determined by the type of use, the duration of the licence and the territory in which publication will take place.[175] Research carried out with a number of TV and film companies revealed that current practices utilize the *standard agreement* but terms may vary. Generally, there were no official set rates but Channel 4 are said to work from an official ratecard.[176] They said that each case would be dealt with separately, the company maintaining full discretion as to whether to deal, so any request for footage would depend on many factors. They would only entertain the needs of the secondary creators if there was an easier system, i.e. less time-consuming and if there was something in it for them. In answer to the question on whether there were any plans to operate a publicly accessible archive for moving images online, it was discovered that Pathe has already done this but for viewing purposes only.[177] This highlights a fear of loosing revenue to pirates making perfect digital clones.

Collective administration is useful for artists who do not wish to manage, administrate and police their intellectual property. However, members transfer their rights voluntarily, leaving room for the unyielding to withhold permission to use a work. One solution for *v.sampling* would be to require *compulsory licensing* of particular portions of a work. For instance, statute could require this form of licence for a number of seconds of a work and the fee could be seen as 'compensation' for the use, defined by statute or an independent third party and managed by collecting societies or by other means. An obvious problem lies with the diverse nature of the works in a multimedia production, wherein the value placed on each component will vary.[178]

These and associated problems, such as the usurping of the copyright owner's control over their work can make the option unfavourable. However, it does have certain advantages in that it could: serve to standardize things and provide legal certainty; reduce transaction costs; promote efficiency; reduce the burden of extensive copyright searches and private negotiations; lead to unhindered dissemination of copyrighted works for reuse; and, vet the power of the copyright owner to *refuse to deal.* The new model of *royalty-free licensing* involves buying licensed images on a non-exclusive basis that can be used for supposedly any purpose, any number of times and throughout the world. If priced equitably, this seems like the perfect solution, but the devil often takes refuge in the small print.[179]

The Creative Commons is devoted to expanding the range of creative work available for others to build upon by offering a range of legally binding licences that permit copying and sharing.[180] While you retain your copyright, these licences allow the licensees to do various acts, which would otherwise be restricted by copyright, that is, they allow the world to distribute, display, copy and webcast your work, provided the licensee lives up to the conditions of the licensor. It is unclear as yet, whether these licences will stand up to the full extent of the law.

To accommodate our ever-growing 'electronic culture', the industry's major stakeholders might do better to take a holistic approach and embrace these chances for exploitation. Lessons can be learned from the record industry's reluctance to entertain on-line services for downloading music. Whatever the form or system of licensing *v.samples*, more often it is the consumer who is dictating what they want and how they should experience it. Will the copyright owners make themselves an island or will they enter the mix?

Appropriationism and postmodernity in a corporate world

'Art is a history of inspired plagiarism and visual art is a history of ingenious adaptation.'[181]

There are a number of identifiable pillars on which the postmodern cultural paradigm stands. The most readily discernible of these is the concept of the 'mix'. Building on art theory during the Modernist period, in which theorists saw all art as in some way incorporating and reacting to the art of the past, the concept of the 'mix' as creation in postmodern theory makes this relationship to the past totally explicit by using *samples* of the pre-existing imagery of past artists in ways which imbue them with new meaning.

> The whole of human development is derivative. We stand on the shoulders of the scientists, artists and craftsmen who preceded us. We borrow and develop what they have done: not necessarily as parasites, but simply as the next generation. It is at the heart of what we know as progress.[182]

It is plain from the previous histories that the postmodern paradigm has been accepted and adopted almost universally in the art world and the media/communications industries. Appropriation can be seen as one of the main modes of expression within this new world-view. Brewster and Broughton link this to the sampling phenomenon through the DJ: 'Because his artistry comes from combining other people's art, because his performance is made from other musicians' performances, the DJ is the epitome of a postmodern artist'.[183]

Several artistic movements in history, such as Cubism and Dadaism, routinely used '*objets trouvé*' in their art. Marcel Duchamp, creator of the famous

L.H.O.O.Q.[184] opined that the act of selection can be a form of inspiration as original and significant as any other.[185] Why, if artists have for 40 years worked with eclectic mixtures of these techniques, do we still have a Copyright Act that imposes rigid categories upon them? Carlin argues that: 'Copyright Law constrains the impulse of modern artists to use, refer, to quote, challenge and praise the imagery that pervades the visual environment, thus placing unacceptable limitations upon artistic activity and free expression'.[186]

A further pillar of postmodern art is that it often consciously includes the viewer; from being left to interpret the work in whatever way they perceive it subjectively, to actually being part of the work itself.[187] Curator, Melissa Feldman, describes the video installations of artist Bill Viola as mental landscapes into which the viewer is physically and psychically thrust. Bill Viola has himself exclaimed:

> This for me is the most exciting thing about working as an artist at this time of history ... the real raw materials are not the camera and monitor, but time and experience itself, and that the real place the work exists is not on the screen or within the walls of the room, but in the minds and heart of the person who has seen it.[188]

Another important consideration when looking at appropriative *digital* art is to recognize that it is technologically led. As is evident, holders of copyright in the moving image are often companies or corporations. This is important, as the production of digital hardware is solely a corporate endeavour, i.e. corporations are the sole purveyors of the means by which digital appropriation can be achieved. With the last decade's rise in corporate consolidation within the media/communications sector, the corporations who purvey the technological means of appropriation (and often advertise their wares on the strength of its copying abilities) are all too often the same corporations who own vast databases of the content being appropriated and which their lawyers are defending so vigorously.[189] Corporations, it seems, are 'hedging their bets': advertising their hardware/software for its appropriative capabilities, as well as protecting their content, through DRM and TPMs.[190]

> ...individuals who create intellectual property have not had the resources or channels of distribution to disseminate their creations. Today, most creators have little choice but to sell their copyright to corporations who then disseminate these works. Does this encourage the creation of new content?[191]

The position of corporate copyright owners has also been bolstered by the trend for continually extending the term of copyright. The effect of this trend is most explicit in US law, where the 'Sonny Bono Act' extended

copyright to 70 years for individuals and 95 years for companies/corpora-
tions. This discrepancy between the rights of individuals and organizations
reveals the clear beneficiaries of this policy: large corporate copyright
holders. Lessig has argued that this policy is unconstitutional:[192]

> The Constitution says that copyrights are to be 'for limited times'. The
> framers initially set those 'limited times' to be quite short – 14 years,
> renewable once . . . This text, the challengers say, forbids the extension
> of existing terms . . . a 'limited' copyright term is no longer limited if
> Congress extends it every time some Mickey Mouse lobbyist asks.[193]

Lessig, here, is criticizing the obvious bias in this policy favouring certain
corporate interests, and their unprecedented influence over Congress. This
influence can be seen to a lesser extent, in the European 70-year rule.[194] In a
quest to reclaim 'the Commons' (i.e. public domain), in his book, Lessig rec-
ommends a radical revision of copyright law.[195] Copyright protection, he
suggests, should be cut to five years, renewable 15 times. Where copyrights
were not renewed, the work would enter the public domain.[196] For Lessig,
The Bono Act was not just another instance of 'fat-cat favouritism but part
of a disastrous trend towards what might be called property-rights
fundamentalism'.[197]

Many of the fans surveyed gave anecdotal evidence of the corporate strategy of threatening legal action and issuing 'cease and desist' notices saying
that their copyright has been infringed, and that expensive legal action will
ensue, even though copyright infringement is clearly not a strict liability
offence. Some companies are fiercely guarding their property even if it means
using their vastly superior economic position to scare individuals into compliance. Jenkins, referring to the privatization of culture writes: 'Media companies are expanding their legal control over intellectual property as far and
as wide as possible, strip-mining our culture in the process'.[198] By ignoring
the reality of appropriative postmodern creation, and, through inaction, pan-
dering to the demands of corporate copyright holders, copyright law is virtually handing the iconographic and polemic infrastructure of our society
over to corporate control. The law must be careful to be seen to show regard
for social, humanistic and democratic values, and ethical concerns. Conversely, if appropriative practices are to be treated as entirely illegal then a
clear message in the form of sound legal guidelines need to be sent to those
who consider it a 'victimless' crime, or not a crime at all. Tushnet warns:

> Pragmatic considerations suggest that copyright law should not stray
> too far from common-sense understandings. If people consider a law to
> be silly and violate it routinely by performing activities that they feel
> are both harmless and central to their lives . . . the law will not be
> respected. Copyright law might be more frequently followed if the lines
> it drew resembled emerging implicit copyright norms.[199]

Conclusion

Postmodern art achieves much of its richness by appropriating elements of past genres, incorporating them into embroideries of fragmentary conflicting styles, mixed in different ways, and placed into different contexts. In our video-saturated world, where moving images pervade our public and private spaces, society has made the transition into acceptance of 'recombinant strategies' in art, entertainment, and technology. If *v.sampling* is an art form, the logical conclusion is that the law must, under certain circumstances allow *v.samples* in order to be 'effective'. As has been pointed out, the act of selection can be as original and significant as any other. Artists quickly become attached to freedom of expression, whatever their medium and video artists are no exception to this. As McKenna so aptly put it: 'The psychology of art has always favoured fragmentary theft, in a way that does not engender loss to the owner'.[200]

The fact that appropriative practices have a long and distinguished history in the arts, and that today this tradition has embraced new technologies, gives them natural appeal for artists. There has not only been a massive surge in credibility, demand and audience appreciation, but there is evidence that there has been a huge increase in both the number and frequency of industry forums/talks on the subject too. Also, the number of educational courses now available to uphold, teach and nurture these practices means there is much support for them and for the endless possibilities for creation spawned from them. These practices are a key component in the make-up or architecture of our emerging digital culture but as we have seen, they are creating problems for copyright owners *and* users.

There are two main dilemmas. First, how should current copyright laws be interpreted? The main difficulties include adapting to new technologies and practices, ambiguous statutory language (e.g. the meaning of 'substantial') and unclear intent behind the laws (e.g. who do they protect?). Second, how should disputes be settled? As has been evident, there have been no cases specifically relating to video sampling and there exist no solid licensing or clearing systems. The threat of legal action is usually enough to deter an artist from *v.sampling* due to marked differences in bargaining power. Hence, the important question is whether the laws provide an appropriate mechanism to satisfy the different interests involved, or at least weighs them against each other. The law's obvious weakness is the lack of predictability and legal certainty for all parties.

The practical and legal ramifications presented to the CDPA by *v.sampling* have yet to be explored. VJing, as a relatively young art form has had no legal battles to date. Until these battles occur it is going to be very difficult to gauge how cases may be handled and what their outcomes might be. On the one hand, a VJ may be breaking the law but, on the other, they are within, as yet, untrodden legal territory. Moreover, VJing is a subculture, operating 'below the radar'. Until someone profits greatly and is sued, the legality of the activity remains uncertain. Here, a judgement in favour of either party would place the government of the day in a precarious, political position. On one side, any relaxation of copyright law would anger powerful media companies who are adamant not to loose their tight grip on their intellectual property. Conversely, strengthening copyright law would only stifle innovation in the creative industries, which is precisely what the UK government ostensibly strives to promote, and with good reason.[201]

Even if companies embrace the sale or licensing of *v.samples* to secondary creators for a proportionate and equitable fee, there still exists no real prospect for either to avail of copyright protection in the new work under the present law. The fact that a VJ's set is performed live, creates very particular problems for gaining copyrights in their work. Fan edits are extremely vulnerable because of their obvious 'substantial taking'.

Unauthorized v.sampling does happen and is extremely popular. Therefore, if secondary creators are unable to sample because of copyright law, then it is doing exactly the opposite of what it set out to do, i.e. to promote creativity and protect artists' rights. By failing to adapt or change the law, the courts or the legislature are leaving the fate of this digital art form in the hands of those corporations who own the works VJs and fans want to sample. By their very nature, visual art forms need to refer to pre-existing imagery within wider society in order to comment upon it. Without access to this cultural imagery, VJing is relegated merely to the role of 'eye candy', unable to engage in any wider socio-political discourse. As Falstrom points out, copyright is supposed to balance the right of the artist to control access to his work against the need for society to experience the benefit from art.[202] Judicial ingenuity will have to be pushed to new limits if the public interest in access to copyright works is not to be hugely diminished.

Notes

1 I.e. the process whereby one can record, store and manipulate in digital form a sound from a previous recording. See Watson, Margaret E: 'Unauthorised Digital Sampling in Musical Parody: A Haven in the Fair Use Doctrine? [1998–1999] 20–21 Western New England Law Review 469, at 472.

2 *Sleepless in Seattle*, 1993, Directed by Nora Ephron, Produced by Tristar Pictures [US].

3 'Contact Europe VJ Festival', Milan 10th–12th May 2003. See Appendix II in thesis, p. 67, 'Sampling the Moving Image: A Legitimate or an Unwanted Art Form?: A Study on the Effectiveness of the UK Copyright Designs and Patents Act 1988 with Regards to the Practice of Video Sampling' (unpublished) (2003). Westminster University Library, 4–12, Little Titchfield Street, London W1W 7UW.

4 Supra [n 3]. See Appendix I of thesis, Question 21, p. 65.

5 Through Fox's London and Los Angeles Offices.

6 Gillette, David and Mauer, Barry: 'Escaping into the Vortex of Imagination: Proposing a Poetics of Creativity and Collage for the Digital Arts.' www.trace.ntu.ac.uk/incubation/level2/speakers/abstracts.htm.

7 This situation is slightly complicated by the work of video artists using instal-

lations, who blur the line between recorded and performed, time-specific video art. VJs could even be said to fall under this category of video art, as some liken their work to installations.

8   I.e. artistic works, dramatic works, film.

9   In statistical science, for example, a *sample* is a section of a given population or data set. Likewise, in the audiovisual industries, a *sample* means an excerpt or clip of a media product.

10 Waters, Peter and Lauren Eade: 'Framed: The risks of sampling Film?' ENT. L.R., Vol. 13, Issue 2, pages 43–44 (2002). www.acrullilaw.com/publications-Detail.asp?pubNo=21.

11 Cutler, Randy Lee: 'Pilfering the Datapool and Other Recombinant Strategies.' www.eciad.bc.ca/~rcutler/.

12 Fox, Barry: 'Digital Movies Knock Out Film in London Screen Duel', *New Scientist*, July 26, 2003, p. 8. Movies generate well over half of their profits through subsequent video release, televization (i.e. video broadcasting) and merchandising. In fact, the 'film' industry may as well be called the 'video and merchandising' industry based on the areas in which it makes most of its profits.

13 This means its signal is read with the same binary coding (i.e. in 1s and 0s) as most computer applications.

14 Digital Versatile Discs.

15 Video Home System, released by JVC in 1976.

16 British Broadcasting Company (later Company changed to Corporation).

17 Although no video cassette recorder until 1957, so all TV was broadcast live.

18 America's National Broadcasting Company.

19 The *portapak* was first developed as a lightweight portable recording device for air-to-ground surveillance during the Viet Nam War.

20 Fifield, George: The Early Video Project; The Paik/Abe Synthesizer. http://208.55.137.252/paikabesynthesizer.html.

21 Paik was reputedly one of the first purchasers of the *portapak*.

22 Supra [n 3]. See Appendix III in thesis, p. 72. Michael Heap (VJ – www.vjs.net) in interview with author, 11 August 2003, St. James' Park, London.

23 Piak, Nam June, *Exposition of Music – Electronic Television*, Galerie Parnass, Wupperatal, Germany, 11–20 March 1963.

24 Piak, Nam June, *Participation TV* (electronic assemblage), 1963.

25 With his friend Mr Shuya Abe, an engineer from Tokyo.

26 Supra [n 20]. Fifield.

27 Ibid.

28 Author of the popular novel, Kesey, Ken: *One Flew Over the Cuckoo's Nest*, Pan Books Ltd (1973).

29 Audio-Visual.

30 So called because of the new practice of overlaying (or 'dubbing') sounds played from one record deck on to the music played on another to create a new and unique sound.

31 Also, later, in 'disco'.

32 For example, Lee 'Scratch' Perry or Grand Master Flash in the 1970s.

33 Scratching is the practice of manually dragging or otherwise rapidly manipulating the speed of an LP to create new variation on the original sound.

34 Stefan, G. is a video artist from San Francisco. He coined the term VJ at Dingwalls niteclub in Camden in 1979.

35 Shamberg, Michael and Raindance Corporation: *Guerrilla Television*, New York, Holt Reinhart and Winston (1971).

36 See the US Supreme Court case, *Sony Corp.* v. *Universal City Studios, Inc*, 464 U.S. 417 (1984). Held: The VCR could legitimately be used for home time-shifting purposes. This was deemed a fair use.

37 Originally released as the *Flashomatic* in 1955 and then the *Space Command* in 1956.

38 Snider, Hart: Thesis on 'Scratch Video – a mutant hybrid of scratch DJ music and Guerrilla TV'. (2000). www.artengine.ca/scratchvideo/evolution_video_portapak.html.

39 Music Television, a television channel.

40 EBN later worked with U2 on their *ZOO TV Tour*, in which they famously phoned George Bush Snr. live on stage during a sell-out concert, whilst projecting a video sample of him onto the largest TV screen ever to be created until then.

41 Supra [n 3]. See Appendix III of thesis p. 72.

42 Steinski had been involved in the audio sampling explosion in the music world.

43 A technique that they called 'density editing'.

44 *And The Motorcade Sped On* (1984), Steinski, Kane and Lazzaro (audiovisual work).

45 The audio component of which was released as a single.

46 Such as those used to create the dinosaurs in the film *Jurassic Park*, 1993, Directed by Steven Spielberg, Produced by Universal Pictures [US] and Amblin Entertainment [US].

47 Manovitch, Lev: *The Language of New Media*, The MIT Press, Cambridge, Massachusetts (2001) p. 144.

48 Supra [n 3]. See Appendix IV in thesis, p. 87. Olivier Sorrentino (aka VJ Anyone – www.anyone.org.uk), in interview with author, 21 August 2003, Old Street, London.

49 Supra [n 3]. See Appendix II in thesis, pp. 68–70.

50 To a point where, for under £1,000, anyone can own video editing and manipulation tools that the artists of the 1980s could only dream of.

51 Such as Apple's 'Final Cut Pro'.

52 Exhibition: Illegal Art: Freedom of Expression in the Corporate Age, is a visual, audio and video show featuring works that challenge the expansion of copyright law and the policing of creative expression. A recent show was held on 7 and 8 February 2003, Buddy, 1542 n, Milwaukee ave, Chicago 773.342.7332.

53 The Institute of Contemporary Arts, The Mall, London SW1Y 5AH.

54 The ICA's September 2003 programme, Exhibition section www.ica.org.uk.

55 Bill Viola's *The Passions* exhibition from 22.10.03 to 04.01.04. The National Gallery, London.

56 Small, independently published magazines for and by fans of a particular movie, TV programme, etc.

57 *Star Trek*, 1966–1969, TV series, Created by Gene Roddenberry, Produced by Desilu Productions Inc. [US] (1966–1967), Norway Corp. and Paramount Television [US] (1968–1969).

58 Only very few copies of these fanzines were distributed around college campuses.

59 The first known example of this being a story about *Star Trek* heroes Captain Kirk and Mr Spock in a homoerotic storyline.

60 Which quickly became considerably cheaper than celluloid and projectors.

61 Anon: *The Disney™ Danger*, www.cultureby.com/books/plenit/html/Plenitude 2p. 16.html.

62 Jenkins, Henry: 'Digital Land Grab', *Technology Review*, Cambridge; Mar/Apr (2000).

63 Branwyn, Gareth: *Jamming the Media: A Citizen's Guide to Reclaiming the Tools of Communication. Chronicle Books* (1997) p. 14.

64 Supra [n 3]. See thesis, pp. 63–66. A web-based questionnaire carried out by the author, which was posted as a hyperlink on a number of fan sites.

65 Star Wars Episode 1: The Phantom Menace (1999). Directed by George Lucas, Produced by 20th Century Fox [US] and Lucasfilm Ltd. [US] Jar Jar Binks, the 'comic relief' character, was virtually cut out of the re-edit. Also, many of the aliens' voices and dialogue were also changed to remove what many fans felt were ethnically stereotypical accents.

66 Kraus, Daniel: 'The Phantom Edit', 11 May 2001 archive.salon.com/ent/movies/feature/2001/11/05/phantom_edit/.

67 One fan is reported to have claimed that aspects of *Star Wars*: Episode 1, were taken from their fan fiction. In copyright law, the plaintiff is more likely to succeed if they can prove that the defendant had access to his or her material and an obvious problem exists with websites, which virtually anyone can access.

68 Rogers, Andrew, *Part 1: The Emergence of a New form of Fan Appreciation*, 18 October 2001. http://www.Zap. 2it.com.

69 Kelly, Kevin and Paris, Paula, 'Beyond Star Wars: What's next for George Lucas', *Wired Magazine*, Issue 5.02 – Feb 1997. www.wired.com/wired/archive/5.02/fflucas.html?pg=4&topic=.

70 Jenkins, Henry: 'The Poachers and the Stormtroopers: Cultural Convergence in the Digital Age' (2003) http://commons.somewhere.com/rre/1998/The.Poachers.and.the.Sto.html.

71 He also pointed out that fans ordinarily comply with orders to shut down their websites.

72 Supra [n 3]. See Appendix I in thesis, Question 6, p. 63.

73 Hudson, Robbie: 'When Hamlet met the A-Team', the *Sunday Times* 4 August 2002. p. 49.

74 Terms of Service for Web site offered by Lucasfilms at, www.fan.starwars.com/~site/TermsOfService.

75 Aka former police investigator Dmitri Puchkov, of St. Petersburg.

76 *Lord the Rings: The Fellowship of the Ring* (2001). Directed by Peter Jackson, Produced by New Line Cinema [US] (an AOL Time Warner company), The Saul Zaentz Company [US] (licensor) (d/b/a Tolkien Enterprises) and WingNut Films [NZ].

77 Walsh, Nick Paton: 'Russia's Cult Video Pirate Rescripts Lord of the Rings as Gangster Film', the *Observer (World Section)*, 22 June 2003, p. 23.

78 There are even some trailers for movies that don't yet exist, such as *Indiana Jones 4*!.

79 *A.I.: Artificial Intelligence* (2001). Directed by Steven Spielberg, Produced by Amblin Entertainment [us], DreamWorks SKG [US], Stanley Kubrick Productions, Warner Bros. [US] The 'Kubrick Edit' is by a fan of Stanley Kubrick (the originator of many of the ideas for the film who died before making it) who felt that they could make an edit more faithful to Kubrick's memory than the one Spielberg released.

80 Supra [n 69], Question 1.1, p. 63.

81 The Directors' Guild of America.

82 Hilden, Julie: *The 'Clean Flicks case': Is It Illegal to Rent Out a Copyrighted Video After Editing it to Omit 'Objectionable' Content?* writ.corporate.findlaw.com/hidden/20020903.html.

83 Rojas, Peter: 'ONLINE: SECOND SITE: HOLLYWOOD: the people's cut', the *Guardian*, 25 July 2002, p. 2.
84 Griffith made films between 1908 and 1930.
85 Griffith revolutionized film editing; he broke scenes, for the first time, into many shots, filming from different angles and distances. He switched between actions at different locations, a style called *cross-cutting*.
86 *The Birth of a Nation*, 1915, Directed by D.W. Griffith, Produced by David W. Griffith Corp. and Epoch Producing Corporation.
87 *Rebirth of a Nation*, 2002, Paul Miller (aka DJ Spooky) (projected audiovisual work). First shown at San Francisco's *Other Minds* Music Festival in 2002, and the Massachusetts Museum of Contemporary Art in 2003.
88 www.djspooky.com/art.html.
89 *The Battleship Potemkin* (1925). Directed by Grigori Aleksandrov and Sergei M. Eisenstein, Produced by Goskino [SU] and Mosfilm [SU].
90 The first sound film to create a sensation was *The Jazz Singer* in which the entertainer Al Jolson sang and spoke in synchronous sound. *The Jazz Singer* (1927). Directed by Alan Crosland (I), Produced by Warner Bros. [US].
91 Movies with synchronized sound.
92 For example John Cage in music, Nam June Piak in Video, Jean Luc Godard and Bruce Conner in Film, Richard Foreman and Robert Wilson in Theatre and William Burroughs in Literature, see John, Carlin: Culture Vultures: Artistic Appropriation and Intellectual Property, 13 Colum. Vla J.L. and Arts (1988) p. 106.
93 Okpaluba, Johnson: Appropriation Art: Fair use or Foul? in McClean, Daniel and Schubert, Karsten: *Dear Images – Art, Copyright and Culture* (Ridinghouse ICA) 2002. p. 199.
94 *A Movie* (1958). Directed by Bruce Conner, Distributed by Canyon Cinema [US].
95 Some critics see this as Conner's prediction for the state of the cinema in the early twenty-first century, and as such, it cannot be said to be entirely inaccurate!.
96 *Koyaanisqatsi* (1983). Directed by Godfrey Reggio, Produced by Institute of Regional Education, Santa Fe.
97 *Powaqqatsi* (1988). Directed by Godfrey Reggio for Institute of Regional Education, Santa Fe, Distributed by Cannon Films [US].
98 Supra [n 21]. See Appendix III of thesis, p. 74.
99 *Zelig* (1983). Directed by Woody Allen, Produced by Orion Pictures Corporation [US].
100 *Forrest Gump* (1994). Directed by Robert Zemeckis, Produced by Paramount Pictures [US].
101 The creator of *Austin Powers: International Man of Mystery* (1997). Directed by Jay Roach, Produced by Capella International [US], Eric's Boy, Juno Pix, KC Medien AG [DE], Moving Pictures [US] and New Line Cinema [US].
102 *The Staggering Stories of Ferdinand De Bargos* (1991). Broadcast by BBC2 (TV Comedy Series).
103 Myers, Michael, quoted in: *Knives out for Affleck's Superhero Saga*, Scotland on Sunday, The Scotsman Publications Ltd, 16 February 2003. p. 8.
104 *Psycho* (1960). Directed by Alfred Hitchcock, Produced by Shamble Productions.
105 *24 Hour Psycho* (1993). Douglas Gordon (projected audiovisual work).
106 *Scream* (1996). Directed by Wes Craven, Produced by Dimension Films [US] and Woods Entertainment [US].
107 *Halloween* (1978). Directed by John Carpenter, Produced by Compass International Pictures and Falcon Films.

108 *Halloween H20: 20 Years Later* (1998). Directed by Steve Miner for Dimension Films [US] and Nightfall Productions [US].

109 *An Affair to Remember* (1957). Directed by Leo McCarey, Produced by 20th Century Fox [US].

110 *The Cable Guy* (1996). Directed by Ben Stiller, Produced by Columbia Pictures Corp. [US] and Licht/Mueller Film Corp.

111 *How to Lose a Guy in 10 Days* (2003). Directed by Donald Petrie, Produced by Lynda Obst Productions, Moviemakers Productions (MMP) [DE], Robert Evans Co. [US] and distributed by Paramount Pictures [US].

112 Section 10 CDPA 1988. A work of 'joint authorship' is defined as a work produced by the collaboration of two or more authors in which the contribution of each author is not distinct from that of the other author or authors.

113 See s.9(2)(ab) CDPA 1988.

114 See s.13B CDPA 1988 and Directive 93/98; Duration of Copyright and Rights in Performance Regulations 1005, S.I. 1995 No. 3297. This is not the case for films made before 30 June 1994 for which the 50-year term remains intact. These designated persons are the principal director, the author of the screen play, the author of the dialogue and the composer of the music specifically created for and used in the film.

115 Sprague, Robert D: 'Multimedia: The Convergence of New Technologies and Traditional Copyright Issues', 71 DENV. U. L. REV. 635, 643 (1994).

116 Supra [n 3]. See Appendix I, Questions 14 and 14.1, p. 97.

117 Section 9 CDPA 1988. The author of an artistic work means the person who creates it. The author of a film was under the 1956 Act and remains under the CDPA 1988, s.9(2)(ab) 'the person by whom the arrangements necessary for the making of the film are undertaken'. In the case of a film, the producer and the principal director.

118 Sections 16–21 CDPA 1988.

119 Sections 17, 21, 19 CDPA 1988 (respectively).

120 Sections 17 (4) CDPA 1988. Note also s.17(2) that copying in relation to a literary, dramatic, musical or artistic work means reproducing the work in any material form. This includes storing the work by electronic means.

121 The Director now has the power to prohibit distribution of any version of his film, other than his own private cut Article 2(1) Council Directive 93/98/EEC (of 29 October 1993), for harmonizing the term of protection of Copyright and certain Related Rights. See also Sterling, J.L.A.: *World Copyright Law*, Sweet & Maxwell (1998), p. 167 and, Cornish, W.R.: *Cases and Materials in Intellectual Property*, Sweet & Maxwell (1999) pp. 406–407.

122 Section 16 (3)(a) CDPA 1988.

123 *Hyperion Records* v. *Warner Music* [1991] unreported.

124 Lord Denning in *Hubbard* v. *Vosper* [1972] 1 All ER 1023, CA.

125 *Produce Records* v. *BMG Entertainment* [1999] unreported.

126 *Designers Guild Ltd* v. *Russell Williams (Textiles) Ltd* [2000] 1 WLR 2416.

127 *Spelling Goldberg Promotions Inc.* v. *BPC Publishing* [1981] RPC 280, CA.

128 *Football League* v. *Littlewoods Pools Ltd.* [1959] ch 637.

129 For example Mr Justice Laddie calls it the 'idea/expression fallacy' in Laddie, Prescott, Vitoris *et al.*: *The Modern Law of Copyright and Designs*, 3rd edition, (Butterworths, London 2000) at 3.74. Mr Justice Laddie believes that whilst there is no copyright in general ideas, an original combination of ideas may constitute a substantial part of a copyright work, at 4.43 citing Lord Hailsham in *L.B. Plastics Ltd* v. *Swish Products Ltd* [1979] RPC 551.

130 *Designers Guild Ltd* v. *Russell Williams (Textiles) Ltd* [2000] 1 WLR 2416 at 2423E.

131 Walravens, Nadia in 'The Concept of Originality and Contemporary Art', in McClean, Daniel and Schubert, Karsten: *Dear Images – Art, Copyright and Culture* (Ridinghouse ICA) 2002, p. 174, citing Sol Le Witt's view from Traite de la propriete litteraire et artistique (Litec, 1994) p. 72.

132 Sections 22–26 CDPA 1988.

133 *LA Gear* v. *Hi-Tech Sports* [1992] FSR 121, CA.

134 Section 22 CDPA 1988.

135 Section 23 CDPA 1988. Copyright in a work is infringed where someone without permission, possess, sells or lets for hire, or exposes for sale or hire, exhibits or distributes or distributes otherwise than in the course of a business to such an extent as to affect prejudicially the owner of the copyright, an infringing copy of the work.

136 Section 24 CDPA 1988.

137 Section 25 CDPA 1988.

138 Section 26 CDPA 1988. Supplying the apparatus to infringe the copyright in a film or to receive visual images conveyed by electronic means will result in liability for the person who supplied the apparatus or any substantial part of it. An occupier of the premises who gave permission for the apparatus to be brought on to the premises may also be liable, as may anybody who supplied the copy of the film used to infringe the copyright.

139 Section 77, The Paternity right; s.80, The Integrity right; s.84; and, s.85 of the CDPA 1988 (respectively). Under s.95 moral rights in the UK subsist for as long as the copyright lasts (save for the right to object to false attribution which expires 20 years after death) and generally remain with the author or pass to his estate on death.

140 Section 78 CDPA 1988. These are subject to the exemptions under s.79.

141 See s.77 for a precise list of the various forms of exploitation which will give rise to the right. For example under s.70(6) the director of a film has the right to be identified whenever the film is shown in public, broadcast or included in a cable programme service or copies of the film are issued to the public.

142 Section 80(2) CDPA 1988.

143 Section 80(2)(b) CDPA 1988.

144 Wienand, Peter: *VJs/Video Jockeying – An Introductory Guidance Note* (National Endowment for Science, Technology and the Arts (NESTA)) (not yet published when sourced; copy obtained privately by the author).

145 *Gilliam* v. *American Broadcasting Co.s Inc* (1976) 538 F2d14 See also the interlocutory decision of Morritt, J. in *Morrison* v. *Lightbond* [1993] EMLR 144 where a 'megamix' if five musical compositions was arguably 'derogatory treatment', and *Tidy* v. *Trustees of the National History Museum* (1997) 39 IPR 501 where summary judgment was refused by Rattee, J. where cartoons were reduced in size.

146 *Consorts Huston and Co.* v. *Turner Entertainment Corp. and TV Channel La Cinq, Cour de Cassation* 28 May 1991, Petites Affiches no. 85, 15 July 1992. See also *Association of Danish Film Directors* v. *Danmark Radio*, Danish High Court, Eastern District, 14th Dept. Docket No. 35/1992. See also: Tackaberry, Paul, *Denmark: Copyright and Moral Rights*, News Section: [1992] 6ENT.L.R E-88.

147 *Clark* v. *Associated Newspapers Ltd* [1998] 1 All ER 959.

148 The US refused to accept moral rights until recent international treaty obligations made this a necessity.

149 For example, the Act explicitly excludes from protection motion pictures, audiovisual works, posters, electronic publications, magazines, newspapers, works of applied art, and several other categories of work.

150 Sections 29–30 CDPA 1988. There is also provision for 'incidental inclusion' under s.31.

151 In determining whether a use is fair the court has to look at four factors, i.e. the purpose and character of the use, the nature of the copyrighted work, the amount and substantiality of the portion used and the effect of the use on the potential market for or value of the copyrighted work.

152 *Campbell* v. *Acuff Rose Music* 510 U.S. 569 (1994). The 2 Live Crew's unauthorized use of the first line of the lyrics of Roy Orbison's song 'Oh, Pretty Woman' was held by the US courts, to be a fair use. In this case, even the commercial nature of their parody did not exclude such a finding.

153 Parody of a particular work, as opposed to the style, is more common.

154 European Directive 2001/29 on the Harmonization of Certain Aspects of Copyright and Related Rights in the Information Society.

155 The Copyright and Related Rights Regulations 2003 came in to force on the 31 October 2003. http://www.hmso.gov.uk/si/si2003/20032498.htm#19.

156 Bently, Lionel: 'Sampling and Copyright: Is the Law on the Right Track?' [1989] JBL 113, p. 411 (in relation to music sampling).

157 Low, Peter: 'Copyright Law and the Ethics of Sampling' (2000), www.lowlife.fsnet.co.uk/copyright. In three parts. Low even claims that crediting the original would undermine the whole artistic aspect of sampling and would therefore be fatal, at part 3:2.

158 Phillips, Jeremy: When is a Fact? [2000] ENT.L.R, Issue 6, Sweet and Maxwell Ltd.

159 In order to justify protection, the author must have utilized her own 'skill, labour and effort', which operates on a *de minimis* principle. Originality requires only that 'the work should not be copied and should originate from the author.' *University of London Press* v. *University Tutorial Press* [1916] 2 ch 601.

160 Per Lord Oliver in *Interlego AG* v. *Tyco Industries Inc and others* [1988] 3 All ER 949 at p. 972.

161 *Interlego AG* v. *Tyco Industries* [1989] 1 AC 217.

162 Section 5B(2) CDPA 1988.

163 Supra [n 93]. Barron, Anne: *'Copyright, Art and Objecthood'*, in McClean, Daniel and Schubert, Karsten, Barron refers to these categories as the, taxonomic medium-specific approach of copyright, reflecting modernist aesthetic prejudices, which are unable to accommodate new art practices.

164 *Metix* v. *Maughan* [1997] FSR 718.

165 *Tate* v. *Fulbrook* [1908] 1 KB 821; Fixation has on occasion been found necessary for artistic works in: *Merchandising Corp of America* v. *Harpbond* [1983] FSR 32 concerning face paint on Adam Ant; *Komesaroff* v. *Mickle and Others* [1998] R.P.C. 204 concerning sand pictures; *Creation Records* v. *News Group Newspapers* [1997] EMLR 444, where the collocation of random unfixed objects was not a collage even though done with artistic intent.

166 *Creation Records* v. *News Group Newspapers* [1997] EMLR 444.

167 Read, Herbert (Editor) and Stangos Nikos (Contributor): Thames and Hudson Dictionary of Art and Artists, 2nd Edition (November 1994).

168 Richard Wilson's *20:50* (1987).

169 Damien Hirst's *'In and Out of Love'* (1991).

170 The Mechanical Copyright Protection Society was formed in 1924; it collects and distributes mechanical royalties to its composer and music publisher members. These are generated from the recording of music on to many different formats. www.mcps.co.uk.

171 The Design and Artists Copyright Society Ltd was formed in 1983 by a group

of artists in order to administer and protect the rights of visual artists in the UK. It is the only organization working for artists and photographers in the UK that deals solely with copyright and artist's rights. www.dacs.co.uk.

172 Video Performance Ltd was set up by the music industry in 1984 to adminis-ter the broadcast, public performance and dubbing rights in music videos. Blanket agreements with TV stations and other programme providers allow full use of the VPL repertoire in return for a fee. www.videoperformance.co.uk.

173 The Directors' and Producers' Rights Society was a collecting society, set up in 1992. www.dprs.org.

174 Prices often depend on, for example the size of the company. I have been told that they charge, on average, £50 a second but are largely no-price-named negotiable dealings.

175 This form of direct licensing is useful with regards to the control retained by the copyright holder.

176 Supra [n 3]. See Appendix VI in thesis, p. 97. Author's e-mail correspondence with a representative from Channel 4, 27 August 2003.

177 Ibid., p. 98.

178 Precisely one reason why the courts have felt the need to adopt a test based on substantiality which is more concerned with quality over quantity. It is also true to say that the more copyrighted works there are in a production, the less value each work contributes individually to the overall scope of the production.

179 For example, there may be ambiguous limits placed on the usage e.g. a royalty free licence will not always include merchandising uses. Also, the customer may be further burdened with the responsibility of clearing additional rights other than just those previously anticipated, if a work is subject to pre-existing agreements or third party rights or interests.

180 www.creativecommons.org (see also for licensing projects, discussions etc.).

181 A spokesperson at a mock trial, in The Institute of Contemporary Arts, The Mall, London: 'The New Honda Ad On Trial: A Case of Plagiarism?' – Fischli and Weiss, Der Lauf Der Dinge (The Way Things Go) London, 22 July 2003.

182 Laddie: 'Copyright: Over-Strength, Over-regulated, Over-rated?' [1996] 5 EIPR 253, p. 260.

183 Brewster, Bill and Broughton, Frank: *Last Night A DJ Saved My Life – The History of the Disc Jockey* (Headline, 2000) p. 21.

184 *L.H.O.O.Q.* (1919) is a 'Rectified Readymade' by Duchamp, which consists of a reproduction of the Mona Lisa with a moustache pencilled on to it.

185 D'Harnoncourt, Anne and McShine, Kynaston: Marcel Duchamp, Prestel, (1989) p. 129.

186 Carlin, John: Culture Vultures: Artistic Appropriation and Intellectual Prop-erty, 13 Colum. Vla J.L. and Arts (1988), p. 2.

187 Gillian Wearing's Signs (1993), A photographic work where people on the street were asked to write down what they were feeling at the time on a sign they would then hold up in front of the camera. Eamonn Mc Cabe: Two hundred people turned up on Brighton beach for an art installation dressed in duffle coats, hats, mittens and scarves on 1 May 2003. The project, called Keep Your Tunic On, was organized by The Guardian newspaper as a parody of the work of Spencer Tunick.

188 www.media-gn.nl/people/johannvdS/martfevi.html.

189 For example: Microsoft, who manufacture PC hardware and software that makes video sampling possible and also own Corbis, a large commercial online image/video bank. Apple, again manufacture computer hardware and software and also own Apple music store and i-tunes which sells downloadable music.

Similarly, Sony tech. division and Sony music division seem to have conflicting interests in these areas.

190 Digital Rights Management and Technological Protection Measures.

191 Besser, Howard: 'Recent Changes to Copyright: Attacks Against the Public Interest' (1998). www.gseis.ucla.edu/-howard/.

192 NB. Bill H.R. 1621/S.505 (The sonny Bono Act), The Copyright Term Extension Act was passed by both the House and the Senate Oct 7, 1998. *Ashcroft* v. *Eldred* case fought in the Supreme Court by Lawrence Lessig, claiming on behalf of Eldred, that the extension of copyright was unconstitutional.

193 Lessig, Lawrence (Professor at Stanford University): '*Copyright Law and Roasted Pig*', 22 October 2002. www.redherring.com/insider/2002/10/roast-pig-copyright-102202.html.

194 See Directive 93/98; Duration of Copyright and Rights in Performance Regulations 1005, S.I. 1995 No. 3297.

195 Lessig, Lawrence: *The Future of Ideas: The Fate of the Commons in a Connected World*, Random House (2001).

196 Except for copyrights on software, which he argues, should only be renewable once.

197 Surowiecki, James: 'Righting Copywrongs, The Talk of The Town', The Financial Page, *The New Yorker*, 21 January 2002, p. 27.

198 Jenkins, Henry: 'Digital Land Grab', *Technology Review;* Cambridge; Mar/Apr 2000: p. 103.

199 Tushnet. R.: 'Copyright, Fan Fiction and a New Common Law', *Loyola of Los Angeles Entertainment Law Journal*, 17 Loy.L.A. Ent.L.J. 651.

200 McKenna, Tyrone: 'Where Digital Music Technology and Law Collide – Contemporary Issues of Digital Sampling, Appropriation and Copyright Law', (1999. p. 11) http://elj.warwick.ac.uk/jilt/00-1/mckenna.html.

201 Creative industries accounted for 7.9 per cent of the UK GDP, 2000. www.culture.gov.uk/creative_industries/default.htm.

202 Falstrom, Carl: 'Thou Shalt not Steal: Grand Upright Music Ltd v. Warner Bros. Records Inc. and the Future of Digital Sound Sampling in Popular Music', [1993–1994] 45 *Hastings Law Journal* 359.

14 Law, music and the creative process

Who is now an author?

Steve Greenfield and Guy Osborn

Introduction

> My starting point is that the meaning of art depends on a specific conjunction of aesthetic, ideological, economic and legal institutions. Until recently, for example, it was taken for granted that 'music' (a particular organisation of sound) was constituted as something fixed, something authored, and something that exists as property. These assumptions reflect the two sides of the bourgeois ideology of art, its simultaneous stress on individual creativity and individual ownership, on Romantic-capitalist ideology which has survived both the rise of the mass media and the development of electronic means of cultural reproduction. During the last two hundred years, though, the contradictions involved in this account of art have become harder and harder to manage.[1]

It is undeniably the case that the development of new technologies has fundamentally altered both the production and the consumption of music. The history of recording technology demonstrates the shift towards a re-recording culture and this has accelerated with the digitization of sound recordings.[2] The way in which music is consumed has been most severely altered by the rapid growth of the Internet as a means of distribution and the advancement of audio compression, MP3 technology. This has forced a fundamental re-evaluation of how we view music; '. . . it could be argued that MP3 is far more transformative than the previous format changes and marketing revolutions in that it changes the relationship between artist and record company'.[3] A key issue for the recording industry is to ensure that it can retain its consumers through offering a differently constructed product. The industry has finally realized that customers may wish to pick and choose the tracks that they buy rather than having them bundled together in the form of an album. The launch of iTunes, the re-emergence of Napster and other similar vehicles for distribution, is an indication of this switch in marketing. This might be viewed as an empowering process that allows consumers to pick and choose only the tracks they want which may well eventually spell the end for the album format. Why pay for the 'filler' when you can select purely the 'killer'?[4] Alternatively this marketing strategy could be seen as a forced attempt to offer a legitimate alternative to a process already instigated by consumers as far back as the cassette era. The relationship between the end user and recording technology is littered with attempts to adapt and embrace the technology beyond its designated purpose;

> The phenomenon of consumers appropriating recording technology, or redefining the uses and reasons for making a sound recording, is one of the most important aspects of sound recording history. Often the process of appropriation was a transgression of boundaries. Underlying many of the different artistic, commercial, scientific and engineering applications of sound recording, for example, is a history of subversion.[5]

The current disquiet within the recording industry is not without historical precedents. The switch from the publishing of sheet music to its recording was in itself a major change in how music was produced, distributed and consumed.[6] The changes in technology have allowed artistic works to be used and adapted in unimagined ways. However, it is not just the consumption of music that is affected by technological change, the mode and means of production of music has been radically altered by the introduction of technology. When the fanzine *Sniffin' Glue* attacked the privileging of musical production by citing a clarion call to learn three chords and then to form a band, it was still based on the idea that at the very least a guitar was needed and (eventually) a means of recording.[7] The development of technology has 'democratized' musical production – now anyone with access to a basic computer and free software can 'form a virtual band' and produce recorded music. So, whilst new technology has altered consumption and allowed new ways of consuming, it has also radically affected production. This is a process of evolution that developed more drastically with the introduction of the sound sampler;[8]

> The digital sampling device has changed not only the sound of pop music, but also the mythology. It has done what punk rock threatened to do: made everyone into a potential musician, bridged the gap between performer and audience. Being good on a sampler is often a matter of knowing what to sample, what pieces to lift off what records; you learn that by listening to music, which makes it an extension more of fandom than musicianship.[9]

This chapter takes as its focus the issue of production. In particular two aspects of traditional copyright theory will be analysed through the prism of contemporary musical practice; originality of composition and the issue of joint authorship. The tension within these two areas is neatly described by Bettig;

First of all, what humans are able to think and create at the current stage of history is due to the contributions of all humanity. The most revolutionary moment of postmodern art is the recognition it produces of the intertextuality of human experience. The concept of individual genius, spontaneous and transcendent, is a mystification that helps perpetuate possessive individualism. Second, very few forms of intellectual and artistic creativity involve an individual creator.[10]

It is essentially this issue of creation, and particularly the question of authorship that we concern ourselves with in this chapter, particularly within the context of intertextual practice and the (im)possibility of single authorship. The chapter deals with the meaning of authorship from the perspective of current musical practice and charts the changing nature of authorship and composition, and the law's difficulty in responding to this.

The changing concept of authorship within the music industry

Copyright ascribes rights to an author, normally an individual, though joint authors are recognized where their individual contribution cannot be isolated.[11] Without authorship and consequent ownership, copyright would lose its economic value and fluidity.[12] However, the idea of individual authorship is not always an easy one to delineate in practice. Consider the film industry (in a wider sense than from a purely copyright perspective) where a number of contributors play a role in the realization of a film, yet only the principal director and producer are credited as authors of the work.[13] This has its roots in auteur theory but conveniently disregards the potential collaborative aspects of film production:

Adherents to the auteur theory accept, of course, that the director of a film requires the assistance of actors and technicians to realize his or her vision, but they contend that the director has final responsibility for the appearance of the film. In effect, therefore, actors and technicians are regarded as the director's amanuenses, making no significant creative contribution of their own.[14]

This collaborative theory, as Arnold terms it, broadly represented the status quo before auteur theory became fashionable in the 1950s, and Arnold attempts to explore the bifurcation between authors and performers (defined as interpreters and executants). In particular, he identifies 'shades of interaction' between the two in drama and music – there is, he argues, a difference between a version of a song where the songwriter provides merely lyrics and melody, and a version of it where the songwriter '. . . provides a full score of the song arranged for guitar, bass, drums, piano, and brass section consisting of alto saxophone, tenor saxophone, trumpet, and trombone, including full details of the tempi, dynamics, and so on'.[15] This tension can be seen in the joint authorship cases of *Stuart* v. *Barrett* [1994] EMLR 448, *Hadley* v. *Kemp* [1999] EMLR 589 and *Beckingham* v. *Hodgens* [2003] EMLR 18.[16] All of these cases involve a different aspect of the same question – who is, or can be, the author of a musical work?

Section 11(3) of the CDPA 1988 provides that; 'In this Act 'work of joint authorship' means a work produced by the collaboration of two or more authors in which the contribution of each author is not separate from the contribution of the other author or authors'. Effectively the key aspects of this are that there needs to be a *collaboration*, that each author *contributes* and that these contributions are *not separate*. In *Stuart* v. *Barrett* the question was whether a situation of collective collaboration existed and whether the 'jamming process' had led to the drummer having a claim on the copyright in the musical work. Here it was accepted that where the musical work transpires as part of a group 'jamming session', all of the group members can be joint authors for the purposes of copyright. This issue is not however always clear cut.

In *Hadley* v. *Kemp* (the Spandau Ballet case) there were two arguments put forward in support of a claim for joint authorship. The first was based upon the collective songwriting process approach, as in *Stuart*. The evidence, however, showed that Gary Kemp, the main songwriter, presented to the rest of the band a finished composition, which the rest of the band were then to perform. The final version of this did not differ significantly from the original 'demo' version presented by Kemp and the claim on this basis failed. The second argument for joint authorship, was, as Coulthard put it, '. . . rather more sophisticated'.[17] This argument centred upon the idea that copyright did not subsist in the song until it was fixed, and that it was fixed when the band as a whole had recorded it and had added their own creative touches to it. Therefore, the argument went, communal joint authorship was shown in this instance. This argument was also rejected on the grounds that the musical work that was reduced to material form by the band was not different to the version that already existed in Gary Kemp's consciousness before fixation. The final approach by the claimants was to argue that each individual band member was an author of the songs by virtue of what they each individually brought to the song, be it their voice (Hadley), drumming (Keeble) and various percussion/other instruments (Norman). This argument was given short shrift on the basis that whilst all the performances were solid and professional there was no evidence, apart from in one instance, of any 'creative originality'.[18] This approach has been subject to criticism, particularly on the basis of the decision in *Godfrey* v. *Lees* [1995] EMLR 307 and the compatibility between the two decisions.[19]

Beckingham, hereafter 'the Bluebells case', is a further illustration of the difficulty of ascribing authorship within the music industry. Unlike *Hadley* v. *Kemp*, this did not involve a member of a band or group, but a session musician. Beckingham, known professionally as Bobby Valentino, was a professional violinist, hired as a session musician to play on the song *Young at Heart* by the Bluebells in 1984. Robert Hodgens of the Bluebells wrote the music and co-wrote the lyrics with Siobhan Fahey of Bananarama. Valentino was paid £75 for performing a violin part, and he signed a consent form for the use of this performance. Some years later, following the song's re-emergence as part of a TV campaign, he claimed joint authorship in the song. The Court of Appeal upheld the High Court decision, rejecting two further claims from Hodgens including one that a fourth ground, that of intention, should be added to the requirements for joint authorship.[20]

All of these cases illustrate that ascribing authorship may be more difficult than first appears – certainly there are various 'shades of interaction'[21] that may give rise to a legal claim of authorship. This becomes even more marked as notions of creativity change, for example the position of a DJ is a good example of the difficulties in determining authorship within a landscape of changing methods of creation:

> The bottom line is that a DJ is an improvisational musician. It just happens that in place of notes he has songs, in place of piano keys or guitar strings he has records. And just like a musician, the DJ's skill lies in how these are chosen and put together. Think of a DJing performance in a compressed time frame and it might help. Where a guitarist can impress an audience by playing a 30 second improvised sequence of chords and notes, what a DJ does takes a lot longer ... and there are now so many records available, and so many mixes of most songs, that a DJ's records are fully analogous to the notes of an instrument.[22]

This of course begs the question of, what, or who, is a creative artist both artistically and then legally?[23] As we have noted above it is the application of technology that has led to new methods of artistic creation which may also lead to a compromise of existing rights.

Technology, digitization and copying

Technology, or perhaps more accurately 'new' technologies, are seen by some as being a threat to traditional notions of musical production.[24] For example, the onset of recorded music was viewed by live musicians as a threat to their livelihoods, and each technological advance has undoubtedly provoked responses based on the threat to the status quo. Music (or at the least certain genres of music) may be viewed on one level as inherently derivative. However, it is the technological advances that have allowed work to be produced that is perhaps even more derivative in that it relies, explicitly, upon not only 'original' musical and literary works of other creators, but also on existing sound recordings. An implication of this has been an attempt by original owners of work to attempt to protect their rights through legal threats and challenges. In particular, the area of sound sampling, and more recently the rise of the process of 'mash ups' or 'bastard pop', has brought the tensions in the area to the fore although, as illustrated below, these inter-textual elements have long been an issue within music and copyright law.

Historically, there have been a number of claims based upon 'new' work allegedly infringing previous work. The crucial aspect of such cases is not that the work is taken wholesale as in a cover version or similar, but that a part of it is taken (usually a riff or a vocal line) and used in the new composition. The key issue is one of *substantiality*. The question is whether the work that has been taken amounts to a 'substantial part' of the original work, an evaluative exercise that involves looking at issues such as the quality and quantity of the material taken (the issues of recognizability) and the intention and purpose of the party 'taking' the work.[25] There have consequently been a number of well publicized disputes and court cases concerning plagiarism and the creation of popular music.

Perhaps most famously, George Harrison's number one hit *My Sweet Lord* was considered to be an infringing copy of Ronald Mack's *He's So Fine*. It was found that Harrison had subconsciously copied from the original 1962 song.[26] Other similar cases, centring upon the alleged taking of the mechanical rights to a song include instances involving bands such as Elastica, whose song *Connection* was alleged to have used the guitar riff from Wire's *Three Girl Rhumba* and whose *Waking Up* was argued to similarly utilize the riff from The Stranglers' *No More Heroes*. Both of these were settled out of court. Copyright ownership allows the owner to exert a significant level of control over any attempts to use the 'new' work in the future. As has been argued elsewhere this can act as a form of censorship by preventing future use and creation, as can be seen by the examples of Kevin Rowland and Spiritualized among others.[27] Similarly, litigation concerning Robbie Williams received great exposure due to his pre-eminence and popularity. The High Court held that his song *Jesus in a Camper Van*, co-written with Guy Chambers infringed the copyright in Loudon Wainwright's *I am the Way (New York Town)*.[28] On the crucial issue of substantiality (see below), the judge noted that the amount taken was indeed significant; 'Jesus in a Camper Van takes the central idea from I am the Way (New York Town), namely that the son of God attracts bad luck by going round saying "I am the Way" and embodies it in virtually identical words'.[29] In the United States, an interesting defence to such an action arose in the case of *Campbell* v. *Acuff-Rose Music* where it was successfully argued that the unauthorized use and adaptation of the original work *Pretty Woman*, by the 2 Live Crew, was permissible on the grounds of fair use in that the new work was a parody and therefore protected. This was despite the fact that the 2 Live Crew piece was produced for commercial gain, and, that in the first instance they had sought authorization to use the original, which had been rejected. This case certainly stretches the boundaries of defining parody and is unlikely to prove to be much use in subsequent cases.

This question of 'copying' has become even more contentious with the development of new technologies that have made the process of musical production both easier and more contentious. The key issue within contemporary musical practice is that of sound sampling. The term 'sampling' denotes the taking of a series of sound samples from various sound recordings and the weaving together of these into a form of musical collage.[30] On one level this is no different in its ethos from the plagiarism debates we note above, and similarly may further 'blur the line between quotation and plagiarism', especially within the context of historical appropriation within black musical cultures;

> Defenders of a musician's right to sample might trace the practice back to its African-American oral culture roots. Keith Miller argued that black oral traditions, particularly the customs of the folk pulpit, involved a significant amount of 'borrowing' from the literary and cultural commons ... Existing works are not viewed as private property but as a 'common treasure' to be drawn upon to create new works.[31]

Similarly Bettig gives the example of hackers and shareware, where individual computer programs may be merely a particular point on a cumulative progression, and a recognition by such 'creators' that a collective and cumulative ethos drives creation. In terms of sound sampling, Frith gives the example of M/A/R/R/S number one hit *Pump up the Volume* which lifted directly from the Stock, Aitken and Waterman produced song *Roadblock*, arguing that this is exactly the same process that musicians have always used, taking sounds and ideas and making something of their own out of it as part of the 'magpie culture' of pop?[32] Peter Waterman argued that there were two key differences in this new form of appropriation – first, that sampling was merely using the same sound to the same effect rather than imitating it, and second, that the appeal of a song based on a sample, *is* the sample rather than the new composition. This second argument takes the recognizability factor of substantiality one stage further. However, while the ethos is perhaps the same as for copying musical and literary works (as noted above), the technology allows this to be taken further, by copying other works and infringing other rights. The technology that underpins the process of sound sampling can be described thus:

> ...changes in music technology relate primarily to a general system for the encoding, storage and manipulation of musical signals (digital, rather than analog)), and to the standardization of a system 'language' or set of machine protocols known as MIDI (Musical Instrument Digital Interface). This enables different components in any music making or recording set-up, such as synthesizers and sequencers, to communicate with each other and with general purpose micro-processors. In general terms, MIDI communications systems enable, for example, a computer

to *control* a keyboard or drum machine, or to *receive*, store and manipulate data (finally, sounds) generated by such an 'instrument' (instruments in this context are often referred to as 'MIDI controllers'). During the time that the musical information (textures, rhythms, melodies, tempi etc.) is stored in digital form, it can be manipulated and edited like other kinds of computer data.[33]

So, digitization and the rise of technology enabling sound sampling allows musicians to use parts of existing sound recordings and adapt them at will. A whole new opportunity for appropriation or creation is thus created. An excellent example of this process in practice is provided by Australian band The Avalanches and their album *Since I Left You*, which is almost totally devoid of what might be termed original source material, but composed of fragments of other sampled recordings. The album is said to have anywhere between 1,000 and 3,500 samples on it, something that caused their US lawyer to spend six months obtaining copyright clearances. The title track of the album, released as a single and reaching the Top 20 in the UK on the back of heavy playlisting, provides an illuminating example of both the process of creation, and also the difficulty of categorizing it in terms of traditional creativity;

> The vocal line is from 'Everyday' by the Main Attraction but there's also a sample of 'Lets do the Latin Hustle' by Klaus Wunderlich. Plus bongos, triangles, snares, tom-toms, cymbals, four or five violins from different records. We get inspired by small parts of records, rarely the whole track. There are at least 1000 samples on the album. In a way, I feel like we haven't played on it at all.[34]

Whilst the source material is a disparate mishmash, the whole is cohesive and sounds fresh and original. As Chater notes, however, even the creator of this work has doubts about his own role within the process and, by association, his position as a creative artist. In legal terms, the question is how (or can) the law be adopted to deal with this intertextual practice.[35] Schumacher illustrates this difficulty with regard to rap music:

> The case of rap also highlights the ways in which notions of authorship and originality do not necessarily apply across forms and cultural traditions – not because of any inherent worth or quality of different musics, but because different musical practices defy the universals of legal discourse.[36]

Rap as a cultural form is predicated upon the use, and revision, of texts as part of creating a new text – rap relies explicitly upon referencing previous work, and as such challenges a number of legal canons. For example, the methodology of rap poses questions about the ownership of sound. Rap as a discourse poses questions about the ownership and meaning of texts and flaunts its very intertextuality. This presents a challenge to both copyright law, to our own understanding of musical practice, and to the idea of authorship itself:

> As the DJ samples, there is a simultaneous critique of the ownership of sound and 'Rockist' aesthetics which remain tied to the romantic ideals of the individual performer. Rap forces an expansion of these definitions of musicality. Its meaning-making practices which rely on intertextual referencing via the sample demonstrate the different ways in which the struggle over originality is waged in divergent musical traditions. Because rap music and the practice of sampling change the notion of origin (the basis of copyright) to one of origin*s*, it becomes transgressive in the Foucauldian sense and an infringement of copyright law in the eyes of the courts.[37]

Rap, and sampling generally, created a new pop aesthetic where copying becomes part of the creative act.[38] There have been a number of legal cases that have touched on the issue of how the law deals with this cultural question – the cases have, however, been inconclusive and illustrate that often a settlement will be made, on confidential terms, rather than attempting to engage in a fruitless legal battle. Perhaps even more fundamentally, these cases do illustrate the potential censorial upshot of copyright law and the difficulty it has in dealing with practices outside of its traditional confines and situated outside capitalist social relations.[39]

Perhaps the apotheosis of this process was reached with the case of the 'Grey Album' in 2004. Rap's intertextuality and the possibilities of technology were given a twist by what has been termed 'bastard pop'. Effectively, here two or more sound recordings are 'mashed' together to create a new work. It is, as Neil McCormick put it, '. . . a genre to erase all genres, existing in a kind of alternative musical universe, where fashion distinctions are blurred and every musical style is interconnected'.[40] This is evidently taking the process of sampling to its logical conclusion, rather like with The Avalanches' approach but being even more upfront of the new creations provenance. For example, one celebrated mash up, *A Stroke of Genius* by the Freelance Hellraiser, was explicit in terms of its use of Christine Aguilera's *Genie in a Bottle* and The Strokes *Hard to Explain* even billing it as *The Strokes v. Christie Aguilera*. The Grey Album took this referentiality even further.

In January 2004, DJ Danger Mouse released a limited run of copies of his new work, *The Grey Album*. Critical response was unanimously favourable; for example, in the US the Boston Globe called it 'the most creatively captivating album of the year', while the NME described it as a 'truly, *truly*, great pop record.'[41] However, whilst the music critics lauded the record, the record industry were far more sanguine. *The Grey Album* was, in fact, part of an aural experiment by DJ Danger Mouse, in which he took the vocals of Jay

Z's *The Black Album* and created the musical backing tracks to these lyrics solely from sounds taken and adapted from the Beatles album *The Beatles* (commonly referred to as '*The White Album*'). For example, '*Encore*' was primarily based on the vocals from Jay Z's '*Encore*' and the vocals and guitar loop from *Glass Onion*, and *What More Can I Say* on slowed down piano from *While My Guitar Gently Weeps* and lyrics from Jay Z's *What More Can I Say*. It ought to be noted at this point that an exposition on paper of this method fails to capture the complexity of the process, and the skills that DJ Danger Mouse has shown. Only by listening to the work can this be appreciated; DJ Danger Mouse has effectively stripped *The White Album* to its constituent parts and re-arranged it using Jay Z's *The Black Album* as its skeleton.

EMI, owners of the Beatles' back catalogue of sound recordings, contacted DJ Danger Mouse and various record stores who were selling the album ordering them to 'cease and desist' as they were in breach of copyright in supplying *The Grey Album*, given that the Beatles' material had not been cleared. This led to a storm of protest, accusations of creative censorship against EMI and an international day of protest, *Grey Tuesday*, organized by the pressure group Downhill Battle. Here hundreds of websites all posted the album for 24 hours, leading to thousands of copies being downloaded. Explaining the reason for this act of civil disobedience, Rebecca Laurie said, 'EMI isn't looking for compensation, they're trying to ban a work of art . . . The record industry has become a huge drag on creativity and it's only getting worse – it's time to take a stand'.[42] This is redolent of copyright acting as a censorial force, as we have noted above and elsewhere. In addition, it is a potent social comment on the use, and re-use, of creative work(s), and a great illustration of both the potentialities of new technology and the limits of authorship and originality within our traditional notions of copyright, and further questions whether concepts such as authorship and originality, as the law understands them, can remain intact;

> Rather than allow it to be used in an attempt to stifle yet another creative form of musical practice, the industry, legislators and the courts need to re-examine copyright law and its commitment to outmoded notions of originality, creativity and ownership, and to balance the economic interests that these ideas support with a recognition of the technologists' capacity to transform musical sounds and their right to make creative use of recorded material in the production of new works.[43]

Conclusion

> By looking at the process of production, we see that technologized music is the product of not just auteur-musicians but of the work of musicians and engineers alike. We cannot go back to some pre-industrial form of music.[44]

This chapter has outlined some of the key technological issues affecting musical practice, and, in particular, the applicability of copyright law. Essentially, it has explored the notions of authorship and originality within contemporary music making and concluded that these concepts are too rooted in a historical romantic tradition of creativity that does not fit in with the methodologies of creativity provided by new technologies. We argue that authorship as a concept is outmoded and that as all work is derivative, copyright 'devices' preventing future use of work should be resisted.

This article is derivative. All academic work is derivative in that it is based on something that has gone before. As academic authors we sample ideas, sometimes literally reproducing them, and pay homage to the earlier creators via the medium of referencing systems. In a broader sense, to prevent work being produced on the basis of referentiality would prevent much great art being produced. Posner cites examples including Milton 'plagiarizing' Genesis for Paradise Lost and Manet 'quoting' from Raphael, Titian, Velasquez and Rembrandt, before adding bravely:

> If these are examples of plagiarism, then we want more plagiarism. They show that not all unacknowledged copying is 'plagiarism' in the pejorative sense. Although there is no formal acknowledgement of copying in my examples, neither is there any likelihood of deception. And the copier has added value to the original – this is not slavish copying.[45]

Similarly with authorship, creative products are essentially social products, often based on prior knowledge, and often produced in an environment where it is difficult to work out an individual's contributions to this endeavour:

> The value added by the laborer and any value the object has on its own are by no means the only components of the value of an intellectual object. Invention, writing, and thought do not operate in a vacuum; intellectual activity is not creation *ex nihilio*. Given this vital dependence of a person's thoughts on the ideas of those who came before her, intellectual products are fundamentally social products. Thus even if one assumes that the value of these products is entirely the result of human labor, this value is not entirely attributable to any particular laborer (or small group of laborers)[46]

The final issue to consider is the applicability of the law – is legislation, common law, or a legalized approach to these questions the optimum way to tackle these areas? Again we see an attempt by the law to deal with cultural issues, by considering not the *cultural* nature of the area but the *commercial*, and again we see a simplistic approach that fails to appreciate the nuances of the area that the law tries to colonize. An added dimension to this is the difficulty that the law has in keeping up with technological developments and the problems of a 'lagging law'. This difficulty has been witnessed with sound sampling, with Napster and other online delivery vehicles and it appears apparent that the law is not a suitable mechanism to deal with such problems. This has manifested itself in an industry response of attempting to deal with this by other means, but effectively heralds another failure of the law.

Notes

1 Frith, S. (1993) 'Music and Morality' in Frith, S. (ed.) (1993) *Music and Copyright* Edinburgh University Press: Edinburgh, 1.

2 Morton tracks the development of the American culture of making sound recordings, allied to the availability of the technology, which developed as a hobby but expanded with the introduction of the eight track and its successor the cassette tape. As he notes 'For the last twenty years, home duplication of commercial records has become an ingrained part of life for many Americans, but its success as a democratized form of activity corresponds with a failure for the record industry. What the record companies lost to cassette recording was the opportunity to introduce a customized or individualized music product on tape. In choosing to make recordings at home, ordinary people have retaken a role, however minor, in determining the ways they receive commercial music culture.' David Morton (2000) *Off the record* Rutgers University Press, p. 169.

3 Carey, M. and Wall, D. (2001) 'MP3: The Beat Bytes Back' *International Review of Law, Computers and Technology* Volume 15, Number 1, 35.

4 Proto punks from California SUM 41 released an LP entitled 'All Killer, No Filler' (2001), the title alluding to the fact that while an LP might usually consist of 4 good songs (killer), often the singles and then padded out with 'filler', their LP had apparently subverted usual industry expectations. Subjectively, it had not.

5 Morton op. cit. n 2, p. 178.

6 See generally Frith, S. (1987) 'The Industrialisation of Popular Music' in Lull, J. (1987) *Popular Music and Communication* Sage: London.

7 Mark Perry's 'Sniffin Glue' was perhaps the definitive punk fanzine. See for example the anthology Perry, M., Petty, M., Rawlings, T. (2000) *Sniffin Glue. The Essential Punk Accessory* Sanctuary Publishing.

8 Trevor Horn indicates that the major technological developments that affected his musical production were string synthesizers in the late 1970s, the Polymoog synthesizer, the rhythm boxes in the late 1980s and most importantly the Fairlight sampler. See Warner, T, *Pop Music Technology and Creativity* (2003) Ashgate.

9 Sanjek, D. (1991) 'Don't have to DJ no more. Sampling and the "autonomous creator"' conference paper quoted in Frith, (1993).

10 Bettig, R. (1996) *Copyrighting Culture. The Political Economy of Intellectual Property* Westview Press, 239.

11 There are of course exceptions – witness in particular the situation as regards to films. Since 1 July 1994 the author of a film is the producer *and* principal director CDPA 1988 s.9(2).

12 Generally on authorship see Bently, L. and Sherman, B. (2001) *Intellectual Property* Oxford University Press: Oxford, chapter 5. Bently and Sherman describe authorship as 'the focal point around which many of the rules and concepts are organized', at p. 108. Further this approach is part of a common law tradition of copyright, in contradistinction to civil law approaches, that is gradually being challenged by globalization and harmonization.

13 This is a fairly recent development as historically the producer was the author (Copyright Act 1956 s.13(10)), but now producer and director are jointly credited. See Arnold, who notes that interestingly the adoption of the auteur theory has helped lead to this shift.

14 Ibid. p. 4.

15 Arnold (2000) p. 6.

16 See generally, Free, D. (2002) '*Beckingham* v. *Hodgens*: The Session Musician's Claim to Music Copyright' *Entertainment Law*, 3 93.

17 Coulthard, A. (1999) 'Copyright in musical arrangements – Spandau Ballet and beyond' *Communications Law* 218.

18 The one exception was the song 'Glow' and the contribution of Norman.

19 See further on this the argument of Coulthard (1999) at p. 221. The case involved an orchestral arranger and accompanist for Barclay James Harvest.

20 See further Free, Ibid, n 16.

21 See Arnold's arguments, ibid.

22 Brewster, B and Broughton, F (1999) *Last Night a DJ saved my life. The history of the disc jockey* Headline: London.

23 Some years ago we visited the Chicago Museum of Contemporary Art. An exhibit there by Felix Gonzales-Torres placed some of these ideas within the context of modern art. The exhibit 'Untitled (The End)' 1990 appeared from a distance as a large block or box; however, closer inspection revealed this to be a number of reams of paper stacked up, all of which were white pieces of paper, some 28″ by 20″, with a black edging. Next to the stack was a notice:

> Untitled (The End) is one in a series of 'stacks' Gonzalez-Torres started producing in 1988. Each stack, comprised of sheets of paper printed with an identical text or image (in this work a black border), stands directly on the floor and resembles a tombstone. Paradoxically, what appears to be a sculpture is actually an edition of prints on paper. The visitor may participate in this work by taking a sheet. The stack, which fluctuates in size, is regularly replenished.

Here the relationship between author and audience is blurred. In addition, what is necessary for a creative act becomes contentious – an issue that becomes more contentious as new technologies allow easier utilization of work in a variety of creative fora.

24 See for example the Royal Society of Arts debate 'Will technology be the death of professional musicians?' 5 February 2003, available online at www.theRSA. org.

25 See CDPA 1988 s.16.

26 *He's so Fine* contained four repetitions of a short musical phrase (Motif A) followed by four repetitions of another short phrase (Motif B). It was found by the court that the combination of the two motifs made it a highly unusual pattern. *My Sweet Lord* used '. . . the same motif A (modified to suit the words) four times, followed by Motif B, repeated three times, not four. In place of *He's So Fine*'s fourth repetition of Motif B, *My Sweet Lord* has a transitional passage of musical attractiveness of the same approximate length, with the identical grace note in the identical second repetition. The harmonies of both songs are identical. *Bright Tunes Music* v. *Harrisongs Music* 420 F Supp. 177 (S.D.N.Y 1976).

27 See Greenfield, S. and Osborn, G. 'Remote Control' in Cloonan, M and Garafolo, R. (2003) *Policing Pop* Temple Press. Also more generally on plagiarism and music, Stone, R. (1993) 'Plagiarism and originality in music: a precarious balance' *Media Law and Practice 51*.

28 Interestingly, the Loudon Wainwright version was itself a parody of the Woody

Guthrie song 'I am the Way' from 1963, the copyright in both of these is owned by Ludlow Music.

29 Quoted in Perry, K. (2000) 'Copycat Singer loses fight over song' *The Guardian* 3 October. It is of course important to consider the importance of the part to the work as a whole. Consider the following excerpts:

> Loudon Wainwright III – I am the Way (New York Town) 4th verse
> Every Son of God gets a little hard luck some time
> Every Son of God gets a little hard luck some time
> Every Son of God gets a little hard luck some time
> Especially when he goes around saying he's the way
>
> Robbie Williams/Guy Chambers – Jesus in a Camper Van Verse 2, 4, 5 etc. (repeated)
> . . . I suppose even the Son of God
> Gets it hard sometimes
> Especially when he goes round
> Saying I am the Way

30 Perhaps the most obvious and indeed dreary examples of sampling can be seen in the works of Jive Bunny and the mastermixers.

31 Bettig, R. (1996) *Copyrighting Culture. The Political Economy of Intellectual Property* Westview Press, p. 237.

32 Frith, S. (1993) 'Music and Morality'. He notes in the chapter that the phrase 'magpie form' is Charlie Gillet's; 'The first question to ask is: how was what M/A/R/R/S did any different from the usual pop practices of copying, quoting and indeed plagiarizing? Hasn't pop always been, in Charlie Gillet's words, 'a magpie form'? Haven't pop writers and producers always used musical elements eclectically, taken sounds and ideas from wherever they could find them? Putting it simply: why is *sampling* a bass line different from *imitating* it?'.

In legal terms the answer to Frith's question would be framed in terms of an additional copyright infringement in the first place, with the sound recording potentially infringed in addition to any infringement of, in this example, a musical work. Frith's example focuses upon the imitation and sampling of a bass line. If lyrics were taken with the bass line there would of course be an additional infringement in terms of the literary work (the lyrics).

33 Durant, A. (1991) 'A new day for music? Digital technologies in contemporary music making', in *Culture, Technology and Creativity* John Libbey: London.

34 Robbie Chater of the Avalanches, cited in Perrone, P. (2001) 'Lost for a definition? Garage Rock party chaos is a good enough start' the *Independent* 16 April.

35 See Bently, L. (1989) 'Sampling and Copyright: is the Law on the Right Track' Parts I and II, *Journal of Business Law* 113 and 405; Tackaberry, D. (1990) 'The Digital Sound Sampler: Weapon of the Technological Pirate or Palette of the Modern Artist?' *Entertainment Law Review* 87; Stone, R. (1993) 'Plagiarism and originality in music: a precarious balance' *Journal of Media Law and Practice*, 51; Bently, L. and Sherman, B. (1992) 'Cultures of Copying: Digital Sampling and Copyright Law' *Entertainment Law Review*, 158.

36 Schumacher, T. (1995) '"This is a sampling sport": digital sampling, rap music and the law in cultural production' *Media, Culture and Society* Vol. 17, 253.

37 Schumacher, Ibid., 266.

38 See here Greenfield, S. and Osborn, G. (2004) 'Copyright law and power in the music industry' and Theberge, P. '(2004) 'Technology, Creative Practice and Copyright', both in Frith, S. and Marshall, L. (2004) *Music and Copyright* Edinburgh University Press: Edinburgh.

39 See our arguments in Greenfield and Osborn (2003) op. cit. n 27 and (2004) op. cit. n 38.
40 McCormick, N (2002) 'Pop eats itself' *The Daily Telegraph* 27 April, accessed at http://www.smh.com.au/articles/2002/04/26/1019441299877.html on 10 July 2004.
41 NME 13 March 2004. See further Theberge (2004) op. cit. n 38.
42 Downhill Battle Press Release 18 February 2004 http://www.downhill battle.org/pressreleases/greytuesday_21904.html, accessed 11 March 2004.
43 Theberge op. cit. n 38, 154.
44 Schumacher op. cit. n 37, 261.
45 Posner, R. (2002) 'On Plagiarism' *The Atlantic Online* (http://www.theatlantic. com/issues/2002/04/posner.htm, accessed 1 October 2003).
46 Hettinger, E. (1989) 'Justifying Intellectual Property' *Philosophy and Public Affairs*, 31.

Index